Readings for

EDUCATIONAL PSYCHOLOGY

Edited by ELLIS BATTEN PAGE
University of Connecticut

In consultation with
Lee J. Cronbach
University of Illinois

Harcourt, Brace & World, Inc.
New York, Chicago, and Burlingame

FOR OUR PARENTS

Library of Congress Catalog Card Number: 64-18307

Printed in the United States of America

Contents

Foreword

A textbook has notable limitations, for it must try to unify dozens of concepts and lines of argument. In educational psychology, such a presentation, emphasizing generally accepted principles and their implications for the school, is, of necessity, incomplete. Some of the needed supplementation must be provided by first-hand observation and some by classroom discussion. But carefully selected readings from original sources can also do much to invigorate the course and deepen the student's understanding.

Education is controversial, and so are the positions taken by psychologists on issues practical or theoretical. Most of these competing positions can be defended logically and all are defended vehemently—and all go beyond present evidence to some degree. A textbook summary of the lines of argument loses this play of speculation and controversy, which is a significant feature of the educational scene. The experience of reading various propositions in the words of their advocates puts the prospective teacher into the center of that tournament of ideas. The student responds eagerly to the opportunity to match his own conceptions against others'; discussion is never dull when the student is testing his wit against a Skinner or a Thelen. And the psychologist-instructor finds uncountable opportunities to renew the question, central to constructive use of his science: How much of this debate is on empirical questions, to be settled by past or future research rather than by force of argument?

A second type of original source material is the psychologist's first-hand account of a study. Through the examination of such sources the student acquaints himself with the texture of original work and learns to appreciate the difference between research and casual observation. A textbook summary of a study can all-too-easily sound like another pronouncement from authority; in an original report the authority clearly lies in the data, not in the writer. To make this distinction clear to the student is an important aim of educational psychology.

In addition, a book of readings can help to clarify a difficult topic by reviewing concepts in language other than the textbook's, and to add interest and a sense of reality by describing actual practices.

The instructor who, recognizing these advantages, proposes to assign readings in the college library encounters much difficulty. Many of the most useful selections turn out to be unavailable, or available in too few copies. Moreover, it is a considerable task to identify highly effective selections. Hence "books of readings" fill a great need.

The volume of selections assembled by Ellis Page reflects his view and mine that the educational psychology course should contribute to the student's general psychological insight, and not lose the grand issues beneath a clutter of detail and technical terminology. The authors he presents are thinkers; beyond that they have little in common. Psychologists, anthropologists, sociologists, and at least one philosopher meet between these covers to offer a provocative symposium. The common element in these writings is their power to open the student's eyes to things he has overlooked in the educational scene.

While many of these selections appear in the end-of-chapter reading lists of my book, it is the discrepancy between the two that requires comment. Some of the reasons are obvious: the text lists include more selections than could be reprinted, and some are too lengthy for reprinting; a few strikingly valuable selections appeared after the publication of my book; a few selections come from sources unlikely to be found in libraries and hence are not suitable for listing in the text. But more important is the fact that Page assembled the readings with a fresh mind, guided by his experience as a teacher, and so discovered a number of superior selections of which I was unaware. The resulting collection engages the educational psychology student in spirited conversation with one after another of the present-day leaders in the field.

LEE J. CRONBACH

Preface

In educational psychology, the use of readings offers some unique advantages. Whereas a textbook must be guided by the author's point of view, a book of readings may cover the whole range of the discipline. Educational psychology is rooted in different professional interests (learning or development); different rules of evidence (empirical or rational); different explanatory systems (stimulus-response or field); different subjects of study (groups or individuals). Especially, educational psychologists differ on goals, and therefore on methods of collecting evidence and reaching conclusions. Such diversity may be well represented in a book of readings, which allows the student to experience at first hand the reasoning of a well-balanced cross-section of contributors to the subject.

Although these readings would serve as an appropriate supplement to any educational psychology textbook, they are especially designed to accompany Cronbach's *Educational Psychology,* Second Edition (Harcourt, Brace & World, 1963). The chapter organization, and consequent balance of topics, are those of Cronbach's text, and the selections themselves are partly based upon reading lists that appear in the text. Those selections not taken from Cronbach's reading lists were chosen because they were considered to be more valuable and appropriate for the purposes of this volume. Editing was aimed to illustrate or complement each textbook chapter, and to achieve Cronbach's stated goals: relevance to school problems, adherence to research, realistic complexity of approach, and clarity of presentation. And Dr. Cronbach, by his comments as the editing progressed, has been most helpful in the efforts to achieve these goals.

Obviously, the several goals are often in conflict. Whereas school problems may be studied in rather loose and subjective ways, carefully designed research is usually conducted in laboratories far removed from the classroom realities. The study that combines great relevance and great rigor, therefore, is rare indeed. Similarly, complexity and clarity seldom exist together. There are few subjects more complicated than teaching and learning, and the complexities are not easily portrayed in words. On the other hand, a glib and appealing presentation may suggest a false simplicity in the subject. Rare is the writer who combines an easy pen with a hard understanding of the subject. We have tried, however, to avoid extreme lapses from relevance or rigor, from complexity or clarity.

In the editor's view, educational psychology at its best is an empirical social science. The more dependable methods are the more scientific methods, with careful manipulation of variables in realistic settings and careful quantification of results. The worthier findings, in this view, are those emerging from applications of such methods.

Yet the present responsibilities of educational psychology encompass more than what may now be built upon scientific research. Educational objectives, personality interactions in the classroom, aesthetic learnings, to name only three examples, have to date so rarely been studied scientifically that educational practice must often rely upon quite different sorts of evidence, such as everyday observation, careful generalization from other settings, and accumulated conclusions from successful practice. Where intelligent social scientists are able to draw upon such "unscientific" systems of evidence to formulate conclusions, their findings will be of considerable value to students.

The only danger for the student lies in his regarding all evidence as equally valid or equally final. It is not, and an effort has been made to suggest in the headnotes to the readings that the student ask searching critical questions about the evidence presented and the conclusions reached. One valuable lesson a book of readings may impart to a student is an awareness of the tentative quality of most evidence. Educational psychology is a fast-changing field in a century of change. The pace of new investigation is ever increasing. Concepts rapidly lose their cutting edges and are replaced by more usable ones, themselves to be replaced. In making the selections we have aimed to retain some of this sense of activity because, first, it may lead some students to conduct experiments in areas where our information is inadequate, and second, it may free students from the false simplicities which can lead to early dogmatism about teaching aims and methods.

ELLIS BATTEN PAGE

February, 1964

B. F. SKINNER

Education and Human Control

> Educational psychology is responsible primarily for the *science* of teaching, as distinct from the philosophy or art of teaching. It therefore has a peculiar responsibility, and Skinner here explains how urgent a responsibility this is. In doing so, he offers a challenge to educators, especially to students of educational psychology.

Science is steadily increasing our power to influence, change, mold—in a word, control—human behavior. It has extended our "understanding" (whatever that may be) so that we deal more successfully with people in nonscientific ways, but it has also identified conditions or variables which can be used to predict and control behavior in a new, and increasingly rigorous, technology. The broad disciplines of government and economics offer examples of this, but there is special cogency in those contributions of anthropology, sociology, and psychology which deal with individual behavior. Carl Rogers has listed some of the achievements to date in a recent paper. Those of his examples which show or imply the control of the single organism are primarily due, as we should expect, to psychology. It is the experimental study of behavior which carries us beyond awkward or inaccessible "principles," "factors," and so on, to variables which can be directly manipulated.

It is also, and for more or less the same reasons, the conception of human behavior emerging from an experimental analysis which most directly challenges traditional views. Psychologists themselves often do not seem to be aware of how far they have moved in this direction. But the change is not passing unnoticed by others. Until only recently it was customary to deny the possibility of a rigorous science of human behavior by arguing, either that a lawful science was impossible because man was a free agent, or that merely statistical predictions would always leave room for personal freedom. But those who used to take this line have become most vociferous in expressing their alarm at the way these obstacles are being surmounted.

Now, the control of human behavior has always been unpopular. Any undisguised effort to control usually arouses emotional reactions. We hesitate to admit, even to ourselves, that we are engaged in control, and we may refuse to control, even when this would be helpful, for fear of criticism. Those who have explicitly avowed an interest in control have been roughly treated by history. Machiavelli is the great prototype. As Macaulay said of

From B. F. Skinner, "Some Issues Concerning the Control of Human Behavior" (Symposium originally with C. R. Rogers), *Science,* 124 (1956), 1057–65. Reprinted in B. F. Skinner, *Cumulative Record* (New York: Appleton-Century-Crofts, 1961). Reprinted with permission.

him, "Out of his surname they coined an epithet for a knave and out of his Christian name a synonym for the devil." There were obvious reasons. The control that Machiavelli analyzed and recommended, like most political control, used techniques that were aversive to the controllee. The threats and punishments of the bully, like those of the government operating on the same plan, are not designed—whatever their success—to endear themselves to those who are controlled. Even when the techniques themselves are not aversive, control is usually exercised for the selfish purposes of the controller and, hence, has indirectly punishing effects upon others.

Man's natural inclination to revolt against selfish control has been exploited to good purpose in what we call the philosophy and literature of democracy. The doctrine of the rights of man has been effective in arousing individuals to concerted action against governmental and religious tyranny. The literature which has had this effect has greatly extended the number of terms in our language which express reactions to the control of men. But the ubiquity and ease of expression of this attitude spells trouble for any science which may give birth to a powerful technology of behavior. Intelligent men and women, dominated by the humanistic philosophy of the past two centuries, cannot view with equanimity what Andrew Hacker has called "the specter of predictable man." Even the statistical or actuarial prediction of human events, such as the number of fatalities to be expected on a holiday weekend, strikes many people as uncanny and evil, while the prediction and control of individual behavior is regarded as little less than the work of the devil. I am not so much concerned here with the political or economic consequences for psychology, although research following certain channels may well suffer harmful effects. We ourselves, as intelligent men and women, and as exponents of Western thought, share these attitudes. They have already interfered with the free exercise of a scientific analysis, and their influence threatens to assume more serious proportions.

. . .

EDUCATION

The field of education will show how nonscientific preconceptions are affecting our current thinking about human behavior.

The techniques of education were once frankly aversive. The teacher was usually older and stronger than his pupils and was able to "make them learn." This meant that they were not actually taught but were surrounded by a threatening world from which they could escape only by learning. Usually they were left to their own resources in discovering how to do so. Claude Coleman has published a grimly amusing reminder of these older practices. He tells of a schoolteacher who published a careful account of his services during 51 years of teaching, during which he administered: ". . . 911,527 blows with a cane; 124,010 with a rod; 20,989 with a ruler; 136,715 with the hand; 10,295 over the mouth; 7,905 boxes on the ear; [and] 1,115,800 slaps on the head. . . ."

Progressive education was a humanitarian effort to substitute positive reinforcement for such aversive measures, but in the search for useful human values in the classroom it has never fully replaced the variables it abandoned. Viewed as a branch of behavioral technology, education remains relatively inefficient. We supplement it, and rationalize it, by admiring the pupil who learns *for himself;* and we often attribute the learning process, or knowledge itself, to something *inside* the individual. We admire behavior which seems to have inner sources. Thus we admire one who *recites* a poem more than one who simply *reads* it. We admire one who *knows* the answer more than one who *knows where to look it up.* We admire the *writer* rather than the *reader.* We admire the arithmetician who can do a problem in his head rather than with a slide rule or calculating machine, or in "original" ways rather than by a strict application of rules. In general we feel that any aid or "crutch"—except those aids to which we are now thoroughly accustomed—reduces the credit due. In Plato's *Phaedrus,* Thamus, the king, attacks the invention of the alphabet on similar grounds! He is afraid "it will produce forgetfulness in the minds of those who learn to use it, because they will not practice their memories. . . ." In other words, he holds it more admirable to remember than to use a memorandum. He also objects that pupils "will read many things without instruction . . . [and] will therefore seem to know many things when they are for the most part ignorant." In the same vein we are today sometimes contemptuous of book learning, but, as educators, we can scarcely afford to adopt this view without reservation.

By admiring the student for knowledge and blaming him for ignorance, we escape some of the responsibility of teaching him. We resist any analysis of the educational process which threatens the notion of inner wisdom or questions the contention that the fault of ignorance lies with the student. More powerful techniques which bring about the same changes in behavior by manipulating *external* variables are decried as brainwashing or thought control. We are quite unprepared to judge *effective* educational measures. As long as only a few pupils learn much of what is taught, we do not worry about uniformity or regimentation. We do not fear the feeble technique; but we should view with dismay a system under which every student learned everything listed in a syllabus—although such a condition is far from unthinkable. Similarly, we do not fear a system which is so defective that the student must *work* for an education; but we are loath to give credit for anything learned without effort—although this could well be taken as an ideal result—and we flatly refuse to give credit if the student already knows what a school teaches.

A world in which people are wise and good without trying, without "having to be," without "choosing to be," could conceivably be a far better world for everyone. In such a world we should not have to "give anyone credit"—we should not need to admire anyone—for being wise and good. From our present point of view we cannot believe that such a world would be admirable. We do not even permit ourselves to imagine what it would be like.

. . .

If we are worthy of our democratic heritage we shall, of course, be ready to resist any tyrannical use of science for immediate or selfish purposes. But if we value the achievements and goals of democracy we must not refuse to apply science to the design and construction of cultural patterns, even though we may then find ourselves in some sense in the position of controllers. Fear of control, generalized beyond any warrant, has led to a misinterpretation of valid practices and the blind rejection of intelligent planning for a better way of life.

Chapter 1

How Psychology Contributes to Education

1-1

RUDOLF FLESCH

Phonics vs. No Phonics

1-2

JOHN B. CARROLL

The Case of Dr. Flesch

RUDOLF FLESCH

Phonics vs. No Phonics

This selection is taken from Flesch's best-selling book, *Why Johnny Can't Read.* Its popularity is understandable, since it is well written and presents research evidence in a simple, understandable manner. Its theme may be shocking to the American citizen and conscientious parent. When truth is so plain, Flesch seems to say, how can our schools persist in error? What is this terrible conspiracy about reading? Be sure to compare the position taken by Flesch with that taken by Carroll in the next selection.

Thomas H. Huxley once described the scientific attitude like this: "Sit down before fact as a little child, be prepared to give up every preconceived notion, follow humbly wherever and to whatever abyss nature leads, or you shall learn nothing."

The attitude of our experts on reading is quite different. Their minds are filled with preconceived notions, they have an utter disregard for facts, and they are unwilling to learn anything.

Whenever the results of phonics and of the word method were compared by tests and experiments, phonics came out on top. . . . Let me repeat that statement and amplify it: In every single research study ever made phonics was shown to be superior to the word method; conversely, there is not a single research study that shows the word method superior to phonics.

I know that this seems an unbelievable claim. Let me explain why I feel justified in making it. Every researcher in every field of science begins his work by surveying the previous research literature in the field. Consequently, almost all research reports are equipped with footnotes and bibliographical references that cover everything that has been done up to that point. A few hours in a library, working back from the latest studies in a given area, are therefore usually enough to check the sum total of research done to solve a given problem.

A few weeks ago I spent two days in the library of Teachers College, Columbia University, tracking down every single reference to a study of "phonics vs. no phonics." I carefully read each one of those papers and monographs. Naturally, it is possible that some item or items in the bibliography have escaped me; but I honestly don't think so. I covered the ground as diligently as I possibly could, looking for scientific evidence *in favor* of the word method.

There was none.

In the books and pamphlets by the "experts" there are plenty of statements referring to those research studies. Usually the findings are called "contradictory." Sometimes a few stray statistics are quoted out of context; sometimes the actual findings are boldly misrepresented. The result is always the same: the preconceived notions are endlessly repeated, the true facts are concealed.

The true facts are these, in chronological order:

In 1913, Professor C. W. Valentine of the University of St. Andrews in Scotland published in the *Journal of Experimental Pedagogy* the results of a brilliant experiment. He had hit upon the idea of solving the "phonics vs. no phonics" problem by teaching his college students to read English words written *in Greek letters.* So he transcribed a passage from Robert Louis Stevenson in Greek letters and gave two groups of twenty-four students each two minutes to decipher it. One group had first been coached in the Greek alphabet, the other had been coached in recognizing the *whole words* in the Stevenson passage, as they looked in Greek letters. Result: Those who had learned the alphabet did 200 per cent better.

Professor Valentine then tried a similar experiment with eight-year-old children at the University Training School in Dundee. The result was the same. It all added up, he reported, to "a striking victory for the phonic method."

In 1916, Miss Lillian B. Currier, a teacher in the public school of Tilton, New Hampshire, wrote a paper called "Phonics or No Phonics?" for the *Elementary School Journal.* (In 1923 she followed it up with another paper under the same title.) Miss Currier had taken two groups of children in first and second grade, and taught one group *with* phonics and the other *without* phonics. She had no statistics to offer but reported that the "non-phonic" children read with more expression and interest, but the "phonic" children were more careful and more accurate in reading the words that were on the page.

Next we come to a report by Mr. W. H. Winch, *Teaching Beginners to Read in England,* published in this country in 1925. Mr. Winch, a leading British educator, carried out a number of statistical experiments with children in first grade. (English children start going to school at five, so that they start to read at what is kindergarten age over here. . . .) There were two groups of children, one taught by the phonic method, the other by the "look-and-say" (that is, whole-word) method. After two months the children were given four tests. The look-and-say group scored 62.8, the phonic group 79.1. Mr. Winch summarized these results simply: "The phonic group has scored a complete victory."

Next study: In the *Elementary School Journal* of May, 1928, Elmer K. Sexton and John S. Herron report on "The Newark Phonics Experiment." Sexton and Herron tested a thousand school children in Newark, New Jersey. In spite of a rather confusing experimental setup, they concluded that the results favored instruction in phonics.

Next: In the October, 1930, *Journal of Education Psychology* Raymond M. Mosher and Sidney M. Newhall report on "Phonic vs. Look-and-Say Training in Beginning Reading." Fifty children in New Haven, Connecticut, were taught by the word method and seventy-three children by the phonic method. The two groups were given ten tests. Eight of the ten tests favored phonics.

Now comes a very interesting story (from *New York State Education,* October, 1930): Miss Helen R. Braem is Head Teacher at Letchworth Village, a state institution for mental defectives. The inmates of that institution are boys under sixteen with an I.Q. of from 30 to 75. Naturally they are very poor readers; they make very little progress at their school which, following the New York State Department of Education, uses the sight-reading (whole-word) method. One nice day Miss Braem hits upon the idea of giving those boys phonics. She digs up some phonic primers and readers and goes to work on an experiment, forming a "Sight Reading Group" and a "Phonic Group." The results are amazing. After one year she observes: "The Sight Reading Group had started reading for two years; the Phonic Group had started it for one year; yet the Sight Reading Group made three times the number of mistakes and took almost three times as long to read the same test." Now that Miss Braem has found the answer to her problem, she decides to help the poor "Sight Reading Group" who were the victims of the experiment. After three years of sight reading she gives them instruction in phonics. Another eight months go by and they have caught up with the boys who got phonics right from the start.

Next, 1931: In the *Peabody Journal of Education* Mr. S. C. Garrison and Miss Minnie Taylor Heard write of "An Experimental Study of the Value of Phonetics." They experimented with about one hundred school children in first and second grade; one half had phonics, the other half had none—or rather, they had the so-called "intrinsic" phonics invented a few years earlier by Professor Gates of Teachers College, Columbia University. At the end, there was a series of tests. Total result: The phonics group scored 58.5, the other group 55.5. Three points in favor of phonics. *And,* Garrison and Heard report, the phonics group was also considerably better in spelling.

Several years pass. Then Mr. Harry L. Tate publishes a paper on "The Influence of Phonics on Silent Reading in Grade I" (*Elementary School Journal,* July, 1937). A group of thirty-six first-graders were taught by the look-and-say method, another group of thirty-seven children were given exactly the same instruction plus fifteen minutes each day of drill and practice in phonics. After two months they were given three tests. Two of the tests ("silent reading" and "paragraph reading") were tests of guessing rather than reading and the word-method children scored slightly better. The third test, however, was a test of "word recognition." In this test the score of the phonic group put them 4.6 months ahead of their "normal reading age," which means, according to Mr. Tate, that they scored *270 per cent better* than the word-method group. In other words, fifteen minutes of phonics for eight weeks had pushed them half a school year ahead of children taught by the usual method. Mr. Tate comments that this result is "overwhelming proof of a reliable finding" and adds: "Phonetic instruction and drill, as judged by the results of the Gates Primary Reading Test, Type 1, is far superior to the look-and-say method in developing the ability to recognize words."

Let's proceed to another study in a somewhat different setting. Sister M. Dorothy Browne, of St. Joseph's College, Adrian, Michigan, writes her doctor's dissertation on "Phonics as a Basis for Improvement in Reading" (Catholic University of America, 1938). How about using phonics for remedial reading? she says. Let's see what phonics can do for sixth-graders. So she gives a ten-minute phonic drill to 160 sixth-graders in six parochial schools in Chicago, Detroit, and Washington, D.C. Another 160 students form a control group with no phonic drill. After nine months the two groups are tested. The "reading age" of the control group is 154.9 (that is, the norm for a child of twelve years and eleven months), that of the phonic-drill group 162.73 (thirteen years and seven months). Ten-minutes-a-day of phonics for nine months has put them eight months of "reading age" ahead of their fellow students. On the basis of her findings, Sister M. Dorothy Browne comes to this conclusion: "The study of phonics is helpful not only to the pupil who is deficient in reading, but is even more effective in stimulating the better reader to further growth."

And now we have arrived at 1939, the publication date of the most extensive and conclusive study of them all. It is the dissertation of Mr. Donald C. Agnew, taking his doctor's degree at Duke University. Mr. Agnew sets out to settle the old controversy once and for all. Those limited experiments with experimental and control groups of first-graders are inconclusive, he feels. Let's take *all* the children in *all* the schools in a city, he says, and find out where they stand at the end of third grade when the effect of reading instruction can really be effectively measured. So one spring he gives tests to all the third-graders in all the schools in Raleigh, North Carolina. Before he does that, he gives to all teachers who ever taught these children an elaborate questionnaire; from the answers he figures for each teacher the exact degree to which she uses phonics in her teaching. Then he works out the statistical relationship between the children's test scores and the amount of phonics they presumably got from their teachers.

The results are a terrific disappointment. They hardly show any differences. Mr. Agnew, in danger of not getting his Ph.D. degree, goes home and ponders. What went wrong? He comes to the conclusion that his basic assumption was wrong, namely, that a little phonics would go a long way. After all, the supervisors of the Raleigh schools are word-method people; they frown on phonics, and there is not one among their teachers who would dare to do a real job of phonics in her class. The value of phonics can only be proven when it is taken seriously and taught systematically.

Fortunately, there is the city of Durham, North Carolina, whose superintendent of schools is a pro-phonics man. All teachers in Durham schools have to teach phonics whether they like it or not. So Mr. Agnew gives another series of tests to some three hundred third-graders in Durham. *Their* teachers have all been teaching more phonics than even the most phonics-minded teacher in Raleigh. (Mr. Agnew has established that fact again with questionnaires.) Nothing could be more conclusive than a comparison of those third-grade test scores in Raleigh and Durham.

Here is the lineup of Mr. Agnew's average test results:

Name of test	*Score of children in Raleigh (word method)*	*Score of children in Durham (phonics)*
Gates A 4	63.31	79.50
Gates A 5	23.85	32.17
Gates B 2	18.11	29.29
Gates B 3	9.29	15.20
Word Pronunciation	53.15	70.17
Gates Type A	4.03	4.08
Gates Type B	4.18	4.18
Gates Type C	4.11	4.61
Gates Type D	4.15	4.38
Pressey Vocabulary	59.26	71.85
Eye-Voice Span	31.89	37.94

As you can see, the Durham children scored higher *in every one of these tests* (except Type B, where the scores were even). In addition, Mr. Agnew also gave them the "Gray Oral Reading Check Test," Set II and Set III. This is a test where the results are measured by the number of errors made in reading. On Set II, the Durham children made on the average 2.35 errors, the Raleigh children made 8.79. On Set III the Durham children made 7.05 errors, the Raleigh children 17.50. (The time scores on these tests showed that the phonics-trained Durham children took a little over a minute to read each set, while the little Raleigh word guessers took considerably less than one minute to make two to four times as many errors.)

Mr. Agnew's conclusions were clear and emphatic:

> Should phonetic methods be employed in the teaching of primary reading? The answer to this question can be given only when the purposes for teaching primary reading have been agreed upon. If the basic purpose in the teaching of primary reading is the establishment of skills measured in this study (namely: independence in word recognition, ability to work out the sounds of new words, efficiency in word pronunciation, accuracy in oral reading, certain abilities in silent reading, and the ability to recognize a large vocabulary of written words), the investigations would support a policy of large amounts of phonic training. If, on the other hand, the purposes of teaching primary reading are concerned with "joy in reading," "social experience," "the pursuit of interests," etc., the investigations reported offer no data as to the usefulness of phonetic training.

I can fully understand Mr. Agnew's outburst of sarcasm, since I worked my way through the same literature. It's exactly as he says: If you want to teach children how to read, you need phonics; if you just want to make them feel good, you don't.

After Mr. Agnew's definitive study, research in "phonics vs. no phonics" came practically to an end. Not, of course, because his conclusive results had made further studies unnecessary—rather, I suppose, because later potential researchers realized that if the Durham-Raleigh results couldn't change the educators' minds, then obviously nothing could.

I have only one more item that will bring the story up to date.

In December, 1943, Dr. David H. Russell reported in the *Journal of Educational Research* a study of first- and second-grade children in Vancouver, British Columbia. There were sixty-one children who were given day-by-day phonic work on sounds and extra practice in handwriting; fifty-five other children were taught little or no phonics. At the end of the experiment both groups were given twelve different tests of reading and spelling. The phonics-trained group did better on every one of those twelve tests. "The table [of test results] clearly reveals," comments Dr. Russell, "that the early and rather direct type of instruction in the phonics group has a favorable influence on achievement in spelling and reading."

Ironically, this same Dr. Russell is . . . the author of *Children Learn to Read* (1949), one of the leading word-method texts. I can't offer any explanation for this astonishing reversal; but then, it's inexplicable anyway how all the high priests of the word method have managed to disregard and by-pass the unanimous findings of Valentine, Currier, Winch, Sexton and Herron, Mosher and Newhall, Braem, Garrison and Heard, Tate, Browne, Agnew, and Russell.

After all this, you possibly expect me now to recite the evidence *in favor* of the word method. But, as I said at the beginning of this chapter, there is none. The story as I told it here is complete; this is the sum total of all experiments ever made. I have left out nothing and I have misrepresented nothing—to the best of my ability as a researcher.

The record is perfectly clear. The facts have been available to anybody in the field for many years. Our "scientific" educators simply don't *want* to know the truth.

JOHN B. CARROLL

The Case of Dr. Flesch

Carroll here discusses the subject of the preceding article: phonics as part of the teaching of reading. His writing is not as simple as Flesch's. Addressed to professional psychologists rather than to anxious parents, it is more technical in language and more qualified in its conclusion. After you have read both articles, try to formulate your own answers to the following questions: Is education simple or complicated? How do we know anything about learning? How can we best learn more? How can the science of psychology best contribute to the improvement of educational practice? These persistent questions are background themes for all of the study of educational psychology and for the balance of this book.

On page 123 of his recent best-selling book *Why Johnny Can't Read* (11), Rudolf Flesch makes the following statement:

> There are only two kinds of experts worth listening to when it comes to reading: linguists and psychologists.

Flesch takes pains to give the impression that he is extremely suspicious of educators, at least educators who have done research on methods of teaching reading, for these are presented as being engaged in a conspiracy to "conceal . . . the true facts" (p. 61), even (he implies) to conceal or ignore the results of their own research studies (p. 68). Educators who have lent their names to series of readers used in elementary schools, or who teach teachers how to teach reading, are especially not to be trusted, Flesch would have us believe.

In view of all this, it is with some trepidation that I undertake to comment on the now celebrated controversy about whether Johnny can read, for there is a possibility that Flesch would class me, along with the current President-elect of the APA [1] (whom he takes to task on page 43), among those "educators and teachers' college professors who happen to be members of the American Psychological Association" (p. 124). On the other hand, I do not think I have at any time been involved, ego or otherwise, in any system of teaching reading. I am not the author of a series of readers, nor do I teach the teaching of reading (except as it may occasionally come up for discussion in seminars on the psychology of language). If anything, I am on record (8, pp. 146–150) as having been mildly critical of some

[1] [Lee J. Cronbach.]

John B. Carroll, "The Case of Dr. Flesch," *American Psychologist,* 11 (1956), 158–63. Reprinted with permission of the American Psychological Association, Inc.

educators' views on reading instruction, and even slightly sympathetic to the "linguistic" approach which Flesch claims to recommend. In any event, I do not feel that any psychologist need feel apologetic about being affiliated with a "teachers' college," where there is as much opportunity as anywhere else for "scholars whose main work is the study of the human mind" —as Flesch characterizes (p. 124) the kind of psychologist who is "worth listening to." I would, in fact, urge psychologists to line up with educators like Gray, Gates, Witty, and others in their defense against the attacks made by Flesch.

For the sake of both the linguists and the psychologists whom Flesch would have people listen to, it is extremely important to have the record set straight. A number of writers have already stated (4, 5, 14) that Flesch has distorted and misrepresented the research evidence concerning the teaching of reading, particularly the research on the role which "phonics" should play in this teaching, and that his accusations have needlessly distracted and embarrassed American educators at a time when the schools have their full share of real rather than fancied problems. It is ironic that this particular attack on educators should have come from one who himself once earned a PhD from a teachers' college.

Members of the American Psychological Association, in confronting this whole matter, may wish to assess Flesch's performance in terms of the following excerpt from the *Ethical Standards of Psychologists,* adopted in 1953.

> The public requires dependable sources of psychological information, and it is in the interest of the profession that the public be well supplied. Psychologists who interpret the science of psychology or the services of psychologists have an obligation to report fairly and accurately. Exaggeration, sensationalism, superficiality, and premature reporting of new developments should be avoided; modesty, scientific caution, and due regard for the limits of our knowledge should characterize all statements.

In getting into this whole matter the array of hypotheses to be examined include the following:

1. That Flesch is right and that most teachers of reading are wrong.
2. That Flesch has, willfully or otherwise, misrepresented research results on the teaching of phonics.
3. That Flesch can't read.
4. That Flesch does not understand elementary statistics.

In order to establish a basis for the analysis which I shall make, it will be useful to sketch briefly the major conclusions which any fair-minded reader can draw from the published research on the question of "phonics vs. no phonics."

First, a little terminological discussion. What is phonics? *Phonics* is not to be confused with *phonetics,* which is the science of speech sounds and has nothing necessarily to do with reading or spelling. It is careless to say that "English is an unphonetic language," as some educators and laymen do, for English (that is, *spoken* English) is just as "phonetic" as any other language, if we mean by that statement that its sounds can be studied scientifically. When educators speak of the teaching of *phonics*, they mean the teaching of relationships or correspondences (regular or irregular) between the sounds of the spoken language and the symbols (or sequences of symbols) which may be used to represent these sounds in the customary orthography or system of spelling. In English orthography, the sound-symbol relationships happen (for historical reasons) to be somewhat more irregular than in those of most other languages, and even the regularities are somewhat more complicated and "unreasonable" than they need to be, as pointed out by the would-be spelling reformers. "Phonics" can be introduced into the teaching of reading at various stages, either at the very beginning, or later. There are various ways of teaching phonics: it can be done in a somewhat mechanical way, teaching the letters of the alphabet and their sounds, then having pupils "sound out" words; it can be done inductively, by presenting children with sets of similarly pronounced words with common orthographic features; or again, it can be done in a rather "incidental" manner (still remotely inductive, however), simply by frequently pointing out the relation between a given sound and a given letter or combination of letters, the while using other methods of teaching reading. The mechanical way of teaching phonics is the "old-style," "conventional" phonics method originated many years ago; it tends to lead to constraints on the kinds of words and sentences which can be introduced in the early stages of reading. (The method of teaching reading advocated by Flesch may be characterized as most nearly resembling old-style, conventional phonics.) The "incidental phonics" method, on the other hand, typically allows flexibility in the introduction of a vocabularly better related to the children's interests and needs.

The opposite of "phonics" is often considered to be the "word," "sight," or "look-and-say" method, which attempts to develop immediate associations between whole words and their spoken counterparts, with no explicit attention to the separate letters or sounds composing these words. A number of other "methods" are described by Anderson and Dearborn (2); actually, all these methods may better be regarded as procedures which may be variously used and combined in a well-balanced reading program.

From the above, it becomes immediately obvious that it is misleading to draw the issue as between "phonics" and "no phonics," and many of Flesch's distortions of research evidence stem from his failure to inform his readers precisely what kinds of "phonics" instruction are involved in the research studies on which he reports.

The major conclusions to be drawn from the research evidence available are as follows:

1. In the first grade of the elementary school, the best plan to follow for the average child is to start the first half-year with various "readiness" activities and familiarization. As children develop interest in reading and appreciation of the use of the written word, they should be gradually taught to recognize a small "sight" vocabulary without necessarily learning any sound-symbol correspondences (9, 15, 20, 21, 22).

2. Possibly in the latter half of the first grade, and certainly in the second year, children will gain somewhat more if inductive or incidental phonics instruction is presented. Failure to introduce phonics in the second grade or later may adversely affect word-recognition skills and spelling (3, 18, 23).

3. Children who are taught *from the beginning* by a conventional, old-style phonic method do not do as well in various reading performances (particularly those involving comprehension) as those taught in the way described in (1) and (2) above; however, the differences are not dramatic, and may or may not be statistically significant (16, 21).

4. Children who are given *no* phonics at all in the first grade do almost as well as those given gradual, incidental phonics instruction, and usually better than those receiving "conventional" phonics instruction. They tend to develop phonic insights and generalizations by themselves (22).

5. The method of instruction makes very little difference for fast, apt learners; the superiority of "incidental phonics" over "no phonics" and "conventional phonics" becomes more marked for low aptitude pupils (15).

6. Many children move out of the elementary school grades without having acquired adequate word-recognition skills based on phonic knowledge; wide differences in "phonic ability" can be detected even at the college level. The extent to which the method of instruction is responsible for these differences is not known (23, 24).

7. Despite what may be taught in schools of education, or recommended in books about the teaching of reading, there are still fairly wide variations in the methods used by teachers, at least according to their statements (6, 19).

To judge from Flesch's Chapter V, which purports to be an exhaustive survey of the literature on "phonics" vs. "no phonics," there is only one issue: which method shall be used, the "phonic" method or the "word" method? He claims to find no evidence whatsoever favoring the word method, and the casual reader of the conclusions cited above might tend to agree with him. We have already commented on the fallacy involved in this reasoning. The reader might persist, however, and ask whether it might not be true that Flesch made an honest mistake in not recognizing that methods are inevitably complex and that there are different varieties of phonic methods and different stages at which the introduction of phonic teaching might or might not be appropriate. Bearing on this point is the bountiful evidence that Flesch misrepresented a number of research studies, going directly counter to their authors' own statements. Such is true for studies by Currier (9), Gates (13), Sexton and Herron (20), Mosher and Newhall (17), Garrison and Heard (12), Tate (21), Agnew (1), and Russell (18).

Start with the Currier and Duguid study (9), published in 1916. True, this is not a rigorous study by contemporary standards, but it was sufficiently well controlled to indicate a trend. According to Flesch, Miss Currier performed a small-scale experiment in a Tilton, New Hampshire public school. Still according to Flesch, "She had no statistics to offer but reported that the 'non-phonic' children read with more expression and interest, but the 'phonic' children were more careful and more accurate in reading the words there were on the page." If we let Miss Currier speak for herself, we learn: "The phonic classes were so concentrated on letter sounds that the attention was diverted from the *sense* of the paragraph to *word pronunciation*. . . . The reading was generally less smooth, slower, and the idea confused." Apparently, Flesch has a high tolerance for confused ideas.

Next let us note how Flesch handles the 1927 experiment of Gates (13), which he says was responsible for the trend away from phonics. According to Flesch (p. 54): "Dr. Gates sets up an experiment: one first grade is taught by his new 'incidental phonics'; another first grade—the control group—is exposed to conventional phonic drills. After a few months, the two groups are tested. Hurrah! The new method has won. And Dr. Gates is on his way to drive phonics out of American schools." On reading the Gates article, we by no means get the impression that Gates thought to himself, "Hurrah! the new method won!" On the contrary, none of the differences between the experimental and control groups were significant, a fact which Gates himself emphasized. There was only a weak trend favoring the "incidental phonics" group. (By present-day standards, the statistical methods used were crude, and not even the *N*'s were reported; nevertheless, there is little if any indication that the null hypothesis should be rejected in any of the comparisons.) Gates himself concluded: "In some of the earlier investigations, as suggested by such titles as 'Phonics or No Phonics' [cf. the title of Flesch's chapter!], it has appeared that there was no choice other than to accept or reject the complete phonetic system. The intelligent procedure is to determine what phonetic drills, devices, etc., are of value."

We now come to the research of Sexton and Herron (20) published in 1928, in reference to which Flesch says (p. 62): "In spite of a rather confusing experimental set-up, they concluded that the results favored instruction in phonics." The experimental set-up would not be confusing to anyone who understands experimental design. In any case, here is what Sexton and Herron actually said: "The teaching of phonics functions very little or not at all with beginners in reading during the first five months. It begins to be of some value during the second five months but is of greater value in the second grade." They point out that ". . . teaching ability has immeasurably more influence on the teaching of reading than has the use or non-use of phonics."

Flesch next reports on the experiment of Mosher and Newhall (17), published in 1930: "Fifty children in New Haven, Connecticut were taught by the word method and seventy-three children by the phonic method. The two groups were given ten tests. Eight of the ten tests favored phonics." True, but if you read the Mosher and Newhall report you will find that none of the differences were statistically significant, and that the two differences which favored the "word method" were the largest of all.

According to Flesch, Garrison and Heard (12) "experimented with about one hundred school children in first and second grade; one half had phonics, the other half had none—or rather, they had the so-called 'intrinsic' phonics invented a few years earlier by Professor Gates of Teachers College, Columbia University. At the end, there was a series of tests. Total result: The phonics group scored 58.5, the other group 55.5. Three points in favor of phonics." Flesch ignores the fact that the PE of this difference is reported as 1.53, a figure which allows us to find that the probability of the chance occurrence of a difference as great as three points is about .19, or nearly one in five. (Garrison and Heard did not report the probability level, but surely Flesch could have done the simple computations and table-referrings required.) One of Garrison and Heard's conclusions reads: "In the teaching of reading it seems probable that much of the phonetic training now given should be deferred till the second or third grades. It appears that work in meaningful exercises which are planned to increase comprehension and to teach discrimination of words is more important than phonetics." I shall not bother to quote other conclusions which Flesch does not include.

The 1937 experiment of Tate (21), to read Flesch's discussion of it, sounds like iron-clad evidence on his side. As he reports it:

> A group of 36 first-graders were taught by the look-and-say method, another group of 37 children were given exactly the same instruction plus 15 minutes each day of drill and practice in phonics. After two months they were given three tests. Two of the tests ("silent reading" and "paragraph reading") were tests of guessing rather than reading and the word-method children scored slightly better. The third test, however, was a test of "word recognition." In this test the score of the phonic group put them 4.6 months ahead of their "normal reading age," which means, according to Mr. Tate, that they scored *270 per cent better* than the word-method group. . . . Mr. Tate comments that this result is "overwhelming proof of a reliable finding" and adds: "Phonetic instruction and drill, as judged by the results of the Gates Primary Reading Test, Type 1, is far superior to the look-and-say method in developing the ability to recognize words."

Let us now report what Tate actually said. To be sure, Flesch did quote Tate accurately, but the quotations were pieced together in a rather forced manner from various portions of the article, and the conclusion cited above was only *one* of Tate's conclusions. Tate queried the teachers of his phonics group, who pointed out that the phonic instruction tended to hold back progress and make some children use their lips too much in silent reading. Tate also laid stress on the results of the sentence-reading and paragraph-reading tests, which favored the non-phonic group. His final conclusions were as follows: "Regular periods for phonics instruction and drill are not desirable. Phonics should be used by the pupil as a tool and not as subject matter to be mastered for its own value." Flesch does not report the fact that this was how Tate really felt about phonics.

Next in chronological order would come the experiment of Dolch and Bloomster (10) on "phonic readiness," which Flesch takes up in his Chapter VI. He calls this the "one single experimental study in which the onset of phonic readiness at seven was discovered" (p. 72). This may be the case, and it is also possible that some educational authorities have misinterpreted this study, as Flesch claims. At any rate, what the experiment *does* show is that ability to make phonic generalizations *without training or guidance from the teacher* probably does not mature until a mental age of seven or greater. The experiment tells nothing, contrary to what Flesch seems to imply, about whether or not children can be taught or guided to use phonics before a mental age of seven. The weight of evidence from other studies suggests that they can.

I have not yet been able to examine in the original Agnew's study (1), which Flesch presents as favoring the conventional phonics approach, but from Anderson and Dearborn's (2) discussion of it I judge that Flesch made too much of small, insignificant differences which appeared to favor conventional phonics, and that he played down too much the clear finding that the non-phonic group read faster on the average. I shall not make an issue of Flesch's treatment of this study, however.

We come now to the last experiment discussed by Flesch, a study by Russell (18) published in 1943. Because it suited his purposes, Flesch reported this particular experiment with reasonable accuracy, but the interpretation of the results hinges on semantics. The children who got "phonic work on sounds" did better on tests than children who got "little or no phonics," but this does not exclude the possibility (in view of the investigator's known views, a high probability) that the "phonic work on sounds" was more in the nature of the "incidental phonics" which had been found effective in other experiments, and not at all the old-fashioned phonic drill advocated by Flesch.

In setting out to make his survey of the literature on the "phonics vs. no phonics" question, Flesch claims he attempted to track down "every single reference." He continues (p. 61): "I carefully read each one of those papers and monographs. Naturally, it is possible that some item or items in the bibliography have escaped me; but I honestly don't think so. I covered the ground as diligently as I possibly could, looking for scientific evidence *in favor* of the word method. . . . There was none." At the end of his literature survey chapter, the like of which has probably never before appeared in a best seller, he tells us (p. 68): "The story as I told it here is complete; this is the sum total of all experiments ever made. I have left out nothing and I have misrepresented nothing—to the best of my ability as a researcher."

The evidence cited above bears on the question of Flesch's misrepresentation of research findings. There is also evidence on Flesch's ability to handle simple statistical data. What about his statement that he "left out nothing"? When I started to check the completeness of Flesch's coverage, I was in much the same position that Flesch seems to have been in, for I had never had occasion to make an exhaustive literature search on this particular problem. With very little difficulty I was immediately able to locate a number of important and pertinent studies. I found that Flesch had completely missed the study of Gates and Russell in 1938 (15), which shows a slight superiority of an "incidental phonics" method over *both* the word method (using little or no phonics) and a method emphasizing conventional phonics—a superiority which is more marked for pupils low in reading readiness. I found that Flesch had omitted the study by Tate, Herbert, and Zeman (22) which found that "incidental phonics" was slightly superior to a method in which all phonics instruction was deliberately excluded. The study by Burt and Lewis (7), published in England in 1946, and casting doubt on the usefulness of phonics instruction for "backward readers" (who *do* turn up in England, despite any impression which Flesch may have given to the contrary), was completely passed by in Flesch's "exhaustive" search, as was also the recent and very pertinent study by McDowell (16). McDowell's study, conducted in parochial schools in Pittsburgh and vicinity, compared a rather systematic "phonetic" method with the method which was regularly used in these schools, and found that the regular method generally yielded slightly superior achievement after three years. (It can be assumed that the regular method itself contained some phonics instruction.)

We shall excuse Flesch for failing to mention two pertinent studies published in 1954 (3, 23) on the chance that they appeared after he submitted his manuscript.

If one could search the length and breadth of the land, one could probably locate a sizable minority of teachers and educational administrators for whom "phonics" is almost an unmentionable word, and who in consequence may be doing less well with their charges than they might do. One might find also a considerable number of teachers and educational administrators who believe, contrary to the research results, that a strict phonic approach is the most efficacious method of teaching reading. If Flesch had wanted to make a constructive contribution to the teaching of reading, he might have used his talents of persuasion and rhetoric in the cause of drawing the attention of these groups to the true importance of "phonics" as *one* of the procedures to be followed in a well balanced program of reading instruction. He could also have performed a much needed service by addressing himself to the parents who are over-anxious about Johnny's difficulties in reading, telling them how they might better cooperate with Johnny's teacher and school authorities, and demonstrating for them some *tested* techniques in helping Johnny learn to read. There is even a possibility that Flesch could have shown teachers how a "linguistic" approach might improve present-day techniques of teaching phonics.

If Flesch had chosen to do these things, instead of what he did, he could still have produced a best seller. The present analysis will give psychologists and their friends the bases for recommending a fate for the best seller under scrutiny here.

REFERENCES

1. Agnew, D. C. The effect of varied amounts of phonetic training on primary reading. *Duke Univer. Res. Stud. Educ.*, 1939, No. 5.
2. Anderson, I. H., & Dearborn, W. F. *The psychology of teaching reading.* New York: Ronald, 1952.
3. Bedell, R., & Nelson, Eloise S. Word attack as a factor in reading achievement in the elementary school. *Educ. Psychol. Measmt,* 1954, 14, 168–175.

4. Bienvenu, H. J., & Martyn, K. A. Why can't Rudy read? *Nat. Educ. Ass. J.*, 1955, 44, 499–500.
5. Brown, S. Dr. Flesch's cure for reading troubles; a cool look at the panacea. *Commentary,* 1955, 20, 162–168.
6. Brownell, W. A. Current practices with respect to phonetic analysis in the primary grades. *Elem. Sch. J.*, 1941, 42, 195–206.
7. Burt, C., & Lewis, R. B. Teaching backward readers. *Brit. J. Educ. Psychol.*, 1946, 16, 116–132.
8. Carroll, J. B. *The study of language.* Cambridge: Harvard Univer. Press, 1953.
9. Currier, Lillian B., & Duguid, Olive C. Phonics or no phonics? *Elem. Sch. J.*, 1916, 17, 286–287.
10. Dolch, E. W., & Bloomster, Maurine. Phonic readiness. *Elem. Sch. J.*, 1937, 38, 201–205.
11. Flesch, R. *Why Johnny can't read, and what you can do about it.* New York: Harper, 1955.
12. Garrison, S. C., & Heard, Minnie Taylor. An experimental study of the value of phonetics. *Peabody J. Educ.*, 1931, 9, 9–14.
13. Gates, A. I. Studies of phonetic training in beginning reading. *J. Educ. Psychol.*, 1927, 18, 217–226.
14. Gates, A. I. A review of Rudolf Flesch, *Why Johnny can't read.* [New York:] Macmillan, [1955].
15. Gates, A. I., & Russell, D. H. Types of materials, vocabulary burden, word analysis, and other factors in beginning reading. *Elem. Sch. J.*, 1938, 39, 27–35; 119–128.
16. McDowell, J. B. A report on the phonetic method of teaching children to read. *Cath. Educ. Rev.*, 1953, 51, 506–519.
17. Mosher, R. M., & Newhall, S. M. Phonic vs. look-and-say training in beginning reading. *J. Educ. Psychol.*, 1930, 21, 500–506.
18. Russell, D. H. A diagnostic study of spelling readiness. *J. Educ. Res.*, 1943, 37, 276–283.
19. Russell, D. H. Opinions of experts about primary-grade basic reading programs. *Elem. Sch. J.*, 1944, 44, 602–609.
20. Sexton, E. K., & Herron, J. S. The Newark phonics experiment. *Elem. Sch. J.*, 1928, 28, 690–701.
21. Tate, H. L. The influence of phonics on silent reading in grade I. *Elem. Sch. J.*, 1937, 37, 752–763.
22. Tate, H. L., Herbert, Theresa M., & Zeman, Josephine K. Nonphonic primary reading. *Elem. Sch. J.*, 1940, 40, 529–537.
23. Templin, Mildred C. Phonic knowledge and its relation to the spelling and reading achievement of fourth grade pupils. *J. Educ. Res.*, 1954, 47, 441–454.
24. Tiffin, J., & McKinnis, M. Phonetic ability and its measurement and relation to reading ability. *Sch. & Soc.*, 1940, 51, 190–192.

Chapter 2

What Teachers Are Trying to Accomplish

2-1

HARRY S. BROUDY

Mastery

2-2

DAVID RIESMAN

Community Pressures on the Schools

HARRY S. BROUDY

Mastery

> "Mastery," we may all agree, is a major goal of teaching. But what is mastery? How do we know it when we have it? How can we produce it? We can best understand professional goals when they are accurately defined, and such definition is a special concern of certain educational philosophers. In this essay a master analyst plies his trade. After you have finished Broudy's article, think about some words that describe other goals of education: "skill," "creativity," "knowledge," "adjustment," "happiness." Do not these goals also need careful, searching scrutiny?

The term "mastery" has a long history both in common usage and in educational parlance. The relations of master-slave, master-servant, master-disciple, master-pupil, and master-self are familiar to most of us. As the origin of the word indicates (*magnus* = great), the master was supposed to be superior to the subject in power or worth, or both.

In the mastery of a craft and the mastery of a subject matter, the superiority is of a person over a skill or over a body of knowledge rather than of one person over another. That Mr. Delta is master of Slave Beta means that Beta obeys the commands of Delta, or that Delta's decisions supersede those of Beta; but if Delta masters the Greek language, it does not mean that he gives orders that the language obeys. Control is the common element in both types of mastery, but presumably we do not mean the same type of control in both cases. The way one can use the Greek language is not identical with the way one can use a slave.

In educational literature mastery signifies control achieved through learning. By learning one is supposed to achieve mastery of a subject (chemistry), a craft (carpentry), or the processes that make up subjects, crafts, and other learned activities. However, we distinguish various outcomes of learning by calling some of them knowledge and others skill. Thus we speak of a person "knowing" chemistry and another as being a "skilled" carpenter.

We do not ordinarily speak of mastering attitudes or appreciations, even though, in analyzing *why* a person has or has not this or that attitude, we may locate the cause in the learning or failure to learn this or that piece of knowledge or acquiring or not acquiring this or that skill.

For example, to appreciate Shakesperian plays it is advisable to know *how* to read Shakesperian English, and to know a great deal *about* Shakespearian drama. But when we use "appreciate" in this sense we mean not

Harry S. Broudy, "Mastery," Chapter 5 in B. O. Smith and R. O. Ennis, eds., *Language and Concepts in Education* (Chicago: Rand McNally, 1961), pp. 72–84. Reprinted with permission.

only that *X* "likes" Shakesperian drama, but also that *X* evaluates it according to certain standards. The late Professor Kittredge of Harvard, for example, was a master of Shakespeare because of his knowledge about Shakespeare. Without it, he might still have liked Shakespeare, but his claim to mastery would be regarded as dubious.

Perhaps we do not use the term mastery in describing attitudinal and emotional learnings because to learn an attitude is not to control it, but rather to be controlled by it, that is, one *is* one's attitudes in a way that one is not identified with his knowledge or his skill.

1. MASTERY WITH RESPECT TO SKILL

If we exclude appreciations from the domain of mastery, we are left with knowledege and skill as relevant to it. We do speak of mastering the art of playing the piano, driving nails, ploughing, sailing a boat, driving a golf ball, and riding a bicycle. These involve skill. Skills have two major aspects: the executive and the judgmental. The former is a sequence of acts involving muscle movements or symbols, or both. This sequence is guided by judgments (the second aspect of skill) in order to achieve some kind of adaptation. The skilled typist makes rapid movements with few waste motions, and adapts the key movements to the copy, the balkiness of the machine, and office distractions.

Clearly, by mastery we mean both aspects of skill. Skills vary in the required proportions of these components. The carpenter needs more of the judgmental factor than does the floor scrubber, and the cotton farmer more than the cotton picker. It would be an odd master of carpentry who was clumsy in the use of a hammer, yet if he lacked adaptive judgment, to say that he had mastered carpentry would be odder still.[1]

What is meant by manipulative or executive mastery is fairly clear. We can describe the growth of a skill in terms of the decrease in the time needed to perform the task, the reduction in the number of errors, and in the effort expended. These criteria are also suitable for judging mastery of the whole skill or craft as well as its component parts. They are the criteria of efficiency, that is, the ratio between effort and results. But when the task in question is a complicated set of operations such as carpentry, the judgmental component is also a factor in efficiency, because the need to choose among alternatives at any state of the operation slows down the execution, and incorrect choices increase both time and the number of errors.

[1] As a matter of fact, this question is academic because the manipulative phase is learned first, so that if anything remains unlearned it is more likely to be the judgmental phase.

The adaptive judgment follows the executive trial because obstacles to the exercise of the skill arise only in the course of the exercise. Some of these can be anticipated in thought, but only *after* they have been encountered in practice. For example, the skilled carpenter can rescue a nail that he anticipates will become bent as it is being driven through a board. This exemplifies adaptive (judgmental) skill (presumably occasioned by his lapse of manipulative adeptness), a skill perfected in response to many misadventures with nails.

Mastery in complex operations would seem to mean, therefore, that the performer has speeded the choosing process. How can this be done?

1. It may be that after much trial and error obstacles are so finely discriminated that each sets off a specific response that will eliminate it. For example, the experienced carpenter will perform automatically specific movements in response to a knot in the way of the nail, to a board that is too brittle, too wet, etc. In this way the need for deliberation is eliminated or greatly reduced.

2. We may say that in the course of long experience the carpenter has classified obstacles into those requiring the use of a chisel, an adz, glue, or braces. Here deliberation is reduced to recognizing the class into which an obstacle is to be placed.

3. Unusual obstacles presumably require thinking, that is, a series of symbolic trials and judgments—for example, the carpenter who is confronted with the problem of joining wood to a new alloy. Thinking does not directly speed the response as do the first two processes, but, if successful, it paves the way for more rapid classification of obstacles, and ultimately for automatic responses to them. It is an indirect way of speeding the process.

Undoubtedly, the highest palm of mastery awaits the *thinking* carpenter, the one who can overcome unusual obstacles. We would, however, have to make some qualifications. First, the thinking carpenter would have to be efficient in the sense of (1) and (2) for *ordinary* obstacles. If this were not the case, he would not be called a master carpenter, but an ingenious amateur. Thinking is the necessary recourse of the novice to make up for his lack of skill; to the expert, thinking is an extension of skill far beyond that which the ingenious amateur can reach by dint of thinking alone.

In the second place, given an unusual problem, if carpenter *A* solves it by automatic responses and carpenter *B* by thinking, which would be judged the greater master? There is little doubt that carpenter *A* would get the nod.

The discussion would seem to indicate that with respect to skill, we mean by mastery efficiency of performance and that this, in turn, means progressively less effort and fewer errors to complete a task. Mastery is achieved by routinizing the component sequences of the task whether they be executive or judgmental.

It may be objected that while this description may be adequate for skills involving physical movements or combinations of physical movements and sensory discriminations, it would not hold for skills involving a high proportion of symbolic materials. Examples of such skills might be mental arithmetic, reciting the multiplication table, and memorizing poetry.

There are two problems here. First, there is the question as to whether efficiency is what we mean when we speak about the mastery of symbolic skills. The other problem is whether the kinds of learning we ordinarily call knowledge, or understanding, or problem-solving are merely skills or involve something other than a skill. We shall postpone the second question until the latter part of this chapter.

If we compare our experience of doing mental arithmetic with riding a bicycle, we note certain differences. For one thing, in doing mental arithmetic (a symbolic skill) we are not aware of using large muscles, although we may feel certain strains around the eyes or in the scalp. Instead we seem to be aware of words representing number processes or images of one kind or another. In riding a bicycle our awareness is pretty much of muscular movement, visual patterns of the road, and sounds on the street. In other words, the content of our consciousness differs with the activity involved. On the other hand, there are some important likenesses. In both types of activity learning is marked by less confusion, less difficulty in keeping the results of the operations from becoming mixed up with each other, and, above all, greater confidence. As a result, the process moves more swiftly and accurately—it becomes more efficient. Operationally, therefore, despite difference in the materials employed, both symbolic and muscular skills are said to be mastered when they can meet the same criteria of efficiency. As to how efficiency is achieved, the analysis already given on page 24 would seem to suffice for the symbolic skills also.

2. MASTERY AND TYPES OF KNOWING

When we speak of mastery, do we mean anything other than skillful performance? Does mastery mean a performance made as automatic as possible? These questions raise some difficulties. Skills, it may be admitted, do have a manipulative phase that can become more or less efficient, and it may be conceded that the judgmental phases of an activity may be telescoped into quick choices among standardized sets of alternatives. Nevertheless, there is such an activity as knowing, and to know *X* is in a sense to master *X*. Is all knowing a kind of doing, a kind of efficient execution of a sequence of prestructured acts, existential or symbolic?

Common sense and technical philosophy hesitate to identify knowing with skillful doing. Both the Realist (e.g., Aristotle or Hutchins) and Instrumentalist (e.g., John Dewey) would shy away from the reduction of knowing to a skill, although for quite different reasons. The Realist would refuse to eliminate the intuitional (or insight) phase of knowing; the Instrumentalist would balk at reducing the complete act of thought to automatic response sequences.

Although the Realist does not deny the importance of careful inference in arriving at judgment, he nevertheless insists that all knowledge ultimately rests on immediate awareness of things in relation. These relations may be perceptual, as when we say "the chair is behind the table"; or they may be conceptual, as when we say "if *A* is north of *B* and *B* is north of *C*, *A* is north of *C*." Whether we understand a sentence, or recognize that *x* is an instance of *X*, or that a certain sentence is a definition, or that a chain of sentences proves something, the content of our consciousness is an insight or a succession of insights into patterns more or less clear, more or less complicated, more or less extensive. Practice and experience may hasten the moment of intuition or insight, but either we have the insight or we do not.[2] Hence the Realist would have to exclude these instances of im-

[2] "In short, the attainment of a concept has about it something of a quantal character. It is as if the mastery of a conceptual distinction were able to mask the preconceptual

mediate knowing (insight) from the realm of skill, so that mastery in conceptual learnings would not mean the same as mastery of a skill.

On the other hand, John Dewey is also clear on the matter of immediate knowing. What the Realist calls "immediate knowing" Dewey calls "understanding," and although he admits that these immediate insights are indispensable to inquiry, he denies their equivalence. Knowing is a term he reserves for that product of inquiry called warranted assertion.[3] To what extent, therefore, would Dewey be willing to equate the process of inquiry with a skill? Certainly he would agree that some materials for thought are worked over and over again so that they no longer need reflection, but he would insist, it would seem, that genuine inquiry and routinized skill are antithetical, for it is the failure or absence of skill that occasions the reflective act in the first place; the settled, the accomplished, the finished—none of these requires thought. Thinking and automatic responses seem to exclude each other.

In the Realist account of knowing there is no overt doing at all. It is, following Aristotle, an immaterial process in which either a sensible or intelligible form is abstracted from its material vehicle. For the Instrumentalist, doing of an overt kind is indispensable to carrying the act of thought to its completion into some kind of verification. But this overt action is subordinated to and guided by symbolic action, for one thing, and it is neither routine nor automatic, for another. Thinking is a *creative* mode of adaptation.

We see, therefore, that the gradualness with which a skill is perfected is contrasted with the all-or-none character of insight, on one hand, while on the other, the creative, adaptive, deliberate aspects of thinking are opposed to the automatic character of a skill. It becomes necessary to examine more closely what might be meant by mastery of an item of knowledge or a body of knowledge, keeping in mind that in the generic sense of the term it means some kind of control. It is certain that having the type of insight called understanding is at least part of what is meant. But this tells us little. For one thing, is there only one or more than one type of knowledge to be mastered or understood? Speaking in the context of school subjects, there seem to be three kinds of statements that we are called upon to understand:

1. Statements of fact, also called existential statements, such as: "there is a cloud in the sky"; "the circumference of the earth is approximately 25,000 miles"; "Washington crossed the Delaware"; "I put sodium into water and it sputtered." These are examples of knowing *that* something or other is or was the case.
2. Statements classifying things into kinds, or indicating the properties

---

memory of the things now distinguished. Moreover, the transition experience between 'not having' a distinction and 'having it' seems to be without experiential content." Jerome S. Bruner, Jacqueline J. Goodnow, and George A. Austin, *A Study of Thinking* (New York: John Wiley & Sons, Inc., 1956), p. 50. See also H. S. Broudy, *Building a Philosophy of Education* (New York: Prentice-Hall, Inc., 1954), p. 220, for a similar observation.

[3] See *Logic: The Theory of Inquiry* (New York: Henry Holt and Company, 1938), Chap. 8.

of certain types of things: "aluminum is a metal"; "all is not gold that glitters"; "homeostasis refers to the efforts of an organism to maintain balance"; "synapse is the point of connection between two neurones."

Definitions, terminology, pigeon holes of one kind or another all help us categorize (classify) our experiences so that we can say "*X* is this sort of thing, or this thing is an *X* kind of thing." Every subject of instruction has material of this kind to be mastered. We may speak of this kind of knowing as knowing *what,* or classificatory, knowledge.

3. Finally, in most subject matters there is some kind of reasoning by which it is argued that one way of looking at experience is more sensible or more logical or more trustworthy than another. For example, in biology the theory of genes and chromosomes (terminology) makes it easier to account for the "facts" of genetics than some other theory. Or the theory of oxidation makes it easier to explain why the iron rusted after the rainstorm and the aluminum did not. Or the theory that Hamilton was a man of aristocratic leaning helps to explain why he advocated certain measures in the early years of the Republic. Or the theory of the unconscious helps to explain why some people have phobias of very specific objects for no reason that they can mention. This may be called theoretical or explanatory knowledge. It may also be called knowing *why,* and it is the most comprehensive of the three kinds of knowledge. Actually, all three are involved with each other, because the terms used in stating facts and theories are concepts and these, in turn, affect what we perceive the facts to be. On the other hand, "aluminum is a metal" describes the way language is used in chemistry, that is, it is a fact about language usage.

There are many interesting logical and psychological differences among these types of knowing. Pedagogically, however, our central problem is how to test for the presence of each type of knowing. It is impossible to inspect directly the contents of a pupil's consciousness; therefore, we have to rely on inferences from his test behavior. What sort of test responses would allow us to differentiate correctly whether or not John is recalling *memoriter,* classifying according to some logical scheme, relating hypotheses to evidence, etc.? We may attack this question by examining in some detail one type of knowing—conceptual—to determine the meaning of two statements: "John knows concept *A*" and "We can infer from response (*R*) that John knows concept *A*."

The justification for not examining all types of knowing intensively lies in what has already been said about the relations among them. All types of knowing involve classification. For example, to know that "it rained here" involves correct classification of wet roads, wet grass, and streaming gutters with the effects of rain. Empirical generalizations are statements about what relations classes of existing objects bear to each other.

Reasoning, inductive or deductive, cannot proceed far without judgments as to what can be classified as premises, propositions, valid and invalid arguments. However, the learning of a concept or the relation among concepts presupposes that the learner can recall, recognize, discriminate, and judge—processes that are involved with varying degrees of importance in all types of knowing. How then are concepts learned?

3. MASTERY OF CONCEPTS

Bruner says that to learn to attain a concept is *"the process of finding predictive attributes that distinguish exemplars from non-exemplars of the class one seeks to discriminate."* [4] Bruner's subjects attained concepts in the following way. There were a large number of cards with various combinations of figures differing in size, color, and content. The experimenter framed a concept in his mind and showed the subject a card that was a correct instance of the concept. For example, the concept might be "large, red, two figures," and a card with two large red triangles might be chosen as a correct example. From the other figures the subject was asked to pick cards that he thought might also be correct examples of the concept, and the experimenter confirmed or failed to confirm each trial. By varying his selections, the subject could eliminate certain characteristics, such as the number and kind of figures, until he hit upon the concept itself. Bruner points out that the strategies used by the learner to attain concepts are not necessarily deliberate or conscious, "although the sequence of behavior showed systematic features of a highly regular and skilled order." [5]

Bruner's subjects developed certain methods for picking the cards in order to eliminate non-defining characters as quickly as possible. We need not go into these in detail. Some used a good deal of deductive reasoning to figure out which card would eliminate the greatest number of possibilities; others used fairly mechanical and systematic scanning to do so. Nevertheless, there was improvement as the method was practiced.

The words "regular" and "skillful" in Bruner's own characterization serve to point out that the way concepts are learned tends to converge upon the skill pattern. One need not say that all concept learning follows this pattern. For example, one could learn the characteristics of a tornado or of aluminum by reading about it or being told about it. But however one learns a concept, operationally the test for mastery would tend to be the speed and accuracy with which one was able to classify new instances correctly. Thus although at first one may have had to think and discriminate carefully in classifying aluminum, or detecting fallacies in syllogistic reasoning, or working out problems algebraically, in time and with practice these are performed with fewer and fewer halts for choices based on deliberation or thinking. It would seem, therefore, that the attainment of concepts and the use of them do not differ from attainment of mastery in skills.

Why then do we hesitate to accept the correct answer to a mathematics problem as proof that the student has mastered the solving of such problems? Why do we insist that he pass in his "work" as well as the answer? Why are we wary about the faultless rendition of the proof of a theorem in geometry? I am certain that it is not entirely founded on suspicions of cheating.

This suspicion does not arise about mastery of manipulative skill. If a boy types well, according to the efficiency criteria, we do not ask whether

[4] Bruner *et al.*, p. 22.
[5] *Ibid.*, p. 241.

he can *really* type well. If he recites the multiplication table flawlessly on a number of occasions, we do not wonder whether he can *really* recite the multiplication table. If he does the computation required for solving algebraic equations, we do not ask, "Can he *really* compute algebraic equations?" But a correct set of answers to questions in chemistry, algebra, history, or in any of the school subjects may leave one with the suspicion that possibly the behavior is the result of rote memory, and this apparently seems not to satisfy the mastery requirement in this context.

What more seems to be required for conceptual mastery may be indicated by examining some of the situations that could be described by the statement "John has mastered the concept of oxidation." This could mean:

(1) John, in response to the cue, "What is oxidation?" replies with a textbook definition of oxidation.

(2) John makes this response (1) when not warned in advance that he would be asked for it, as on an examination.

Is response (1) a reliable index of understanding (conceptual mastery)? Examinations in many subjects are constructed every day as if it were. Presumably it is assumed that this response is typical of what the learner would respond in the class of situations calling for the concept of oxidation. Nevertheless, a large body of common sense and expert opinion would not regard either response as a reliable index, although (2) would be regarded as more reliable than (1).

(3) John responds with a paraphrase of the definition in the text—with or without specific preparation for the cue.

This is regarded as an advance over (1) and (2) because it eliminates somewhat the possibility that John has succeeded by rote memory alone. Presumably by a sequence of tests one could find out whether John's paraphrase had or had not become stereotyped or memorized. Our suspicions would be heightened if the precise wording were repeated, although logically is one justified in concluding that rote memory of definitions or paraphrases of definitions is evidence of non-understanding? Latin masters who frowned on use of the trot (pony or crib) may have been justified on moral grounds, but certainly in some instances the trot furnished more understanding than did the original text, and the memorized trot translation no more belied this than did the honest and laborious translation by another pupil prove that he *did* understand what he had worked out.

(4) John replies with ordinary examples of oxidation: burning, rusting, spontaneous combustion.

(5) John replies with an unusual example (one not in the text and not discussed in class—e.g., cellular respiration).

(6) John, when presented with an instance of oxidation, categorizes it properly (instance taken from the text or from common experience).

(7) John categorizes properly an unusual or unfamiliar case of oxidation.

Responses (4–7) are regarded as good evidence of understanding, because the giving of an example necessitates that John *select* from his experience an item having attributes that set oxidation apart from other chemical processes. The same principle would apply, of course, to John's ability to identify a chemical operation as an instance of oxidation.

Nevertheless, responses (5) and (7) would carry special conviction because of the word "unusual." Ordinary examples of oxidation can be memorized from the text or can be recalled from the teacher's discussion. These might also be used to make identifications, provided the sample to be identified was identical with or very similar to the items that had been learned as examples of oxidation.

This is not the case with unusual examples and specimens. Logically, of course, nothing more is involved in giving an extraordinary example than an ordinary one. Logically, rusting exhibits the attributes of oxidation as well as does cellular respiration. Psychologically and pedagogically, however, the difference is enormous. For one thing, that a student shows awareness of materials not specifically studied is itself a sign of scholastic initiative that is not lost on the teacher. But, more important, the citing of cellular respiration as an instance of oxidation signifies an ability to identify the attributes of the concept in situations that do not permit easy identification with what is already familiar. Further, it may be a hint of response (8) in which John seems to be able to relate oxidation to kindred chemical principles.

The probability that John can give unusual examples and identify unusual specimens by chance or practice apart from understanding is virtually zero. Conversely, with the attributes of the concept clearly before him, it would be unlikely for John to fail in any but the most doubtful cases.

We shall not discuss in detail the type of response called experimental. Once more, whether John could perform an experiment to illustrate or to demonstrate oxidation would be inconclusive if it were a familiar experiment, and virtually conclusive if it were a highly unusual one.

(8) John responds by launching into a discussion of oxidation in terms of valence, chemical bonds, the periodic table, and reduction.

(9) John can carry on this discussion with an experienced chemist who asks questions and puts out leads.

The series of responses (1–8) vary in the degree to which the correct answer could have been the result of rote memorization or practice. Note that our dissatisfactions with the earlier responses are not that they are swift, but they might be "unthinkingly" so; not merely that the pupil might not have thought out his answer, but rather that he *could* not think it out in unfamiliar or unpracticed instances.

Response (9) constitutes evidence that would convince even the most skeptical schoolmaster that John *understands* oxidation and is not merely skillful in reinstating memorized or practiced verbal patterns on three counts: First, the solving of unfamiliar and unusual problems has not been practiced. Second, the solution involves apprehending something as an instance of a general principle or law, and this is an act of insight that has to be enacted anew in each fresh situation. Finally, in discussing oxidation with an expert, the likelihood that the learner has had a chance to rehearse the dialogue is remote.

What then is the factor in test behavior that distinguishes "knowing" responses from merely correct ones? It seems to be a *flexibility* of the response, an *adaptiveness* to requirements of the task by fine discriminations and judgments of fitness and relevance. To test this we use situations in which the learner has to respond discriminatingly and with unpracticed (not yet automatic) responses. Even in tests of knowing facts, where simple recall would seem to be an adequate test, discrimination and flexibility are not wholly absent. Otherwise machines and parrots would be judged to "know" facts.

Knowing at any level, even the rapid recognition involved in the judgmental aspect of a skill, seems to denote an awareness of the cue, stimulus, or problem in a context. Discrimination and flexibility are the *behavioral* criteria of adequate knowing, but apparently we find it difficult to account for such adaptiveness of the response without *presupposing that the actor is aware of a context that justifies and makes sense out of his acts.*

"Knowing that," "knowing what," "knowing why," simple and complex skills, symbolic and muscular skills all vary in the phenomenological (awareness) context in which they occur. The context shrinks to practically nothing in a well-established muscular skill, such as swimming, and swells enormously when we are thinking through a problem in juvenile delinquency. In mathematics, the context is a set of definitions, postulates, and their deductive relations. In science, empirical statements and theories furnish the context. In riding a bicycle, it is a sensory-motor-perceptual field.

When, therefore, we speak of mastery in the sense that knowing something is to master it, we mean (1) an awareness of an appropriate context that grounds the adaptive response and (2) efficiency in making that response.

4. MASTERY OF SCHOOL SUBJECTS

What is involved in the mastery of school subjects? School subjects vary with respect to the type of contexts of which the pupil is to be aware. History, for example, deals largely with contexts made up of series of cause-effect sequences. The events are particular and not specific; therefore, the logical context is not highly structured. Each event has a name, location, date, antecedents, and consequences, and there is no way of deducing these items of information from any principle. There is no necessary relation among "voyage to the new world," "Columbus," and "1492." There is plenty of thinking to be done in the study of history, but the recall factor in historical competence must always remain high. Hence, without constant repetition of the materials, history learnings are doomed to vagueness, if not oblivescence, no matter how well they have been taught.

In empirical sciences, such as chemistry, geography, and economics, the prescription calls for more conceptual and inferential mastery and for less efficiency in recall than is needed in history. For one thing, the particular facts dealt with are really *classes* of particulars. Geology is concerned with igneous rocks, not this or that igneous rock; economics with the consumer, not with Mr. A, an individual consumer. Nevertheless, definitions, experiments, descriptions, hypotheses, diagrams, and tables have a given content that has to be recalled to permit fruitful thinking in these areas.

This may explain why science teachers lean so heavily on recall as a test of competence. To know terminology and to be able to repeat rules and laws are so important as means to adequate learning that they are often taken as reliable signs of such learning despite the notorious fact that they need not be. What saves the situation from becoming ludicrous is that the good student understands *and* memorizes, while the really poor student does neither. The damage, one may surmise, comes to and from the mediocre pupil who, finding it impossible to understand and think in a subject matter, resorts to memorization. This he can do well enough to pass examinations and perhaps even to enter college.

In the deductive sciences, such as mathematics, and some phases of grammar and physics the premium is clearly on conceptual contexts. But even here there is content to be recalled if the pupil's work is to be consistently satisfactory. For example, in proving that the opposite angles formed by intersecting lines are equal, it is necessary to recall that a straight line forms an angle of 180 degrees as well as the axiom about the addition and subtraction of equals. In Euclid, one has to remember which theorems have already been proved, so that one can decide whether or not a given theorem may be used for proof of new theorems. Furthermore, certain constructions, approaches, gambits, and procedures for solving mathematical problems come, in time, to be recalled so readily as to render the procedures semiautomatic.

In other words, school subjects require mixtures of contexts, but not the mixing up of them. Because only ingeniously devised tests can give us reliable clues as to what contexts are in fact guiding the responses of the student, there is always the danger that the pupil will operate from inappropriate contexts—perceptual instead of conceptual—without the teacher knowing it.

Another danger, of course, is that because teachers test for one type of context, others will not be learned at all. For example, if tests in literature are of the factual variety, the appreciative outcomes may not accrue simply because students have detected what "pays off" in one instructor's grading system. There is also the possibility that some teachers are not too clear as to the outcomes they seek.

Sophistication about the diverse types of competence involved in the various school subjects may help to prevent confusion about what kind of context-awareness the pupil is to have, how to achieve it, and how to test for it. We may want automatic responses on the multiplication table, but interesting details about the costumes of the Eskimos might be studied for acquaintance rather than for long-term retention or for use in problem-solving. Sophistication in these matters can prevent a teacher from believing that he has produced one kind of mastery when, as a matter of fact, he has produced another. This is important because all learning seems to gravitate toward the form of the routinized skill, following what might be called the law of the least noetic effort. It may be expected that regardless of what the teacher is trying to teach, the pupil will convert it into that form of knowing or skill that is most congenial to him. If he has difficulty with theories, he will convert them into factual statements; if he cannot achieve an insight, he may resort to practicing a skill. Conversely, the lazy student may wish to substitute easy generalizations for skill.

The same sophistication is needed for testing the results of learning, because here also all evaluation tends toward the least ambiguous form of test items (the factual) and not all modes of mastery are tested with equal validity by items of this sort.

Both in school and out the term "level of mastery" is frequently used to indicate that mastery is a matter of degree. By levels of mastery we may be referring to (1) the efficiency of the response, (2) the area over which control is exercised, or (3) the level of control employed. The first type is exemplified by *A* typing faster than *B;* the second by *X* who can use three tools compared to *Y* who can use only one. As to level of control employed, this would seem to refer to the amount or degree of judgment among alternatives that a task entails. Earlier in the chapter it was pointed out that even choices can be routinized, that is, reduced to the type of mastery in levels (1) and (2). Accordingly, it would seem as if what might be meant by "high level" mastery is the sort of judgment and decision that demands a high order of theoretical competence as well as efficiency.

Accordingly, we say that a physician has a higher level of mastery of medicine than the nurse. His theoretical context is so well developed that the novel, the peculiarities of the individual case, baffle him only until he can fit them into his theoretical framework. Because he may fear the effects of a narcotic on the digestive system of his patient, he may vary its amount or eliminate it altogether. Or the pattern of blood pressure, pulse, temperature, and other data may induce him to increase the dosage. Such adaptiveness based on theory is not expected from the nurse. Similarly, the auto mechanic is not expected to display the flexible control of automotive problems characteristic of the automotive engineer.

But between two physicians or between two automotive engineers, he who is the greater master categorizes faster, more accurately, on fewer cues, and with less cognitive or noetic strain. In other words, if we keep the theoretical level constant, differences in mastery are differences in skill; if we keep efficiency of response constant, differences in mastery correspond to differences in the levels of theoretical insight required to get the correct response.

In summary then:

1. The meaning of mastery, although it always connotes control, varies with the type of learning outcome.
2. Mastery involves a judgment about the context of which the learner is supposed to be aware (the phenomenological factor).
3. Mastery involves a judgment about the adaptive behavior that tests the presence of the appropriate context.

4. Finally, mastery can be characterized as insightful action made habitual. The level of mastery is judged by the strength of the habit, given equal insight; and on the insight, given equally well-established habit.

DAVID RIESMAN

Community Pressures on the Schools

Goals of teaching and curriculum content are decided by many persons: teachers, administrators, professional groups, and members of the community. In this selection a sociologist writes about the pressures to conformity exerted by some communities upon secondary schools. He discusses the problem of teacher freedom and professional courage especially in the "controversial" field of social studies. With his acute sense of social change, Riesman claims to see certain major shifts in these pressures.

. . . It is obvious that not all secondary school systems are alike: they differ as much among themselves as colleges do. A few big-city and suburban public high schools (such as Boston Latin, Winnetka's New Trier, the Scarsdale schools, New York City's High School of Music and Art or Stuyvesant High, etc.) have quite as much of a tradition of intellectual distinction and even as devoted and protective alumni as all but a small handful of private schools—and offer a far better education than many colleges do. Occasionally, as happened in Pasadena, such schools may lose a fight for freedom and experimentalism, but they recognize the fight as theirs.

In many ways the high schools are today in the position the colleges were a hundred years ago. In their need to monitor idly prankish youth, in their "collegiate" razzle-dazzle of sports and dating, in their fear of being called "godless," in their need (not financial but political) to accept whoever comes, in their unavoidable concern with morals, they recall many vignettes we have of nineteenth-century college life. Of course, the differences are great, too: the high schools today involve the whole community in a way that even the colleges with the most vociferous subway alumni neither did nor do; and one could argue that in some ways high school youth is presently more mature and more sober than college youth of the collegiate generations. Moreover, when we read W. Lloyd Warner's *Democracy in Jonesville* and August B. Hollingshead's description of the same Midwest small town in *Elmtown's Youth,* we are reminded of still another feature of the early American college, namely, its emphasis on parental social stand-

From David Riesman, "Secondary Education and 'Counter-cyclical' Policy," Chapter 3 in *Constraint and Variety in American Education* (Lincoln: University of Nebraska Press, 1956), pp. 107–54. Reprinted with permission.

ing as the basis for seating and even for honors; for these books show the high school and its teachers to be almost completely dominated by the "better element," to the extent of influencing grades given and such honors as leading the band, according to the social-class position of the family. The same theme of class (and in the South, caste) domination of the schools appears in other books of the Warner group, such as Allison Davis and John Dollard's *Children of Bondage,* and in John Gillin's chapter on "The School in the Context of the Community" in *Education and Anthropology.*

WHICH PUBLIC RUNS THE SCHOOLS?

Other studies, however, have shown rapid democratizing tendencies to be at work in the control of the schools just as these tendencies have also, in hardly more than a generation, altered the high school from a college preparatory institution for one-fifth or so of the teen-agers (or an occasional terminal institution for the girls) to the taken-for-granted pattern for four-fifths or more. In a number of communities the school boards have become highly democratic in the sense of reflecting, with at least equal voice, the less educated and the less privileged strata. Thus, in one New England manufacturing city, the superintendency and the school board have become the symbols, even more than such an office as the mayoralty, of ethnic and class conflict, with the Irish and to a lesser degree the French Canadians getting their revenge on the Beacon Hill–type snobs of earlier generations. Since the lower-class parent has no interest in the schools, save as a political symbol, unless his own children are of school age, this means that the superintendent of schools must, if he lasts that long, educate a new group of constituents every few years—a totally different situation from that of the private school headmaster who has managed to cultivate a self-perpetuating body of trustees.[1]

Likewise, an unpublished study done on the West Coast has shown how the school board in an expanding industrial town became the most representative agency in the town, speaking not only for the newcomer industrialists but for the farmers and others of lesser education who didn't want to see any "new-fangled notions" in the schools, any more than they wanted to see the town's water monkeyed with by fluoridation—this last being, as I mentioned in my second lecture, an issue on which the more parochial have in some towns mobilized to defeat the more cosmopolitan and science-minded higher status groups.

The handful of studies we have (including the Lynds' close scrutiny of the control of the "Middletown" schools) do not allow us to triangulate the entire area or even readily to interpret the data we already have; thus, we

[1] I am indebted for materials on the politics of the "Bay City" schools to as yet unpublished memoranda by James Shipton and Peter and Alice Rossi. Another study, done by Neal Gross, Ward Mason, and their colleagues at the Harvard School of Education, includes case studies of the role of New England school superintendents in coping with a wide variety of publics, including their teachers. The pressures to which they respond, moreover, are not merely local. For educators, despite what some of their university critics say, *can* read, and are not unaffected by the philosophies of education that emanate from the cultural and scientific centers.

know that Middletown and Elmtown are (or were) to some degree company towns and possibly not representative even of their regions. We do know that there are schools so located as to be able to profit from a balance of powers in the community—that is, to be powers themselves, able to give a cagey and purposeful superintendent quite a free hand within very broad limits—so long at least as no dramatic issue presents a group in the community with a chance to make trouble for him and capture votes and symbolic vindications for itself. Indeed, the teachers themselves, in alliance with school board members, have been known to drive a superintendent out, though on the whole they tend to stay out of fights at the hierarchy's peak and, like the conscientious civil servants they often are, to fall into line with any workable mandate from "downtown."

In rural areas, matters are again different. Warren Peterson found, in his study of women high school teachers in Kansas City, that many had entered the Kansas City system after sad experiences of rural and small-town politics, where a single shift in the school board might eliminate a school principal and virtually dispossess his teachers; in comparison, a metropolitan school system offered the security of tenure, often enforced by a union, as well as greater opportunity to specialize.

ALTERED PATTERNS OF PRESSURE ON THE TEACHER

The harassment of the public school teacher has been traditional in the smaller American communities, but this used to take the form (particularly if the teacher was a woman) of policing her private life, her smoking and gallivanting and church-going, without much direct interference in her conduct of the classroom. Today, especially in the larger places, the teacher is much freer to lead her own private life, but what we might term her academic freedom is under a great deal of pressure. Lack of concern over the teacher's private life reflects the general urbanization of America and the decline of puritanical vigilance over teachers, ministers, and other exemplars; meanwhile, however, concern over the teacher as a person has taken on a new aspect; the teacher is required today to be a "good guy," warm and friendly, not too eccentrically dedicated to interests in which the community cannot share. Moreover, the personality of the teacher has become more closely intertwined with the subjects taught: the high schools, which could remain fairly remote from immediate community preoccupations when attended only by a few, are now under a service-minded pressure to teach the social studies, and in many places they are also under pressure to teach a kind of syncretistic and neutral religion, as well as to teach tolerance, democracy and citizenship, and all other good things.[2]

Teaching these topics, which contain more obvious dynamite than the limited traditional curriculum did, however, both draws on what is in the papers and risks getting into them. High school teachers can become labeled

[2] In smaller communities, as Wilbur Brookover points out in *The Sociology of Education,* the high schools also have in the past borne much of the obligation to furnish entertainment—through sports, debates, plays, music, etc.—a function from which the mass media, the county clubs, and do-it-yourself are gradually relieving them.

by their students as "controversial" as soon as any discussion in the social area gets at all heated or comes close to home.[3] While a college student usually has to take the trouble to write home before he can get a parent steamed up about what a teacher has said in class, and in fact is quite likely to protect his teacher against his less enlightened parents, the secondary school student is still living at home with parents whose jealousy of the teacher is not mediated by distance either of space or of status. The high school teacher has in fact lost relative status in recent years as more and more parents are themselves high school graduates. And while the kindergarten teacher gains admiration because she can control several dozen preliterates whose mothers cannot always manage even one, the high school social studies teacher has a harder time being one-up on American-born parents who can claim to know as much as she about civics or UNESCO.

THE SOCIAL STUDIES AS A CASE IN POINT

Considering this situation in an essay a few years ago, I proposed that social studies be abandoned in the public schools, since they could not, without more protection for the teachers, be taught with any vigor or candor, and that without this they were apt to become sheer piety or, as they are called in one school, the "social slops." Rather than having the teachers assign news-magazines and deal with current debates, or try to show that the Brazilians or even the Chinese are human, too, and live in an interesting way, I suggested they stick to languages, mathematics, and the arts. These are disciplines that can be taught without political compromise (other than that of allowing poor students to pass), and they can be adequately, if sometimes crushingly, taught by a person who is neither courageous nor inspiring.[4]

John Dewey, with his orientation towards problem-solving as the principal basis of thought, and towards the school as a factor in the life of the community, would probably have regarded my view as an unwarranted concession to reaction. He might have pointed out, as many of my critics

[3] A number of investigations have asked high school students what they consider as the qualities of a good teacher; this "consumer research" indicates a preference for clear explanations, good discipline and impartiality (no pets), good grooming, consideration for pupils' feelings, patience and kindness. These are hardly the qualities easiest for the dedicated social science teacher to cultivate! See, e.g., Sister M. Theophane and Arlene Rasor, "Good Teaching as Seen by Junior High School Pupils," *School Review,* Vol. 54 (1956), pp. 72–75.

[4] My article, "Some Observations on Intellectual Freedom," appeared in *The American Scholar,* Vol. 23 (1954), pp. 9–25, and is reprinted in *Individualism Reconsidered and Other Essays,* pp. 123–138.

Patrick Hazard has in correspondence made a point I fully agree with, namely that the arts can, if illuminatingly taught, be quite as controversial—even as "political"—as the social sciences, but for most teachers, regrettably, the invitation to controversy is a latent one in the arts and an unavoidable one in the social studies. I am also aware that teachers of such allegedly non-controversial subjects as French and algebra, basketball and shop, do often manage to convey social attitudes all the more effectively by pretending not to—convey them by side-comments or even by the way they conduct themselves in class; it would often be well to have such unexamined attitudes clarified and counterposed by social studies teachers who make explicit their preference for detached factuality as against side-of-the-mouth indoctrination.

did, that even today perhaps no more than a quarter of our high school students go on to college, and the rest if social studies were abandoned would get no formal orientation in a confusing world. And, just because the social studies do connect, if not taught too badly, with contemporary themes, they may occasionally help the teacher make contact with students for whom the traditional curriculum seems meaningless and remote—students who would otherwise drop out of school or, what is worse, remain physically present while learning how to evade the school's requirements—thus, in effect, preparing themselves to do the same in the jobs they will hold later on.

"FACTS" VERSUS "VALUES"

My attitude on this matter has also been influenced by a chain of reflections set off by Max Weber's influential argument that the social scientists must eschew values in their work, and must in that sense separate their work from their personal lives and their unarguable preferences. It struck me that Weber's position was an understandable one for a German professor who feared among his colleagues and students the development at the close of the First World War of a romantic anti-democratic movement; he wanted to caution them that the world of the future required of them a stoical factuality, a rational appraisal of the new situation rather than a self-indulgent reaction against it. Today, among many in the avant-garde universities of this country, such a position is no longer progressive, and social science teachers who confront uncommitted, city-wise students who wouldn't dream of fighting city hall are often likely to emphasize the role of values in research and to attempt to smoke out the evasions and self-deceptions of empiricism.[5] But in many Southern or denominational colleges the situation is in this country today very much like that which Weber faced forty years ago: in these relatively unemancipated places youngsters arrive crammed full of values—their parents' and townsfolk's—but very shy on facts; and it is obviously an achievement to bring some detachment into their perspective, some sublimation of naive, often chivalric vehemence. At the same time, by stressing his hard factuality, a college teacher in such a setting may escape censure, at least outside of the areas of greatest passion such as race relations or Communism, where presentation even of facts, no matter how judiciously, may be regarded as subversive.

The same possibility is open to the high school social studies teacher, who may present a model of dispassionateness to students still deeply imbued with the unthought-out values they grew up with, or the sometimes more frivolous opinions they have picked up from the peer-group or the media. Such an approach has its obvious dangers, first in not safeguarding the teacher or the students from community vigilantes, and second in its relative narrowness of range, for there will be some students in almost every school who would profit from seeing the way an informed and conscientious

[5] For fuller discussion, cf. my article (written in collaboration with Nathan Glazer), "Some Observations on Social Science Research," in *Individualism Reconsidered*, pp. 467–483.

teacher himself decides "loaded" questions rather than simply "giving both sides." While such complexity can more readily be handled in college than in the secondary schools, we are still a long way from sending every student to college, or even every bright student. Thus, it is likely that the social studies teacher can be emancipating for many of his students even if the best he can do is to introduce a bit of data and a bit of respect for it.

CAN WE LEAVE IT TO THE "DOCUMENTARY" MEDIA?

I did, however, assume when I wrote my criticism of high school social studies that such introduction did not need to be made within the confines of the school, and that the high school students would be exposed to many of the themes of the social studies outside of school, particularly through the mass media. Radio and TV are censored, too, as the schools are, but the veto groups which affect them, being national in scope, are sometimes less parochial than the vested interests which can curb a public school teacher—or indeed see to it that there is nothing to curb. Many of the enthusiasts for educational TV, including myself, have hoped to provide intellectual challenge for young people through a still-young medium, not bound by tradition or tied to the school boards. In sober moments, however, I realize that countervailing power must be sought within, as well as outside, the schools. If teachers cannot occasionally make contact with a student's mind, the teachers will be dead on their feet and the young in their care will be stultified, no matter what programs "Omnibus" puts on. The school teacher may lack prestige in the eyes of the community at large, but the school as an institution has an unavoidable impact on the child—an impact almost as great as that of his parents. This is of course not an argument against experimentation with the media. Perhaps a TV program can be, for a sharecropper's child growing up in the dead-end schools of our Black Metropolises, something of the catalyst that pulp fiction was for Richard Wright (as he describes his grim upbringing in *Black Boy*), namely, an escape from the all-too-omnipresent "reality" into another world of fantasy and imagination. But at present we know that most such children will find what is vacuous in the media to confirm their street and school experience, rather than to prevail against it.

NO ROAD BACK

All these considerations have brought me around to conceding that there is no presently viable alternative to some high school social studies programs—quite apart from the moral and practical problem of abandoning a program, for whatever good reasons, at the same time that it is under attack from conservatives who want to go back to the old-fashioned curriculum and from reactionaries who want the social studies revamped to drill the students in their version of Americanism. For those who are going on to college, the social studies might well be postponed, but for those who are not—and they cannot simply be consigned to vocational courses—the high schools have perforce become an *ersatz* college with all that implies in curricular and extra-curricular patterning. Nevertheless, I cannot comfortably resign myself to a dilemma in which teachers are forced, in a setting far less protected than that even of relatively unfree colleges, to take positions (including text adoptions) that may get them into trouble with vigilante groups on the one side or their own consciences on the other. Some school teachers have felt I was patronizing them in discouraging courageous behavior on their part, but of course I have nothing but praise for those who willingly take the risks involved in intrepid social studies teaching. But no school system can count on possessing even a minority of such teachers—for perhaps the majority, in fact, the dilemmas I have been discussing will scarcely exist, so encapsulated are they in the uncriticized values of their local communities.

FIGHTING FIRE WITH WATER

The schools' vulnerability is in part a matter of the rhetoric of community controversy. Suppose, as now often happens, a demand is made for religious instruction in the schools. The superintendent or school principal is against this: he thinks it can only be mushy, not truly religious—that, if anything, it will turn the kids against religion and against each other. To explain all this would take time and require some audience sophistication, while his critics will label him as "godless" if he resists. Or, to take another instance, there was a typical letter a short while ago (March 12, 1956, by Nancy McGannon) in the Chicago *Daily News* attacking the President of a division of the Illinois Education Association for resisting one of the Broyles Bills requiring all teachers to take a loyalty oath; the writer said she couldn't understand how academic freedom was abridged and ended by declaring: "I'm afraid there are a lot of parents and taxpayers who do not understand it." It is hard to imagine this "parent and taxpayer" writing a similar letter about her inability to grasp the import of one of the Hoover Commission reports or the Report of the President's Council of Economic Advisors, yet the "parents and taxpayers" do suppose that they can advise on matters having to do with education. When the President of the Illinois Education Association sought to answer her, the reply took nine paragraphs; it spelled out the ambiguity of requiring a special test oath of teachers, while at the same time it met the parent on the common ground of patriotism and anti-Communism. The very fact that the more complex positions take longer to state puts the teacher on the defensive to start with, for at best the teacher's position will be given equal chronological time and that will not suffice for clarification (unless she has the rare ingenuity for putting complex matters simply). The closer a word is to a blow, the greater its impact in the short run and the harm is done; in many controversies over the schools, there is no long run, little distance between the partisans, and few constitutional barriers to impetuosity.

POWER OF THE PRESS

One important barrier, however, is perhaps implicit in what has already been said, namely, a liberal and enterprising press (broadcasting, because of its lack of permanence and its usual political irrelevance or neutrality, usually matters less). A vigorous press—even a good student paper—can act as a counter-cyclical force in its own right, and alter the patterns of public rhetoric in favor of the more complex as against the mindless. I have been repeatedly struck with the influence of the local papers on the climate of freedom or miasma at particular universities. A few colleges are so secure as not to be hurt or helped by the press (for instance, Harvard's Corporation and Overseers would in any case be more influenced by the *Herald-Tribune* than by the Boston *Post* or Hearst papers); and many are so benighted as not to learn from any source that freedom is as necessary to a college as a library or stadium. But when I compare in the Middle West the free state universities with the beleaguered ones, it seems to me that Wisconsin professors profit by reading Evjue's *Capital Times* (or the liberal Milwaukee paper) as breakfast-table reminders of support—profit, too, from knowing that waverers might even be intimidated from going against the current. Minnesota profits (as does Iowa) from the open-minded Cowles press in much the same way. By contrast, professors at Ohio State pick up the Columbus *Dispatch* anxiously, worrying what it might imply to other professors, and the administration, about how Senator Bricker, or some other regent, feels about their last speeches or books or even classroom comments. The reactionary professors feel heartened by the paper to vent their venom on the liberals; waverers get confused. Plainly enough, if a professor were sure neither administration nor regents nor state legislators pay the slightest attention to the paper, he would view its attacks as a joking matter rather than as a nightmare. However, it is sometimes hard to know which comes first: for a liberal press, as at Madison, may be as much the result as the cause of a free spirit among the faculty.

THE TWILIGHT CASE OF THE JUNIOR COLLEGE

In spite of what I have just said about the occasionally large or even disproportionate influence of the local paper on a university, it remains true that the colleges, including those which are publicly controlled, are much less within the purview of the parish than are the high schools. There are intermediate cases which illuminate this difference, and I was recently involved in one of them. It was the sort of subterranean academic freedom case that is common today, where the individual faculty man seeks to avoid national publicity, though it might vindicate him, lest it also make it harder for him to get another job while in addition embarrassing colleagues and superiors who are men of good will but are not exactly spoiling for a fight. The man in question, a sociologist, had been given a contract to teach in a junior college controlled by a large metropolitan school system, but before he could begin, police and FBI reports on his alleged radical past reached headquarters and his contract was revoked. In discussing the case with headquarters people, Everett Hughes and I found a great concern lest harm unjustly befall the instructor—the concern one might find in a decent paternalistic business—but virtually no realization that any principle was at stake, any issue of academic or intellectual freedom transcending the individual or the school system. For the officials had grown up in the secondary school world where teachers are employees; they said in effect that they had no trouble getting teachers and that it was unreasonable to expect them to investigate complaints about a man who hadn't actually entered the system. Had he actually started, I know they would have been protective of him as a member of the team, but they felt little responsibility to anything so abstract as freedom of opinion.

The case made me realize that, as the junior college movement spreads, we may see many twilight colleges, which appear free from the perspective of the high school but almost unprotected and even obscurantist from the perspective of the traditional private college. And at many of these junior colleges, as at some of the state or poorer private institutions, the chief academic freedom issues that arise do not involve ideas or associations, but rather the right of professors to flunk students who are plainly inadequate but who arguably may gain from postponing their entry on the job market.

What I have said should not be taken to mean that public institutions have no means of professional defense against the customer. Many of the big state institutions, if their presidents know their business, are more than a match for any single pressure group in the state; the University of Minnesota, for example, with its extensive services to the state, its great prestige, and its alumni holding virtually all state offices, is quite a power in its own right. (Lewis Dexter and Theodore Caplow have called other such cases to my attention.) But I am saying that the junior college which grows up from below, without an academic board of its own but bound to the secondary school system, may share the vulnerabilities of the latter and not create for the students who go there any sharp increase in illumination.

THE COUNTERVAILING POWER OF THE SCHOOLS

And yet, despite all I have said, despite all the pressures and pieties to which the schools must be subservient, we know from a great accumulation of public opinion data that differences of education differentiate Americans more sharply than any other single factor. The college-educated person, whatever his religion, race, or region, tends to become internationalist and cosmopolitan in outlook, to be liberal on civil liberties issues, and in general to be tolerant. (If he terms himself a conservative, it is rather because of his stand on economic and social welfare issues.) By contrast, the person who has gone only to grammar school is frequently xenophobic and suspicious—against giveaway programs and ties to foreign countries or to "foreigners" within this country. The high school and junior college graduates are between these extremes.

It is hard to separate out the effects of further schooling from the causes: we know from Kinsey's studies that the high school boy who will in all probability go to college already has different sexual patterns from the boy who will not. Income alone, apart from motivation, is not decisive, and it is clear that schooling attracts some and repels others at every point in the educational career. Certainly, one factor in the influence of high school and college is sheer size and movement; as the Junior Division *Bulletin* (of the University of Nebraska) states: college will bring "a mingling with young people from other communities and from foreign countries, whose backgrounds are different from yours and from whom you will learn just as they will learn from you" (p. 7, 1955–56). We know that this growth of mutual understanding by no means happens as a regular thing, but, coupled with whatever broadening influence the teachers have, it does make the feeling of the bigot that teachers and education in general must be watched at least a comprehensible if not forgivable one. We who are college teachers are all too aware how little impact we and our ideas ordinarily have on the young, but the polls show us that we are part of an apparatus in our society that sorts people out into very different styles of life and thought.

And even at the secondary school level, as I have already implied, the teachers are not quite so powerless in controlling the customers as might appear. . . .

. . . Public-school teachers have done better than professors in organizing into unions which overleap the local community—this is, as just implied, in part because they are not academic, not attached to specific disciplines. In the state education departments, teachers have powerful lobbies. And in the National Education Association and the nationally known teachers colleges, the embattled teachers have begun to find support when they get into a local jam. . . .

Chapter 3

An Introduction to the Learning Process

3-1

JOHN W. M. WHITING

Theories of Learning and Behavior

3-2

ARDEN N. FRANDSEN

Learning: An Integration of Theories

M. WHITING

of Learning and Behavior

This essay compresses much of what is known about learning into a few succinct pages. As such, it will serve as a review for those who have studied learning, and as an introduction for those who have not. What are the kinds of learning with which the school especially deals? What implications for new research in educational psychology are implicit in Whiting's summary? After reading this article, study carefully the next selection for a more expanded overview of ideas about learning.

Research in the process of learning may be divided into three general areas of interest which may be referred to as *primary learning, secondary learning,* and *social learning.* Although my major interest is in the latter two, it is in the field of primary learning that the basic principles and concepts have been developed—principles upon which secondary and social learning depend. It is necessary therefore to briefly review and summarize the various theories and concepts which have been developed in the field of primary learning.

PRIMARY LEARNING

Research in primary learning has been carried on in the laboratory under carefully controlled conditions with animals as subjects. Dogs, rats, cats and pigeons have been the species most generally used. Primary drives such as hunger, thirst or pain from electric shock have been characteristically employed for motivation; relatively simple stimuli such as buzzers or lights have been preferred to more complex ones and, similarly, relatively simple responses such as salivation, maze running, or pressing a bar.

Pavlov (5) was, of course, the father of learning theory and his experiments are so well known that they need not be described. It should be pointed out, however, that he viewed learning as essentially a process of stimulus substitution. A stimulus, which he called an unconditioned stimulus, was chosen which could be counted on to evoke a response. This was then paired repeatedly with a neutral or conditioned stimulus until the latter gained power to evoke the response. It should be noted that the stimulus situation was experimentally varied and the response controlled, and

John W. M. Whiting, "Theories of Learning and Behavior," in Wesley Allinsmith and Judy F. Rosenblith, eds., *The Causes of Behavior: Readings in Child Development and Educational Psychology* (Boston: Allyn and Bacon, 1962). Reprinted with permission.

that contiguity between the unconditioned and the conditioned stimulus was considered to be the crucial event for learning.

In the United States quite a different view of learning was originally evolved by E. L. Thorndike (9), and developed by Hull (2), Skinner (7), N. E. Miller (3, 4), and Spence (8). This view, generally referred to as the reinforcement theory of learning, emphasizes motivation and reward. The experimental model which best expresses this view is provided by a hungry animal in a box learning to make some response (such as pressing a lever) to get a pellet of food. Rather than controlling the response and changing the stimulus as was the case in Pavlov's experimental design, the stimulus is held constant and the responses permitted to vary freely. This type of theory views learning as a process of response selection rather than stimulus substitution. Furthermore, reward following a correct performance is held to be crucial in this theory, mere contiguity between the conditioned and unconditioned stimulus is held to be insufficient.

A third view of learning is the *S-R* contiguity theory of Guthrie (1). The basic postulate of this theory is that complete learning takes place whenever a response occurs in the presence of a stimulus. Neither the presence of an unconditioned stimulus nor a reward is required. Guthrie accounts for the fact that learning is often continuous rather than a sudden "all or none" process by the fact that an organism is not perceiving all the stimuli in a situation on any given trial and gradual improvement results from more and more stimuli getting associated with the response.

The application of gestalt psychology is best exemplified by Tolman (10). Learning in Tolman's view involves changes in cognition rather than the strengthening of *S-R* connections. Vivid or salient stimuli (events) which are repeatedly perceived by an organism to be in a consistent spatial or temporal relation to one another give rise to the belief that these events will be so related in the future. Improvement in performance thus depends upon the increasing adequacy and validity of the cognitive map which guides and directs the performance.

MOTIVATION AND PERFORMANCE

Since the consequences of learning can be measured only if the organism does something, a complete theory of learning must contain principles governing performance. That is, it must concern itself with factors such as motivation, generalization and response competition as well as with acquisition. Hull has been most explicit in this regard and has assumed that the amplitude, latency, resistance to extinction and probability of occurrence of any act is a joint function of learning and motivation.[1]

Generalization is another performance principle of considerable importance. This principle is concerned with the progressive decrement in the strength of a habit as the stimuli in test situations are made more dissimilar from those present during learning. It provides a basis for some of the complex problems involved in symbolic mediation. This principle has also

[1] As he expresses it: ${}_sE_r - f({}_sH_r) \times f(D)$ where ${}_sE_r$ is the term relating to performance, ${}_sH_r$ to accumulated learning, and D to current motivation.

been used by Miller, by Sears (6), and by Whiting and Child (11), to account for the Freudian mechanisms of displacement and projection.

Response competition or conflict between simultaneously evoked habits is a final performance principle which should be mentioned. Ambivalence, insecurity and anxiety may be defined as special cases of response competition.

SECONDARY LEARNING

As the term is being used here, secondary learning refers to the special principles which govern the so-called acquired drives and acquired rewards —that is, those motives and rewards which are learned rather than innate. Since these concepts are particularly relevant to the reinforcement theory of learning, it is the followers of Hull who have done most systematic work in this area.

Acquired drives may be divided into two classes which may be termed conditioned primary drives and purposive acquired drives. Fear provides a model for the conditioned primary drive. Neutral stimuli associated with pain become danger signals which come to evoke fear. When fear has been established, the organism will learn to avoid or to escape from the dangerous situation.

The concept of purposive acquired drives is derived from the assumption that a conflict between goal expectancies produces insecurity which will motivate an organism to solve the conflict. Dependency, aggression, and achievement are examples of acquired drives which have recently been accounted for in this manner.

Acquired rewards or token rewards are like acquired drives, learned rather than innate. It is generally held that the process of acquisition results from simple association of some neutral stimulus with some primary reward. Thus if a mother always smiles as she nurses the baby, her smile comes to be in itself rewarding. Tokens of value such as money gain their reward value in a somewhat more complicated manner, but presumably the process is not different in principle.

SOCIAL LEARNING

Culture and society provide some special circumstances or learning conditions which all children must face in growing up. Three factors in particular are important in this regard. First, rewards and punishments are administered by people, generally parents, who are perceived by the child to be similar to himself and whom he is generally taught to imitate. As a consequence, self-other discriminations, role adoption, projection, and the complicated process of identification and the internalization of values become central problems which any theory of social learning must face.

Secondly, the progressive maturation of the child from infancy to adulthood results in the child at first learning habits which he must later be forced to relinquish. For example, the child first learns to be dependent, then to be self-reliant and responsible. He may be permitted to have temper tantrums as an infant and then must learn to control his aggression as an older child. These shifts in parental attitude produce conflicts which in many instances have enduring effects.

Thirdly, all human children are brought up into a society of people who speak a language. Theories of social learning have scarcely begun to account for the implications of this fact. The transmission of systems of belief and value by formal or informal and often unintended instruction, transfer of training by verbal mediation, and the learning of the cognitive structure involved in planning are only some of the problems deriving from the symbolic behavior of human beings which an adequate theory of social learning must account for.

Justice obviously cannot be done in such a brief review to the theories here presented. Many of the fine points have had to be omitted; others have no doubt been distorted by condensation. Furthermore, many important contributors to certain facets of the learning process have not been mentioned at all. It is hoped that this review will serve as a skeleton outline of the major viewpoints held by learning theorists and the problems which face investigators concerned with learning and behavior.

A brief bibliography of important works on learning and behavior.

1. Guthrie, E. R. *The Psychology of Learning.* New York: Harper, 1935.
2. Hull, C. L. *The Principles of Behavior.* New York: Appleton-Century, 1943.
3. Miller, N. E. and Dollard, J. *Social Learning and Imitation.* New Haven: Yale University Press, 1941.
4. Miller, N. E. Learnable drives and rewards. In S. S. Stevens (ed.), *Handbook of Experimental Psychology.* New York: Wiley & Sons, 1951.
5. Pavlov, I. P. *Conditioned Reflexes.* (Trans. by G. V. Anrep.) London: Oxford Press, 1927.
6. Sears, R. R., *et al.* Some child-rearing antecedents of aggression and dependency in young children. *Genet. Psychol. Monogr.*, 1953, 47, 135–234.
7. Skinner, B. F. *The Behavior of Organisms; an Experimental Analysis.* New York: Appleton-Century, 1938.
8. Spence, K. W. Theoretical interpretations of learning. In S. S. Stevens (ed.), *Handbook of Experimental Psychology.* New York: Wiley & Sons, 1951.
9. Thorndike, E. L. *The Fundamentals of Learning.* New York: Teachers College, 1932.
10. Tolman, E. C. *Purposive Behavior in Animals and Men.* New York: Appleton-Century, 1932.
11. Whiting, J. W. M. and Child, I. L. *Child Training and Personality.* New Haven: Yale University Press, 1953.

ARDEN N. FRANDSEN

Learning: An Integration of Theories

In reading conflicting explanations of the theories of learning, students are sometimes confused or discouraged. In this selection Frandsen blends many of the theories into a persuasive and harmonious whole. His explanation of the two-factor theory is particularly illuminating, and his seven conditions for effective learning provide material for interesting comparisons with other authors.

Despite the fact that scientific appraisals reveal that today's children equal or exceed the scholastic attainments of their parents at the same ages [1], parents and the popular press often challenge teachers to justify their new methods of teaching. For example, observing the "rat tending" and other unusual individual and social activities of the children who participated in a diet experiment with Reddie and Blue Boy, a parent whose elementary school experiences had been restricted largely to teacher-directed drill might blame such "progressive" methods for his immature child's unfortunate deficiencies in reading, spelling, and arithmetic, or for his resistance in conforming to rigid parental discipline at home. One parent claims that the happiness of his young children is the product of their frustration-free lives; but a neighbor wonders if these children are being disciplined sufficiently to prepare them for the "harsher realities" he foresees for them as adults. Still another critic, the writer of a popular book, apparently thinks that in American schools phonics has been abandoned for the word method in teaching children to read; as a consequence, he challengingly asserts that the method of teaching reading is entirely wrong [11]. A defender of the current methods, however, who believes that phonics, rather than being abandoned, has become part of a more comprehensive approach, explains that a proper combination of the word method in the initial stages, the introduction of phonetic and other word-analysis techniques as children mature, and the emphasis throughout on reading for meaning develops the proficiency in reading characteristic of the great majority of American school children.

As a basis for meeting such challenges and for intelligent interpretation of such controversies, teachers need to understand the scientifically established theories and conditions of effective learning. Also, it is from understanding these theories and conditions of learning that creative teachers are able to invent new and more effective ways of teaching and child guidance.

In attaining the objectives of the elementary school, children acquire several different kinds of behavior patterns. These patterns include . . . combinations of knowledge and understandings, skills and competencies, attitudes and interests, and habits and action patterns—with both intellectual and emotional components. Moreover, the curriculum content comprises study in several different areas, such as language, reading, arithmetic, social studies, natural science, and arts, and includes child development goals as well. As a general guide to teachers in creating conditions for effective learning of these different behavior patterns in all these curriculum areas, we shall attempt to formulate a comprehensive and practical outline of learning principles. In achieving this purpose, we shall be eclectic in our consideration of learning theories, but we shall try to achieve an integration rather than a collection of ideas. We shall strive to anchor our formulation securely to the pertinent observational facts and experiments in psychology and education.

THEORIES OF LEARNING

In the attempts to understand and to control learning, three different approaches or schools of thought have evolved: the conditioned-response theory, of which one particular view has been systematically developed and comprehensively applied to practical learning situations by Guthrie [4, 5, 6]; the "trial-and-error" or "effect" theory of Thorndike, which for application to teaching has been given modern interpretations by both Thorndike [22] and Gates [2]; and the gestalt or "insight" theory, of which the applications have been elaborated by Hartman [8], Lewin [12], and Wheeler and Perkins [24]. Within these three approaches there are several particular theoretical formulations [10]. Most of the writers who have developed theories within any one of these general approaches have attempted to encompass all the pertinent facts known about learning within their systems of explanation, and with results which, I believe, would be considered at least logical. This is not surprising, because, as Guthrie has remarked, "Theories are not true or false, they are useful or less useful." It would appear, however, that each of the three general theories, because of its particular emphasis, is most adequate or useful for explaining a different phase of learning or learning situation. And since we are concerned here with developing a formulation of learning theory which will have maximum usefulness as a guide to teaching, we shall examine the theories from this point of view.

Differences in the learning situations to which the three learning approaches have been applied are illustrated diagrammatically in Figure 1.

In stating the principle of conditioning, Guthrie writes that "a combination of stimuli which has accompanied a movement will on its recurrence tend to be followed by that movement" [6, p. 23]. In diagramming this formulation, we may assume that (R_1) is a reaction which has occurred in response to the pattern of stimuli (S_1) and (S_2) or (S_3), (S_1) being already adequate (because of innate development or prior conditioning) to elicit (R_1). Next time this pattern of stimuli is presented or only a significant part of it—only (S_2) or (S_3), which originally were not adequate to elicit (R_1) —is presented, (R_1) will tend to recur. In this way a person may learn to make a given response to an extended range of stimuli.

In the trial-and-error situation, the individual is confronted with (S_1), to which he has no habitual or adequate response immediately available. By making several "provisional tries" [10, p. 335]—(R_1), (R_2), (R_3), etc.—he discovers from the effects of each trial a suitable response. The insight situation does not differ basically from the trial-and-error situation, except that the learner is often assumed to perceive or to conceptualize (correctly or incorrectly) the meaning of the total situation before acting. Mentally or vicariously he has anticipated the consequences of making (R_1), (R_2), or (R_3) to (S_1), and he chooses without overt trials what he assumes will be an adequate response in the situation. The insight explanation does not differ fundamentally from the trial-and-error explanation, because in the latter also it is assumed that each response is made in the light of at least partial

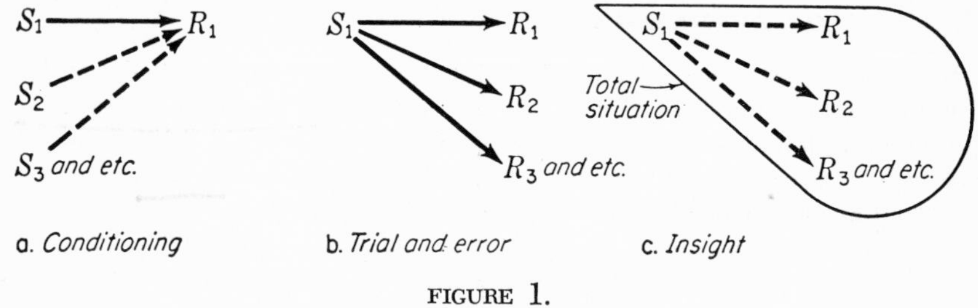

FIGURE 1.

Diagrams of three kinds of learning situations and behavior

and tentative insight. It is assumed that each provisional trial is guided by hypotheses about the expected outcomes, "to be confirmed or denied by its success or failure" [10, p. 336]. In the historical development of learning theories, however, it is the gestalt (or configural) psychologists who have emphasized the perceptual and cognitive (or meaning) aspects of learning.

To clarify further the contributions to explanations of learning of these three general theories, an example of how each explains a learning activity may be helpful.

Example of conditioning. Peter, a child of three years, was taught by Dr. M. C. Jones [21, pp. 428–429] to make the same kind of pleasurable and emotionally confident response which he made to a friendly adult or a well-liked food also to a rabbit, which had previously elicited marked fear. The friendly adult and the food at lunchtime—(S_1) in the diagrammatic illustration of conditioning—already evoked a comfortable and pleasurable reaction; and when the rabbit—(S_2), which in this instance is the conditioned stimulus—was in successive trials moved closer to Peter so that it gradually became a significant part of the combination of stimuli leading to comfort and pleasure, it also came to elicit this reaction in place of fear. Peter could finally stroke the rabbit with one hand and eat with the other.

Many school situations are analogous to this example. When the first grade child enters school, because it is his first long absence from home and because the school is new and strange, he may feel timid. But if his teacher is warm, friendly, and reassuring, and does not press him too quickly into new or difficult activities, he responds to her with feelings of security and confidence; and very shortly this response to his teacher is extended to all school situations of which she has been a significant part. In general, the formula for teaching by conditioning, according to Guthrie, is: When a response has been elicited by a combination of stimuli (already adequate and to-be-conditioned stimuli) frequently enough to make the conditioned stimulus a significant part of the combination, then, if only a part of the combination (the conditioned stimulus), is represented, the response tends to recur [5, p. 26]. In Guthrie's treatment of conditioning, the only essential considered fundamental is that of contiguity (or nearness) between the conditioned stimulus and the desired response. And only one trial would be required for learning if in that trial the conditioned stimulus served as the significant stimulus in eliciting the conditioned response. But adventitious stimuli often interfere, and thus the usual need for several trials.

Example of trial-and-error learning. Trial-and-error learning is rather dramatically illustrated in a simple experiment reported by Miller and Dollard [15]. Under the bottom edge of the center book on the lower shelf of a 4-foot-long bookcase containing books of similar color and size a flat piece of candy is hidden. A six-year-old girl fond of this particular candy is brought into the room and told that a piece of candy is hidden under one of the books in the case, and that she may have it to eat if she is able to find it. As she searches, she is directed to return each book after looking under it. Motivated by her appetite for the candy and by the challenging, gamelike problem, she makes several goal-directed trials [15, pp. 14–16]:

> First, she looks under a few books on the top shelf. Then she turns around. After a brief pause, she starts taking out the books on the lower shelf, one by one. When she has removed eight of these books without finding the candy, she temporarily leaves the books and starts looking under the magazines on the top shelf. Then she returns to look again on the top shelf under several of the books she has already picked up. After this, she turns toward the experimenter and asks, "Where is the candy?" After a pause, she pulls out a few more books on the bottom shelf, stops, sits down, and looks at the books for about half a minute, turns away from the bookcase, looks under a book on a nearby table, then returns and pulls out more books. Under the thirty-seventh book which she examines, she finds the piece of candy. Uttering an exclamation of delight, she picks it up and eats it. On this trial, it has taken her 200 seconds to find the candy.
>
> She is sent out of the room, candy is hidden under the same book, and she is called back again for another trial. This time she goes directly to the lower shelf of books, taking out each book methodically. She does not stop to sit down, turn away, or ask the experimenter questions. Under the twelfth book she finds the candy. She has finished in 86 seconds.

On the third trial, she goes almost directly to the right place, finding the candy under the second book picked up. She has taken only 11 seconds.

On the following trial, the girl does not do so well. Either the previous spectacular success has been due partly to chance, or some uncontrolled factor has intervened. This time the girl begins at the far end of the shelf and examines 15 books before finding the candy. She has required 86 seconds.

Thereafter, her scores improve progressively until, on the ninth trial, she picks up the correct book immediately and secures the candy in three seconds. On the tenth trial, she again goes directly to the correct book and gets the candy in two seconds.

Her behavior has changed markedly. Instead of requiring 210 seconds and stopping, asking questions, turning away, looking under magazines, searching in other parts of the room, picking up wrong books, and making other useless responses, she now goes directly to the right book and gets the candy in two seconds. She has learned.

From Miller and Dollard's description of this child's learning behavior, we note that, as signs of learning progress, there were gradual though uneven reductions in the number of provisional trials and in the time required. It seems safe to infer also that the child's concept of the solution to the problem became clearer and more differentiated, and that she became more confident in her approach.

Often it is helpful to both the learner and his teacher to see a graphic portrayal of some phase of the progress made at each trial. Figure 2 demonstrates the progress of this child in terms of the number of books examined, showing an error score for each trial.

For interpreting such examples of learning, Thorndike, over a period of a half century of experimenting and theorizing, has developed several principles, which constitute his trial-and-error, or "connectionist," theory of learning [2, 22]. (1) In this instance, the child, motivated by her desire for the candy and by the challenging task, is in a state of "readiness," or is mentally set by the directions for a certain kind of searching behavior. (2) A "multiple and varied attack" on the problem begins; she tries provisionally book after book and makes other explorations as well in her search for the candy. (3) According to the "law of effect," the responses followed by motive satisfaction are selected for continued use (learned), and those attended by dissatisfaction are eliminated. In this instance, the obviously unrewarding explorations are quickly eliminated, and eventually only the book covering the candy is picked up. (4) It is also assumed in the theory that with repeated "exercise" of the correct stimulus-response connections, and when accompanied by "belongingness," or motive satisfaction, these connections are strengthened. The learning curve shows that by the ninth trial the S-R connection between perception of the right book and picking it up has been so strengthened that there is no longer any competition from any other book or exploratory effort. (5) Two supplementary principles should be mentioned as being significant, especially from the point of view of teaching activities analogous to this one. First, the correct S-R connection would have been learned more readily if the significant stimulus had been more "indentifiable"—if the correct book had been marked distinctively instead of resembling all the other books on the shelf. And second, if this six-year-old child had had readily "available" such a counting response as "seventh book from the left on the bottom shelf," she would have mastered the problem more quickly. (6) Another important aspect of the theory is the assumption that, on meeting other situations which have elements in common with this one, the child will respond by "analogy" with a pattern of behavior similar to that found successful in this searching problem. (7) Also, on subsequent occasions, we may expect that only a part of the total situation will be necessary to elicit this problem-solving approach; that is, "associative shifting" (shifting the response to fewer or even, at first, inadequate cues) will occur.

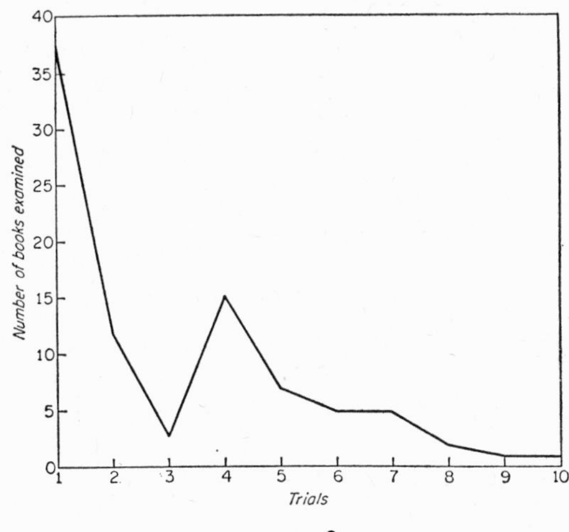

FIGURE 2.

Learning curve for six-year-old girl's trial-and-error efforts to find candy under a certain book in a bookcase

(From N. E. Miller and J. Dollard, *Social Learning and Imitation* [New Haven, Conn.: Yale University Press, 1941] p. 15. Reprinted with permission.)

In the attempt to bring out all Thorndike's explanatory concepts of learning, the interpretation of this illustration has become somewhat strained. The central feature of this theory is the law of effect. Finding herself in a problem situation—(S_1) in (b) of the diagram presented earlier—the child tries out as responses (R_1), (R_2), (R_3), etc., and on the basis of the effects, she discovers an adequate mode of adjusting to this and to similar situations. In both the subject-matter and the child development aspects of the curriculum, much of the child's learning may be readily explained according to this general theory. The child will learn and use those responses which he perceives are correct and which he experiences as motive-satisfying. And it should be remarked in passing that rewarding desired behavior has been found much more effective than punishing undesired behavior in developing desirable behavior.

Example of learning with insight. Using the Obstacle Peg Test shown in Figure 3 with 74 two- to six-year-old children, Harter [7] demonstrated both overt, trial-and-error learning and, in some of these children, insight learning.

Confronted with the device pictured—an 8¼-inch-diameter grooved board containing within the grooved path three unremovable pegs with differently colored tops—each child is asked, "Slide the red ball [pointing to the red peg top] to the red hole in the center [pointing again]." Since the pegs are not removable, the task can be accomplished only by sliding the otherwise interfering yellow and green pegs out of the way into the grooves at 2, 3, 4, or 5.

Of the 74 children tested, 53 succeeded by overt, trial-and-error moves and 21 failed, within the five minutes allowed. That maturity is one factor determining success in this task is indicated by the fact that the successful group exceeded the failing group both in average chronological and in average mental age. But at this time our interest is especially in insight learning, the role of which in this solution-learning problem is suggested in two ways. (1) The successful group made fewer moves than did the failure group; apparently a better perception of the problem as a whole, or insight into it, made their moves surer. (2) Of the 50 children in the successful group who were given a second trial, "thirty-two made no trial-and-error moves"; the insight or understanding achieved on the first trial served as a sufficient cognitive guide for clearing the path and moving the red peg without error directly to the center hole.

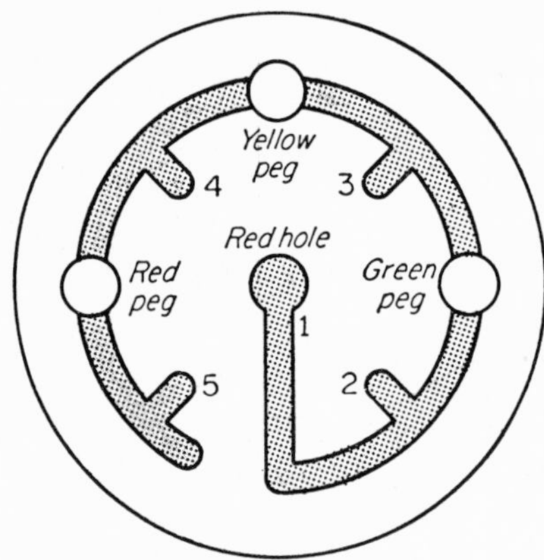

FIGURE 3.

Obstacle Peg Test, illustrating trial and error and insight learning: "Slide the red peg to the No. 1 hole"

(From G. L. Harter, *J. Genet. Psychol.*, 38 [1930] 362.)

According to gestalt, or insight, psychologists, the important changes constituting learning are perceptual and cognitive (or mental). Hartmann, in explaining this instance of learning, would probably say that the children in the Obstacle Peg Test situation, as a result of their goal-directed observation and thinking, progressed perceptually "from a relatively undifferentiated, homogeneous stage to a more elaborate and internally differentiated condition" [8, p. 202]. Insight was achieved in that "the point of the situation" was seen by a process of organizing or reorganizing perceptual patterns of the significant elements in the situation in relation to the goal. Lewin [12, pp. 224–229] would speak of these perceptual changes as changes in "cognitive structure." A "previously vague and unstructured area becomes cognitively structured and specific." According to his views, learning is a process of differentiating the relatively unstructured, and the "cognitive maps" or mental guides thus constructed and reconstructed become guides to more adequate action in problem situations. As a child first observes the Obstacle Peg Test, he probably perceives it as an undifferentiated pattern of pegs and grooves. But as he observes this vaguely structured situation, because he is goal-directed to slide the red peg to the center hole, he reorganizes his perception and concept of it. Mentally he differentiates the clear path from the side paths for the obstructing pegs; and guided by this specifically structured "cognitive map," he executes the pattern of moves required.

Much of the child's problem-solving learning in school can be thus explained. In application to motor skills, for example, Hartmann writes that the "heart of such learning lies in the vivid sensory perception of this structure (the configuration of action required in performance of the motor skill) and its essential reproduction in the pattern of movement of the body of the learner" [8, p. 188]. Similar analyses could be made of the process of identifying the meaning of words in reading, of understanding concepts in science and social studies, of problem solving in arithmetic, of achieving a satisfying result in creative art—indeed, for every aspect of the curriculum. With the modern emphasis on meaning, generalizing, and applying principles in school learning, this explanation of learning is favored.

Insight and trial-and-error learning. This analysis of learning by insight is not, as has already been mentioned, inconsistent with the trial-and-error explanation. In fact, the two views may be harmonized as one. In our particular integration of the two approaches to learning, however, the perceptual aspects, or, in Lewin's terminology, the changes in cognitive structure, predominate in what we shall call learning. Thorndike's law of effect, which in the trial-and-error theory accounts for the selection of right responses and the elimination of wrong responses, needs to be extended. In addition to motive satisfaction or dissatisfaction, the selection-and-elimination process is guided also by the learner's perception of the effects of each provisional trial. This perceptual factor is of crucial importance.

A TWO-FACTOR THEORY OF LEARNING

Having noted that so-called "trial-and-error" and "insight" learning are fundamentally similar, we left with only two basic kinds of learning, which Mowrer [16, 18] has designated as (1) "conditioning," or stimulus substitution—(a) of Figure 1—and (2) "problem solving," or response substitution—(b) and (c) of Figure 1. According to Mowrer, habits, knowledge, understandings, language, motor skills—all voluntary behavior mediated by the central nervous system—are acquired by problem solving. Emotional learning, including love, anger, fear, anxiety, etc., and also secondary motives, interests, likes and dislikes, and attitudes are acquired by conditioning. In these emotional learnings the autonomic nervous system is important in mediating responses which are largely involuntary. In problem solving, the law of effect is an important explanatory principle; in conditioning, "contiguity," in agreement with Guthrie, is the only explanatory principle needed.

Tuttle [23] has expressed a similar view in saying that there are two kinds of learning: (1) "intellectual" learning—of skills, memorized facts, and reasoning; and (2) "affective" learning—of attitudes, drives to action, appreciations, interests, morals, tastes, and standards. These two kinds of learning may occur separately in sequence (conditioning leading to problem solving, or vice versa), but they also occur frequently in intertwined, simultaneous relationships.

How a six-year-old boy came to fear a frog, and the patterns of behavior he learned in dealing with it, illustrate conditioning and problem solving combined. As the child, who had theretofore exhibited only interest and cu-

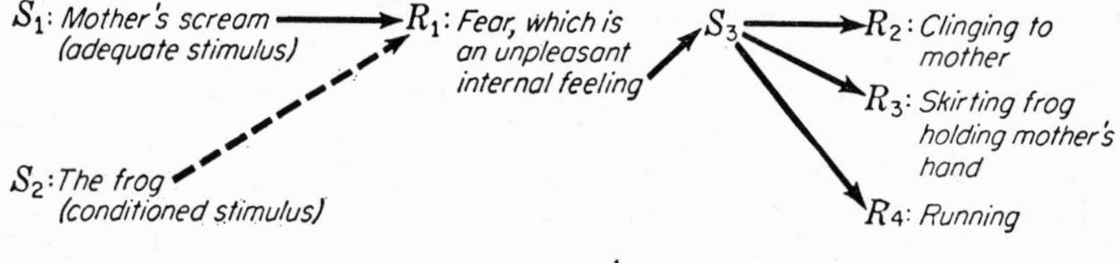

FIGURE 4.

Two-factor learning theory diagrammed: a conditioned fear response becomes internal stimulus (S_3) *for varied responses* (R_1), (R_2), *and* (R_3).

riosity about frogs, was about to cross a grass-covered irrigation ditch with his mother on the way to their car, a lively frog hopped out of the ditch. The mother, with a scream of terror, jumped back away from the frog; and the boy, in response to his mother's scream, also scampered back and clung to her. Then, resuming the approach to the car, the child, who had now, like the mother, been conditioned to fear the frog, met the problem by joining his mother in a path skirting widely around it, choosing to hold his mother's hand on the side away from the frog. When it was discovered that the child had forgotten his cap in the house they were leaving and must return for it, he this time reacted to his newly conditioned fear of the frog by running very quickly on the part of the path where the frog had appeared.

Figure 4 presents diagrammatically the two-factor-theory explanation [17] of this instance of learning. In the diagram, (S_1) is an adequate stimulus for eliciting fear in this child. In this instance, because the theretofore nonfrightening frog was a significant part of a combination of stimuli—(S_1) and (S_2)—eliciting fear, it also, even without the mother's demonstration of fear, became a conditioned stimulus for exciting fear in the child. This fear will presumably always occur in the boy as a response to frogs until a substitute response is learned. But the fear response is also a stimulus as an unpleasant internal condition. The child will attempt to allay it by varied problem-solving efforts. In this case, he responded first by clinging to his mother; second, by taking a path to avoid the frog and by holding his mother's hand; and third, by running quickly past the frog.

Definition of learning. With this background for an eclectic approach to learning, we are now ready to attempt an integrated statement of what learning is—and, since we are primarily concerned with teaching, of the essential conditions for effective learning. Guided by both Melton [14, pp. 667–668] and Munn [19, p. 374], we may define learning as "a change in experience or behavior resulting from purposeful observation, overt activity, or thinking, and accompanied by motivational-emotional reactions, which results in more adequate satisfaction of the motivating conditions." In the meaning of the phrase "experience or behavior" we explicitly include perceptions, cognitions, overt actions, motivational-emotional feelings, and attitudes. In typical learning situations, such as learning to recognize the meaning of new words in reading, the child is changing in many ways. Vague visual-stimulus patterns are being differentiated into meaningful percepts. Cognitive structures which determine how new words and ideas shall be perceived are being organized. Verbal- and visual-action patterns are being differentiated and connected with the appropriate stimulus patterns. And important motivational-emotional attitudes are developing simultaneously. While he is learning to read by problem solving, the child is also acquiring interest and confidence in, or distaste for and anxiety about, the activity, depending on the conditioning aspects of the situation.

By saying in our definition of learning that the changes achieved result in more adequate satisfaction of motives, we imply an emphasis upon the motivational, purposive, and goal-directed nature of learning. Since both intellectual and emotional learnings are involved in typical instances of learning, we shall need, according to Mowrer, a theory which encompasses both problem solving and conditioning. This Mowrer's two-factor theory of learning accomplishes. But before we adapt it to an integrated formulation as a guide to teaching, we shall first describe the two aspects separately.

Problem-solving learning. Descriptively, problem-solving learning involves the following phases: (1) A motivated person, who, upon meeting (2) a situation—(S_1) in (b) or (c) of Figure 1—to which he cannot adjust adequately on the basis of either innate behavior patterns or prior learning, (3) makes multiple, goal-directed, provisional tries. (4) Experiencing the effects of these trials, both perceptually and as motive satisfaction or dissatisfaction, he (5) selects ("differentiates" or "integrates"), often from several trials, a pattern of behavior which promises to meet the motivating conditions more adequately. (6) When this or a similar situation arises again, the more adequate pattern will recur more directly and with less attention and effort. The central feature in this learning behavior is the perceptual experience which results in changing the cognitive structure (or mental map) for reacting to the situation; and the persistence of this new cognitive structure constitutes the learning that has taken place. As illustrations of this concept, the child's trial-and-error search for candy and the solution by insight of the Obstacle Peg Test may be recalled.

As a further exercise in applying this pattern of analysis, we may consider how a five-year-old learns to articulate *g* correctly so that he pronounces gun as "gun" rather than as "dun." In a friendly, nonthreatening relationship with an adult (*conditioning confidence*), he may be made interested in saying "gun" just as the adult does (*motivation*). But he is at first unable to do so (*problem*). As leads to goal-directed trials, he may observe the adult's pronunciation more closely, or be guided by the adult's explanation and demonstration of where to place his tongue and lips and how to use his throat in saying "gun" (*teacher-guidance of goal-directed trials*). As he perceives that his own attempts are coming to resemble more closely the adult model or that they still deviate from it, he repeats with slight or with more radical modifications his attempts to articulate the word, and experiences more or less satisfaction of mastery and approval (*perception of effects* and *motive satisfaction*). Often, while his attention is on pronouncing the word, he fails to perceive the results of his trials. He can be helped in this respect by a mirror or sound recorder (*perception of effects*). Out of these repeated goal-directed trials, in which his perceptions of the effects of preceding trials become guides for performance in subsequent trials, he differentiates and integrates—both cognitively and as a motor pattern—a satisfying response for the situation (*pattern selection*). Finally, in addition to habitually pronouncing gun as "gun," he may now, even without special training, say "go" instead of "doe" (*transfer*).

A little reflection will reveal that much of the teacher-directed learning in the elementary school conforms to this pattern of analysis. As examples, the following may be mentioned: in *language,* improvement of articulation, correct usage, understanding of meanings of words and more complex verbal expressions, learning how to make a speech or write a composition, etc.; in *handwriting,* understanding of how letters are formed, improvement in legibility and speed, and improvement in such features as uniformity of slant and alignment, quality of line, and spacing; in *spelling,* learning how to learn to spell words, mastery of the 3,000 to 5,000 most needed words, learning how to use the dictionary, and recognition of the correctness or incorrectness of words spelled in writing; in *reading,* learning independent recognition of words, improvement in comprehension and speed of reading, vocabulary development, and learning how to adapt reading to a variety of purposes and uses; in *arithmetic,* learning the combinations, acquiring understanding of and skill in problem solving, and understanding the uses of arithmetic; in *science,* acquiring understanding of and skill in using concepts; in *art* and *music,* acquiring skills, knowledge, and understanding; in *health* and *physical education,* acquiring motor skills, knowledge, and understanding; and in *development of healthy personality, character,* and *social behavior,* understandings, knowledge, techniques, and skills. In all these activities, the learning is basically by trial and error or by problem solving.

Conditioning. In all the above-mentioned areas there are also important motivational-emotional components. These components, such as interests, appreciations, and attitudes, are learned by conditioning. That is, when reading, social studies, music, art, or other activities are made a part of a combination of stimuli already adequate for leading to satisfying uses, mastery, pleasure, approval, and other gratifications, then these subjects, or parts of them, also become effective as conditioned stimuli in arousing interest and appreciation. As Pressey has written, "An interest grows with tropical lushness in the warm sun of success and approval. It withers if not so nourished and stimulated, may even be blighted by only one devastating experience if instead of success and approval it meets ridicule or contempt and failure" [20, p. 156].

The motivational-emotional components in interests and appreciations, however, are not learned as isolated elements; what a person *does* to satisfy his interest or to escape anxiety or a feared object, he learns to do by problem solving, as was illustrated in the case of the child's fear of the frog, mentioned earlier. We are reminded again that, typically, learning by problem solving and by conditioning are going on simultaneously. Our formula for teaching interests, appreciations, and attitudes, since they involve motivational-emotional components, should therefore include, besides the principle of contiguity from conditioning, the principle of "effect" or motive satisfaction from problem-solving learning.

In general, then, to develop interest in a new activity, associate it with conditions which already lead to motive satisfactions, and arrange that the adaptive responses made in this situation be rewarding.

Deriving the conditions for effective learning. In this essentially eclectic consideration of learning theories, an adaption of Mowrer's two-factor theory has provided a basis for integrating traditional theories into a concept of learning comprehensive enough to cover both its intellectual and emotional aspects. From the conditioning theory an explanation of the learning of interests, emotions, and attitudes has been derived. Explanations of problem-solving learning have drawn from the trial-and-error theory the concepts of multiple provisional trials and of the role of motive satisfaction or dissatisfaction in selecting responses, and from the insight theory the concept of perception and cognition as guides to behavior. Restating a definition of learning based on this integrated theory, it may be said that learning results from reacting purposefully to environmental and self situations, and that learning involves a change or reorganization of an individual's perceptual, cognitive, and motivational-emotional structure which may be utilized as a guide to more adequate adjustments to the given situations and to related situations. As deductions from and elaborations of this theory and definition, we shall now formulate a practical outline of learning principles for application to teaching.

ESSENTIAL CONDITIONS FOR EFFECTIVE LEARNING

For elementary school children to learn effectively to read, to understand arithmetic or social studies, to acquire appropriate social techniques, or to learn effectively in any of the areas previously outlined, at the same time acquiring confidence as learners and interests in many learning activities, the following conditions are considered essential: (1) sufficient mental maturity and an appropriate pattern of abilities; (2) teacher-guidance in focusing attention on (a) goal-directing hypotheses (mental sets leading to identification, discrimination, and differentiation of stimulus clues, and to tentative formulation of means-to-goal response patterns), (b) efficient modes of attack, and (c) adjustments in goals or standards to the progress of the learner; (3) practice which consists of provisional trials or hypothesis-guided self-activity oriented toward discovery, differentiation, and integration of more effective patterns of behavior; (4) perception of the effects of each trial, with provision for checking the correctness and adequacy of each and for revising subsequent efforts in the light of clear perception of the results of previous goal-directed attempts; (5) provision for transfer of training, which involves emphasis upon meanings, the inductive learning of principles, the interorganization and expansion of these principles, and their useful application; (6) motivation, which arouses, sustains, directs, and determines the intensity of learning effort, and which in cooperation with perception of the effects defines and evaluates the consequences of provisional trials; and (7) freedom from anxiety and distorting attitudes which impair or prevent effective learning. How these conditions determine effectiveness of learning will first be illustrated by an example. This will be followed in subsequent chapters by experimental data supporting the validity of the principles and indicating further applications of them.

An example: learning manuscript writing. To illustrate the conditions of effective learning, we may apply them to a plan for teaching first grade children manuscript writing. Considerable research indicates that manuscript writing is well suited to the maturity level of primary grade children. Hildreth says that, in comparison to cursive writing, it is easier to learn, is adjusted to the growth tendencies of children, is immediately legible, and aids in learning to read and to spell [9]. Thus the first condition, that of "sufficient maturity and an appropriate pattern of abilities," is at least partially met. First grade children will differ, of course, in the patterns of their abilities, and some may have specific handicaps in perception or motor skills which make even manuscript writing difficult.

Teacher-guidance in focusing attention on goal-directing hypotheses implies teacher-guidance in how to write. This is usually provided by setting forth models to imitate and by demonstrations or explanations. Since there are usually several ways to perform a skill, not all equally efficient, the research on efficient modes of attack in learning the elementary school subjects should be consulted for suggestions. In this instance, Lewry, in an article on improving manuscript writing in the primary grades, supplies us with a good model [13]. Guided by the criteria of simplicity and of most frequent use in primary reading materials, he developed the system which is presented in Figure 5 and which we shall use as our model in this instance.

By presentation of this model on the blackboard or in a smaller model at each pupil's seat, by teacher-demonstration of how the letters are formed, and by some verbal explanation, the child is helped to discriminate and to comprehend the stimulus clues (the model) to which he is to react, and to conceive a mental guide (or cognitive structure or map) for making appropriate goal-directed responses.

The practice begins with writing content in which the child is interested and which is so restricted in length and difficulty as to ensure some degree of initial success.

Perhaps not just at the beginning, when too great complexity of goal might arouse anxiety, but as soon as some progress in forming the letters correctly has been made, attention is called to an efficient mode of attack in forming letters. Lewry marked letters with numbers and arrows, as shown in Figure 5, to indicate an efficient order and direction of movements in forming the letters. The teacher may guide pupils in acquiring this mode of

abcdefghijklmnopqrst
uvwxyz ABCDEFGHI
JKLMNOPQRSTUVWXYZ

Order and direction of movement: a b c d e

FIGURE 5.

Letter models for teaching mode of attack in manuscript writing

(From M. E. Lewry, *Elem. Sch. J.*, 47 [1947] 508–15. Reprinted by permission of The University of Chicago Press.)

attack by demonstrations and accompanying verbal explanations. As the pupils make progress in formation of letters and come to feel some confidence and comfort in using manuscript in "creative" writing, new goals and standards are introduced; otherwise plateaus in the progress curve would occur. These new goals, added periodically throughout the primary grades, should include learning to space more closely between letters within a word and to space more widely between words, greater uniformity of slant and alignment, even quality of line, and improvement in speed. Individual characteristics of style develop as variations from these essentials for legibility and efficiency.

If skill in manuscript writing is to be achieved, practice will, of course, be necessary. Both short, daily periods of systematic, teacher-guided practice and practice in writing in a variety of school activities should continue at least throughout the primary grades and may well be extended beyond this period [9]. But practice alone, though necessary for learning a skill, is not sufficient, as will be demonstrated later. For practice to be effective, there must also be continuous attention to goal-directing ideas—ways and techniques for improving. At least a part of each practice period should be used for actively discovering, differentiating, and integrating more effective writing techniques, rather than merely for passive repetitions of response patterns already achieved, which may be relatively good or poor. To manage practice efficiently, the teacher will need to consider such factors as length of each practice period and suitability of content from the points of view of interest, difficulty, and amount for each lesson. These factors will be elaborated in a later general discussion of the conditions for effective learning.

To provide for perception of the effects of each trial, the pupil, with the help of his teacher, will check, following each trial at achieving a manuscript-writing objective (or at least periodically during each practice period), to see whether his performance meets the standards of his model or goal. Has he confined himself to the simple circles, straight lines, and curves indicated in Figure 5, or has he used irregular ovals and unnecessary curves? Has his progression from left to right been inefficient, as in making the stem before the circle in writing *d*? Has he spaced properly between words, etc.? Perception of the effects of each trial makes possible corrections that lead to continuous improvement or confirm the already accomplished correct patterns. At first the teacher will need to help children individually so as to check the adequacy of their performances, but they should also be taught to check or "proofread" for themselves so that they may become independent in using this important condition for effective learning.

In learning manuscript writing, as in most learning activities, consideration of the provision for transfer of training multiplies the efficiency of each practice period. In learning to write the 26 lower-case letters, for example, it is conceivable that a pupil might see them as 26 different characters, each one consisting of several different features to be meticulously copied. But this would be a very wasteful procedure, because there are not 26 different formations; there are only three, as an inductive examination of the letters will reveal. All the letters consist of simple circles or part circles; straight lines—perpendicular or horizontal; and simple curves, as in *f* or *j*. At the outset, as a part of the teacher-guidance in goal-directing ideas, the teacher should show by demonstration and verbal explanation that all the letters are simply variations of circles, lines, and curves. Since these formations are already within the repertory of skills of primary grade children, the single letters also are familiar forms, not requiring meticulous copying. Other transfer advantages derive from practicing with words needed and therefore used in writing, and from practicing on words or letters which overcome specific difficulties for particular children.

In motivating children to practice handwriting, perhaps the best incentive is to provide for using the skill in writing one's name, in labeling various objects, and, eventually, in creative writing. It is also possible to arrange conditions so as to appeal to the child's desire for mastery, knowledge of progress, and teacher approval.

If the child feels generally secure at school, where he is away from home perhaps for the first time, if he is successful in his initial attempts, sees himself making satisfactory progress, finds opportunities to use his developing skills, and is approved by a warm, friendly teacher for his efforts, he is likely to be conditioned to respond to handwriting practice with interest and confidence. But if he is denied these satisfactions, if in his initial efforts he is perplexed, or experiences failure and criticism, he may become anxious and self-distrustful, and may need to avoid handwriting as an escape from an anxiety-provoking situation. Or, if he is expected to learn to "write," and regards manuscript as mere "printing," he may resist acquiring the skill.

An example of such interfering attitudes is the experience of a six-year-old child who went timidly away to the first grade with her confidence bolstered by the fact that she could already write her name. But during the "writing lesson," when the teacher wrote each child's name on the board in manuscript, she was disturbed to find that it was not written in the way she had learned to write it. Among other variations, *a* was written in Lewry's simple style, rather than in the more complicated form she had learned. This was so disturbing that she actually went to the board and with her hand erased the name as written by her teacher, saying that it was not her name. This, of course, would not be the time to help this child learn a simpler and more efficient way of manuscript writing. The need for supporting her confidence with the skill brought from home was more important at this particular time; later, when she had found security in her new relationships at school and confidence from her growing skills, she would be ready to change with satisfaction her way of writing.

Consideration of the need for developing and maintaining interest and confidence in school children reminds us that too much pressure too early to acquire efficient modes of attack, and too much conscientious checking of errors, may, rather than make learning more effective, impair learning efficiency. In making a beginning in manuscript writing, children should perhaps be left free for some time to use their crude achievements in writing activities. Eventually there will be many evidences of self-confidence and even questions from the children about how to improve some feature of their writing. These are the signs of readiness for accepting new standards and for substituting more effective modes of attack for less efficient ones.

Analyses similar to this analysis of manuscript teaching could be made for any school learning activity. If the teaching includes adequate consideration as to (1) maturity and abilities, (2) teacher-guidance in showing or in arranging conditions for self-discovery of how to accomplish learning goals efficiently, (3) practice, (4) perception of the effects of provisional trials, (5) provision for transfer, (6) motivation, and (7) freedom from anxiety and distorting attitudes, the conditions for effective learning will have been provided. Such analyses are useful in evaluating a new method of teaching. These conditions serve as guides in developing one's own methods of providing for effective teaching. In instances of failure to learn, one may very well investigate to determine which one or combination of these conditions is not being provided. And in striving for improvements in teaching, teachers may well consider ways of providing more adequately for these essential conditions of effective learning.

REFERENCES

1. Finch, F. H., and V. W. Gillenwater: "Reading achievement then and now," *Elem. Sch. J.*, 49: 446–454, 1948–1949.
2. Gates, A. I.: "Connectionism: present concepts and interpretations." *The Psychology of Learning*, pp. 141–164. 41st Yearbook of the Nat. Soc. Stud. Educ., Part II. Chicago: Distributed by the University of Chicago Press, 1942.
3. Gurnee, H.: *Elements of Social Psychology*, Farrar & Rinehart, New York, 1936.
4. Guthrie, E. R.: "Conditioning: a theory of learning in terms of stimulus response and association." *The Psychology of Learning*, pp. 17–68. 41st Yearbook of the Nat. Soc. Stud. Educ., Part II. Chicago: Distributed by the University of Chicago Press, 1942.
5. ———: *The Psychology of Learning*, Harper, New York, 1935.
6. ———: *The Psychology of Learning*, rev. ed., Harper, New York, 1952.
7. Harter, G. L.: "Overt trial-and-error in problem solving of pre-school children," *J. Genet. Psychol.*, 38: 361–372, 1930.
8. Hartmann, G. W.: "The field theory of learning and its educational consequences." *The Psychology of Learning*, pp. 165–214. 41st Yearbook of the Nat. Soc. Stud. Educ., Part II, Chicago: Distributed by the University of Chicago Press, 1942.
9. Hildreth, Gertrude: "Should manuscript writing be continued in the upper grades?" *Elem. Sch. J.*, 44: 85–93, 1944.
10. Hilgard, E. R.: *Theories of Learning*, Appleton-Century-Crofts, New York, 1948. See also Second Edition, 1956.
11. "How Johnny reads" (editorial), *Time*, June 20, 1955, pp. 55–56.
12. Lewin, K.: "Field theory and learning." *The Psychology of Learning*, pp. 215–242. 41st Yearbook of the Nat. Soc. Stud. Educ., Part II. Chicago: Distributed by the University of Chicago Press, 1942.
13. Lewry, Marion E.: "Improving manuscript writing in primary grades," *Elem. Sch. J.*, 47: 508–515, copyright 1947 by the University of Chicago. Reprinted by permission of the University of Chicago Press.
14. Melton, A. W.: "Learning," in W. S. Monroe: *Encyclopedia of Educational Research*, Macmillan, New York, 1952.
15. Miller, N. E., and J. Dollard: *Social Learning and Imitation*, Yale University Press, New Haven, Conn., 1941.
16. Mowrer, O. H.: *Learning Theory and Personality Dynamics*. Ronald, New York, 1950.
17. ———: "Learning theory," *Rev. Educ. Res.*, 22: 475–495, 1952.
18. ———: "On the dual nature of learning—a re-interpretation of 'conditioning' and 'problem-solving,'" *Harv. Educ. Rev.*, 17: 102–148, 1947.
19. Munn, N. L.: "Learning in children," in L. Carmichael (ed.): *Manual of Child Psychology*, Wiley, New York, Copyright, 1954.
20. Pressey, S. L., and F. P. Robinson: *Psychology & the New Education*, Harper, New York, 1944.

21. Ruch, F. L.: *Psychology and Life*, Scott, Foresman and Company, C
Copyright, 1948.
22. Thorndike, E. L.: *Human Learning*, Appleton-Century-Crofts, New
1931.
23. Tuttle, H. S.: "Two kinds of learning," *J. Psychol.*, 22: 267–279, 1946.
24. Wheeler, R. H., and F. T. Perkins: *Principles of Mental Development*, Crowell, New York, 1932.

Chapter **4**

The Stream of Development

4-1

PAUL H. MUSSEN AND MARY C. JONES

Late- and Early-Maturing Boys

4-2

LETA S. HOLLINGWORTH

Children Above 180 IQ: Child D

PAUL H. MUSSEN and MARY C. JONES

Late- and Early-Maturing Boys

Knowledge of development depends upon data. If our knowledge is to be adequate, investigations must be carefully planned and executed. Some of the selections you have read are based upon rational considerations. The present correlational study, however, is empirical, measuring on the one hand the physical characteristics of the students, on the other their behavior, and relating the two measurements. After reading this article, consider the question: Have the authors proved that the physical differences *cause* the other differences? How can one be sure? If they did not prove cause, would their study be without value?

While many intensive case studies show that personal and social adjustment during adolescence may be profoundly influenced by rate of physical maturation, there is a scarcity of systematic data on the relationship between the adolescent's physical status and his underlying motivations, self-conceptions and interpersonal attitudes. There is, however, a small body of evidence which demonstrates that greater physical maturity is associated with greater maturity of interest among girls (10) and that early-maturing boys differ from their late-maturing peers in both overt behavior and reputational status. In one study (8) in which a staff of trained observers assessed a large group of adolescents on a number of personality variables, boys who were consistently retarded in physical development were rated lower than those who were consistently accelerated, in physical attractiveness, grooming, and matter-of-factness; and higher in sociability, social initiative (often of a childish, attention-getting sort), and eagerness. Reputation Test (11) data indicated that classmates regarded the late-maturing boys as more attention-getting, more restless, more bossy, less grown-up and less good-looking than those who were physically accelerated.

On the basis of these findings, it may be inferred that adult and peer attitudes toward the adolescent, as well as their treatment and acceptance of him, are related to his physical status. This means that the sociopsychological environment to which late-maturers are subjected—and consequently the social learning situations they encounter—may be significantly different from that of their early-maturing peers. As a consequence, according to the ratings summarized above, they acquire different patterns of overt social behavior. It seems reasonable to hypothesize that groups differing in physical status will also differ in more covert aspects of behavior and personality.

Paul H. Mussen and Mary C. Jones, "Self-Conceptions, Motivations, and Interpersonal Attitudes of Late- and Early-Maturing Boys," *Child Development*, 28(2) (1957), 243–56. Reprinted with permission.

Indirect evidence relevant to this hypothesis comes from an investigation of the long-term consequences of physical acceleration or retardation during adolescence. Jones (6) found that group differences in physique had practically disappeared by the time her early- and late-maturing subjects reached their early thirties. Nevertheless, young adults who had been physically retarded adolescents differed from those who had been accelerated in several important psychological characteristics. In general, it appeared that the adult subjects could be described much as they had been during adolescence. Thus, those who had been early-maturers scored higher on the good impression, socialization, dominance, self-control (low score on impulsivity), and responsibility scales of the California Personality Inventory, while those who had been slow in maturing scored higher on the flexibility scale. On the Edwards Personal Preference Schedule, early-maturers scored significantly higher on the dominance scale, while the late-maturing were high in succorance. Jones concludes that the early-maturing "present a consistently favorable personality picture with regard to . . . important social variables" (6). Moreover, there was some evidence that these men had attained more stable vocational adjustments than those who had been late in maturing. These group differences in later adjustment suggest that the sociopsychological atmosphere in which the adolescent lives may have profound immediate and enduring effects on his personality structure as well as on his overt behavior.

The present study was designed to investigate the relationship between maturational status and certain important, covert aspects of personality during late adolescence. Personality structure was assessed by means of the Thematic Apperception Test (TAT) which seems to be the most appropriate and sensitive instrument for this purpose. More specifically, on the basis of the literature reviewed above and other general works on the psychology of adolescence (1, 4, 5), we formulated and tested a series of propositions relating to differences between the physically retarded and the accelerated in self-conceptions, underlying motivations, and basic interpersonal attitudes. These variables were translated into TAT categories—needs (n), press (p), and descriptions (defined briefly in Table 1)—and the score of early- and late-maturers in each of these categories were compared. The propositions and the rationale underlying them, together with the TAT variables involved, follow.

1. In view of their obvious physical retardation, relatively unfavorable reputations and disadvantageous competitive position in many activities, the late-maturing boys are more likely to have feelings of inadequacy. Hence, more boys in this group than in the early-maturing group are likely to have negative self-conceptions (TAT category: *negative characteristics*).

2. The adolescent in our culture generally desires more independence and adult status. This may be the source of a major problem for the late-maturer, however, since he is often regarded and treated as a small boy by adults and peers and is not likely to be granted independence as early as physically accelerated boys. Therefore, it may be anticipated that more late- than early-maturers regard adults, particularly their parents, as domi-

TABLE 1

Number of early- and late-maturers scoring high in TAT variables

TAT variable	*Definition of variable*	*High early-maturers*	*High late-maturers*	*Chi square value*	*p*
PROPOSITION 1					
Negative Characteristics	H^{Ed} is described in negative terms (e.g., imbecile, weakling, fanatic)	5	13	6.80	<.01
PROPOSITION 2					
p Dominance 1	H forced by parents to do something he doesn't want to	4	8	1.73	.09
p Dominance 2	If prevented by parents from doing something he wants to	6	8	.31	>.30
p Dominance 3	Total instances of H's being forced by parents to do something and/or prevented from doing something	7	11	1.46	.11
p Rejection	H rejected, scorned, or disapproved of by parents or authorities	5	11	3.69	.03
PROPOSITION 3					
n Aggression 1	H is aggressive in physical, asocial way	8	3	3.88	.02
n Aggression 2	H is mad at someone, argues	7	4	1.52	.10
n Aggression 3	Total of all H's aggressive actions	11	8	1.26	.10
n Autonomy 1	H leaves home	7	10	.75	.20
n Autonomy 2	H disobeys or defies parents	7	11	1.46	.11
n Autonomy 3	Total of instances in which hero leaves and/or defies his parents	3	9	4.16	.02
PROPOSITION 4					
n Affiliation 1	H establishes good relations with his parents	8	8	.00	>.50
n Affiliation 2	H falls in love, has a romance, marries	9	14	2.66	.05
n Affiliation 3	Total instances in which H establishes and/or maintains friendly relations	8	12	1.46	.11
PROPOSITION 5					
n Succorance	H feels helpless, seeks aid or sympathy	7	12	2.43	.06
p Nurturance 1	H is helped, encouraged, or given something by parents	5	8	.93	.18
p Nurturance 2	H is helped, encouraged, or given something by someone else (not parents)	8	14	3.88	.02

TAT variable	Definition of variable	*High early-maturers*	*High late-maturers*	*Chi square value*	*p*
PROPOSITION 6					
n Achievement	H attempts to attain a high goal or to do something creditable	9	10	.02	>.50
n Recognition	H seeks fame and/or high prestige status	9	8	.28	>.30
PROPOSITION 7					
Denial of Feeling	S states that picture elicits no thoughts or feelings	9	5	2.43	.06

Ed *H stands for hero.*

nating, forcing them to do things they don't want to or preventing them from doing things they want to do (high scores in *p Dominance*). Moreover, the parental treatment these boys experience and parental refusal to grant them independent status may be interpreted as personal rejection. Hence, we predicted that more late-maturing boys would score high in *p Rejection.*

3. These feelings of being dominated and rejected may result in attitudes of rebellion against the family and in feelings of hostility. We therefore expected that more of the late-maturing group would reveal strong aggressive needs (high scores in *n Aggression*) and desires to escape from (*n Autonomy—leaving parents*), or to defy, the family (*n Autonomy—defying parents*).

4. On the basis of the data indicating that slow-maturers showed a great deal of social interest (although often of an immature kind), we hypothesized that more members of this, than of the early-maturing group would reveal strong interests in friendly, intimate interpersonal relationships (high scores in *n Affiliation*).

5. Assuming that, as Jones and Bayley (8) suggest, the social initiative and attention-getting devices of the late-maturers are of a compensatory nature, we would expect this group to be basically dependent and to have strong needs for support from others. These should be manifest by higher scores in TAT *n Succorance* and *p Nurturance.* The latter may be considered a most indirect measure of dependence, a kind of wish-fulfilling view of the world as helpful and friendly.

6. The early-maturer, being regarded and treated as more adult, is more likely to become self-confident, and to acquire high status goals. For these reasons, we predicted that more of the physically accelerated would give evidence of high achievement goals (high scores in *n Achievement*) and concern with personal recognition (high scores in *n Recognition*).

7. Late-maturing boys in our culture probably face more problems of personal adjustment than do their early-maturing peers. As a result of this, they may become more aware of their problems, and, as the high degree

of flexibility of young adults who had been retarded in maturing suggests, more insightful. Hence we predicted that they would be more willing and able than early-maturers to face their own feelings and emotions (low scores in the TAT variable *denial of feeling*).

In summary, we attempted to test seven propositions related to differences in the personalities of early- and late-maturing boys. It was hypothesized that more late-maturers would score high in variables relating to negative self-conceptions, dependence, aggression, affiliation, rebelliousness, and feelings of being dominated and rejected. More early-maturers, on the other hand, were expected to reveal strong achievemnt and rcognition needs, feelings of personal success, and tendencies toward denial of feelings.

PROCEDURE

The 33 seventeen-year-old male subjects of this investigation were members of the Adolescent Growth Study which included a normal sample of boys in an urban public school system (3). The subjects of the present investigation represented two contrasting groups, selected on the basis of their physical maturity status: 16 of them had been among the most consistently accelerated throughout the adolescent period; the other 17 had been among the most consistently retarded.[1] All of them took the Thematic Apperception Test, which provides the basic data of this study, at age 17.

The TAT consisted of 18 pictures: nine from the Murray set which is now standard (cards 1, 5, 6, 7BM, 10, 11, 14, 15, 17); five pictures from the set generally used in 1938 when these data were collected (a man and woman seated on a park bench; a bearded old man writing in an open book; a thin, sullen, young man standing behind a well-dressed older man; a tea table and two chairs; an abstract drawing of two bearded men); and four designed especially for this investigation (the nave of a large church; a madonna and child; a dramatic view of mountains; a boy gazing at a cross which is wreathed in clouds).

The tests were administered individually. Each card was projected on a screen while the subject told a story which was recorded verbatim. Standard instructions were given for the Murray cards, and subjects were asked to describe the feelings elicited by the other four pictures. Most of the stories were brief, consisting of only one or two sentences.

As we noted earlier, each of the personality variables involved in the seven propositions was translated into a TAT scoring category. The scoring scheme involved counting the relevant needs, press, and description of the heroes of the stories, the assumption being that the storyteller has identified with the hero: the hero's needs are the same as the boy's; the press that impinge upon the hero are the ones that affect the boy telling the story.

[1] The present sample includes 27 of Jones and Bayley's (8) 32 subjects (the 16 most consistently retarded and 16 most consistently accelerated boys in the study). The other five boys had not taken the TAT at age 17. The six subjects who were in the present study but not in Jones and Bayley's study are the three "runners-up" from each end of the physical maturity distribution, i.e., the three who were closest to the 16 most accelerated cases and the three cases next to the 16 most retarded.

A total of 20 needs, press, and descriptive categories, each defined as specifically as possible, was developed in the analysis of the protocols. A score for each subject for each TAT category was derived by counting the number of stories in which it appeared. A list of the categories used, together with brief descriptions of them, is found in Table 1.

To test the reliability of this analysis, one of the authors (PM) and another psychologist[2] independently scored 15 complete protocols (300 stories). The percentage of interrater agreement was 90, computed by the usual formula (number of agreements divided by number of agreements plus number of disagreements).

In order to eliminate bias, the scoring used in the present study was done "blind," that is, independently of knowledge of the subject's maturational status.

RESULTS

Frequency distributions of the scores of all subjects were made for all the TAT variables. Each distribution was then dichotomized at the point which most nearly enabled the placing of half of the 33 subjects above, and half of them below, the dividing point. Subjects having scores above this point were considered high in this particular variable; those with scores below that point were considered low in this variable. Chi square tests were used to test the seven propositions, i.e., to ascertain whether or not high scores in certain TAT variables were in fact more characteristic of one group (late- or early-maturers) than of the other.

Table 1 lists the TAT variables, the number of late- and early-maturers with high scores in the variable, the chi square value obtained and the level of significance. It should be noted that the hypotheses tested were one-sided hypotheses, while the chi square value is in terms of a two-sided hypothesis. When chi square has only one degree of freedom, the square root of chi square has a distribution which is the right hand half of a normal distribution. In order to test a one-sided hypothesis, the chi square test must be converted into the equivalent value in terms of a unit normal deviate (2). The levels of significance reported in Table 1 were evaluated in these terms.

Table 1 shows that, as had been predicted, more late-maturing than early-maturing boys revealed feelings of inadequacy and negative self-concepts, i.e., scored high in the TAT variable *negative characteristics.* Hence proposition 1 was confirmed. This finding is consistent with the frequently made clinical observation that retardation in physical maturation may be an important source of personal maladjustments and attitudes of inferiority.

Proposition 2 stated that more late-maturers regard their parents as highly dominating and rejecting. The evidence summarized in Table 1 substantially supported this proposition. While the difference was not statistically significant, more late- than early-maturers scored high in *p Dominance by parents* (total). There was a marked difference between the groups in the variable which involves parental domination by forcing the child to do

[2] We are indebted to Dr. Virginia B. Ware for her participation in this aspect of the study.

something he does not want to do (*p Dominance by parents, forcing*). However, examination of the data with respect to the variable *p Dominance by parents* (*prevention*) makes it necessary to reject that part of the proposition which maintains that late-maturers are more likely to view their parents as highly restrictive of their activities.

That aspect of proposition 2 which deals with feelings of rejection was confirmed by our data. Compared with the early-maturing group, a significantly greater proportion of the late-maturers told stories in which the hero was rejected by parents or authority figures. These feelings of rejection may stem from different sources. In some cases, the parents' behavior may make it clear that they are disappointed in their physically retarded son whom they regard as immature. The boy, perceiving this attitude, may interpret it as rejection. In other cases, parental reluctance to allow the late-maturing boy to establish his independence may lead to considerable tension in the family and the boy's feelings of rejection may simply reflect the ongoing parent-child conflict.

It is possible that earlier in their teens, soon after the physical changes of adolescence became apparent, many of the early-maturing boys also experienced conflicts with their parents, arising from difficulties in establishing their independence or in handling emerging heterosexual interests. At that time they too may have felt dominated or rejected. However, by the age of 17, when these data were collected, these boys were ordinarily treated as adults and granted more freedom. Hence, they were more likely to have resolved many of their conflicts with their parents and to feel accepted and independent.

The hypothesis (part of proposition 3) that more late-maturers would be highly aggressive was rejected on the basis of the evidence given in Table 1. In fact, the differences between the two groups on all the TAT aggression variables were in the opposite direction from the prediction. High scores in the variables relating to aggression of the most overt and violent type were significantly more frequent among the early-maturers, and more members of this group also scored high in measures of milder (verbal) aggression and of total aggression. While late-maturers may experience more problems of adjustment and greater frustrations than their early-maturing peers, they apparently do not manifest greater aggressive motivation. It may be that their own feelings of inadequacy or fears of retaliation and punishment for aggression inhibit their expression of hostile feelings, even in fantasy. On the other hand, the early-maturers who feel more secure personally, and recognize their own relatively advantageous physical and social status, may feel freer to express their aggressive needs. Since aggression is a culturally stereotyped masculine trait, it seems possible that the physically accelerated, being accepted as mature and identifying readily with adult males, are more likely to acquire this characteristic. In any case, the finding that early-maturers express higher aggressive motivation during late adolescence seems consistent with Jones' finding that, as young adults, they score high on the dominance scale of the Edwards Personal Preference test (6). Perhaps the relatively strong aggressive motivation of the early-maturer, or the mature sex-role identification it may imply, serves as a basis for the development of later qualities of leadership and persuasiveness (7).

As Table 1 indicates, the other aspect of proposition 3 was confirmed: a significantly greater proportion of late- than of early-maturers displayed strong motivations to escape from, or defy, their parents. These may be essentially aggressive reactions, stemming from feelings of parental domination and rejection, or they may reflect the late-maturers' awareness of their strife with their parents whom they perceive as blocking their drives for independence. These strong needs for escape and defiance may also be considered evidence of a generally immature way of handling parent-child conflicts. Perhaps, by the age of 17, the early-maturers have already resolved many of their conflicts with their families and/or have learned to handle these in less rebellious and in more direct and mature ways.

Proposition 4 stated that, compared with their early-maturing peers, more late-maturers would manifest strong needs for establishing close social contacts with others. While there was some confirmatory evidence, the results were not clear-cut. When all affiliative needs were considered together (score for *n Affiliation—total*), the group differences were in the predicted direction, but not statistically significant. Examination of the protocols revealed that almost all instances of affiliation concerned either parents or the opposite sex; there were very few stories involving close, friendly associations between like-sexed peers. The two major types of affiliation were scored separately. As Table 1 shows, late-maturers did not differ from early-maturers with respect to need for affiliation with parents, but a significantly greater proportion of the former group displayed strong motivation for heterosexual affiliation.

In view of the late-maturers' strong feelings of inadequacy and dependent needs (see below), it is surprising that a greater proportion of this group did not exhibit strong needs to establish and maintain close bonds with their parents. This may be due to the late-maturers' more intense conflicts with their parents at this age (17 years), their fears of being rejected and dominated by them, and their generally defiant attitudes which prevent them from admitting, even in fantasy, their strong underlying needs to form close contacts with them.

The significant difference between the groups in *n Affiliation* (*love, romance, marriage*) is subject to several possible interpretations. For one thing, this category may refer to general needs to establish close relations with others (with peers or adults other than parents) and not merely to desire for contact with the opposite sex. The set of stimulus cards may not have been adequate to elicit responses indicative of more general affiliative needs; hence, these were expressed through responses in the heterosexual affiliation category. If this is true, proposition 4 was confirmed, and the late-maturers' high scores in this variable indicate their greater general interest in establishing and maintaining friendly relationships.

It is also possible that the late-maturers' strong affiliative needs are actually directed only toward members of the opposite sex, i.e., that *n Affiliation* (*love, romance, marriage*) measures specifically heterosexual interest. Assuming that this is true, there is another plausible explanation for the discovered difference. As we saw earlier, the late-maturer may be afraid to admit that he desires close association with his parents. He may also feel that his immaturity and poor reputational status prevent him from establishing successful social relationships with like-sexed peers. Hence, he may "displace" his affiliative needs to members of the opposite sex, who, in his fantasies, may seem more responsive.

A third possible explanation of the difference is based on Jones and Bayley's findings that the late-maturers show less overt interest in girls and are regarded as less good-looking (8). From these data, it may be inferred that the physically retarded probably do not have successful and rewarding experiences with girls. Hence their heightened need for affiliation with the opposite sex, expressed in the TAT, may reflect their attempts to satisfy in fantasy needs which they cannot satisfy adequately in reality.

The data were generally supportive of proposition 5 which stated that late-maturers are likely to have strong underlying dependent needs. A higher proportion of this group than of their early-maturing peers scored high in *n Succorance,* the difference between the two groups approaching statistical significance ($p = .06$). Furthermore, high scores in the category involving receiving help and support from others (not including parents) (*p Nurturance—non-parents*)—an indirect measure of dependent needs—were significantly more characteristic of the physically retarded than of the physically accelerated. In view of the late-maturers' attitudes toward their parents, discussed above, it is not surprising to find that perceptions of parents as kindly and supportive (high scores in *p Nurturance—parents*) were not significantly more common in this group than in the early-maturing group.

On the basis of the data involving the TAT variables *n Achievement* and *n Recognition,* we rejected proposition 6 which stated that more early-maturers would be self-confident and have high needs for achievement and personal recognition. In our culture there is strong pressure to develop needs for achievement and personal recognition, and, according to our results, these needs and feelings may become intense regardless of—or perhaps in spite of—the child's maturational status, feelings of personal adequacy, dependency, and adjustment to parents.

Two interesting incidental findings from the TAT data seem to be consistent with the proposition that more early- than late-maturers are likely to be self-confident. Seven boys in this sample of 33 adolescents told stories in which the hero was helpful or kind to someone else (*n Nurturance*). Of this group, six were early-maturers, while only one was a late-maturer ($x^2 = 2.09$, $p = .07$). Insofar as *n Nurturance* may be a measure of the storyteller's own feelings that he can accept an active, mature role, more of the accelerated group feel self-assured with respect to having attained mature status.

The other incidental finding which seems to support proposition 6 is based on responses only to card 1 of the Murray series which depicts a young boy contemplating a violin which rests on a table in front of him. Eight of the subjects spoke of the boy (the hero) as a prodigy or a genius.

Of these, seven were early-maturers; only one was physically retarded ($x^2 = 5.25$, $p = .01$). If the attribution of this prestige status and accomplishment to the hero reflects the subject's own feeling that he has been an achiever, it follows that more of the physically accelerated have positive self-concepts. In view of the small number of cases involved, both of these findings must be considered tentative, but they do offer some evidence in support of proposition 6.

Proposition 7, which stated that relatively few of the physically retarded boys are unwilling or unable to face their own feelings and emotions, received some support from the TAT data summarized in Table 1. A smaller proportion of the members of this group than of the physically accelerated group specifically denied that the pictures evoked any feelings or emotions (e.g. "It doesn't make me think of anything"). While this variable may not adequately measure *denial of feeling* as a major defense mechanism, this result seems to indicate that late-maturers are more sensitive to their own feelings and more ready to admit and face them openly. Since these qualities are basic to the development of psychological insight, it may be inferred that late-maturers, as a group, are more likely to become insightful individuals.

DISCUSSION

The results of the study support the general hypothesis that, in our culture, the boy whose physical development is retarded is exposed to a sociopsychological environment which may have adverse effects on his personality development. Apparently, being in a disadvantageous competitive position in athletic activities, as well as being regarded and treated as immature by others, may lead to negative self-conceptions, heightened feelings of rejection by others, prolonged dependent needs, and rebellious attitudes toward parents. Hence, the physically retarded boy is more likely than his early-maturing peer to be personally and socially maladjusted during late adolescence. Moreover, some of his attitudes are likely to interfere with the process of identification with his parents, which is generally based on perceptions of them as warm and accepting (9). This, in turn, may inhibit or delay the acquisition of mature characteristics and attitudes which are ordinarily established through identification with parents. Fortunately for the late-maturers' subsequent adjustments, they seem more willing and able to face their feelings and emotions. This may be a result of their awareness of others' attitudes toward their immaturity or their feelings of personal inadequacy and dependency.

The physically accelerated boys, on the other hand, are likely to experience environmental circumstances which are much more conducive to good psychological adjustment. Hence, their psychological picture, as reflected in their TAT stories, is much more favorable. By the time they were 17, relatively few early-maturers harbored strong feelings of inadequacy, perceived themselves as rejected or dominated by parents or authorities, or felt rebellious toward their families. As a group, they appeared to have acquired more self-confidence and had probably made stronger identifications with mature adults. Hence, they perceived themselves as more mature individuals, less dependent and in need of help, and more capable of playing an adult male role in interpersonal relationships.

These findings assume additional, probably greater, importance when they are considered in the light of Jones' findings on the early adult (age 33) adjustments of boys who had been retarded or accelerated in physical maturing (6). It should be recalled that by this age physical differences between the two groups had practically disappeared. Certain important psychological differences were noted, however, and these were consistent with the differences at age 17, reported in the present study. For example, the responses of the early-maturing group to two paper-and-pencil tests, revealed that, as young adults, they were more dominant, more able to make a good impression and more likely to be turned to for advice and reassurance; more self-controlled; and more willing and able to carry social responsibility. In short, they present a general picture of psychological maturity. Moreover, more of the early-maturers seemed to have made successful vocational adjustments. In contrast to this, when the late-maturers became adults, they tended to be highly dependent individuals who could be described, on the basis of their test responses, as tending to be rebellious, touchy, impulsive, self-indulgent, and insightful. Most of these characteristics are indicative of poor adjustment and psychological immaturity. Fewer members of this group had made good vocational adjustments.

The striking correspondence between the two descriptions of the groups, derived from different kinds of tests and collected at widely separated periods of time, lends further support to Jones' conclusion that "the adolescent handicaps and advantages associated with late- or early-maturing appear to carry over into adulthood to some extent" (6). It seems clear that many attitudes of adolescent personality (patterns of motivation, self-conceptions, and attitudes toward others) characteristic of late- and early-maturing boys are relatively stable and durable rather than situational and transitory. This may be attributable to the fact that in our culture adolescence is generally a critical and difficult period of adjustment. Within a relatively brief interval of time, the child must work out numerous complex and vitally important personal problems—e.g., adaptation to his changed biological and social status, establishment of independence, vocational adjustment. In dealing with these problems, he may acquire new behaviors and personality attributes which have broad ramifications, not only on his current adjustment, but also on his subsequent development. If the adolescent can cope with his problems without too much inner stress and turmoil, his self-esteem, feelings of adequacy, and consequently his subsequent adjustment, are likely to be enhanced. On the other hand, if his problems induce great tension and anxiety, he is likely to feel frustrated and inadequate, and, if these feelings are maintained, to adjust less satisfactorily as an adult.

Obviously, the adolescent's success or failure, as well as ease or tension, in handling his problems will be determined to a large degree by the sociopsychological forces to which he is subjected during this time, and these, as we have seen, may be significantly related to his rate of maturation. Thus, physical status during adolescence—mediated through the sociopsychological environment—may exert profound and lasting influences on personality. For this reason, many aspects of the adult's behavior and personality seem consistent with his adolescent adjustments, attitudes and motivations.

Insofar as our results permit generalization, they suggest that some important aspects of motivation, such as needs for achievement and personal recognition, are not significantly affected by maturational status. It may be that among subjects whose achievements are strongly encouraged and rewarded from very early childhood, the need to achieve becomes powerful and resistant to change even in the face of feelings of helplessness and inadequacy. The latter may inhibit the achievement-oriented overt behavior of some late-maturers, but the underlying motivation to achieve seems as strong in this group as it is among the physically accelerated.

In conclusion, it should be noted that, although rate of maturing and associated factors may affect personality development, the relationship between physical status and psychological characteristics is by no means simple. A vast number of complex, interacting factors, including rate of maturation, determines each adolescent's unique personality structure. Hence, in any specific instance, the *group* findings of the present study may not be directly applicable, for other physical, psychological, or social factors may attenuate the effects of late- or early-maturing. For example, an adolescent boy who is fundamentally secure and has warm, accepting parents and generally rewarding social relationships may not develop strong feelings of inadequacy even if he matures slowly. Analogously, the early-maturing boy who has deep feelings of insecurity, for whatever reasons, will probably not gain self-confidence simply because he matures early. In summary, in understanding any individual case, generalizations based on the data of the present study must be particularized in the light of the individual's past history and present circumstances.

SUMMARY

The present investigation was designed to test seven propositions concerning the relationship between rate of physical maturation and important aspects of personality structure, specifically, self-conceptions, underlying motivations, and basic interpersonal attitudes. The TAT protocols of 33 seventeen-year-old boys—16 who had been consistently physically accelerated throughout adolescence and 17 who had been consistently retarded—were analyzed according to a scoring schema involving 20 needs, press, and descriptive categories. The scores of early- and late-maturers in each of the categories were compared.

An earlier study (8) demonstrated that late-maturing boys are more likely than their early-maturing peers to encounter a generally unfavorable sociopsychological environment. Analysis of the data of the present study indicates that this situation may have adverse effects on the personalities of the physically retarded. These boys are more likely to have negative self-conceptions, feelings of inadequacy, strong feelings of being rejected and dominated, prolonged dependency needs, and rebellious attitudes toward parents. In contrast, the early-maturing boys present a much more favorable psychological picture during adolescence. Relatively few of them felt inadequate, rejected, dominated, or rebellious toward their families. More of them appeared to be self-confident, independent, and capable of playing an adult role in interpersonal relationships. Early- and late-maturing groups did not differ significantly from each other in needs for achievement or personal recognition.

These findings make it clear that rate of physical maturing may affect personality development in crucially important ways. However, it is important to note that in any particular case the effects of early- or late-maturing may be significantly modified by the individual's psychological history and present circumstances.

REFERENCES

1. Farnham, M. L. *The adolescent.* New York: Harper, 1951.
2. Fisher, R. A. *Statistical methods for research workers.* (7th Ed.) Edinburgh: Oliver & Boyd, 1938.
3. Jones, H. E. Observational methods in the study of individual development. *J. Consult. Psychol.,* 1940, 4, 234–238.
4. Jones, H. E. *Development in adolescence.* New York: Appleton-Century, 1943.
5. Jones, H. E. Adolescence in our society. In *The family in a democratic society, Anniversary papers of The Community Service Society of New York.* New York: Columbia Univer. Press, 1949. Pp. 70–82.
6. Jones, Mary C. The later careers of boys who were early- or late-maturing. *Child Developm.,* 1957, 28, 113–128.
7. Jones, Mary C. A study of socialization at the high school level. In preparation.
8. Jones, Mary C., and Bayley, Nancy. Physical maturing among boys as related to behavior. *J. Educ. Psychol.,* 1950, 41, 129–148.
9. Payne, D. E., and Mussen, P. H. Parent-child relations and father identification among adolescent boys. *J. Abnorm. Soc. Psychol.,* 1956, 52, 358–362.
10. Stone, C. P., and Baker, R. G. The attitudes and interests of premenarcheal and postmenarcheal girls. *J. Genet. Psychol.,* 1939, 54, 27–71.
11. Tryon, Caroline M. Evaluation of adolescent personality by adolescents. *Monogr. Soc. Res. Child Developm.,* 1939, 4, No. 4.

LETA S. HOLLINGWORTH

Children Above 180 IQ: Child D

The preceding article told of developmental trends in a group of adolescents. The stream of development can also be illuminated by individual case studies. Leta Hollingworth studied many extremely bright children, but none more remarkable than D. What is your image of a brilliant child? Sickly? Unbalanced? Blind to beauty? Read the investigator's simple records, and study D's own childhood work. How would you deal with D if you were his elementary teacher?

Child D is a boy, born March 9, 1910. He was first described by Terman, who tested him in 1917. D . . . was brought to the attention of the writer by the principal of the Horace Mann Kindergarten (Teachers College, Columbia University) as being a child of remarkable endowment. He was at that time 7 years 4 months old and had a Mental Age of 13 years 7 months, with an IQ of 184 (S–B).

FAMILY BACKGROUND

D is descended from Russian Jews in the paternal branch and from English Jews in the maternal branch.

Father. D's father immigrated to America at an early age. He is a high school graduate and was a student of engineering but abandoned these studies in the third year to do newspaper work, and later entered the advertising business in a large city. His leisure is spent in writing, and he has published a number of books, including three novels and a philosophical drama dealing with religion. His first book, a novel, was published when he was 21 years old. He was 28 when D was born.

Mother. D's mother went to school for only a few weeks and has been largely self-taught. Before marriage she was statistician and registrar in a large philanthropic organization. She has published stories, reviews, and poems, and a book on education. She has always taken part personally in the education of D. She was 26 years old when D was born. D is an only child.

Leta S. Hollingworth, "Child D," Chapter 7 in *Children Above 180 IQ* (Yonkers: World Book Company, 1942). Reproduced with permission of the estate of Dr. Harry Hollingworth.

Noteworthy relatives. Noteworthy relatives beyond the first degree of kinship include the following: a chief rabbi of Moscow, who was exiled for aiding the Nihilists; a distinguished lawyer; a man who by his own efforts became a millionaire; a concert pianist; a composer and virtuoso; a writer; and "a relative decorated for science in Poland."

The maternal great-grandfather was a famous rabbi who compiled and published a Jewish calendar covering a period of 414 years. This calendar contains, in regular order, the exact period of every new moon's appearance, the sabbaths, festivals with scriptural portions for each, and the equinoxes of the solar year according to the prescribed and authorized Jewish laws and corresponding to dates in the common era. The tabulations have been carefully compiled from various works of ancient rabbinical astronomers, with annotations in Hebrew and English.

This rabbi was also the great-grandfather of the four first cousins of D, whose intelligence quotients have been taken, and who rated 156, 150, 130, and 122, respectively. A second cousin in the maternal line yielded at the age of 6 years an IQ of 157.

PRESCHOOL HISTORY

D cut his first tooth at 4 months of age. He could say words at 8 months and talked in sentences at 11 months. In November, 1910 (8 months), he said "little boy" when his shadow appeared on the wall. D could stand, holding to chairs, at 9 months of age, and he walked alone at 11 to 12 months. At the age of 18 months, while sitting on his mother's lap as she sat before a typewriter, he learned to read by looking at the letters. The records kept by the mother indicate that he "learned to read and count in 1911." One such record reads, "October 11, counts all day long."

At 8 months of age D strung in succession 5 yellow and 5 red balls and then began on blue, when the activity was interrupted. In March, 1912, he was using words to express relationship, such as "will" and "shall" (correctly), "but," "and," "my," "mine." At 2 years 6 months his vocabulary (incomplete) was 1690 words.

D's earliest memory goes back to 2 years of age, when he saw a rat and thought it was "a little brownie." An example of the quality of the questions asked by D in the first 36 months of life is one he asked in October, 1911 (19 months): "Has every door two knobs?" "Why?" His mother reports: "He was always asking unexpected questions."

This child was not placed in school at the usual age because he did not fit into the school organization. At the time he should have entered kindergarten D could read fluently and could perform complicated arithmetical processes. His intellectual interests were far beyond those of even the highly selected children of a private kindergarten. Therefore, his parents kept him out of school and obtained the companionship of other children for him by sending him to a playground.

D was first seen by the present writer [L. S. H.] while he was attending this playground, in the year 1916–1917. It is very interesting to note how D made social contacts with the other children while pursuing his own interests. For instance, he published a playground newspaper called "The Weekly Post."[1] He composed, edited, and typed this paper, issued at intervals, and it had a regular playground circulation.

TRAITS OF CHARACTER

No faulty traits of character have been ascribed to D by parents or teachers interviewed. He was rated for character by Terman's method under Terman's direction, with a result of 1.93 from parents' estimates and 1.90 from teachers' estimates (the median score, for comparison with average children, being 3.00). D is thus rated by parents and teachers alike as well above the average in character. The desirable traits most often mentioned are refusal to lie, loyalty to standards once adopted, readiness to admit just criticisms, unselfishness, and amiability.

MENTAL MEASUREMENTS

General intelligence tests of D show the following results:

Date	*Birthday age of D*	*Stanford-Binet MA*	*Stanford-Binet IQ*	*Army Alpha points D*	*Army Alpha points Norm*	*Thorndike test for freshmen (points) D*	*Thorndike test for freshmen (points) Norm*
August, 1917	7–4	13–7	184				
January 29, 1921	10–11			185 (Form 5)	—		
				Passed all for Superior Adult			
June, 1922	12–3					106	70–80

It is thus seen how greatly D surpasses the average child in mental tests. In the five years which have elapsed since D's first test there has been no tendency to become mediocre. At the age of 7 years he showed an IQ of 184; at the age of 11 years he exceeded by a wide margin on Army Alpha the median score for postgraduate students in first-rate universities; at 12 years he far exceeded the median score of college freshmen on Thorndike's test for that group. The validity of these scores is consistently borne out by the school history.

PHYSICAL MEASUREMENTS AND HEALTH

The following measurements, as of May, 1922, were made in the gymnasium of the high school attended by D:[2]

[1] A facsimile of a page from this paper is reproduced on page 244 of the author's book, *Gifted Children* (The Macmillan Company, New York, 1926).

[2] A note shows that on March 16, 1926, at just 16 years of age, D's height was 71.5 inches and his weight 115 pounds, stripped. EDITOR.

Weight (lbs.)		Height (in.)		Ht.-Wt. Coefficient	
D	Norm	D	Norm	D	Norm
76.0	82.8	64.0	57.7	1.19	1.44

D's health has always been excellent and no physical defects are known to his parents. He is rated as very stable nervously. His slenderness has been rated as a defect by one examiner; although he greatly exceeds the norm in height, he falls below in weight. He is therefore very tall and slender in appearance, which is characteristic of his father and uncles.

MISCELLANEOUS CHARACTERISTICS

Diversions. At the age of 7 years D's favorite amusements were skating, "Mechano," reading, playing ball, writing, tabulating, solitaire, chess, and numerical calculation in all its forms. As development has proceeded, he has continued most of these recreations, turning more and more, however, to games of intellectual skill. He likes other children and likes to be with them; he has established relations with them by editing newspapers for them, teaching them about nature, and the like. Play in the sense of mere purposeless sensorimotor activity has not been enjoyed by him.

Imaginary land. From the age of about 4 years to about the age of 7, D was greatly interested in an imaginary land which he called "Borningtown." He spent many hours peopling Borningtown, laying out roads, drawing maps of its terrain, composing and recording its language (Bornish), and writing its history and literature. He composed a lengthy dictionary—scores of pages—of the Bornish language. The origin of the words "Borningtown" and "Bornish" is not known. It seems possible that D's imaginary land may have arisen out of the mystery of being born.

Gift for music. D has had piano lessons for several years, and he has displayed remarkable ability to deal with the mathematical aspects of music. A sample is shown of his musical composition, illustrating his understanding of musical symbols and his ability to interpret through this medium. He composed music before he had any instruction in playing musical instruments. He read certain booklets which came with Ampico and decided to compose. He can compose music which he cannot himself play.

Gifts for form and color in drawing. D's talent for color, for drawing and design, has been marked from the time he could wield a pencil. His drawings, paintings, and designs would fill a book by themselves. A sample of his original work at the age of 10 years is reproduced.

This conventionalized bird is a fragment from his decoration for the chest in which he kept his "scientific work" at that time. This oblong chest he painted Chinese red, with three figures on the front. These were the conventionalized bird here shown, a conventionalized nest with eggs, and a

FIGURE 1.

Part of a composition by D at age 8 years 7 months

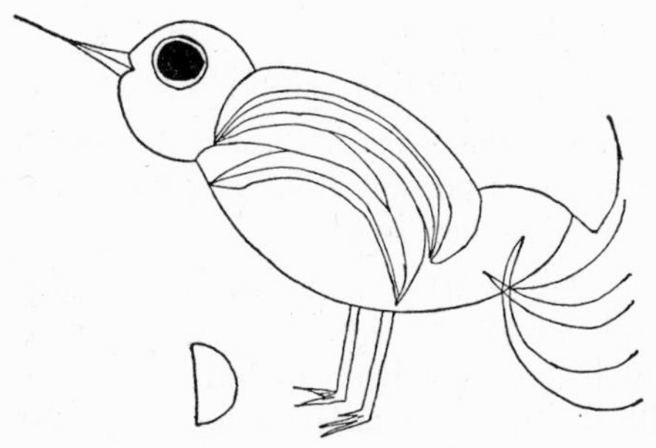

FIGURE 2.

Drawn by D at age 9 years 9 months

conventionalized butterfly—all painted in striking combinations of yellow, blue, green, and red.

D loves color, and one of his favorite playthings has been a sample folder of silk buttonhole twists of three hundred shades. Between the ages of 8 and 9 years he would go over and over these, classifying the colors in various ways, scoring them for beauty, and renaming them to satisfy his appreciation of them. Some of these names will give an idea of his appreciation:

spotted pale	dark darking green
darkling green	regular green
shame blue	paper white
spoiled pink	apron blue
soft light pink	beau yellow
meadow beauty pink	visitor's green
cat black	alien white
royalest red	feeling blue

One of his favorite games (aged 8 to 9 years) was to assign a numerical value to each of the 300 shades and then to list them for "highest honors." "Royalest red" nearly always won in these contests.

Origination of new concepts and new words. From earliest childhood D has felt a need for concepts and for words to express them that are not to be found in dictionaries. His occupation in this field he calls "wordical work." Some examples are recorded by his mother in the following note dated December, 1916.

> Was having his dinner and being nearly finished said he didn't care to eat any more, as he had a pain in his actum pelopthis. He explained that his actum pelopthis, actum quotatus, serbalopsis, and boobalicta are parts of the body where you sometimes have queer feelings; they don't serve any purpose. He said he also had a place called the boobalunksis, or source of headaches; that the hair usually springs out from around the herkadone; that the perpalensis is the place where socks end, and the bogalegus is the place where the legs and tummy come together. He also named one other part, the cobaliscus or smerbalooble, whose function is not explained. The definitions are exactly as he gave them in each instance.

On February 23, 1917, his mother wrote:

> He has not referred to these places since. I do not know where he got the idea for such names, unless possibly from *The Water Babies*. He would probably refer them to some Bornish source.

The invention and classification of the Bornish language already referred to is another example of D's "wordical work." He has also invented hundreds of words which have not been included as Bornish. An example of his handwriting, illustrative of words he has invented, classified, and recorded for pleasure, is here shown.

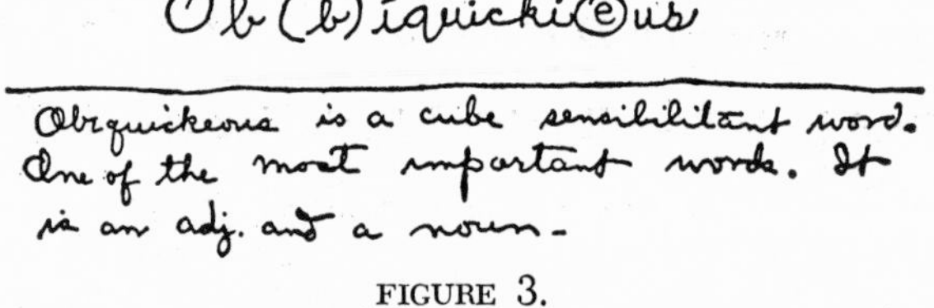

FIGURE 3.

One of D's verbal inventions

Invention of games. D has invented many games. To illustrate this aspect of his mental capacity, there are his designs for three-handed and four-handed checkers.[3] D held that these would be better games than two-handed checkers because they are more complicated. A description of the games invented by D, together with his mathematical calculations concerning the chances and probabilities in each, would fill many pages.

Calculation and mathematical ingenuity. It is difficult to say that D is more gifted in one mental function or group of functions than in others, for his ability is so extraordinary in all performances that without means of measurement one cannot tell in which he deviates farthest from the average.

However, it is to be observed that the quantitative aspects of experience have always played a very striking role in all his performances. Even in his dealing with color he turned to mathematics and made his values quantitative. Throughout childhood he spent hours playing with numerical relationships. These calculations cover hundreds of pages. There is reproduced here a sample of such work, chosen at random from scores of like material. There is no doubt in the mind of the present writer [L. S. H.] that D could, by practice with short-cut methods, easily become a lightning calculator. By the age of 12 years D had finished college entrance requirements in arithmetic, algebra, geometry, and trigonometry, all with high marks.

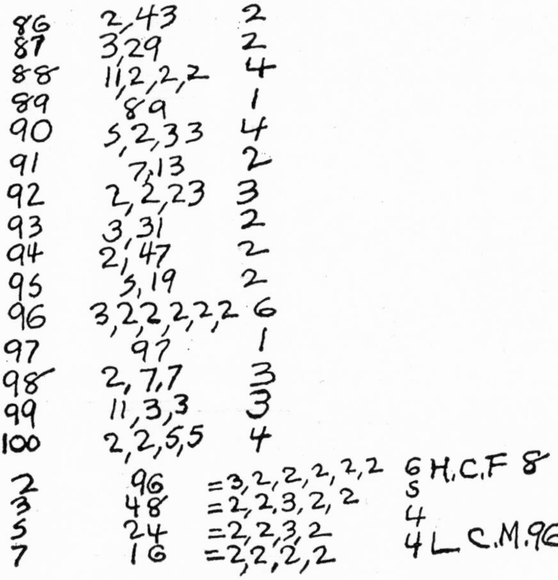

86 2,43 2
87 3,29 2
88 11,2,2,2 4
89 89 1
90 5,2,3,3 4
91 7,13 2
92 2,2,23 3
93 3,31 2
94 2,47 2
95 5,19 2
96 3,2,2,2,2,2 6
97 97 1
98 2,7,7 3
99 11,3,3 3
100 2,2,5,5 4
2 96 =3,2,2,2,2,2 6 H.C.F 8
3 48 =2,2,3,2,2 5
5 24 =2,2,3,2 4
7 16 =2,2,2,2 4 L.C.M. 96

FIGURE 4.

Playing with numbers, Child D, age 7, to find what number under 100 has the greatest number of factors, counts up factors in each and awards "highest honors" to 96.

[3] See *Gifted Children,* pages 246–247.

```
Classification of birds seen in summer 1918.  Classified in Feb.,
1919. "Proper Scientific Name" is the improved name given by D--.

Found  Name          Genus        Scientific            Proper Scien-
Here   (Popular)     or,etc.      N  a  m  e            tific Name.        Equal
*... Towhee.......Species....Erythopthalmus........Pipilo Eryth.......**?..
X...Wh.-eyed Towhee...Sub-Species...E.Alleni..P. Leucopthalmus........***..
X...Green-tailed " ...Genus... Oreospiza.............Pipilo...........**?..
X...Blue Grosbeak... Species...Caerulea.............Cyanea............***..
*...Indigo Bunting..   "    ...Cyanea..............Caerulea..........***..
X...Painted   "   ...  "   ......Ciris..............Pictus............**?
X...Lark Bunting....   "   ..Calamospiza Melanocorys...Melanospiza Leucoptera
                                                                      ***...
*...Barn Swallow..     "   ...Erythrogastra.........Leucurus...........***..
*...Tree    "    ...Genus.....Iridoprocne............Hirundo...........***..
*...Red-eyed Vireo..Species...Olivacea.............Erythropthalmus....Yes..
....Wood Warblers..Family...Mniotiltidae.......... Dendroicidae.......**?..
*...Black & White Warbler..Species..Varia..........Striata............**?..
*...Yellow Warbler..Species...Astiva..............Xantho or Auro.......Yes..
*...Sh.-Billed Marsh Wren..Genus..Cistothorus....Telmatotytes. ....... ? ..
*...Red-br. Nuthatch..Species..Canadensis......Borealis...............Yes..
                                            ....Erythrogastra..........**?..
*****************************************************************************.
```

FIGURE 5.

A sample of D's classifications

SPECIES (G.) J A N. F E B. M A R. A P R. M A Y J U N E JULY A U G. S E P T.
1 15 31 1 15 28 1 15 20 31 1 10 15 20 30 1 10 15 20 31 1 10 15 20 30 1 10 15 20 31 1 10 15 20 31 1 10 15 20 31

HOLBCEL'S GREBE (RARE)
HORNED " (CON.)
PIED-BILLED " ("INFALL)
LOON (F. ")
" BLACK-THR. (R)
" RED-THR. (F. CCN)
PUFFIN (V.R.)
BLACK GUILLEMOT (")
MURRE (")
" BRUNNICH'S (R.)
RAZOR-BILLED AUK (F.C.)
DOVEKIE (")
SKUA (V-R.)
JAEGER POMARINE (F.C.)
" , PARASITIC (")
" , LONG-TAILED (")
GULL, IVORY (CAS.)
" , KITTAWAKE (CO)
" , GLAUCOUS (RATH. R)
" , ICELAND (")
" , KUMLIEN'S (F.C.)
" , GR. BL.-BACKED (")
" , HERRING (AB.)
" , RING-BILLED (R.R.)
" , LAUGHING (CON.)
" , BONAPARTE'S (")
" , LITTLE. CASUAL (WHEN?)
" , SABINE (CAS.)
TERN, GULL-BILLED (")
" , CASPIAN (F.C.)
" , ROYAL (CAS.)
" , CABOT'S (ACC.)
" , TRUDEAU'S " (WHEN?)
" , FORSTER'S (CAS.)
" , COMMON (")
" , ARCTIC (")
" , ROSEATE (COM.?)
" , LEAST (")
" , SOOTY (ACC.)
" , BLACK (")

FIGURE 6.

One of D's records of observations: life cycles of birds

Tendency to classify and diagram. To classify the data of experience has always been one of D's chief interests. One such tabulation was of parts of speech in various stories and poems.[4] Figure 5 is a sample taken from many pages of reclassification of birds. The caption, "Proper Scientific Name," represents the name considered by D to be better than those now recognized by ornithologists. His classifications of words, numbers, colors, musical notes, objects, and so forth would fill a large volume. He often constructs diagrams to clarify or condense meaning.

Interest in science. By the age of 10 years D's chief interest had come to center in science and it continued to center there. His classifications of

of the problem: "Determine the appearance of a finger, F, to two eyes, E_R and E_L, focussed on a pole R at point P_S along lines $E_R R$ and $E_L R$."

Thru R pass plane PL // to the plane of the eyes. Draw a line from E_L (which is nearer to F than E_R) to F, cutting PL in O. Draw $E_R O$; thru F pass a plane // to PL and crossing $E_R O$ in A. Thru A pass F' // F.

F' and F are the positions of F to E_R and E_L.

D.

So it can be shown that 2 other eyes would see F in positions F and F''.

∴ 4 eyes focused on R see F as F, F, F', and F''.

D.

FIGURE 7.

Copy of work done by D "For Fun," March 28, 1921, aged 11 years 1 month

moths, birds, and the like and his observations of their life cycles are "monumental." There are volumes of these recorded observations as in Figure 6.

Figures 7 and 8 illustrate his interest in physical science. They have been taken from his notebooks and state problems which occurred spontaneously to him and for which he tried experimentally to find solutions. During a

[4] *Ibid.*, page 245.

Discussion

of the determination of the course of a freed tack, T, connected with other tacks by rubber bands.

A.Fig.1.

When connected to a tack T' by band B.
Draw T T_1 or L.
T freed will travel along L, answer.

B.Fig.2.

When connected to 2 tacks T' and T'' by 2 bands B and B'.
Answer: Along L, the bisector of T' and TTT''.

C.Fig.3.

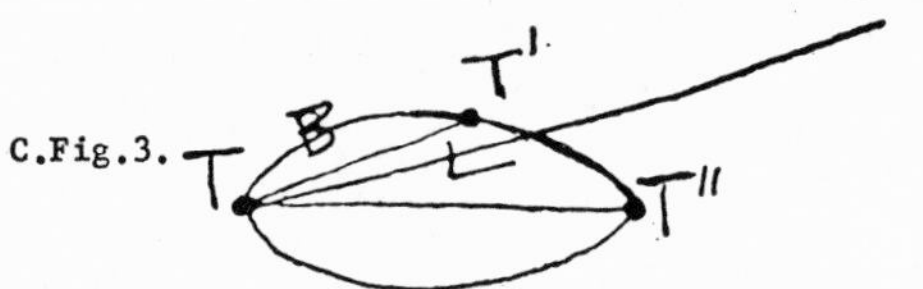

The same as B, but only 1 band B.
Answer same as to B.

D.Fig.4.

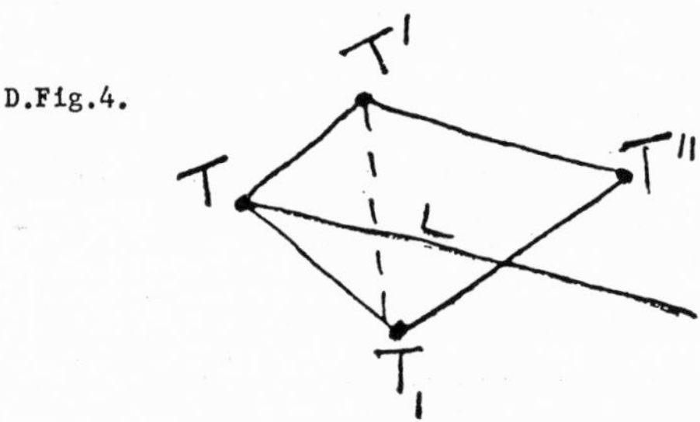

When connected to 3 tacks by any number of bands.
Draw T' T_1, and treat as in B and C.

D.

FIGURE 8.

The path of a tack: Work done by D at age 11 years

series of experiments "to determine the path of a tack," it is reported that "the house was full of tacks" which had been used in attempting solutions.

SCHOOL HISTORY

In the September following his ninth birthday D entered upon formal instruction in the junior high school. In the autumn following his tenth birthday he entered senior high school, from which he was graduated at the age of 12 years, with a scholastic record which won for him two scholarships.

He was admitted to a large Eastern college at the age of 12 years 6 months (1922–1923), and made a superior record throughout the course. It was very interesting to see that D continued to discover means of obtaining social contacts in spite of the great difficulties due to his extreme youth and his intellectual deviation. Thus it is not easy to plan how a 12-year-old boy might successfully participate in college athletics when the median age of college freshmen is over 18 years, but this problem was not too difficult for D. He presented himself to compete for the post of coxswain on the freshman crew where, other things being equal, light weight is an advantage.

He was graduated from college, with Phi Beta Kappa honors, in 1926, at the age of 16 years 2 months. At that time he was ambitious for a career in science.

[EPILOGUE]

D undertook graduate work, with distinction, in the field of chemistry. He became an industrial chemist with an important position in the research phases of the motion-picture industry. Word has been received of his death in September, 1938 [at the age of twenty-eight].

Chapter 5

Differences in Pupil Characteristics: Illustrative Cases

5-1

HOWARD S. BECKER

Social Class Variations in the Teacher-Pupil Relationship

5-2

ELSE FRENKEL-BRUNSWIK

Case Study of an Authoritarian Family and Child

HOWARD S. BECKER

Social Class Variations in the Teacher-Pupil Relationship

Some pupil differences are related to the parents' educational background, the father's occupation, and the financial situation at home. Some differences are linked to national background, race, and neighborhood. A new teacher may be upset to discover that not all students care about the qualities he values. After interviewing 60 teachers working with children from poorer neighborhoods, the sociologist Becker gives his impression of the frictions presented by conflicting values. Do these very differences provide the teacher with one of his best opportunities to help his pupils?

The major problems of workers in the service occupations are likely to be a function of their relationship to their clients or customers, those for whom or on whom the occupational service is performed.[1] Members of such occupations typically have some image of the "ideal" client, and it is in terms of this fiction that they fashion their conceptions of how their work ought to be performed, and their actual work techniques. To the degree that actual clients approximate this ideal the worker will have no "client problem."

In a highly differentiated urban society, however, clients will vary greatly, and ordinarily only some fraction of the total of potential clients will be "good" ones. Workers tend to classify clients in terms of the way in which they vary from this ideal. The fact of client variation from the occupational ideal emphasizes the intimate relation of the institution in which work is carried on to its environing society. If that society does not prepare people to play their client roles in the manner desired by the occupation's members, there will be conflicts and problems for the workers in the performance of their work. One of the major factors affecting the production of suitable clients is the cultural diversity of various social classes in the society. The cultures of particular social-class groups may operate to produce clients who make the worker's position extremely difficult.

We deal here with this problem as it appears in the experience of the

[1] See Howard S. Becker, "The professional Dance Musician and His Audience," *American Journal of Sociology*, LVII (September, 1951), pp. 136–44 for further discussion of this point.

Howard S. Becker, "Social Class Variations in the Teacher-Pupil Relationship," *Journal of Educational Sociology*, 25 (1952), 451–65. Reprinted with permission.

This paper is based on research done under a grant from the Committee on Education, Training, and Research in Race Relations of the University of Chicago.

functionaries of a large urban educational institution, the Chicago public school system, discussing the way in which teachers in this system observe, classify and react to class-typed differences in the behavior of the children with whom they work. The material to be presented is thus relevant not only to problems of occupational organization but also to the problem of differences in the educational opportunities available to children of various social-classes. Warner, Havighurst and Loeb [2] and Hollingshead [3] have demonstrated the manner in which the schools tend to favor and select out children of the middle classes. Allison Davis has pointed to those factors in the class cultures involved which make lower-class children less and middle-class children more adaptable to the work and behavioral standards of the school.[4] This paper will contribute to knowledge in this area by analyzing the manner in which the public school teacher reacts to these cultural differences and, in so doing, perpetuates the discrimination of our educational system against the lower-class child.

The analysis is based on sixty interviews with teachers in the Chicago system.[5] The interviews were oriented around the general question of the problems of being a teacher and were not specifically directed toward discovering feelings about social-class differences among students. Since these differences created some of the teachers' most pressing problems they were continually brought up by the interviewees themselves. They typically distinguished three social-class groups with which they, as teachers, came in contact: (1) a bottom stratum, probably equivalent to the lower-lower and parts of the upper-lower class; (2) an upper stratum, probably equivalent to the upper-middle class; and (3) a middle stratum, probably equivalent to the lower-middle and parts of the upper-lower class. We will adopt the convention of referring to these groups as lower, upper and middle groups, but it should be understood that this terminology refers to the teachers' classification of students and not to the ordinary sociological description.

We will proceed by taking up the three problems that loomed largest in the teachers' discussion of adjustment to their students: (1) the problem of *teaching* itself, (2) the problem of *discipline,* and (3) the problem of the *moral acceptability* of the students. In each case the variation in the form of and adjustment to the problem by the characteristics of the children of the various class groups distinguished by teachers is discussed.

I

A basic problem in any occupation is that of performing one's given task successfully, and where this involves working with human beings their

[2] W. L. Warner, R. J. Havighurst, and W. J. Loeb, *Who Shall Be Educated?* (New York: Harper and Bros., 1944.)

[3] August Hollingshead, *Elmtown's Youth* (New York: John Wiley & Sons, 1949).

[4] Allison Davis, *Social-Class Influences Upon Learning* (Cambridge: Harvard University Press, 1950).

[5] The entire research has been reported in Howard S. Becker, "Role and Career Problems of the Chicago Public School Teacher" (unpublished Ph.D. dissertation, University of Chicago, 1951).

qualities are a major variable affecting the ease with which the work can be done. The teacher considers that she has done her job adequately when she has brought about an observable change in the children's skills and knowledge which she can attribute to her own efforts:

> Well, I would say that a teacher is successful when she is putting the material across to the children, when she is getting some response from them. I'll tell you something. Teaching is a very rewarding line of work, because you can see those children grow under your hands. You can see the difference in them after you've had them for five months. You can see where they've started and where they've got to. And it's all yours. It really is rewarding in that way, you can see results and know that it's your work that brought those results about.

She feels that she has a better chance of success in this area when her pupils are interested in attending and working hard in school, and are trained at home in such a way that they are bright and quick at schoolwork. Her problems arise in teaching those groups who do not meet these specifications, for in these cases her teaching techniques, tailored to the "perfect" student, are inadequate to cope with the reality, and she is left with a feeling of having failed in performing her basic task.

Davis has described the orientations toward education in general, and schoolwork in particular, of the lower and middle classes:

> Thus, our educational system, which next to the family is the most effective agency in teaching good work habits to middle class people, is largely ineffective and unrealistic with underprivileged groups. Education fails to motivate such workers because our schools and our society both lack *real rewards* to offer underprivileged groups. Neither lower class children or adults will work hard in school or on the job just to please the teacher or boss. They are not going to learn to be ambitious, to be conscientious, and to study hard, as if school and work were a fine character-building game, which one plays just for the sake of playing. They can see, indeed, that those who work hard at school usually have families that already have the occupations, homes, and social acceptance that the school holds up as the rewards of education. The underprivileged workers can see also that the chances of their getting enough education to make their attainment of these rewards in the future at all probable is very slight. Since they can win the rewards of prestige and social acceptance in their own slum groups without much education, they do not take very seriously the motivation taught by the school.[6]

As these cultural differences produce variations from the image of the "ideal" student, teachers tend to use class terms in describing the children with whom they work.

Children of the lowest group, from slum areas, are characterized as the most difficult group to teach successfully, lacking in interest in school, learning ability, and outside training:

> They don't have the right kind of study habits. They can't seem to apply themselves as well. Of course, it's not their fault; they aren't brought up right.

[6] Allison Davis, "The Motivation of the Underprivileged Worker," *Industry and Society,* ed. William F. Whyte (New York: McGraw-Hill Book Co., 1947), p. 99.

> After all, the parents in a neighborhood like that really aren't interested. . . . But, as I say, those children don't learn very quickly. A great many of them don't seem to be really interested in getting an education. I don't think they are. It's hard to get anything done with children like that. They simply don't respond.

In definite contrast are the terms used to describe children of the upper group:

> In a neighborhood like this there's something about the children, you just feel like you're accomplishing so much more. You throw an idea out and you can see that it takes hold. The children know what you're talking about and they think about it. Then they come in with projects and pictures and additional information, and it just makes you feel good to see it. They go places and see things, and they know what you're talking about. For instance, you might be teaching social studies or geography. . . . You bring something up and a child says, "Oh, my parents took me to see that in the museum." You can just do more with material like that.

Ambivalent feelings are aroused by children of the middle group. While motivated to work hard in school they lack the proper out-of-school training:

> Well, they're very nice here, very nice. They're not hard to handle. You see, they're taught respect in the home and they're respectful to the teacher. They want to work and do well. . . . Of course, they're not too brilliant. You know what I mean. But they are very nice children and very easy to work with.

In short, the differences between groups make it possible for the teacher to feel successful at her job only with the top group; with the other groups she feels, in greater or lesser measure, that she has failed.

These differences in ability to do school work, as perceived by teachers, have important consequences. They lead, in the first place, to differences in actual teaching techniques. A young high school teacher contrasted the techniques used in "slum" schools with those used in "better" schools:

> At S———, there were a lot of guys who were just waiting till they were sixteen so they could get out of school. At L———, everybody—well, a very large percentage, I'll say—was going on to secondary school, to college. That certainly made a difference in their classroom work. You had to teach differently at the different schools. For instance, at S———, if you had demonstrations in chemistry they had to be pretty flashy, lots of noise and smoke, before they'd get interested in it. That wasn't necessary at L———. Or at S——— if you were having electricity or something like that you had to get the static electricity machine out and have them all stand around and hold hands so that they'd all get a little jolt.

Further, the teacher feels that where these differences are recognized by her superiors there will be a corresponding variation in the amount of work she is expected to accomplish. She expects that the amount of work and effort required of her will vary inversely with the social status of her pupils. This teacher compared schools from the extremes of the class range:

> So you have to be on your toes and keep up to where you're supposed to be in the course of study. Now, in a school like the D——— [slum school] you're just not expected to complete all that work. It's almost impossible. For instance, in the second grade we're supposed to cover nine spelling words a week. Well, I can do that up here at the K——— ["better" school], they can take nine new words a week. But the best class I ever had at the D——— was only able to achieve six words a week and they had to work pretty hard to get that. So I never finished the year's work in spelling. I couldn't. And I really wasn't expected to.

One resultant of this situation—in which less is expected of those teachers whose students are more difficult to teach—is that the problem becomes more aggravated in each grade, as the gap between what the children should know and what they actually do know becomes wider and wider. A principal of such a school describes the degeneration there of the teaching problem into a struggle to get a few basic skills across, in a situation where this cumulative effect makes following the normal program of study impossible:

> The children come into our upper grades with very poor reading ability. That means that all the way through our school everybody is concentrating on reading. It's not like at a school like S——— [middle group] where they have science and history and so on. At a school like that they figure that from first to fourth you learn to read and from fifth to eighth you read to learn. You use your reading to learn other material. Well, these children don't reach that second stage while they're with us. We have to plug along getting them to learn to read. Our teachers are pretty well satisfied if the children can read and do simple number work when they leave here. You'll find that they don't think very much of subjects like science, and so on. They haven't got any time for that. They're just trying to get these basic things over. . . . That's why our school is different from one like the S———.

Such consequences of teachers' differential reaction to various class groups obviously operate to further perpetuate those class-cultural characteristics to which they object in the first place.

II

Discipline is the second of the teacher's major problems with her students. Willard Waller pointed to its basis when he wrote that "Teacher and pupil confront each other in the school with an original conflict of desires, and however much that conflict may be reduced in amount, or however much it may be hidden, it still remains." [7] We must recognize that conflict, either actual or potential, is ever present in the teacher-pupil relationship, the teacher attempting to maintain her control against the children's efforts to break it.[8] This conflict is felt even with those children who present least

[7] Willard Waller, *Sociology of Teaching* (New York: John Wiley & Sons, 1932), p. 197.

[8] Although all service occupations tend to have such problems of control over their clients, the problem is undoubtedly aggravated in situations like the school where those

difficulty; a teacher who considered her pupils models of good behavior nevertheless said:

> But there's that tension all the time. Between you and the students. It's hard on your nerves. Teaching is fun, if you enjoy your subject, but it's the discipline that keeps your nerves on edge, you know what I mean? There's always that tension. Sometimes people say, "Oh, you teach school. That's an easy job, just sitting around all day long." They don't know what it's really like. It's hard on your nerves.

The teacher is tense because she fears that she will lose control, which she tends to define in terms of some line beyond which she will not allow the children to go. Wherever she may draw this line (and there is considerable variation), the teacher feels that she has a "discipline" problem when the children attempt to push beyond it. The form and intensity of this problem are felt to vary from one social-class group to another, as might be expected from Davis' description of class emphases on aggression:

> In general, middle-class aggression is taught to adolescents in the form of social and economic skills which will enable them to compete effectively at that level. . . . In lower-class families, physical aggression is as much a normal, socially approved and socially inculcated type of behavior as it is in frontier communities.[9]

These differences in child training are matched by variation in the teachers' reactions.

Children in "slum" schools are considered most difficult to control, being given to unrestrained behavior and physical violence. The interviews are filled with descriptions of such difficulties. Miriam Wagenschein, in a parallel study of the beginning school teacher, gave this summary of the experiences of these younger teachers in lower-class schools:

> The reports which these teachers give of what *can* be done by a group of children are nothing short of amazing. A young white teacher walked into her new classroom and was greeted with the comment, "Another damn white one." Another was "rushed" at her desk by the entire class when she tried to be extremely strict with them. Teachers report having been bitten, tripped, and pushed on the stairs. Another gave an account of a second grader throwing a milk bottle at the teacher and of a first grader having such a temper tantrum that it took the principal and two policemen to get him out of the room. In another school following a fight on the playground, the principal took thirty-two razor blades from children in a first grade room. Some teachers indicated fear that they might be attacked by irate persons in the neighborhoods in which they teach. Other teachers report that their pupils carry long pieces of glass and have been known to threaten other pupils with them, while others jab each other with hypodermic needles. One boy got angry with his teacher and knocked in the fender of her car.[10]

upon whom the service is being performed are not there of their own volition, but rather because of the wishes of some other group (the parents, in this case).

[9] Allison Davis, *Social-Class Influence Upon Learning*, pp. 34–35.

[10] Miriam Wagenschein, "Reality Shock" (unpublished M. A. thesis, University of Chicago, 1950), pp. 58–59.

In these schools a major part of the teacher's time must be devoted to discipline; as one said: "It's just a question of keeping them in line." This emphasis on discipline detracts from the school's primary function of teaching, thus discriminating, in terms of available educational opportunity, against the children of these schools.

Children of the middle group are thought of as docile, and with them the teacher has least difficulty with discipline:

> Those children were much quieter, easier to work with. When we'd play our little games there was never any commotion. That was a very nice school to work in. Everything was quite nice about it. The children were easy to work with. . . .

Children of the upper group are felt hard to handle in some respects, and are often termed "spoiled," "overindulged," or "neurotic"; they do not play the role of the child in the submissive manner teachers consider appropriate. One interviewee, speaking of this group, said:

> I think most teachers prefer not to teach in that type of school. The children are more pampered and, as we say, more inclined to run the school for themselves. The parents are very much at fault. The children are not used to taking orders at home and naturally they won't take them at school either.

Teachers develop methods of dealing with these discipline problems, and these tend to vary between social-class groups as do the problems themselves. The basic device used by successful disciplinarians is to establish authority clearly on the first meeting with the class:

> You can't ever let them get the upper hand on you or you're through. So I start out tough. The first day I get a new class in, I let them know who's boss. . . . You've got to start off tough, then you can ease up as you go along. If you start out easy-going, when you try to get tough they'll just look at you and laugh.

Having once established such a relation, it is considered important that the teacher be consistent in her behavior so that the children will continue to respect and obey her:

> I let them know I mean business. That's one thing you must do. Say nothing that you won't follow through on. Some teachers will say anything to keep kids quiet, they'll threaten anything. Then they can't or won't carry out their threats. Naturally, the children won't pay any attention to them after that. You must never say anything that you won't back up.

In the difficult "slum" schools, teachers feel the necessity of using stern measures, up to and including physical violence (nominally outlawed):

> Technically you're not supposed to lay a hand on a kid. Well, they don't, technically. But there are a lot of ways of handling a kid so that it doesn't show —and then it's the teacher's word against the kid's, so the kid hasn't got a chance. Like dear Mrs.———. She gets mad at a kid, she takes him out in the hall. She gets him stood up against the wall. Then she's got a way of chucking

the kid under the chin, only hard, so that it knocks his head back against the wall. It doesn't leave a mark on him. But when he comes back in that room he can hardly see straight, he's so knocked out. It's really rough. There's a lot of little tricks like that that you learn about.

Where such devices are not used, there is recourse to violent punishment, "tongue lashings." All teachers, however, are not emotionally equipped for such behavior and must find other means:

The worst thing I can do is lose my temper and start raving. . . . You've got to believe in that kind of thing in order for it to work. . . . If you don't honestly believe it it shows up and the children know you don't mean it and it doesn't do any good anyway. . . . I try a different approach myself. Whenever they get too rowdy I go to the piano and . . . play something and we have rhythms or something until they sort of settle down. . . . That's what we call "softsoaping" them. It seems to work for me. It's about the only thing I can do.

Some teachers may also resort to calling in the parents, a device whose usefulness is limited by the fact that such summonses are most frequently ignored. The teacher's disciplinary power in such a school is also limited by her fear of retaliation by the students: "Those fellows are pretty big, and I just think it would take a bigger person than me to handle them. I certainly wouldn't like to try."

In the school with children of the middle group no strong sanctions are required, mild reprimands sufficing:

Now the children at Z——— here are quite nice to teach. They're pliable, yes, that's the word, they're pliable. They will go along with you on things and not fight you. You can take them any place and say to them, "I'm counting on you not to disgrace your school. Let's see that Z——— spirit." And they'll behave for you. . . . They can be frightened, they have fear in them. They're pliable, flexible, you can do things with them. They're afraid of their parents and what they'll do to them if they get into trouble at school. And they're afraid of the administration. They're afraid of being sent down to the principal. So that they can be handled.

Children of the upper group often act in a way which may be interpreted as "misbehavior" but which does not represent a conscious attack on the teacher's authority. Many teachers are able to disregard such activity by interpreting it as a natural concomitant of the "brightness" and "intelligence" of such children. Where such an interpretation is not possible the teachers feel hampered by a lack of effective sanctions:

I try different things like keeping them out of a gym period or a recess period. But that doesn't always work. I have this one little boy who just didn't care when I used those punishments. He said he didn't like gym anyway. I don't know what I'm going to do with him.

The teacher's power in such schools is further limited by the fact that the children are able to mobilize their influential parents so as to exert a large degree of control over the actions of school personnel.

It should be noted, finally, that discipline problems tend to become less important as the length of the teacher's stay in a particular school makes it possible for her to build a reputation which coerces the children into behaving without attempting any test of strength: [11]

> I have no trouble with the children. Once you establish a reputation and they know what to expect, they respect you and you have no trouble. Of course, that's different for a new teacher, but when you're established that's no problem at all.

III

The third area of problems has been termed that of *moral acceptability,* and arises from the fact that some actions of one's potential clients may be offensive in terms of some deeply felt set of moral standards; these clients are thus morally unacceptable. Teachers find that some of their pupils act in such a way as to make themselves unacceptable in terms of the moral values centered around health and cleanliness, sex and aggression, ambition and work, and the relations of age groups.

Children of the middle group present no problem at this level, being universally described as clean, well dressed, moderate in their behavior, and hard working. Children from the "better" neighborhoods are considered deficient in the important moral traits of politeness and respect for elders:

> Where the children come from wealthy homes. That's not so good either. They're not used to doing work at home. They have maids and servants of all kinds and they're used to having things done for them, instead of doing them themselves. . . . They won't do anything. For instance, if they drop a piece of cloth on the floor, they'll just let it lay, they wouldn't think of bending over to pick it up. That's janitor's work to them. As a matter of fact, one of them said to me once: "If I pick that up there wouldn't be any work for the janitor to do." Well, it's pretty difficult to deal with children like that.

Further, they are regarded as likely to transgress what the teachers define as moral boundaries in the matter of smoking and drinking; it is particularly shocking that such "nice" children should have such vices.

It is, however, the "slum" child who most deeply offends the teacher's moral sensibilities; in almost every area mentioned above these children, by word, action or appearance, manage to give teachers the feeling that they are immoral and not respectable. In terms of physical appearance and condition they disgust and depress the middle-class teacher. Even this young woman, whose emancipation from conventional morality is symbolized in her habitual use of the argot of the jazz musician, was horrified by the absence of the toothbrush from the lives of her lower-class students:

> It's just horribly depressing, you know. I mean, it just gets you down. I'll give you an example. A kid complained of a toothache one day. Well, I thought

[11] This is part of the process of job adjustment described in detail in Howard S. Becker. "The Career of the Chicago Public School Teacher," *American Journal of Sociology,* LVII (March, 1952).

I could take a look and see if I could help him or something so I told him to open his mouth. I almost wigged when I saw his mouth. His teeth were all rotten, every one of them. Just filthy and rotten. Man, I mean, I was really shocked, you know. I said, "Don't you have a toothbrush?" He said no, they were only his baby teeth and Ma said he didn't need a toothbrush for that. So I really got upset and looked in all their mouths. Man, I never saw anything like it. They were all like that, practically. I asked how many had toothbrushes, and about a quarter of them had them. Boy, that's terrible. And I don't dig that crap about baby teeth either, because they start getting molars when they're six, I know that. So I gave them a talking to, but what good does it do? The kid's mouth was just rotten. They never heard of a toothbrush or going to a dentist.

These children, too, are more apt than the other groups to be dishonest in some way that will get them into trouble with law enforcement officials. The early (by middle-class standards) sexual maturity of such children is quite upsetting to the teacher:

One thing about these girls is, well, some of them are not very nice girls. One girl in my class I've had two years now. She makes her money on the side as a prostitute. She's had several children. . . . This was a disturbing influence on the rest of the class.

Many teachers reported great shock on finding that words which were innocent to them had obscene meanings for their lower-class students:

I decided to read them a story one day. I started reading them "Puss in Boots" and they just burst out laughing. I couldn't understand what I had said that had made them burst out like that. I went back over the story and tried to find out what it might be. I couldn't see anything that would make them laugh. I couldn't see anything at all in the story. Later one of the other teachers asked me what had happened. She was one of the older teachers. I told her that I didn't know; that I was just reading them a story and they thought it was extremely funny. She asked me what story I read them and I told her "Puss in the Boots." She said, "Oh, I should have warned you not to read that one." It seems that Puss means something else to them. It means something awful—I wouldn't even tell you what. It doesn't mean a thing to us.[12]

Warner, Havighurst and Loeb note that "unless the middle-class values change in America, we must expect the influence of the schools to favor the values of material success, individual striving, thrift, and social mobility." [13] Here again, the "slum" child violates the teacher's moral sense by failing to display these virtues:

Many of these children don't realize the worth of an education. They have no desire to improve themselves. And they don't care much about school and schoolwork as a result. That makes it very difficult to teach them.

That kind of problem is particularly bad in a school like ———. That's not

[12] Interview by Miriam Wagenschein. The lack of common meanings in this situation symbolizes the great cultural and moral distance between teacher and "slum" child.

[13] *Op. cit.*, p. 172.

a very privileged school. It's very under-privileged, as a matter of fact. So we have a pretty tough element there, a bunch of bums, I might as well say it. That kind you can't teach at all. They don't want to be there at all, and so you can't do anything with them. And even many of the others—they're simply indifferent to the advantages of education. So they're indifferent, they don't care about their homework.

This behavior of the lower-class child is all the more repellent to the teacher because she finds it incomprehensible; she cannot conceive that any normal human being would act in such a way. This teacher stresses the anxiety aroused in the inexperienced teacher by her inability to provide herself with a rational explanation for her pupils' behavior:

We had one of the girls who just came to the school last year and she used to come and talk to me quite a bit. I know that it was just terrible for her. You know, I don't think she'd ever had anything to do with Negroes before she got there and she was just mystified, didn't know what to do. She was bewildered. She came to me one day almost in tears and said, "But they don't want to learn, they don't even want to learn. Why is that?" Well, she had me there.

It is worth noting that the behavior of the "better" children, even when morally unacceptable, is less distressing to the teacher, who feels that, in this case, she can produce a reasonable explanation for the behavior. An example of such an explanation is the following:

I mean, they're spoiled, you know. A great many of them are only children. Naturally, they're used to having their own way, and they don't like to be told what to do. Well, if a child is in a room that I'm teaching he's going to be told what to do, that's all there is to it. Or if they're not spoiled that way, they're the second child and they never got the affection the first one did, not that their mother didn't love them, but they didn't get as much affection, so they're not so easy to handle either.

IV

We have shown that school teachers experience problems in working with their students to the degree that those students fail to exhibit in reality the qualities of the image of the ideal pupil which teachers hold. In a stratified urban society there are many groups whose life-style and culture produce children who do not meet the standards of this image, and who are thus impossible for teachers like these to work with effectively. Programs of action intended to increase the educational opportunities of the under-privileged in our society should take account of the manner in which teachers interpret and react to the cultural traits of this group, and the institutional consequences of their behavior.[14] Such programs might profit-

[14] One of the important institutional consequences of these class preferences is a constant movement of teachers away from lower-class schools, which prevents these schools from retaining experienced teachers and from maintaining some continuity in teaching and administration.

ably aim at producing teachers who can cope effectively with the problems of teaching this group and not, by their reactions to class differences, perpetuate the existing inequities.

A more general statement of the findings is now in order. Professionals depend on their environing society to provide them with clients who meet the standards of their image of the ideal client. Social class cultures, among other factors, may operate to produce many clients who, in one way or another, fail to meet these specifications and therefore aggravate one or another of the basic problems of the worker-client relation (three were considered in this paper).

In attacking this problem we touch on one of the basic elements of the relation between institutions and society, for the differences between ideal and reality place in high relief the implicit assumptions which institutions, through their functionaries, make about the society around them. All institutions have embedded in them some set of assumptions about the nature of the society and the individuals with whom they deal, and we must get at these assumptions, and their embodiment in actual social interaction, in order fully to understand these organizations. We can, perhaps, best begin our work on this problem by studying those institutions which, like the school, make assumptions which have high visibility because of their variation from reality.

ELSE FRENKEL-BRUNSWIK

Case Study of an Authoritarian Family and Child

In this selection Else Frenkel-Brunswik describes a boy who grew up in a "traditional" authoritarian family. Apparently warped by the attitudes in his home, Karl exhibits aggressive behavior, a reflection of his parents' insecurity and fear. Their enforcement of rules that he cannot understand makes him resent all authority, and their ethnic prejudices cause him to reject those who are unlike himself. What do you feel the classroom teacher might do for Karl and for those who will live with him? How can he help Karl to channel his aggressions and become better adjusted to his environment?

One of our most ethnocentric child subjects is an eleven-year-old boy whom we shall call "Karl."

PARENTS AND HOME ATMOSPHERE

Karl's father comes from an authoritarian family and is a mechanic. Karl's father and paternal grandfather were born in this country, whereas the child's paternal grandmother came from Germany. The paternal grandparents died when Karl's father was four years old, and the father was reared by the great-grandparents, who owned a large farm and a wholesale store and "who were rich but not generous with their money."

Karl's mother was born in this country, and so was her father, while her mother was born in Scotland. Karl's maternal step-grandfather was a notary. Karl's maternal grandmother had divorced her husband shortly after Karl's mother was born. In fact, Karl's mother had a succession of stepfathers, one of whom, a combination of musician and laborer, also played an important role for her. She finished the eighth grade, whereas Karl's father's education stopped even before he had reached this level.

The interviewer describes the home as crowded with overstuffed and dreary oak furniture, with lace doilies on the tables. All this perhaps represents a concerted effort on the part of the parents to stress their middle-class identification and to avoid the possibility of being grouped with the underprivileged. This anxiety stems at least partially from the fact that the socioeconomic history of the family is unstable and that there was some loss of

Reprinted from Else Frenkel-Brunswik, "Differential Patterns of Social Outlook and Personality in Family and Children," Chapter 22 in *Childhood in Contemporary Cultures*, edited by Margaret Mead and Martha Wolfenstein, by permission of The University of Chicago Press.

status as compared to the previous generation. There is, however, no evidence of poverty. The family lives in a six-room flat and owns a car and two radios.

The mother's background has much less stability than the father's. "I grew up in big cities and in one hotel after another." Generally, such geographical instability seems relatively common in ethnocentric homes. Both parents, furthermore, report their own parents as foreign-born. This, too, is significantly more often the case with parents of prejudiced than of tolerant children. As a group trend, it may be taken to indicate that the parents still see themselves entangled in the process of assimilation. Apparently as a counterbalance, they stress their "belonging," through both their social aspirations and the rejection of what is considered socially inferior.

Both of Karl's parents had been exposed to strict discipline. The father does not like to talk about his own father, whom he describes as a drunkard and psychopath who deserted his family. He is much more ready to discuss his grandfather, by whom he was raised:

> My grandfather was really strict. He had thirteen children, and even when they were grown up, there wasn't one of them that would talk back to him, and he could handle any of them.

The father of our boy grew up knowing little but work. His grandfather was anxious to see his grandson go to school and even to have his voice trained. Karl's father did not live up to any of his grandfather's ambitions, doing relatively simple work, although he still believes he will one day accomplish a great deal by an invention. He asserts that his occupation is only temporary, since he is likely soon to make a big mechanical invention. This aspiration remains on a fantasy level, since there is little evidence of any concrete work toward the goal.

The idea of achieving fame some day is still alive in the fantasies of Karl's mother as well. Though having worked mainly in factories and being a waitress at the time of the interview she prides herself on her talents, such as photography, composing, and writing. There is here the same kind of unrealistic fantasy to which attention will be called in discussing Karl himself.

In discussing their children, Karl's parents emphasize that they made rules for them which had to be strictly obeyed. For instance, the children had to be in bed "sharp at six without fail." Asked whether the children ever have tantrums, the mother says:

> I should say not. They had better not. If they got mad, I just sat them on a chair and said to stay there until they could behave. I guess they never really had tantrums.

This is at variance with Karl's own statements, according to which he has outbursts of temper. Either this is mere boasting on his part, or the mother's denial of his ever deviating from what she considers good behavior is a distortion of fact; we are inclined to favor the latter interpretation. Apparently along the same line is the mother's statement about Karl, who is obviously a rather weak child, that "he has a strength but he hides it."

Both parents also report that they have used spanking as a disciplinary measure. To quote the mother: "The boys are more afraid of their father than of me; I guess because he is stronger." She seems not to realize that her children are overtrained and welcome the more severe punishment by their father. The father appears considerably worried about what the interviewer might have guessed about the children's relation to him: "It seems like Karl is afraid of me."

It is the father who represents in the family the rigid dichotomizing of the sex roles, which is, as we shall see, one of the characteristics of the authoritarian milieu: "Boys shouldn't do work in the home, though it's all right for a man to be a chef or a baker. The best of them are men." He apparently feels that it is considered appropriate for a man to be a chef and thus to enter the field of women only if there is assurance that he will excel.

The mother, in explaining her children's personality, relies heavily on astrology. She tells us that the personality of Karl's brother, whom we shall call Bill, can be explained by the fact that "he was born under the sign of The Twins." About Karl she says: "He is a dreamer of far places. He will go far and wide. The stars show that." The dependence on fate and the feeling of a mystical connection with supernatural forces has been found typical of the ethnocentric milieu (1, 4), the exaggerated ideas of self-importance going hand in hand with an underdeveloped self-reliance.

Both parents are ethnically extremely prejudiced. They consider the Negroes America's biggest problem, and the father adds: "Dig up Roosevelt and let him help settle it." He is concerned that the Negroes "want to go everywhere." The mother tells how, at the time she was a waitress, she personally took it on herself to put Negroes in their place. She would give them a glass of water and then ignore them:

> When they went out, we smashed the glass behind the counter good and hard so they were sure to hear it. The Chinese and Japanese should be separate too.

About the Jews the mother says:

> The Bible says they will always be persecuted. You know it wasn't a small thing they did—crucifying Christ—God said they would be punished till the end of time.

This line of argument is the more surprising because in the discussion about religion it is not the mother but the father who stresses the importance of religion, as does Karl himself.

KARL'S SOCIAL BELIEFS

Karl is an unusually fat and passive boy with a history of many illnesses. The parents' ethnocentrism is shared by Karl, who in many other respects mirrors fascistic attitudes. We begin with quotations from that part of his interview record that deals with attitudes toward minority members. Karl says about Negroes:

> They make trouble, start wars. I wouldn't mind having all the Negroes in Oakland and all the white people in a different state. I would like to have a couple for good fighters. They are good fighters when they fight with a knife. Like somebody starts a fight and you have a gang with some Negroes to fight with you on your side with knives and guns.

Like most of the ethnocentric children, Karl is in favor of segregation of the outgroups, and, like some of them, his statements show implicit envy of characteristics ascribed to minority groups. Karl admires the physical power, strength, and aggressiveness of the Negroes. He rejects them and does not want them to mix with his own group, but he wants them as protectors—we might almost say as bodyguards—in fights against other boys. His passivity and relative immobility also give direction to the stereotype he has about the Jews:

> They think they are smart and go anywhere they please. They think they are hot. They dress up in all kinds of jewelry. Some just kidnap girls and boys and use them for slaves.

Some characteristics of this image of the Jews, such as their alleged social dominance and their exhibitionism of wealth, are common in ethnocentric children. We find, however, in Karl's statements some emphases and elaborations which, as we shall see, are rooted in his own specific conflicts. Thus the mobility and the enslaving motif is very personal with Karl. We have just heard him express the desire to use Negroes as his fighting slaves. The theme of fighting recurs again and again in Karl's description of minority groups. Although children not uncommonly ascribe aggressiveness to Negroes, it is most unusual for them to mention this quality in descriptions of the Chinese. Karl, however, stresses the point that Chinese are "good fighters"; and about the Filipinos he says: "They are good fighters and definitely good to go through jungles with." As we shall see, the preoccupation with jungles, where one can be lost and subject to deprivation, and the preoccupation with animals dominate Karl's fantasy in general.

Like many of the ethnocentric children, Karl sees general avarice and acquisitiveness as the cause of the last war, while the democratic-minded children specify in greater detail the wants of the different countries. Most of the children in our study think that there will be wars in the near future, but Karl, along with a great many of the ethnocentric children, takes this fact as natural and inevitable: "I think so because there's always going to be a war." As do over two-fifths of the high-scoring and a considerably smaller proportion of the low-scoring children, he thinks that we won the last war because of the atom bomb, ascribing a magical quality to its destructive potential. Equalitarian children refer more often in this context to better resources and the better equipment of America in general.

It is evident that Karl is at least in partial sympathy with Hitler and that his concern is only about the wrongs Hitler might have done to Americans. He states: "He was a little bit O.K. Sometimes he got a little bit too mean and did dirty stuff like putting lighted matches in the toenails of Americans." This partial sympathy with Hitler does not prevent Karl from exercising his extreme punitiveness toward the Germans: "We should put all the Germans and Japs on an island and put an atom bomb to it."

He considers America's biggest problem the fact that "a lot of people are getting mad because everybody is starting war against each other." This is the recurrent fighting theme, this time in the form of an assumption of an almost chaotic war of all against all.

In Karl's response to another interview question we find a further dominant theme—fear of deprivation, especially food deprivation. Karl is against strikes because "if grocery stores go on a strike, we won't have no food. Farmers can go on a strike, and there will be no food, and we will have to grow our own food." Ethnocentric children frequently manifest this particular fear. It is especially exaggerated in Karl but has, as we have ascertained, no basis in real food deprivation.

Karl's attitude toward the social scene and his role in it is best characterized by the one-sidedness of his answer to the interview question, "How would you like to change America?":

> I would like to have a filling station every couple of blocks or so and palm trees and grass along the streets and lawns in front of people's houses and have the back yards all cleaned up and flowers growing. Every store should have all kinds of candy and bubble gum. They wouldn't have no fights in the neighborhood. The cops would take them all in. At Fleishacker's [an amusement park] have nice warm water [in the swimming pool] and the zoo cleaned up. Every day there would be hay for the animals that eat hay and the lions would have lots of meat every day for breakfast and lunch.

As are many of our ethnocentric children, Karl is concerned with cleanliness and external beautification, the removal of aggressive groups, and with having a constant flow of supplies. The only beings for which he shows concern are, characteristically, animals rather than people. His emphasis on rigid order as well as on the regularity in the appearance of streets and other objects contrasts sharply with his emphasis on, and even open advocacy of, turmoil and chaotic aggression, as noticed above.

Equalitarian children, on the other hand, are better able to remove themselves from the pressure of overanxiety about immediate needs. They are more likely to penetrate to such underlying and more general aspects of human welfare as justice and equality, lower prices and higher wages, and moral and ethical values in general.

Before leaving the topic of Karl's beliefs, we should like to point to the similarity between his statements on this subject and those of his brother Bill, older by one year. These differences exist in spite of the fact that the two boys had no opportunity to discuss the subject between the respective interviews. Like Karl, Bill thinks that "we should kick out the colored people from San Francisco" because they get drunk and kill people. He feels that the German war criminals "should all have been hanged and not put in prison." Like his brother, he wants to put "the Japs on an island and throw bombs on them." He considers food to be America's biggest problem, and his main concern in this context is the problem of the rationing of sugar.

KARL'S AND HIS BROTHER'S ATTITUDES TOWARD SCHOOL, FAMILY, AND SEX ROLES

The stereotypical approach to social and ethical challenges, with all its inherent inhibitions, carries over into such related, more specific areas as the conception of teachers, parental roles, sex roles, and so forth. The ambivalent submission to authority, found to be typical of ethnocentric children, is revealed in Karl's statement about teachers. An initial stereotyped denial of criticism, "I like everything about teachers," is followed by the mention of victimization and unjust treatment by teachers: "A lot of them make you go to the principal's office or out of the room for something you didn't do. I had that happen lots of times."

When asked in another context to describe the perfect boy, Karl starts off with a request for obedience to teachers. The craving for a complete surrender to authority is also exhibited in his brother Bill's statement about the kind of teacher he doesn't like: "Those who tell you in a nice way instead of being strict and then don't make you mind." Bill's ideal teacher would be "a man who would be strict," or, as second choice, a woman if "she was very strict." While the emphasis on negative aspects or on strictness seems to be a specific characteristic of ethnocentric children, the tolerant, by contrast, tend more often to emphasize positive traits in the ideal teacher, such as being helpful, laughing at jokes, and the like.

The attitude of ethnocentric children to the teacher appears to be but one of the aspects of a more generalized hierarchical conception of human relations, according to which the weak are expected to exhibit a self-negating surrender to the strong. Karl seems unaware of the fact that he himself succeeds only very partially in fulfilling the strict requirement of submissive obedience. Obviously, he is possessed by destructive and by no means dormant forces which are in part directed toward the very authorities to which he demands allegiance but which are, to an even larger extent, diverted to objects considered by him as underdogs.

In discussing the pupils he likes and dislikes, Karl seems exclusively concerned with the possibility of being attacked by one of the other boys, whereas his brother Bill stresses conventional values, such as politeness and obedience, values also emphasized by Karl in other contexts. Equalitarian children, . . . on the other hand, stress companionship, fun, common interests, and understanding as traits desired in friends.

Both Karl and his brother Bill stress, as do a relatively large proportion of the ethnocentric children, that money helps one to have friends. For Bill, money possesses magical evil attributes:

> It is the root of all evil. It's bad luck to be born with money. If your parents tell you to put it in a bank and you keep it until you are grown up, it's bad luck.

Bill proceeds to describe the disaster which befell several of his acquaintances after they saved their money. This is in line with the general tendency prevalent in the ethnocentric subjects to subscribe to all manner of superstitious statements, to see evil forces at work everywhere, and readily to anticipate doom and catastrophes.

Karl is one of the very few children who would prefer to have a private tutor rather than go to school. He explains that he would like to avoid the effort involved in getting ready to go to school, "to have to pack a lunch and hop a bus." Bill, however, rejects the idea of tutors as "just for rich people, and they are no good." This latter quotation exemplifies the resentment, frequent in ethnocentric subjects, against what they consider oppressors from above, a view which goes along with their fear that those below, such as the minority groups, may rise some day and take over in a fearful revenge.

Both boys have a rigid conception of sex roles, stressing politeness in girls. As Bill points out, "If a boy is talking, they shouldn't butt in." For him the best friend for a boy is a boy, for a girl, a girl. They both reject girls who are discourteous or aggressive toward boys, for example, "If she pulls a boy by the arm and tells him to take her to a show or some place." Although dichotomizing of sex roles is to a certain extent general at this age, children scoring low on ethnocentrism do so to a much lesser degree, stressing more the point that boys and girls should behave naturally with each other. They also do not differentiate their descriptions of a perfect boy from that of a perfect girl as much as do the prejudiced children.

Asked what he would consider a perfect father, Karl, in line with many of the ethnocentric children, speaks mainly of the material benefits this kind of father would provide: "He will let you do anything you like and let you get any kind of food you like and let you take a girl out. Will give you about two dollars every day." Asked how he would like to change his own father, he states emphatically that "my father is good to me" but then goes on immediately to say that he would like to get more money from him to be able "to go to a show or dinner or any place I want." In almost every context he manifests this exploitive-manipulative approach to people.

As is often the case in ethnocentric boys, Karl's hostility is more directly expressed toward the mother than toward the father. When asked how he would like to change his mother, he starts off with "to make her nice," then proceeds to tell what he wants from her, such as "a car." That he is, on the whole, more oriented toward his father is probably related to the fact that the father is more powerful, in a position to provide more goods, and also better able to protect. This kind of dependency is often found to reduce open feelings and expressions of hostility.

While Karl sees people, and especially those in authority, primarily as "deliverers of goods," to use a term of Fenichel's (3), Bill expects mainly regimentation from them. Thus a perfect father is for him one who, if asked for something, "ought not to give it to you right away." Bill denies that he has any desire to change his parents. There is ample evidence, from his interview and especially from his Thematic Apperception Test stories, of Karl's underlying hostility toward the parents. On a "blind" over-all interview rating of attitudes toward parents, Karl earns the extreme rating of "6" with respect to both parents, representing the rater's impression that he is obsessed by the feeling of being threatened and victimized by their hostility. Bill receives a rating of "5"; this is only one step closer to the opposite extreme, "1," which would indicate an affectionate, secure, companionable relationship as seen by the child.

Both boys are assigned an extreme rating on "externalization of values," a category covering opportunism, conventionality, status-concern, and explicit condemnation of those who do not conform.

Both boys tell of corporal punishment at home, and both of them prefer to have their father rather than their mother punish them. Bill comes out with the explicit explanation that his mother "is a little too soft-hearted." In discussing this topic in general, both boys favor very severe punishment of children for relatively minor misconduct and seem only too ready to advocate intervention of the juvenile court in such cases. According to Karl, children should be punished for "talking back to grownups" and for breaking windows: "You should go to Juvenile one year for that."

In Karl a greater readiness toward explosive fits of aggression is revealed in his descriptions of how he reacts in anger: "I do anything I can—bite, pull hair, kick, tear into them." Bill, however, reports that he tries to control his anger as well as he can, mostly by going out of the field. Both explosive outbursts and frantic efforts of control are typical of our ethnocentric children.

Though both boys have shown some tendency to idealize their parents stereotypically and to stress their goodness, neither of them chooses any of the members of the family as companions on a desert island. Karl, of course, stresses first food and water and also that he would take along a girl. From the dreams that Karl relates, as well as from the Thematic Apperception Test, it is evident that he connects the idea of a girl with feeding her or being fed by her and, furthermore, that a girl means to him safety and absence of possible threats felt in connection with boys or men.

Along the same line are Karl's recurrent dreams, "it's about going with a girl for dinner," and about people getting murdered and hanged. The childhood memories he relates are full of mishaps and catastrophes. He remembers having fallen in a pond, recalls seeing his father kill a chicken that ran about without its head, seeing men killing turkeys, and seeing a crate of eggs broken under a truck.

Among his fears he lists his fear of wild animals, of high buildings, of drunken men, of "death in some dark night." He mentions that usually it is the girls who are especially afraid of the dark. When asked whether he wants to be a girl, he denies it but adds the stock projective answer: "Some guys want to be girls." The feminine identification which can be discerned behind much of the aggressive façade is apparent in the interviews and is especially evident in the Thematic Apperception Test.

KARL'S THEMATIC APPERCEPTION TEST STORIES

The rigidification of the child's personality originally induced by the stress on self-negating submission and on the repression of nonacceptable tendencies not only leads to stereotypy; eventually the inherent pattern of conflict may result in a more or less open break between the different layers of personality and in a loss of control of instinctual tendencies by the individual. This contrasts rather sharply with the greater fluidity of transition and intercommunication between the different personality strata which is typical of the child in the more permissive home. The emotional makeup and the rigidity of defense, lack of insight, and narrowness of the ego of the authoritarian personality even carries over into the purely cognitive domain. Here, too, ready-made clichés tend to take the place of realistic spontaneous reactions.

Karl's TAT stories are full of murder and gore, much more so than the usual stories of children of his age. In practically every story a murder is committed under quite extraordinary circumstances. For example, a man who won in a race is "shot in the back five times" while he was "laying in bed, tired from his hard job." Two of the stories, to be further interpreted later, follow:

> It looks like murder. I saw a couple of murder pictures. A girl is down at the dock at night watching them unload freight. There is a man with a cane that is the girl's friend, and he is walking behind her. She had been gambling and won $200. This other man was trying to get the money off her. It was hid somewhere on her. The man with the cane presses on the cane, and a knife comes out. He stabs the man with the gun in the wrist, and the girl calls the cops, and they come and take him away in the patrol wagon to jail. He tries to break away but can't. That night he went to the electric chair, and the girl had the money safe to keep the rest of her life.

> Oh, gads! Sure is murder [cheerfully]. The man was in gambling. He believed the gambling table was crooked. He said it was, and the man behind the gambling table said it wasn't, and he had a whip and started whipping the other in the face. The U.S. Navy guy came in. It was a friend of his. He had a gun, and he shot the bull whip out of the man's hand. The cops came, and the Navy guy told the cops what happened. The guy that owned it was arrested for having a crooked place, and it was turned into a big Safeway store and people went there and bought stuff. And the army guys got $250 for finding out the man had a crooked wheel. The guy in the middle died from bleeding too much.

Usually it is the men who are shot, and only in one story "a lady is hit in the back with a knife." In this case the woman is killed because she betrayed a man. In most of Karl's stories, however, the women manage to be safe and to get food and money.

In almost every one of Karl's stories food is mentioned in a general way or specifically, for example, peanuts, waffles, double-decker cones, etc., and there is reference to specific amounts of money, such as $200, $25, $250, $550,000, $400, 10¢. Usually the person who has the money is in great danger of being deprived of it and of being killed in the process.

Neither the role of the aggressive man nor that of the passive man seems to be workable in these stories. The man who is passive and in possession of some fortune is usually attacked in some surprising way, from behind or while asleep, and is destroyed. The aggressive man, on the other hand, is regularly caught by the police and sentenced at the least to life-imprisonment; more often, he is executed in the electric chair. The earlier story, in which the "crooked place was turned into a big Safeway store," obviously reveals Karl's deep-seated longing that all the dangerous men will be removed and that he will be allowed to be passive and surrounded by food, without fear of aggression and without the ensuing necessity for being aggressive himself. This is also the way he imagines girls to be. Even though the girls are, in the stories, in the more enviable position, not even they are always safe.

Here again we find the preoccupation with animals. In the stories they are being fed, as they were in Karl's projected ideal of America which was quoted earlier. The feminine identification is apparent in the description of the "mother ape that had just laid a baby." Not even the animals and not even the baby ape are safe, since a man tries to "sock the baby ape with his gun."

Of the two types of men, the passive and the aggressive, Karl basically seems to feel closer to the former. In one story he describes in detail how a passive boy who always is being hit by a tough boy "had taken exercises from a guy that helps you make muscles." It is this same passive boy who feeds the animals. We thus have evidence both of insecurity about masculinity and of feminine identification, also manifested in the occurrence of many phallic symbols and castration threats and in an apparent embarrassment about body build and genital organs. In a swimming scene described by Karl he is careful to point out that the boys have swimming suits under their clothes and thus do not have to undress. Karl's stories are not only exaggerated versions of the stories common in ethnocentric boys in general but also have similarities to the stories of overt homosexuals.

Concerning the formal aspects of Karl's stories, the following can be said. They are long and flowing, presenting no necessity for probing on the part of the examiner. In spite of this fluidity, however, the form level of the stories is very low. They are neither coherent nor structured, and what seems like imagination is really a kind of ruminative repetition of the same themes over and over again. Karl is at times aware of this repetitiveness, and he starts one of his stories with the words, "another murder story." One of our foregoing stories begins, "Sure is murder," and the interviewer comments here that Karl makes this introduction with evident cheerfulness. The repetitiveness extends even to such details as numbers: the number $250 occurs in several stories, and other numbers are similar to it. The stories are, furthermore, utterly unrealistic as far as general plausibility is concerned, and they stray away to a marked degree from the content of the picture, which, after the first few sentences, is frequently lost from sight entirely.

The image of the world found in Karl and in most of our ethnocentric subjects—the projection of the hostility they feel toward their parents, and their feeling that the world is a dangerous and hostile place—coincides with the image of the world which Wolfenstein and Leites (15), found in American movie melodramas. This may represent a common fantasy which in the more "typical" Americans, for whom the powerful father is more imaginary than actual, is present at the most archaic levels only.

Bill's stories contain topics similar to those of Karl, such as quarreling, food, money, ambivalence toward the mother, catastrophes, and unhappy endings. But he is at the same time more constricted, and a great deal of encouragement and probing are necessary to lead him away from a mere description of the picture.

Remembering the evidence from the interviews, it appears that Bill is the more disciplined, not to say regimented, of the two boys and the more cautious, even though perhaps the one who will put his biases more readily into action if the opportunity is offered. On the other hand, social upheavals of a major order may be necessary to bring an individual such as Karl to the fore. Lacking these, he may very well lead an inconspicuous, unsuccessful life, ridiculed and baited by his fellows, and possibly even passing over into a state of slow disintegration.

DISCUSSION OF FAMILY INFLUENCE

From this material we gain the impression that the total outlook, just described, seems to a very appreciable extent to have its root in the authoritarian home. Family relationships in such homes are commonly based on roles clearly defined in terms of demands and submission. Execution of obligations rather than affection is the basis of smooth functioning in such homes. Furthermore, there is a stress on stereotyped behavior and on adherence to a set of conventional and rigid rules. The intimidating, punitive, and paralyzing influence of an overdisciplined, totalitarian home atmosphere may well exert a decisive influence upon the thinking and creativity of the growing child. The impoverishment of imagination seems to be analogous to that apparent under totalitarian social and political regimes. At the same time, the consideration of the responses to threats in childhood may reveal much about the ways in which individuals react to threats in adult life.

Intensive experiences in later life are undoubtedly in themselves capable of superseding both earlier influences and the individual predispositions to a certain extent, however, so that no direct or exclusive causal relationship between family structure, attitudes of children, and rise of totalitarianism may be assumed. We must also bear in mind that social conditions and institutions have, in turn, an impact of their own on the family structure.

It is primarily the fact that the home discipline in authoritarian homes is experienced as overwhelming, unintelligible, and arbitrary, demanding at the same time total surrender, which makes for the apparent parallelism with authoritarian political and social organizations. The similarity becomes even more evident if we consider that the child, by virtue of his objective weakness and dependence, is entirely at the mercy of the parental authorities and must find some way to cope with this situation. We found that parents in the authoritarian group frequently feel threatened in their social and economic status and that they try to counteract their feelings of marginality by an archaic and frequently unverbalized need for importance. It is noteworthy that what seems to matter is not so much the actual status on the socioeconomic ladder or the objective marginality within a certain class; what seems decisive in this respect is, rather, the subjective way in which these conditions are experienced and allowed to build up to certain vaguely conceived aspirations. Recent data further suggest that the status concern of individuals susceptible to authoritarianism is quite different from a realistic attempt to improve their position by concerted effort and adequate means-goal instrumentality. An example was given earlier by the rather naïve hope of Karl's father of becoming an "inventor." In addition, we frequently find such aspirations taking the form of an unspecific expectation that help will come from a sudden change in the external situation or from an imaginary person who is strong and powerful.

Authoritarian disciplinary rules seem to have one of their major roots in such vaguely anticipatory, yet inefficient, states of social unrest on the part of the parents rather than in the developmental needs of the child. The parents expect the child to learn quickly certain external, rigid, and superficial rules and social taboos. At the same time they are impatient, demanding a quick execution of commands that leaves no time for finer discriminations and in the end creates an atmosphere comparable to acute physical danger. The rules to be enforced are largely nonfunctional caricatures of our social institutions, based on a misunderstanding of their ultimate intent. In many ways one may even speak of a defiance of culture by external conformity. In any event, the rules are bound to be beyond the scope and understanding of the child. To compel the child into an obedience of the rules which he is thus unable to internalize may be considered one of the major interferences with the development of a clear-cut personal identity.

The authoritarian form of discipline is thus "ego-destructive," in that it prevents the development of self-reliance and independence. The child, being stripped of his individuality, is made to feel weak, helpless, worthless, or even depraved. Parents and parental figures, such as teachers or other authorities, acquire the threatening, distant, and forbidding quality which we have observed in the case of Karl. Disciplining, controlling, and keeping one in line are considered to be their major role. It seems to be largely the resultant fear and dependency which discourage the child in the authoritarian home from conscious criticism and which lead to an unquestioning acceptance of punishment and to an identification with the punishing authority. As we have seen, this identification often goes as far as an ostentatious glorification of the parents. As we have learned from psychoanalysis, however, repressions of hostility cannot be achieved without creating emotional ambivalence, at the least. Thus children who seem most unquestioningly to accept parental authority at the same time tend to harbor an underlying resentment and to feel victimized, without becoming fully aware of this fact. The existing surface conformity that lacks genuine integration expresses itself in a stereotypical approach devoid of genuine affection, so that the description of the parents elicited by interview questions is more often characterized by the use of exaggerated clichés than by expressions of spontaneous feelings. In ethnocentric subjects the range of responses tends to be generally rather narrow and without the variations commonly found in the description of real people. Only the more palpable, crude, and concrete aspects are mentioned.

. . .

In describing the minority groups and the social scene in general, our paradigm of an ethnocentric, authoritarian child, Karl, exhibits rigid dichotomizing, aggressiveness, fear of imaginary dangers or threats of deprivation, and exaggerated adherence to conventional values, such as cleanliness and order. The same themes also occur in his stated attitudes toward parents and friends as well as in the projective material, especially his Thematic Apperception Test stories.

. . .

Toward parents, teachers, and authorities in general Karl at the surface demands total submission, and he approves of whatever they do; but underlying resentment and hatred against them are only too apparent in the projective material. This discrepancy is but one of the many breaks and discontinuities found in Karl and in ethnocentric children in general. Another discrepancy is evident in Karl's explicit stressing of conventional values, which is combined with an implicit leaning toward destructive and chaotic behavior. In fact, there seems to be vacillation between a total adoption and a total negation of the prevalent values of our society.

Still another conflicting set can be discerned between Karl's strained effort to appear as a masculine boy interested in girls and his underlying identification with the opposite sex. Instead of being oriented toward girls as objects of cathexis, he envies them because he thinks of them as less in danger of being attacked and as being fed and given other material benefits. As becomes apparent especially in the Thematic Apperception Test, to be a boy or a man means to him to be in danger. If a man is passive, he may not get the necessary supplies and is helplessly exposed; if he is aggressive, he is punished. Doom is thus inevitable for him. All through the material produced by our ethnocentric children there is evidence of panic lest food or money run short. In persons possessed by such fears, human relations are liable to become unusually manipulative and exploitive. Other persons, authorities, and even the magic forces of nature will, of necessity, be seen mainly as deliverers of goods. Aggression against those considered strong and powerful must then be repressed; at least in part, this aggression will be diverted toward those who can neither deprive nor retaliate.

. . .

In analyzing and interpreting our material, extended use has been made of psychoanalytic hypotheses. Depth psychology has challenged the dominance of the phenotype and has sharpened our eyes to the underlying dynamic patterns. Because of this shift, we can discern in Karl the passivity behind his aggressive violence, the feminine identification and latent homosexuality behind the protestation of his heterosexual interests, the chaos behind his rigid conformity. But since the façade is also an essential part of the psychological makeup, we must think of personality in terms of "alternative manifestations" (5). These are quite self-contradictory in Karl, as they are in most prejudiced children. It is the inherent conflict and anxiety concerning the social, sexual, and personal role of the individual which must be seen at the root of the ensuing desperate avoidance of all ambiguity with its dire consequences for the fate of man.

. . .

Karl's parents reveal the feelings of "social marginality" which are so common in the ethnocentric family. It is obviously in defense against the possibility of being grouped with the underprivileged that they rigidly identify with the conventional values of the class to which they try to hold on. The strict home discipline they are trying to enforce is in part in the service of these narrow social goals; beyond this, it is perhaps a revengeful repetition of the situation to which they themselves were exposed in the unstable socioeconomic history of the family.

. . .

In the context of American culture, Karl and his family are deviants. Fat, fearful Karl is certainly the opposite of the ideal American boy. Most of his and of his family's attitudes are counterpoints to prevailing or consciously espoused American attitudes. Externalization and hostile exclusion are features which they adopt from the wide variety of possibilities, offered within the culture as a whole. Other features contrasting with the major American pattern are their emphasis on hierarchical rather than equalitarian relations, their anxiety about the availability of material goods, and their belief in mystical forces and apprehension about catastrophes as against confidence in one's own efforts and in the collaboration of the environment.

To understand all this, we remember that Karl and his family are caught in an unsuccessful struggle for social status, a status they cannot achieve through their own efforts. Thus they adhere rigidly to some absolute status values which oversimplify the social and cultural realities of our civilization. This renders them helpless and perverts their view of the social scene, making them susceptible to totalitarian propaganda.

It must be specially emphasized that the compulsive type of conformity with its all-or-none character which we have observed in the family of Karl differs in several ways from genuine and constructive conformity. It is excessive, compensating as it does for feelings of marginality and the attendant fear of becoming an outcast and serving the function of covering up the resentment toward the social system as a whole, unconscious as this resentment may be. The lack of a genuine incorporation of the values of society in the authoritarian milieu accounts for the rigidity of the conformity. At the same time it accounts for a certain unreliability, the readiness to shift allegiance altogether to other authorities and other standards. The adherence to the letter rather than to the spirit of the social institutions, which further characterizes the compulsive conformist, issues from his distortion and simplification of the system of norms and commands in the direction of what one may call unidimensional interpretation.

REFERENCES

1. Adorno, T. W., Frenkel-Brunswik, E., Levinson, D. J., and Sanford, R. N. 1950. *The Authoritarian Personality*. New York: Harper & Bros.
2. Burgess, W. 1948. "The Family in a Changing Society," *American Journal of Sociology,* XIII, No. 6, 417–23.
3. Fenichel, O. 1945. *Psychoanalytic Theory of Neurosis.* New York: W. W. Norton & Co.
4. Frenkel-Brunswik, E. 1949*a*. "A Study of Prejudice in Children," *Human Relations,* I, No. 3, 295–306.
5. ———. 1949*b*. "Intolerance of Ambiguity as an Emotional and Perceptual Personality Variable," *Journal of Personality,* XVIII, No. 1, 108–43.
6. ———. 1951. "Patterns of Social and Cognitive Outlook in Children and Parents," *American Journal of Orthopsychiatry,* XXI, No. 3, 543–58.
7. ———. 1954. "Social Research and the Problem of Values: A Reply," *Journal of Abnormal and Sociol Psychology,* XLIX, No. 3, 466–71.
8. Frenkel-Brunswik, E., and Havel, J. 1953. "Prejudice in the Interviews of Children: Attitudes Toward Minority Groups," *Journal of Genetic Psychology,* LXXXII, No. 1, 91–136.
9. Luchins, A. S. 1942. *Mechanization in Problem Solving: The Effect of "Einstellung."* ("Psychological Monographs," Vol. LIV, No. 6.)
10. Mead, Margaret. 1949. *Male and Female*. New York: William Morrow Co.
11. Murray, H. E., and Workers at the Harvard Psychological Clinic. 1938. *Explorations in Personality*. London: Oxford University Press.
12. Ogburn, W. F. 1953. "The Changing Functions of the Family." In *Marriage and the Family,* ed. R. F. Winch and R. McGinnis. New York: Henry Holt & Co.
13. Rokeach, M. 1943. "Generalized Mental Rigidity as a Factor in Ethnocentrism," *Journal of Abnormal and Social Psychology,* XLVIII, No. 2, 259–78.
14. Winch, R. F., and McGinnis, R. (eds.). 1953. *Marriage and the Family*. New York: Henry Holt & Co.
15. Wolfenstein, Martha, and Leites, Nathan. 1950. *Movies: A Psychological Study*. Glencoe, Ill.: Free Press.
16. Zimmerman, C. C. 1948. *Family and Civilization*. New York: Harper & Bros.

Chapter 6

Assessing Readiness: Personality and Motivation

6-1

PHILIP W. JACKSON
AND JACOB W. GETZELS

Dissatisfaction with School Among Adolescents

6-2

ROBERT L. EBEL

Are Important Objectives Testable?

PHILIP W. JACKSON and JACOB W. GETZELS

Dissatisfaction with School Among Adolescents

The authors here raise the question, How do students who are "satisfied" with school differ from those who are "dissatisfied" with school? Locating two extreme groups, one very satisfied and one very dissatisfied, the investigators subject them to various other tests. How are the results of this study valuable to a teacher having both satisfied and dissatisfied students in his classroom? Do Jackson and Getzels show us how to *produce* satisfaction, or how to predict it?

The problem of dissatisfaction with school among children is of theoretical and practical significance to both psychologists and educators. At the theoretical level dissatisfaction with school becomes part of a broader area of inquiry which aims at an understanding of the individual's functioning in an institutional setting and which includes studies of staff morale, role conflict, productivity, and the like. At a practical level the question of why children like or dislike school is directly related to the immediate problems of school dropouts, grouping procedures, planning for the gifted child, and the like.

As might be expected, a social phenomenon as important as dissatisfaction with school is not without its explanatory hypothesis. Some of these spring from empirical findings, while others appear to be part of our cultural ethos. Educational studies that point to an empirical linkage between school failure and school dropouts, and industrial studies that demonstrate a relationship between low morale and decreased output, lead one to suspect that reduced effectiveness in school (i.e., low scholastic achievement) would be a natural concomitant of dissatisfaction with the institution. Thus one would expect to find heightened dissatisfaction among students who have low ability or who are unable for one reason or another to deal adequately with scholastic material.

More recently it has been suggested (although never adequately demonstrated) that many successful students with high ability are dissatisfied with their school experiences; the term "boredom" is often linked with the term "gifted child" in current expositions by educators. The boredom problem

Philip W. Jackson and Jacob W. Getzels, "Psychological Health and Classroom Functioning: A Study of Dissatisfaction with School Among Adolescents," *Journal of Educational Psychology,* 50 (1959), 295–300. Reprinted with permission of the American Psychological Association, Inc.

This study was supported by a research grant from the United States Office of Education. The present report is an expanded version of a paper read at the American Psychological Association meeting, Cincinnati, Ohio, September 1959.

among "gifted" combined with the failure experiences of the low ability child suggests that the greatest number of dissatisfied students is to be found among extreme ability groups. Those who are low in ability and achievement would be expected to show dissatisfaction because of the numerous frustrations they experience in the classroom. Those who are high in ability and achievement would be expected to show dissatisfaction because of the relative lack of stimulation which they experience in the classroom.

Both of these explanations (or, more accurately, hypotheses) contain the implication that dissatisfaction with an institution arises out of the individual's interaction with that institution. An alternative explanation might be that the individual brings a set toward satisfaction or dissatisfaction *to* the institution—that it is a reflection of a more pervasive personal orientation and that success or failure experiences within the institution have a limited influence upon it. This hypothesis obviously places more emphasis than do the earlier ones upon psychological variables, as opposed to environmental variables, in understanding dissatisfaction with school. The research described here was designed to test the relative merit of these alternative views.

PROBLEM

The purpose of this investigation is to examine the differences in psychological functioning and classroom effectiveness between two groups of adolescents—those who are satisfied with their recent school experiences and those who are dissatisfied.

SUBJECTS AND PROCEDURE

The Ss of this investigation were two groups of adolescents identified from among 531 students enrolled in a Midwestern private school. These students were divided into five class groups ranging from the prefreshmen to the senior year of high school. In this institution a single grade, the prefreshmen, is substituted for the usual seventh and eighth grades. The instrument used to select the experimental groups, called the Student Opinion Poll, was a 60-item opinionnaire designed to elicit responses concerning general satisfaction or dissatisfaction with various aspects of school—viz., the teachers, the curriculum, the student body, and classroom procedures. The following are sample items, one in each of the four areas.

3. While there are some differences among them, most teachers in this school are:
   a. Very inspiring
   b. Quite inspiring
   c. Somewhat inspiring
   d. Not inspiring
16. Most of the subjects taught in the school are:
   a. Interesting and challenging

b. Somewhat above average in interest
c. Somewhat below average in interest
d. Dull and routine

14. From the standpoint of intellectual ability, students in this school are:
    a. Too bright—it is difficult to keep up with them
    b. Just bright enough
    c. Not bright enough—they do not provide enough intellectual stimulation
15. The freedom to contribute something in class without being called upon by the teacher is:
    a. Discouraged more than it should be—students do not have enough opportunity to have their say
    b. Encouraged more than it should be—students seem to be rewarded just for speaking even when they have little to say
    c. Handled about right

The instrument was scored by giving one point each time the S chose the "most satisfied" response to a multiple-choice item. Thus, the possible range of scores was from 0 to 60. For the total school population the mean score on the Student Opinion Poll was 37.30; the standard deviation was 9.57. The experimental groups were chosen as follows:

Group I—the "dissatisfied" group—consisted of all students whose score on the opinionnaire was at least one and a half standard deviations *below* the mean of the entire student body. This group contained 27 boys and 20 girls.

Group II—the "satisfied" group—consisted of all students whose score on the opinionnaire was at least one and a half standard deviations *above* the mean of the entire student body. This group contained 25 boys and 20 girls.

The experimental groups were compared on the following variables:

1. *Individual intelligence tests.* In most cases this was the Binet. A small number of children were given the Henmon-Nelson, the scores of which were converted by regression equation into equivalent Binet scores.

2. *Standardized verbal achievement test.* The Cooperative Reading Test was used. Prefreshmen and freshmen were given Test C_1, Form Y; older students were given C_2, Form T.

3. *Standardized numerical achievement tests.* Because of differences in the curricula of the various grade groups it was not possible to administer the same test of numerical achievement to all Ss. The following tests were given according to grade placement:

Prefreshmen—Iowa Everypupil Arithmetic Test, Advanced Form O.
Freshmen—Snader General Mathematics Test.
Sophomores—Cooperative Elementary Algebra Test, Form T.
Juniors—Cooperative Intermediate Algebra Test.
Seniors—Cooperative Geometry Test, Form 2.

4. *California Personality Test.* Two forms of this instrument were used. The intermediate form was given to prefreshmen; the secondary form was given to all of the older groups. Two subscores were obtained, "personal adjustment" and "social adjustment."

5. *Direct Sentence Completion Test.* Ss were asked to complete 27 sen-

tences of the type: "When I saw I was going to fail I . . . .," or, "I think my father is . . . ." Each sentence was given a plus or minus score depending upon the presence or absence of morbid fantasy, defeatism, overt aggression, and the like. The total score was the summation of the individual sentence scores.

6. *Indirect Sentence Completion Test.* This instrument was identical with the Direct Sentence Completion Test except that proper names were inserted for the pronoun "I," thus changing it from a "self-report" to a "projective" instrument. Boys' names were used in the male form of the instrument and girls' names in the female form. The instrument was presented as a "thinking speed" test. To reinforce this notion Ss were asked to raise their hands when they were finished and the elapsed time was written on their test booklet. This instrument was administered approximately two weeks prior to the administration of the Direct Sentence Completion Test.

7. *Group Rorschach.* Cards III, IV, IX, and X were projected on a screen. For each picture the S was presented with 10 responses and was asked to choose the three which he thought to be most appropriate. Each list of 10 contained four "pathological" responses. The S's score was the number of nonpathologic responses among his 12 choices. This group technique follows that desribed by Harrower-Erikson and Steiner (1945).

8. *Teacher ratings.* Each student was given three ratings by his present teachers. These ratings included: (*a*) his general desirability as a student; (*b*) his ability to become involved in learning activities; and (*c*) his possession of leadership qualities. Teachers were required to place all of their students on a five-point scale so that Categories 1 and 5 each contained one-twelfth of the students; Categories 2 and 4 each contained one-fourth of the students; and Category 3 contained one-third of the students. The values 5, 8, 10, 12, and 15 were assigned to the categories and were used in quantifying the ratings.

9. *Adjective Check List.* From a list of 24 adjectives each student was asked to choose the 6 which best described his characteristic feelings while attending classes in particular school subjects. The list contained 12 "positive" (e.g., confident, happy, eager, relaxed) and 12 "negative" adjectives (e.g., bored, restless, misunderstood, angry). The use of the negative adjectives by the experimental groups was analyzed both quantatively and qualitatively.

RESULTS

With the exception of the adjective check list the results of all comparisons are shown in Table 1. Contrary to popular expectations the "satisfied" and "dissatisfied" students did *not* differ from each other in either general intellectual ability or in scholastic achievement. Those differences which did appear were linked to psychological rather than scholastic variables. More specifically, each of the test instruments designed to assess psychological health or "adjustment" was effective in distinguishing "satisfied" from "dissatisfied" students within one or both sex groups.

For both sexes the experimental groups were differentiated by their scores

TABLE 1

Mean scores, standard deviations, and t *statistics for satisfied and dissatisfied adolescents on dependent variables* [a]

	BOYS					GIRLS				
	Dissatisfied ($N = 27$)		*Satisfied* ($N = 25$)			*Dissatisfied* ($N = 20$)		*Satisfied* ($N = 20$)		
	$\overline{x}$	s	$\overline{x}$	s	t	$\overline{x}$	s	$\overline{x}$	s	t
IQ	134.85	14.58	136.44	14.59	ns	128.45	15.06	128.00	11.45	ns
Verbal Achievement	49.96	8.69	50.68	7.87	ns	50.63	9.11	52.28	6.76	ns
Numerical Achievement	50.35	9.75	52.17	10.52	ns	47.78	8.61	48.50	10.26	ns
Calif. Personal Adjust.	45.58	9.82	53.40	7.63	3.18 **	47.90	13.03	54.76	9.25	1.86 *
Calif. Social Adjust.	44.85	11.37	51.84	8.93	2.45 **	47.00	13.15	55.76	7.89	2.50 **
Direct Sentence Comp.	46.93	10.58	49.25	10.02	ns	46.65	12.01	54.00	5.73	2.53 **
Indirect Sentence Comp.	47.19	9.61	51.29	6.95	1.75 *	49.60	10.35	53.47	7.97	ns
Group Rorschach	48.35	10.66	47.44	10.30	ns	47.35	11.35	54.16	8.32	2.15 **
Teacher Rating I: Desirability as a student	8.94	1.83	10.35	1.70	2.85 **	9.84	1.91	10.05	1.59	ns
Teacher Rating II: Leadership qualities	9.01	2.08	10.13	1.96	2.00 *	9.91	2.37	10.04	1.24	ns
Teacher Rating III: Involvement in learning	9.09	2.14	10.23	1.69	2.14 **	9.67	2.32	10.33	2.11	ns

* Significant at the .05 level. ** Significant at the .01 level.

[a] With the exception of IQ, all scores were based upon parameters of the total student body from which the experimental groups were drawn. The scores of all tests were transformed to T scores with a mean of 50 and a standard deviation of 10. For the total population the teacher ratings have a mean of 10 and a standard deviation of 2. The mean IQs for the total school population are: boys, 132, and girls, 128.

on the California Test of Personality. The experimental groups of boys were further differentiated by their responses to the Indirect Sentence Completion Test. For girls additional differences appeared in their responses to the Direct Sentence Completion Test and the Group Rorschach.

On all of these test variables the "satisfied" group attained the "better" score—i.e., the score signifying a more adequate level of psychological functioning. It is also worthy of note that whenever a significant difference appeared, the mean score of the total student population fell between the mean scores of the experimental groups. Thus, the variables that differentiate the experimental groups tend also to distinguish them from the total population of students.

In addition to showing differences on psychological health variables, "satisfied" and "dissatisfied" boys were perceived differently by their teachers. On all three of the teachers' ratings the "satisfied" boys received more favorable judgments than did "dissatisfied" boys. The fact that this result does not appear to be true for girls lends support to the popular expectation that boys are more likely to express their negative feelings publicly than are girls. This hypothesis receives some confirmation from the results of the adjective check list which are described below.

TABLE 2

Number of subjects choosing negative adjectives when asked to describe typical classroom feelings

	BOYS			GIRLS		
Adjective	*Dissatisfied* ($N = 27$)	*Satisfied* ($N = 25$)	*Chi square*	*Dissatisfied* ($N = 20$)	*Satisfied* ($N = 20$)	*Chi square*
Inadequate	19	16	ns	17	7	10.42 **
Ignorant	19	13	ns	15	3	14.54 **
Dull	25	16	6.36 *	16	9	5.60 *
Bored	24	13	8.61 **	20	13	8.48 **
Restless	20	15	ns	19	9	11.90 **
Uncertain	20	21	ns	17	13	ns
Angry	15	4	8.76 **	13	4	8.29 **
Unnoticed	19	5	13.25 **	7	4	ns
Unhelped	18	8	6.24 *	9	6	ns
Misunderstood	16	5	8.31 **	5	2	ns
Rejected	12	3	6.66 **	4	0	ns
Restrained	17	2	16.91 **	9	3	4.29 *

* Significant at the .05 level. ** Significant at the .01 level.

In Table 2 are shown the number of Ss who chose negative adjectives when asked to describe their typical classroom feelings. As they are arranged in Table 2 the adjectives reflect the rankings of four judges who were asked to rank the words on the degree to which they involved an implicit or explicit criticism of others. The 12 adjectives were typed on separate cards and were accompanied by the following directions:

On the following cards are a number of negative adjectives which a person might use to describe himself. Rank these adjectives on the degree to which they involve an implicit or explicit criticism of others. For each adjective ask the question: If a person used this adjective *to describe himself* would he also be implicitly or explicitly criticizing others? Give a rank of 1 to the adjective which would be *least* critical of others and a rank of 12 to the adjective which would be *most* critical of others.

Four psychologists served as judges. The average rank order correlation among the four sets of judgments was .84. The adjectives are presented in Table 2 according to the ranked sum-of-ranks of the judges. The adjective "inadequate" was judged as being most free of criticism of others, while the adjective "restrained" was judged as involving the greatest amount of criticism of others.

As might be expected, the use of negative adjectives was far more frequent among dissatisfied students than among satisfied students. Four adjectives seemed to discriminate equally well between the experimental groups for both sexes; these were: "bored," "angry," "restrained," and "dull."

An examination of Table 2 also suggests the existence of sex differences in the students' description of their typical classroom feelings. Remembering the classificatory scheme by which the adjectives are ranked in Table 2, it appears that dissatisfied girls are somewhat less likely than dissatisfied boys to use negative adjectives involving implicit criticism of others. Dissatisfied boys, on the other hand, are less likely than dissatisfied girls to be distinguished from their satisfied counterparts by the use of adjectives *not* involving implicit criticism of others. If one thinks of criticism directed towards others within Rosenzweig's schema of "intropunitiveness" and "extrapunitiveness" (Murray, 1945), then the observed sex differences may be conceptualized by saying that dissatisfied girls are more *intropunitive* than satisfied girls; dissatisfied boys are more *extrapunitive* than satisfied boys.

This difference in the direction of aggression may provide a context for the obtained differences in teacher ratings discussed earlier. If the dissatisfied boy is more likely than his female counterpart to lay the blame for his dissatisfaction upon others in his environment, particularly school authorities, it is reasonable to expect that he would be viewed as somewhat less than completely desirable by the classroom teacher. The dissatisfied girl, on the other hand, seems more willing to direct her negative feelings inward, thus avoiding the additional risk of counter-aggression by school authorities or by other adults.

DISCUSSION

Two major conclusions are suggested by the findings of this study. First, dissatisfaction with school appears to be part of a larger picture of psychological discontent rather than a direct reflection of inefficient functioning in the classroom. It is almost as if dissatisfaction were a product of a pervasive perceptual set that colors the student's view of himself and his world. Second, it appears that the "dynamics" of dissatisfaction operate differently for boys and girls. Boys seem to project the causes of their discontent upon the world around them so that adults are seen as rejecting and lacking in understanding. This tendency to blame adults may be one reason why these boys are seen as less attractive by teachers than are satisfied boys. Girls, on the other hand, are more likely to be self-critical, turning blame for their dissatisfaction inward. Feelings of inadequacy, ignorance, and restlessness more sharply differentiate satisfied and dissatisfied girls than is the case with boys. This tendency to be intropunitive may partially explain why teacher ratings fail to distinguish between our two experimental groups of girls.

The atypicality of the sample population used in this research places a number of limitations upon the inferential statements which can be made on the basis of these findings. Fortunately, however, the major portion of the investigation has recently been replicated using seventh and eighth grade lower-class Negro adolescents as Ss (Spillman, 1959). The findings of the latter study are essentially the same as those reported here. Again the psychological rather than the intellectual or scholastic variables discriminated between satisfied and dissatisfied students. The findings with respect to the use of negative adjectives were not as clear-cut but, again, every intropunitive adjective was used more frequently by dissatisfied girls as compared with dissatisfied boys, while the latter exceeded the girls in their use of extrapunitive adjectives.

It should be noted that even the most satisfied students made some use of negative adjectives when asked to describe their typical feelings in the classroom. Also, the average member of the satisfied group expressed some dissatisfaction on one-sixth of the questions in the Student Opinion Poll. These two observations should serve as ample cautions against the danger of interpreting any sign of dissatisfaction with school as symptomatic of deeper psychological difficulties. Apparently, some degree of dissatisfaction is the rule rather than the exception. Nonetheless, the responses of the extremely disgruntled group of students leaves little doubt that dissatisfaction with school, like beauty, is frequently in the eye of the beholder.

SUMMARY

This investigation examines the differences in psychological functioning and classroom effectiveness between two groups of adolescents—those who are satisfied with their recent school experiences and those who are dissatisfied. The major findings point to: (*a*) the relevance of psychological health data rather than scholastic achievement data in understanding dissatisfaction with school; (*b*) the importance of differentiating the attitudes of dissatisfied girls from those of dissatisfied boys, the former being characterized by feelings of personal inadequacy, the latter by feelings critical of school authorities. Rosenzweig's concepts of intropunitiveness and extrapunitiveness are applied to these findings and a relevant theoretical framework is proposed.

REFERENCES

Harrower-Erikson, M. R., & Steiner, M. E. Large scale Rorschach techniques. Springfield, Ill.: Charles C Thomas, 1945.

Murray, H. A. *Explorations in personality.* New York: Oxford Univer. Press, 1938.

Spillman, R. J. Psychological and scholastic correlates of dissatisfaction with school among adolescents. Unpublished master's thesis. Univer. of Chicago, 1959.

ROBERT L. EBEL

Are Important Objectives Testable?

Some educators and laymen argue that certain educational outcomes cannot be measured. In this excerpt from a longer article, Ebel takes the opposite position. This is so condensed and effective a statement of an important position that it bears the closest study and thought. Why is measurement important in education? Why is good quantification the hallmark of successful science?

Recommendation: *When any outcome of education is claimed to be important but unmeasurable, inquire concering the clarity with which it has been defined. If an operational definition is possible, the outcome can be measured. If not, its claim to importance cannot be verified.*

Education is a complex process which results in complex, and often subtle, outcomes. It is not surprising, therefore, that writers sometimes mention the existence and importance of intangible outcomes of education. Such writers are likely to suggest that the intangible outcomes of education are difficult to measure and may be entirely unmeasurable.

An alternate view is based on two propositions. (*a*) A human trait is measurable, in at least an elementary sense, if the assertion that one person possesses more of it than another can be independently verified by two or more observers. This means that, if having more or less of a trait makes any observable difference, that trait is measurable. (*b*) In order to be important, an outcome of education must make an observable difference in the behavior of persons who have attained different degrees of it. If attaining an alleged goal of education does not change the overt behavior of the person who attains it in any way, on what basis can it be said to be important?

To say that all important outcomes of education are potentially measurable is not to say that all can be measured easily. But it is to say that any

From Robert L. Ebel, "The Relation of Testing Programs to Educational Goals," *The Impact and Improvement of School Testing Programs, Yearbook 1962* (Chicago: National Society for the Study of Education, 1962), pp. 28–44. Reprinted with permission.

THE CO-OP
BOOK STORE
— SALES RECEIPT —

25 MAR 68

$04.95 —
$00.25 TAX

THE CO-OP
BOOK STORE
— SALES RECEIPT —

25 MAR 68

$04.95 —
$00.25 TAX

distinction between the tangible and the intangible outcomes of education, between the measurable and the nonmeasurable, is spurious.

Why is this point so often misunderstood? Two possible reasons can be suggested. The first is that we use vague, undefined, general terms in talking about the goals of education—terms like character, citizenship, open-mindedness, creativity, excellence, and adjustment. Now there is nothing wrong in the use of general terms to express general ideas. On the contrary, it would be impossible to do otherwise. And statements invoking general terms do serve a useful purpose at some levels of discourse. But we err if we assume that there exists somewhere real, clearly definable, important, human characteristics corresponding to each of the many names we use in describing human behavior. We err further if we think that our main task is that of discovering the true natures of these characteristics rather than that of defining what we mean when we use these trait names. We err most grievously if we attribute difficulty in measuring these named characteristics to limitations in our techniques of testing instead of attributing it to vagueness or lack of agreement as to what the name signifies.

Any unambiguous definition of a quantitative attribute clearly implies a method of measuring it. Conversely, any test or other means of quantifying an attribute implies a definition of it. If we know how to specify the method for determining which member of any pair of persons possesses the greater amount of the attribute in question, we know both what the attribute means and how to measure it. But if the method remains to be developed, we not only lack measurements of the attribute but also a clear idea of what the attribute means.

A second reason why some outcomes of education are held to be unmeasurable may be that the measurement is thought to refer properly only to processes which meet all the requirements for fundamental physical measurement. Some writers, like B. Othanel Smith,[1] have concluded that mental testing leads to numbers which are not measurements at all. Others, like Lorge [2] and Comrey,[3] recognize the value in quantitative processes which do not involve equality of units or an absolute zero. Bergmann and Spence [4] have pointed out that *fundamental* measurement of some attributes of great interest to us is unattainable in principle. But if this were taken to mean that these attributes are unmeasurable, we should have to find some other term for our successful and useful processes of dealing with them in quantitative terms.

A third reason for denial of the measurability of some important educational outcomes may be the opportunity it provides for committed anti-scientists to re-emphasize the limitations of scientific methods. Further, the measurement of human traits opens the door to evaluations and judgments,

[1] B. Othanel Smith, *Logical Aspects of Educational Measurement.* New York: Columbia University Press, 1938.

[2] Irving Lorge, "The Fundamental Nature of Measurement," in *Educational Measurement.* Edited by E. F. Lindquist. Washington: American Council on Education, 1951.

[3] Andrew Comrey, "Mental Testing and the Logic of Measurement," *Educational and Psychological Measurement,* XI (Autumn, 1951), 323–34.

[4] Gustav Bergmann and Kenneth W. Spence, "The Logic of Psychophysical Measurement," *Psychological Review,* LI (January, 1944), 1–24.

which, since they might be unfavorable, are sometimes feared. Thus, there may be some elements of defensiveness in the opposition to probings of the human mind—some comforting shelter to be found in attributing impenetrable mysteries to the human spirit—which encourage belief in narrow limitations to the scope of educational measurements.

The practical limitations of effective educational measurement are real and many, as anyone who has labored to improve educational measurements can testify. But they are not fixed eternally by the nature of man, nor is it useless to try to overcome them. The possibility of measuring the degree of attainment of all important outcomes of education does exist.

Recommendation: *Include in the school testing program tests for all the educational outcomes which the school is actually working to achieve.*

If a school includes tests of such things as attitudes, interests, and values in its testing program, it implies a concern for these things as educational goals. The tests may have limitations, and the school's efforts to educate toward these educational goals may be somewhat uncertain, but the fact that students are tested on them implies that the school regards them as important. Hence, a testing program *can* recognize nonintellectual goals. In so far as the school program purposefully pursues such goals, and in so far as available evaluation techniques permit, it *should* include measures of nonintellectual educational outcomes in its testing program.

What do we mean when we speak of nonintellectual goals? Plato [5] suggested *emotional* and *volitional* goals, for he identified affection (emotion) and conation (will), in addition to cognition (intellect), as three aspects of the human soul. Spencer [6] discussed *moral* and *physical,* along with *intellectual* goals, as aspects of education. The authors of the NSSE Yearbook on *Learning and Instruction* [7] included chapters on motor learning, interests, motives and attitudes, aesthetic responses, and personal and social adjustment, as well as on the more conventionally intellectual aspects—information, concepts, generalizations, and problem-solving.

It seems clear that none of these goals of education is purely nonintellectual or wholly devoid of intellectual content. But it seems equally clear that the emphasis placed on intellectual goals has varied from age to age, usually in response to social pressures. In recent years there has been a sharp increase of emphasis on personal and social adjustment. Even so, there has been more concern for excellence than for adjustment. One can applaud or deplore the current emphasis on intellectual achievement as an objective of education. From the point of view of this chapter, it is a desirable emphasis which deserves continuing support.

Recommendation: *Let the school testing program emphasize the cogni-*

[5] Rupert C. Lodge, *Plato's Theory of Education.* London: Kegan Paul, Trench, Trubner & Co., 1947.

[6] Herbert Spencer, *Education: Intellectual, Moral and Physical.* New York: A. L. Burt Co., 1861.

[7] G. Lester Anderson and Others, *Learning and Instruction.* Forty-ninth Yearbook of the National Society for the Study of Education, Part I. Chicago: Distributed by the University of Chicago Press, 1950.

tive outcomes of education, in recognition of the school's central, fundamental, all-pervasive goal of intellectual development.

It may be appropriate to mention here that any paper-and-pencil test is essentially an intellectual task. Whatever the name of the test, whatever it purports to measure—attitudes, interests, values, character, personality, adjustment—the examinee who seeks to perform well on such a test will respond to it as thoughtfully and as wisely as he can. He will report what he knows or thinks about his attitudes, interests, values, and the like, or what he believes he ought to report. Such a test is, for him, a test of self-knowledge and self-understanding. It may or may not indicate how these attributes affect his behavior in daily life.

Reference has already been made to the intellectual component of most educational goals. While one cannot maintain physical health and vigor or develop motor skills solely by thinking about them, it does help to have and to be able to use the knowledge relevant to the attainment of such goals. This point is stressed persuasively in the recent publication of the Educational Policies Commission: [8]

> The purpose which runs through and strengthens all other educational purposes—the common thread of education—is the development of the ability to think. This is the central purpose to which the school must be oriented if it is to accomplish either its traditional tasks or those newly accentuated by recent changes in the world. To say that it is central is not to say that it is the sole purpose or in all circumstances the most important purpose, but that it must be a pervasive concern in the work of the school. Many agencies contribute to achieving educational objectives, but this particular objective will not be generally attained unless the school focuses on it. In this context, therefore, the development of every student's rational powers must be recognized as centrally important (p. 12).

The Educational Policies Commission, in a section on "Developing Rational Powers," notes the importance of the "inquiring spirit." This is a gentler term than *skepticism* or *critical thinking* but involves the same approach to education. Unfortunately, it is not the approach favored by some among those who stress the nonintellectual goals of citizenship, character, attitudes, values, interests, appreciations, or personal and social adjustment. Nor is it the approach of those who would define educational goals in terms of an extensive catalog of desired responses to particular situations.

Those who warn against overemphasis of intellectual goals sometimes are reflecting concern, not over the neglect of other goals, but over pressure on students who find it difficult to achieve goals of any kind. Education should be enjoyable, they argue, not stressful. The child's happiness is as important as his intellectual development, perhaps more so, they say. Surely the emphasis on intellectual excellence can be overdone. To some extent such overemphasis is self-defeating and, hence, self-correcting. But overemphasis on moment-to-moment happiness is equally dangerous.

[8] *The Central Purpose of American Education.* Washington: Educational Policies Commission of the National Education Association, 1961.

Chapter 7

Assessing Readiness: Abilities

7-1

JULIAN C. STANLEY, JR.

Testing Has a Long History

7-2

JOHN W. GARDNER

The Identification of Talent

JULIAN C. STANLEY, JR.

Testing Has a Long History

Although testing has a "long" history, its growth into a major educational force is recent and explosive. This article, part of a longer chapter on test history, will permit you to see the first stumbling steps toward good measurement, taken in the early years of some persons still living. Stanley's account, part of a new text, may explain why thinking about testing, even by some senior educators, is still misled and confused in the 1960's.

Measurement and evaluation have played a far more prominent role in human history than is generally recognized. . . . Some of the earliest records of the use of various testing devices are found in the Bible, although they generally had no reference to education. One illustration will suffice:

> And the Gileadites took the passages of Jordan before the Ephraimites: and it was *so,* that when those Ephraimites which were escaped said, Let me go over; that the men of Gilead said unto him, *Art* thou an Ephraimite? If he said, Nay; then said they unto him, Say now *Shibboleth:* and he said *Sibboleth:* for he could not frame to pronounce *it* right. Then they took him, and slew him at the passages of Jordan: and there fell at that time of the Ephraimites forty and two thousand.[1]

Here indeed is an old "final examination," though in a field other than education. Doubtless, today's measurement experts would point out that, in spite of its high degree of objectivity, it had certain questionable features: it was oral, it was very short, and the "mortality rate" was excessively high!

The sole test of a man's being a Gileadite was his using the *h* sound in the word *Shibboleth.* Notice that it was a one-question test which yielded for each examinee a score of "right" or "wrong," and that the consequences of failing the exam were rather extreme. It is possible, however, that other paths have been taken if the Gileadites had different attitudes towards the Ephraimites. This illustrates the fact that measurement is always a means to an end and never an end in itself. The uses made of measurement always depend on the broader contexts of values, goals, and purposes of the measurers. The Gileadites seem to have been satisfied with their examination, although a modern-day tester would have his doubts. Isn't it possible that some true Gileadites failed and some true Ephraimites passed? Isn't it

[1] *Judges.* Chap. 12, Verses 5–6, King James Version.

possible than an examiner might have made a wrong judgment on the basis of only one question? These are, of course, questions touching on the principles of test validity and reliability.

In education, some form of measurement is inevitable and is, indeed, inherent in the teaching process. Consider the constant evaluative role of the classroom teacher as he goes about determining the degree of scholastic and social growth of pupils in order to make hundreds of major and minor educational decisions each year. . . . Measuring devices are also indispensable to the guidance counselor, the school administrator, the curriculum planner, and the professional researcher. Here we will discuss the historical events and practical necessities which determined modern trends in educational measurement. . . .

A. FORERUNNERS OF MODERN EDUCATIONAL MEASUREMENT

PSYCHOPHYSICS: "PHYSICS OF THE MIND"

A turning point in the history of psychology occurred in 1879 when Wilhelm Wundt established the first laboratory for experimental psychology at the University of Leipzig, Germany. The rise of *scientific* psychology, as opposed to the traditional *philosophic* psychology, was intimately related to the use of objective measuring devices. Although Wundt interested himself in questions concerning the physiology of sensory processes, reaction times, and word association, he also inherited and extended the psychological legacy known as "psychophysics." [2] This field had been opened 20 years earlier by another German, Gustav Fechner, who saw in psychophysics "an exact science of the functional relations of the dependency between mind and body." [3] Up to this time physics had made great progress in measuring such objective attributes as length, weight, time, temperature, and volume. Fechner came to believe that certain purely "mental" or psychological processes, such as sensation, perception, and feeling, could be accurately measured. According to Fechner, scales measuring them would be definitely and mathematically related to the strength of the sensation-producing stimulus under investigation.

For example, a psychophysicist might be interested in developing a scale of brightness as perceived by a person, using units of "just-noticeable-differences" (j.n.d.'s) in the intensity of the source of light the individual sees. Fechner's Law states that the degree of sensation is related to the actual magnitude of the physical stimulus in a certain specific mathematical way.[4] In this case the magnitude of perceived brightness, as measured in j.n.d.'s, should be that mathematical function of the actual intensity of the light, as measured in a physical unit such as candlepower.

[2] G. Murphy. *Historical Introduction to Modern Psychology.* (Rev. ed.) New York: Harcourt, Brace & World, 1949, pp. 155–156.

[3] As quoted in J. P. Guilford. *Psychometric Methods.* (2nd ed.) New York: McGraw-Hill, 1954, p. 3.

[4] E. G. Boring. The beginning and growth of measurement in psychology. *Isis,* 1961, 52 (168), pp. 238–257.

Fechner also developed several procedures, now known as "psychophysical methods," for determining units of just-noticeable-differences. His basic law has not gone unscathed over the years, however, and its revision and extension in the light of experimental findings continues to be a lively source of debate among researchers.[5]

In 1927 L. L. Thurstone extended the classical psychophysical measuring operations in his "law of comparative judgment,"[6] which allowed the investigator to "measure" a psychological characteristic such as "attitude toward war" for which no known corresponding physical measure could be obtained. Obviously, you could not weigh an individual's attitude toward war in ounces or measure its length in inches, whereas you could determine how bright the light actually was versus how bright it seemed to the observer.

The new psychophysics asked such questions as "How strong is this man's attitude towards the Negro?" "How good are these essays relative to one another?" "What judgment factors underlie preference for movie stars—beauty? gender? type of role? color of hair?" In order to answer these questions, Thurstone and others abandoned the original physical reference point and the original criteria of weight, length, temperature, and volume.

Just as the physical intensity aspect of the psychological response was made unnecessary for certain purposes, the new field of *response-response* investigation developed. If responses made on an attitude scale indicated that an individual hated war, what did this suggest about his responses in other areas? Would he have more intensely negative attitudes than a person with neutral feelings toward war? What about his intelligence, his open-mindedness, his needs for love or dominance, his political views? Thus psychology directed some of its efforts away from the development of directional *stimulus-response* laws, where the stimulus produces the response ($S \rightarrow R$), in favor of the development of *response-response* relationships ($R \leftrightarrow R$) that do not have directionality.

GALTON AND THE STUDY OF HUMAN DIFFERENCES

Coincident with the blossoming of Wundt's experimental psychology laboratory in Leipzig, a slightly different tradition was developing in England under Sir Francis Galton (1822–1911). Although the psychophysicists were interested in determining universal psychological processes and treated the response differences between subjects as so much "experimental error," Galton worked in the intellectual tradition of Darwinian biology, with its emphasis on *variation*, both between and within species. We see in Galton's work the beginnings of a concern for *individual differences*, which has been a keystone in the history of psychological and educational testing. From his "laboratory of anthropometry," established in London in 1882, came studies of topics such as word association, mental imagery, and the genetic basis of genius. To facilitate his research, Galton invented several statistical

[5] See, for example, Psychophysics: one hundred years after (symposium commemorating the 100th anniversary of the publication of Fechner's *Elemente der Psychophysik*). *Psychometrika*, 1961, 26 (1), pp. 3–63.

[6] L. L. Thurstone. A law of comparative judgment. *Psychological Review*, 1927, 24, pp. 273–286.

devices, the most important of which was a graphical method for finding the degree of relationship between two variables (height and weight, for example).[7] As later refined by his colleague, Karl Pearson, this device became the now-classic *product-moment coefficient of correlation.*

THE EARLY HISTORY OF SCIENTIFIC MEASUREMENT IN AMERICAN EDUCATION

Oral questioning dates back to the beginnings of human language; Socrates used it effectively in the fifth century B.C. to "draw out" his students, and until the coming of inexpensive pencils and paper after the middle of the nineteenth century, oral examinations were standard in our schools. Some countries today still require oral final examinations by law.[8] Our own universities harbor vestiges in the form of "thesis orals." Television features oral-quiz "giveaway" programs, though the contestants are often chosen in advance by means of written tests. Not until the present century did writing instruments largely replace glib or faltering tongues.

The first important steps toward the scientific use of measurement in education were taken by Horace Mann more than a century ago.[9] This prominent New England educator, famous for his doctrine of free, compulsory, and universal education, had a remarkable understanding both of the importance of examinations and of the limitations of the ones then being used. His penetrating analysis of the weakness of the oral examinations then in vogue and of the superiority of written examinations can hardly be improved by today's specialist in educational measurement. Mann showed clearly where oral examinations were lacking, employing those concepts which have become the cornerstones of today's theories, and which are now known as validity, reliability, and usability. . . .

Another American educator who understood both the value and the limitations of examinations was Emerson E. White, educational writer and school administrator. In 1886 he wrote, "It may be stated as a general fact that school instruction and study are never much wider or better than the tests by which they are measured." [10] In the same volume (pages 197–198) he enumerated several "special advantages" of the written test:

> It is more impartial than the oral test, since it gives all the pupils the same tests and an equal opportunity to meet them; its results are more tangible and reliable; it discloses more accurately the comparative progress of the different pupils, information of value to the teacher; it reveals more clearly defects in teaching and study, and thus assists in their correction; it emphasizes more distinctly the importance of accuracy and fullness in the expression of knowledge . . . it is at least an equal test of the thought-power or intelligence of pupils. . . .

[7] G. Murphy. *Op. cit.*, pp. 117–122.

[8] J. C. Stanley. College studies and college life in Belgium. *College Board Review*, 1960, No. 40, pp. 10–14.

[9] H. Mann. Report of the annual examining committees of the Boston grammar and writing schools. *The Common School Journal*, 1845, 7 (21), pp. 326–336.

[10] E. E. White. *The Elements of Pedagogy*. New York: American Book Company, 1886, p. 148.

These views of Mann and White appear surprisingly modern and show how far general practice is apt to fall behind the theory of the pioneer thinker. And even though measurement specialists now tend to shy away from the early enthusiasm for the ordinary written test, pointing out that many of the cited limitations of the oral tests also hold in some degree for written tests, the best thinkers of yesteryear were often far ahead of many persons today.

The actual improvement of existing tests and other measuring instruments has always lagged far behind theory, and school practice has been farthest behind of all. In spite of the marked superiority of written examinations over oral, pointed out by Mann as early as 1845, teachers moved neither to adopt the former nor to improve the latter. It is interesting to note, however, that by 1864 an enterprising English schoolmaster, the Reverend George Fisher, had proposed the widespread use of objective and standardized measures of academic attainment. Reverend Fisher outlined the practice of the new system in his school as follows: [11]

> A book, called the "Scale-Book," has been established, which contains the numbers assigned to each degree of proficiency in the various subjects of examination: for instance, if it be required to determine the numerical equivalent corresponding to any specimen of "writing," a comparison is made with various standard specimens, which are arranged in this book in order of merit; the highest being represented by the number 1, and the lowest by 5, and the intermediate values by affixing to these numbers the fractions ¼, ½, or ¾. So long as these standard specimens are preserved in the institution, so long will constant numerical values for proficiency in "writing" be maintained. And since facsimiles can be multiplied without limit, the same principle might be generally adopted.
>
> The numeral values for "spelling" follow the same order, and are made to depend upon the percentage of mistakes in writing from dictation sentences from works selected for the purpose, examples of which are contained in the "Scale-Book," in order to preserve the same standard of difficulty.
>
> By a similar process, values are assigned for proficiency in mathematics, navigation, Scripture knowledge, grammar, and composition, French, general history, drawing, and practical science, respectively. Questions in each of these subjects are contained in the "Scale-Book," to serve as types, not only of the difficulty, but of the nature of the question, for the sake of future reference . . .

Apparently, Fisher was too far advanced for his times, since his incisive work seems not to have attracted a widespread audience. As Leonard P. Ayres put it, "progress in the scientific study of education was not possible until people could be brought to realize that human behavior was susceptible of quantitative study, and until they had statistical methods with which to carry on their investigations." [12]

Although Ayres felt that Sir Francis Galton's great contributions had

[11] From a letter quoted in E. Chadwick. Statistics of educational results. *Museum, A Quarterly Magazine of Education, Literature, and Science.* 1864, 3, pp. 479–484.

[12] L. P. Ayres. History and present status of educational measurements. *Seventeenth Yearbook of the National Society for the Study of Education, Part II.* Bloomington, Illinois: Public School Publishing Company, 1918, p. 10.

largely met these two needs, he credits J. M. Rice with being the "real inventor of the comparative tests." [13] A young American ex-physician turned zealous researcher, Rice had studied pedagogy in Germany and had been influenced by experimental psychologists at the Universities of Leipzig and Jena. His great concern for the quality of contemporary education prompted him to conduct two large studies of spelling achievement in various U.S. cities. In each study, he administered his own specially constructed tests to all students under rather uniform conditions. The volume of his purely personal delving is awesome even in this day of mass research; he secured test results on 13,000 children under his own direction and on 16,000 more by mail, his researches spanning 16 months and 21 cities.[14] Though this first approach to test standardization falls somewhat short of modern practice, it promoted Rice's aim of making education more scientific.

The conclusion to his first article on the results of his investigations sets forth the value of what we now call "norms": "Whether or not the spelling in a particular locality is actually below the average can be learned only by comparing the results of an examination conducted *on the same basis* in many localities. By examining children in any one city, on a set of arbitrarily selected words, the question cannot be solved, because the results in other places, on the same list of words, would remain an unknown quantity. A common standard is offered, however, by a . . . test such as I have undertaken" [15] (italics added). How obvious to us now, but how radical then!

Far more than just a tester, Rice was a pioneer in what later came to be known as progressive education. He was, during the years 1891–1899, a relentless investigator of American education, publishing a series of 20 articles in the *Forum,* a leading literary magazine. The educational leaders of the time were anything but cordial to him, and for many years little progress was made beyond Rice's own work.

If Ayres credits him with the invention of educational measurement, he awards the title, "father of the educational testing movement," to Edward L. Thorndike. During his distinguished and prolific career at Columbia's Teachers College, Thorndike was concerned with many phases of the measurement movement. In addition to his very influential publications on statistical methods in education and his pioneer work on college entrance intelligence tests, Thorndike and his students were responsible for nearly all of the early standard achievement tests and scales. The year 1910 saw the publication of the Thorndike Handwriting Scale,[16] the first of its kind. It consisted of formal writing samples of children in grades five through eight, arranged in an equal-unit, fifteen-category scale of increasing quality (see Figure 1). Two years earlier Stone had reported his doctoral research on elementary school arithmetic,[17] in which he employed instruments that

[13] *Ibid.,* p. 11.

[14] J. M. Rice. The futility of the spelling grind: I. *Forum,* 1897, 23, pp. 163–172.

[15] *Ibid.,* p. 172. See also J. M. Rice. The futility of the spelling grind: II. *Forum,* 1897, 23, pp. 409–419.

[16] E. L. Thorndike. Handwriting. *Teachers College Record,* 1910, 11 (2), pp. 83–175.

[17] C. W. Stone. *Arithmetical abilities and some factors determining them.* New York: Columbia University, 1908.

SCALE A

A SCALE FOR HANDWRITING OF CHILDREN IN GRADES 5 TO 8

The unit of the scale equals approximately one-tenth of the difference between the best and worst of the formal writings of 1,000 children in grades 5–8. The differences 16–15, 15–14, 14–13, etc., represent equal fractions of the combined mental scale of merit of from 23 to 55 competent judges.

QUALITY 18. SAMPLE 125

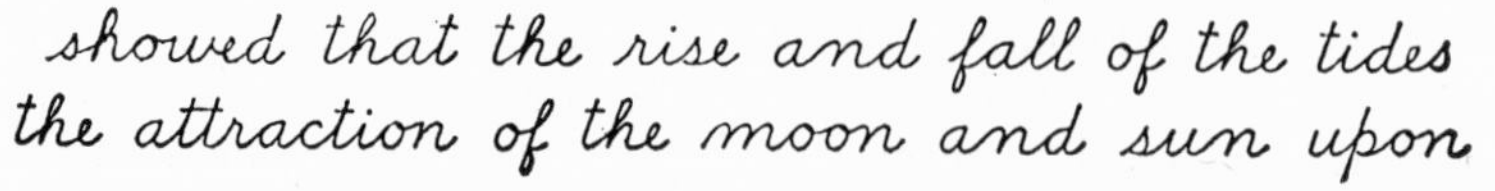

showed that the rise and fall of the tides
the attraction of the moon and sun upon

QUALITY 11. SAMPLES 23 AND 45

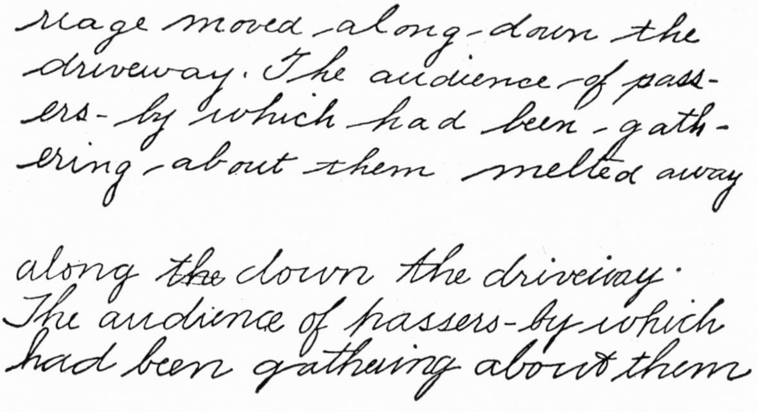

rage moved along down the
driveway. The audience of passers-by which had been gathering about them melted away

along ~~the~~ down the driveway.
The audince of passers-by which
had been gathering about them

QUALITY 4. SAMPLE 121

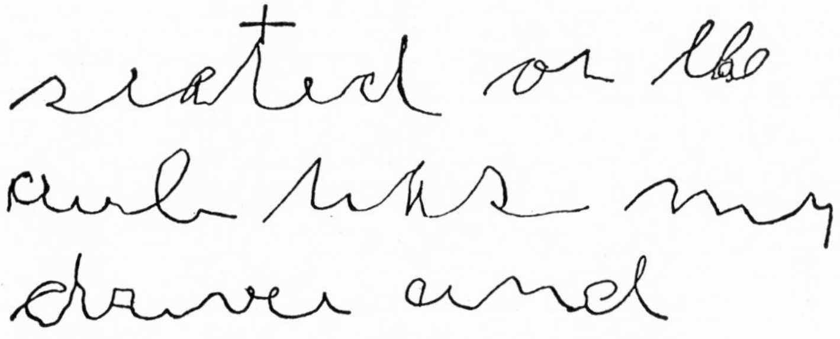

seated on the
[illegible] [illegible] my
drawer and

FIGURE 1.

Excellent, average, and poor handwriting

(From E. L. Thorndike, *Handwriting* [New York: Teachers College, Columbia University, 1910].)

became widely known as "Stone's Standard Tests."[18] A section from an early derivative of the Stone test is reproduced in Figure 2. The next few years saw the appearance of scales and tests in many other fields.

FIGURE 2.
A speed test of arithmetic, composed of exceedingly homogeneous items (published in 1913)

COURTIS STANDARD RESEARCH TESTS

Arithmetic Test No. 1 Addition — SCORE: No. Attempted ______

Series B Form 1 — No. Right ______

You will be given eight minutes to find the answers to as many of these addition examples as possible. Write the answers on this paper directly underneath the examples. You are not expected to be able to do them all. You will be marked for both speed and accuracy, but it is more important to have your answers right than to try a great many examples.

927	297	136	486	384	176	277	837
379	925	340	765	477	783	445	882
756	473	988	524	881	697	682	959
837	983	386	140	266	200	594	603
924	315	353	812	679	366	481	118
110	661	904	466	241	851	778	781
854	794	547	355	796	535	849	756
965	177	192	834	850	323	157	222
344	124	439	567	733	229	966	525
537	664	634	572	226	351	428	862
695	278	168	253	880	788	975	159
471	345	717	948	663	705	450	383
913	921	142	529	819	174	194	451
564	787	449	936	779	426	666	938
932	646	453	223	123	649	742	433
559	433	924	358	338	755	295	599
106	464	659	676	996	140	187	172
228	449	432	122	308	246	281	152
677	223	186	275	432	634	547	588
464	878	478	521	876	327	197	256
234	682	927	854	571	327	685	719
718	399	516	939	917	394	678	524
838	904	923	582	749	807	456	969
293	353	553	566	495	169	393	761
423	419	216	936	250	491	525	113
955	756	669	472	833	885	240	449
519	314	409	264	318	403	152	122

(From J. C. Stone, *The Teaching of Arithmetic* [New York: Sanborn, 1922], p. 234. Reprinted with permission of the L. W. Singer Company, Inc., Syracuse, New York.)

[18] J. C. Stone. *The teaching of arithmetic.* New York: Benj. H. Sanborn, 1922, p. 228.

B. THE HISTORY OF MODERN ACHIEVEMENT TESTS

STUDIES OF THE UNRELIABILITY OF SCHOOL MARKS AND EXAMINATIONS

Tests designed to determine a student's mastery of a given academic area are as old as formal education itself. Only in the last half-century or so, however, have techniques been developed in an effort to insure a maximum of objectivity in the assessment of school achievement. We have already sketched some of the scientific and practical concerns which established the intellectual climate for a tremendous blossoming of education measurement. But good arguments in favor of new methods do not always assure their adoption because first existing methods must be shown to be inadequate. Certainly a factor that greatly spurred the development and use of standard tests was a series of studies begun after the turn of the century. These clearly documented the questionable status of the forms of educational measurement then in use.

Course marks proceed directly from some forms of measurement by the teacher. Sometimes these are explicit, but a mark may often be the result of some tacit and subjective value scale particular to the teacher or department. The need for reform in college marking was sharply brought to public attention by Professor Max Meyer,[19] an experimental psychologist educated at the University of Berlin who reported on the marks assigned by 40 teachers over a five-year period at the University of Missouri. He found such astonishing variations as 55 per cent of *A*'s in philosophy and only 1 per cent in Chemistry III, while there were 28 per cent failures in English II and none in Latin I. Franklin Johnson [20] found a similar situation at the University of Chicago High School, where he was the Principal; in a two-year period the marks in German showed 17.1 per cent *A*'s and 8.4 per cent *F*'s, the marks in English, however, showing 6.5 per cent *A*'s and 15.5 per cent *F*'s. And even when the ability differences of the various groups were allowed for, much of this inconsistency in marking could be more readily attributed to varying marking severity than to varying subject difficulty. In short, school marks appeared highly subjective and arbitrary, the mark assigned often seeming more a function of the *personality of the instructor* than of the *performance of the student*. Without exception further studies elsewhere showed similar results. This was certainly disturbing, if not, as Thorndike suggested, actually "scandalous." [21]

But the evidence presented by later studies was to be even more damaging. Although the departmental variations in grading could be partially accounted for by variations in the background, intelligence, and application of the students in those departments, such factors clearly could not be held responsible for differences when several persons were marking the same student's paper and, least of all, when the same person marked the same paper on two different occasions. Many convincing studies revealed great variability of marks under both conditions.

[19] M. Meyer. The grading of students. *Science*, August 21, 1908, 27, pp. 243–250.

[20] F. W. Johnson. A study of high-school grades. *School Review*, 1911, 19, pp. 13–24.

[21] E. L. Thorndike. Measurement in education. *Twenty-First Yearbook of the National Society for the Study of Education, Part I*, 1922, p. 2.

Perhaps the most striking of the early investigations were those of Daniel Starch, a pioneering applied psychologist. In one of these studies [22] they analyzed facsimiles of the same geometry paper marked independently by 116 high-school teachers of mathematics. The grades given ranged from a low of 28 per cent to a high of 92. Certainly, if high-school teachers could not agree any more closely in mathematics, supposedly one of the most objective subjects, the situation was poor indeed.

Later studies confirmed the early findings. In one of the most spectacular,[23] 100 English teachers were asked to mark a composition and also to indicate the grade level in which they would expect that quality of work. As shown in Table 1, the percentage values varied from 60 to 98, averaging about 87 per cent, the estimated grade location varying from the fifth grade

TABLE 1

The estimated grade-value and percentage marks assigned to an English composition by one hundred teachers (after Falls)

Grade value	PERCENTAGE MARK *60–64*	*65–69*	*70–74*	*75–79*	*80–84*	*85–89*	*90–94*	*95–99*	*Total*
XV								2	2
XIV									0
XIII							1	2	3
XII					1		2	3	6
XI			2			6	5	2	15
X			1	3	8	4	7	1	24
IX	1		1	1	8	4	4	3	22
VIII			2	2	2	3	4	3	16
VII				2	2	2	1		7
VI	1				1	1		1	4
V	1								1
Total	3		6	8	22	20	24	17	100

to the junior year of college, averaging about the beginning of the tenth grade. As a matter of fact, the composition was the best one found by a survey committee at Gary, Indiana, and was written by a high-school senior whose special interest was journalism and who was already a correspondent for some of the Chicago newspapers. It seems reasonable to suppose that many of these English teachers would seldom, if ever, have as good a composition submitted by one of their own pupils. Yet the typical one of these teachers considered it grade "B" for the tenth grade!

Starch [24] also presented the problem in a different and even more unfavorable light. He found that college instructors assigned different marks

[22] D. Starch and E. C. Elliot. Reliability of grading work in mathematics. *School Review*, 1913, 21, pp. 254–259.

[23] J. D. Falls. Research in secondary education. *Kentucky School Journal*, 1928, 6, pp. 42–46.

[24] D. Starch. Reliability and distribution of grades. *Science*, October 31, 1913, 38, pp. 630–636.

when they *regraded their own papers* without knowledge of their former marks. Later, Ashbaugh [25] had 49 college seniors and graduate students, the latter with teaching experience, rate a seventh-grade arithmetic paper on a percentage basis three times, at intervals of four weeks between ratings. The lack of consistency in scoring can be appreciated when it is mentioned that only one of the 49 students gave the same total score on all three trials and only seven gave the same total score on any two successive trials. The average variation between pairs of scores on successive trials was 8.1 points between the first and second trials, and 7.3 points between the second and third trials. These are *averages*. Many of the markers had considerably larger discrepancies.

In a similar study, another researcher [26] found that 28 experienced high-school English teachers differed widely, after an interval of two months, in their grading of an English composition which they believed was written by an eighth-grade pupil, but actually was part of a new and still unfamiliar standard composition scale. He found that 15 teachers who gave passing marks the first time failed the paper the second time, and that 11 teachers who gave failing marks the first time passed the paper the second time. Studies involving English composition are especially significant, because an essay examination is a series of compositions, and when English teachers who presumably have more than ordinary skill in this field can find only limited agreement both with others, and with themselves in a second trial, a more refined technique is called for.

A HALF-CENTURY OF DEVELOPMENT

We may conveniently take 1908 and the publication of Stone's arithmetic tests [27] as the advent of the modern achievement testing movement. The next ten years represented a period of slow but substantial development of printed, objectively scored, and standardized instruments for achievement testing in a number of subject areas. The major problems facing the early test-makers were not so much in theory and technique as in gaining a more favorable opinion among educators as to the value of standardized measuring instruments. The outlook of those early educational psychologists who championed the use of precise measurement in education was put forth by Thorndike in a now classic paper: [28]

> Whatever exists at all exists in some amount. To know it thoroughly involves knowing its quantity as well as its quality. Education is concerned with changes in human beings; a change is a difference between two conditions; each of these conditions is known to us only by the products produced by it—things made, words spoken, acts performed, and the like. To measure any of these

[25] E. J. Ashbaugh. Reducing the variability in teachers' marks. *Journal of Educational Research*, 1924, 9, pp. 185–198.

[26] C. E. Hulten. The personal element in teachers' marks. *Journal of Educational Research*, 1925, 12, pp. 49–55.

[27] Stone, 1908, *op. cit.*

[28] E. L. Thorndike. The nature, purposes, and general methods of measurements of educational products. *Seventeenth Yearbook of the National Society for the Study of Education, Part II*, 1918, p. 16.

products means to define its amount in some way so that competent persons will know how large it is, better than they would without measurement. To measure a product well means so to define its amount that competent persons will know how large it is, with some precision, and that this knowledge will be conveniently recorded and used.

Large-scale testing was first done in the City of New York Survey, 1911–1913, and then soon after by other large cities.[29] In 1915, the National Educational Research Association was founded. Among its constitutional goals was the "promotion of the practical use of educational measurement in all educational research" and, by 1918, a substantial bibliography of tests and test-oriented research had appeared.[30]

Monroe,[31] an effective promoter of educational research, saw 1920 as marking the "beginning of the widespread use of objective tests in American schools." By the end of the decade there were more than 1300 tests available for teachers and researchers.[32] At the same time, investigators became less concerned with stressing scoring objectivity and concentrated more on developing the wider range of item forms needed for tests of higher mental abilities. The true-false item form may have been objective, but usually it required little more than rote memorization on the part of the pupil. For educators interested in measuring abilities such as understanding, comprehension, and critical analysis, new types of items had to be developed and, for the first time, questions were raised as to the reliability and validity of the standard tests: Is this test a consistent measure of a student's knowledge of arithmetic, or will his score fluctuate greatly? Does this test adequately cover the subject matter presented by the teacher? Are the scores obtained in accord with the teacher's own judgments? New statistical methods and research techniques had to be designed to help answer such questions.

In the same decade, a number of textbooks were published which supplemented or replaced E. L. Thorndike's original *Introduction to the Theory of Mental and Social Measurements*.[33] At the same time, teachers were urged to construct their own achievement examinations for subject areas not covered by published and standardized tests. McCall[34] was among the first to suggest that classroom teachers employ the so-called "new-type" examination, and, in effect, that they should adopt the objective measurement principles of the professional. These were indeed days of consolidation, extension, and innovation in achievement testing.

With the thirties, educational measurement passed from adolescence into

[29] D. E. Scates. Fifty years of objective measurement and research in education. *Journal of Educational Research,* 1947, 41, pp. 241–264.

[30] E. Bryner. A selected bibliography of certain phases of educational measurement. *Seventeenth Yearbook of the National Society for the Study of Education, Part II,* 1918, pp. 161–190.

[31] W. S. Monroe. Educational measurement in 1920 and 1945. *Journal of Educational Research,* 1945, 38, pp. 334–340.

[32] W. W. Cook. Achievement tests. *Encyclopedia of Educational Research* (Rev. ed.). New York: The Macmillan Co., 1952, page 1461.

[33] New York: Bureau of Publications, Teachers College, Columbia University, 1904.

[34] W. A. McCall. A new kind of school examination. *Journal of Educational Research,* 1920, 1, pp. 33–46.

maturity.[35] The number of tests developed, standardized, and published increased tremendously. Organizations such as the Cooperative Test Service were established to supply, administer, and score achievement tests. By 1940, there were over 2600 achievement tests [36] available for all the traditional subject areas—reading, math, science, and language, as well as in the areas of health, commerce, aeronautics, and engineering.[37] Evidence that educational measurement was coming of age is seen in the extensive bibliographies of tests and scales that appeared in this decade; the outstanding volumes are listed in Buros' *Mental Measurements Yearbook* series [38] which offers timely catalogues of published tests with expert critiques and extensive research bibliographies. It is an invaluable reference.

Educational measurement specialists began to think differently in the thirties: In 1935 Lindquist, later to become one of the country's outstanding leaders in measurement, warned that "it is . . . important that the *limitations* of present measuring instruments be more adequately recognized. Even the best of the tests now being provided fall far short of measuring all of the desirable outcomes of instruction in any field of subject matter." [39] Similarly, reports of the famed Eight Year Study, under the auspices of the Progressive Education Association,[40] declared that educational measurement had overemphasized the testing of limited areas of knowledge and skills, excluding other important educational objectives. Tyler pointed out that educational objectives must ultimately be conceived of as changes in pupil behavior patterns and that adequate "evaluation" of pupil progress requires devices capable of measuring broad areas of learning. Accordingly, these investigators showed how assessment procedures could be developed to measure the attainment of such objectives as critical thinking, social sensitivity, aesthetic appreciation, and personal and social adjustment.

The so-called "evaluation movement," as exemplified in the work of Lindquist and Ralph Tyler, who also became highly prominent, had a profound influence on educational measurement. Not only did it point out that existing testing devices neglected traditionally significant realms of student behaviors, but it also led to more adequate assessment of higher mental processes, such as application and analysis, and broad areas of nonintellectual skills and learnings, such as interests and attitudes.

The Second World War, like the First, stimulated the further development of rigorous measurement practices, not only through the demands of military classification, but also because the war unified many research efforts under the auspices of the government. Construction of the College Entrance Examination Board examinations, which were first inaugurated

[35] W. S. Monroe. *Op. cit.,* p. 340.

[36] W. W. Cook. *Op. cit.,* p. 1461.

[37] A. D. Woodruff and M. W. Pritchard. Some trends in the development of psychological tests. *Educational and Psychological Measurement,* 1949, 9, pp. 105–108.

[38] O. K. Buros (Ed.) *The mental measurements yearbook.* Highland Park, New Jersey: Gryphon Press, 1938–1965.

[39] E. F. Lindquist. Cooperative achievement testing. *Journal of Educational Research,* 1935, 28, p. 519.

[40] E. R. Smith and R. W. Tyler. *Appraising and recording student progress.* New York: Harper & Brothers, 1942.

around the turn of the century, was taken over by the Educational Testing Service in 1947. ETS was responsible, in 1957, for the development of the Sequential Tests of Educational Progress (STEP), a "battery" of tests designed to measure achievement in several broad areas at various levels from Grade 4 through the sophomore year of college. This followed the tradition of the well-known Stanford Achievement Tests, Metropolitan Achievement Tests, Iowa Every Pupil Tests, and California Achievement Tests, which have, for years, been revised continually.

Since the Second World War, measurement experts have worked to increase the precision and usefulness of their instruments and to improve educational and psychological measurement theory. The momentum towards rigorously scientific methods was increased by the founding of two quarterly professional journals in the late thirties and early forties: *Psychometrika,* "devoted to the development of psychology as a quantitative rational science," and *Educational and Psychological Measurement,* "devoted to the development and application of measures of individual differences." In the late 1940's and the 1950's, many important books appeared which discussed testing theory and practice. A few of the more noteworthy are F. L. Goodenough's *Mental Testing, Its History, Principles, and Application,*[41] J. P. Guilford's *Psychometric Methods,*[42] Gulliksen's *Theory of Mental Tests,*[43] E. F. Lindquist's *Educational Measurement,*[44] and L. J. Cronbach and G. C. Gleser's *Psychological Tests and Personnel Decisions.*[45] A number of textbooks also appeared which were designed to introduce college students to educational and psychological testing, and to develop teacher's skills in the construction and use of classroom examinations.

The concerns of today's specialist in educational measurement are many. Continued efforts are being made to develop and standardize new and more efficient achievement tests, to carry on research concerned with their reliability and validity, and to develop new statistical procedures for use in test construction and data analysis. A recent review of research publications reveals a variety of endeavor: Test development, testing techniques, scoring problems, achievement tests as predictors, evaluative studies, characteristics of achievement tests revealed through factor analysis, and personality characteristics and achievement testing.[46] The concerns of educational achievement measurement are vast, and we hope that this account may add to your understanding of the subject.

[41] New York: Rinehart, 1949.

[42] (2nd Ed.) New York: McGraw-Hill, 1954.

[43] New York: Wiley, 1950.

[44] Washington: American Council on Education, 1951.

[45] Urbana: University of Illinois Press, 1957.

[46] J. C. Merwin and E. F. Gardner. Development and application of tests of educational achievement. *Review of Educational Research,* 1962, 32, pp. 40–50.

JOHN W. GARDNER

The Identification of Talent

Are there dangers in using tests to assess readiness for college? Are there better alternatives? Psychologist Gardner here presents a broad view of testing as a way of selecting students for greater opportunity. Why does he feel that objections to testing will not disappear as tests become better and better?

"My boy is something of a genius," said the Scarsdale commuter to his seat companion on the 5:26 P.M. train. He wasn't speaking metaphorically, he wasn't joking and he wasn't consciously boasting. He said it in a matter-of-fact way, as he might have said, "My boy has a pet hamster." After pausing long enough to let his companion express a decent interest, he went on to report the basis for his judgment—the very high scores his youngster had made on a scholastic aptitude test.

Geniuses used to be rare. Today, thanks to popular interpretation of test scores, every elementary or secondary school has its quota.

The chief instrument used in the search for talent is the standardized test. It would be surprising if the tests were not the object of considerable hostility. They have been. They are unpopular for a number of reasons.

Many people have an aversion to being the subject of mental diagnosis. In some this aversion to the tests is defensive: they fear precise appraisal of their own (or their children's) capacities. In others the aversion is simply a normal reaction to what they consider an invasion of privacy.

Many fear that the tests will be inaccurate—that they will come up with an appraisal of Johnny that isn't fair to Johnny's talents. The fact that the tests may have high statistical reliability and validity does not quiet this apprehension. A neighbor of mine, an investment banker, said, "They tell me the tests are right 95 per cent of the time, but suppose my Billy is in the remaining 5 per cent?"

Apprehension is fostered by the fact that it is very hard for those without professional training in psychology to understand the processes of mental measurement. No one wishes to be judged by a process he cannot comprehend.

To some degree, fear of the tests is a fear of the potentialities for social manipulation and control inherent in any large-scale processing of individuals. The tests bring vividly to mind the hazards of a society which deals with the individual as a statistic. The investment banker quoted earlier put it this way: "I just resist the idea that my boy's life can be changed by a mark made electronically on a slip of paper a thousand miles away by an anonymous person or machine, acting on criteria unknown to me, and using a measuring instrument I can't comprehend." In short, there is not only fear of the tests but fear of the unknown bureaucracy which handles the testing and acts on the results.

No one concerned with the future of testing can afford to ignore these sources of anxiety. On the other hand, even if these sources of concern were to disappear, the hostility toward the tests would probably remain. *The tests are designed to do an unpopular job.* An untutored observer listening to critics lash out at the imperfections of the tests might suppose that the criticisms would be stilled if the tests were perfected. Not at all. As the tests improve and become less vulnerable to present criticism, the hostility to them may actually increase. A proverbial phrase indicating complete rejection is, "I wouldn't like it even if it were good." With the tests, the more appropriate phrase might be, "I wouldn't like them *especially* if they were good."

As a matter of fact some of the tests are excellent even today—within the limits for which they were designed. The development of standardized tests is one of the great success stories in the objective study of human behavior. Anyone who understands the problems of mental measurement must be impressed with the technical achievement these instruments represent.

It is now objected that the tests give an advantage to the individual of good family background and place the individual of poor background at a disadvantage. This is true in some measure. But it must never be forgotten that the tests introduced an objectivity into the measurement of human abilities that never before existed. Before the tests were developed a great many people seriously believed that the less-educated segments of society were not *capable* of being educated. And the view is still prevalent in many societies.

An acquaintance of mine who recently visited a provincial school in France reported, "The teacher seemed to find it impossible to separate his judgment of a pupil's intelligence from his judgment of the pupil's cleanliness, good manners, neatness of dress and precision of speech. Needless to say, his students from the upper and upper middle social classes excelled in these qualities." Before the rise of objective tests American teachers were susceptible—at least in some degree—to the same social distortion of judgment. Against this background, modern methods of mental measurement hit the educational system like a fresh breeze. The tests couldn't see whether the youngster was in rags or in tweeds, and they couldn't hear the accents of the slum. The tests revealed intellectual gifts at every level of the population.

This is not to say that the tests completely eliminate unfair advantage for the young person of privileged social background. They do not. But they are more fair than any method previously used.

Anyone attacking the usefulness of the tests must suggest workable alternatives. It has been proved over and over again that the alternative methods of evaluating ability are subject to gross errors and capable of producing grave injustices. Whatever their faults, the tests have proven fairer and more reliable than any other method when they are used cautiously within the limits for which they were designed.

The best achievement and aptitude tests are remarkably effective in sorting out students according to their actual and potential performance in the classroom. But even in this context they are far from perfect, and any system of identification of talent which assumes them to be perfect will commit grave mistakes.

Of all mistakes made in using the tests, perhaps the worst are made in trying to apply the results beyond the strictly academic or intellectual performances for which the tests were designed. Such mistakes occur for quite understandable reasons. The scholastic aptitude and achievement tests are almost the only really effective tests we have. Everyone knows that there are other powerful ingredients in successful performance—attitudes, values, motives, non-academic talents—but we have no reliable way of measuring these other ingredients. The temptation is almost overwhelming to lean too heavily on the effective—but limited—measures we do possess.

This error produces grievous difficulties when we try to identify young people who will exhibit high performance in later life. Performance in later life places heavy emphasis on precisely those attributes not measured by scholastic aptitude and achievement tests. The youth who has these unmeasurable traits—e.g., zeal, judgment, staying power—to a high degree may not be identified in school as a person of high potential but may enjoy marked success in later life. Similarly, the young person extremely high on scholastic attributes which the tests can measure but lacking in other attributes required by success in life may prove to be a "morning glory."

Anyone who has spent his life around colleges can cite many examples of such apparent (but not necessarily real) shifts in potential. They are usually not nearly so perplexing as we pretend. Many years ago a talented youngster named Rennie D. was brought to my attention by his fond mother. Rennie was a gifted child of the most readily identifiable sort. He was extremely articulate, extremely quick in schoolwork. He was also lazy, self-indugent, flaccid and infantile in his emotions and personality; but these didn't interfere with his school performance. He was good-looking in a clean, open, pudgy way, and teachers loved him not only for his brightness but for his amiability. He sailed through school and college and graduated *magna cum laude*, as his mother assured me he would. But in the twenty years since then he hasn't done a blessed thing.

We like to say that this is puzzling, but in fact it is not. Scholastic aptitude is a central ingredient in school performance and Rennie had it to a high degree. But there are other crucial ingredients in adult performance and apparently he lacked them.

Fortunately, such cases are rare. The "early bloom, early fade" pattern is not common. Most youngsters who show early gifts bear out their promise in some measure. But Rennie is a vivid reminder that the tests were not designed to test success in life.

We now know enough about the tests to suggest rules for minimizing the hazards and maximizing the benefits of these instruments.

By all odds the most important rule is that the tests should not be the sole reliance in identifying talent. Judgments of the youngster's aptitudes and achievements should be based on many kinds of evidence. The tests are one kind of evidence. School grades are another kind. The teachers' written judgments of the student represent another kind of evidence. The judgments of deans, principals and counselors who have had dealings with the child may be useful. The important thing to be borne in mind is that every known measure of aptitudes and achievements has some failings. Only by drawing upon a considerable variety of evidence can we be certain that our judgment is well-rounded and fair to the young person.

An equally important rule is that diagnosis of the young person's aptitudes and achievements must be a continuing process. It is not enough to say that the child has been tested. Has he been tested lately? Has he been tested consistently over the years? We should no more accept a test score that is several years old than we would accept a health report that is several years old. It would be misleading to suggest that repeated testings must be made because we expect major variations in the youngster's aptitudes from year to year. The truth is that his aptitudes will probably remain pretty stable. But at any given age level, a test score may not be a precise reflection of his aptitude. The test used that year may not have been a good one. The score may have been inaccurately calculated. Or it may have been inaccurately recorded. The same requirement of repetition is relevant in the case of school grades and all the other measures on which a judgment is to be based. Any one of them may have been less than accurate in a particular year, and repeated appraisals correct such inaccuracies. And quite aside from inaccuracies in appraisal, the student himself may change from year to year—if not in aptitude then in achievement, in motivation and in many of the other dimensions on which judgments are necessarily based.

Still another important rule is that crucial judgments on the youngster's future should not be based entirely on intellectual gifts. We have pointed out that traits of personality and character are of central importance in the child's later performance. And there are many kinds of socially valuable talent—e.g., in art and music—which are not measured by the tests. All of these should carry due weight in any decisions which are made. This is so obvious that one might wonder why it needs to be mentioned—but the plain fact is that the easiest, laziest thing to do is to sort youngsters out by their scholastic aptitude scores and forget the complications. Teachers should not only combat this laziness; they should actively seek out other dimensions of talent, they should be constantly on the alert for the other attributes that promise to strengthen and guide performance in later life.

The sorting out of individuals in a society is an exceedingly serious business—and a potentially explosive one. No stone should be left unturned to insure that decisions are based on a wide range of evidence, carefully gathered and sifted. And precisely because the consequences for the individual are so serious, the final weighing of evidence, the final judgment that puts it all together, must be made by a qualified and responsible human being rather than by a machine. With all the rich evidence of human fallibility, with all the folk wisdom about human errors in judgment, people still insist that the final decisions concerning their fate be made by their fellow humans.

Diagnosis of an individual's future capacity to perform remains a hazardous undertaking. There are mysteries in individual development which we are far from understanding. Through repeated appraisals of the youngster at various ages, through the use of a variety of measures, through the pooling of many judgments, we are simply acknowledging the complexity of the subject and proceeding with the caution which that complexity dictates.

And it cannot be emphasized too often that the greatest enemy of such caution is the apparent simplicity and efficiency involved in assigning a single number to each youngster. The rapid and efficient handling of large numbers of individuals exerts tremendous pressure toward oversimplified diagnosis, toward the summation of individual attributes in a single index number and toward complete dependence on that number as a key to the individual's fate. Considerations of efficiency must not be allowed to falsify our diagnoses nor to narrow our conception of talent.

Chapter 8

The Interpretation and Application of Ability Tests

8-1

ARTHUR D. MORSE

The Search for Hidden Talent

8-2

ROBERT J. HAVIGHURST AND BERNICE J. NEUGARTEN

The School as a Sorting and Selecting Agency

ARTHUR D. MORSE

The Search for Hidden Talent

This article describes a social experiment aimed at uncovering talent that would otherwise be neglected. Morse discusses some of the academic and behavioral results of making one underprivileged urban high school the object of much special attention, in the form of extra counselors, talented teachers, and enrichment programs. What actual differences in the handling of students has the experiment brought into the school? What would be accomplished if an effort of this quality were expended on all schools?

A boy whom we will call Manuel is 17 years old. Born in Puerto Rico, he arrived in New York with his parents, his brother and sister during the tidal wave of immigration which brought more than 600,000 of his countrymen to the city.

Manuel lives in a dismal tenement crowded with relatives. His father no longer lives with the family and rarely contacts them. His mother has a low-salaried job. She can speak a little English but everyone speaks Spanish in the apartment. There is a television set but there are no books or English-language newspapers. There is no privacy.

The family life of his relatives unfolds before him. He sees and hears them as they love and as they squabble. Crowded conditions and life on the edge of poverty increase their tensions. Nothing is hidden.

For all that, Manuel is not a member of a gang. He has no weapons. He has never been in trouble with the police. He is a junior at George Washington High School. Contrary to the journalistic stereotype it is not a "blackboard jungle." Its 4,700 students, 40 percent of whom are Negroes or Puerto Ricans, respect the handsome colonial building and it 40-year tradition.

Last year Manuel passed every course. In spite of his environment he has achieved self-respect and he is liked by his classmates, whatever their color or family background. There is a good possibility that he will attend college.

Manuel is an example of the hidden talent uncovered by New York City's Demonstration Guidance Project. Its results have implications for all the underprivileged areas of the United States.

Launched in 1956 by the Board of Education's Commission on Integration, the project had as its objective "the early identification and stimulation of able students from low status socioeconomic homes."

It has been established that economically and socially privileged children score higher on intelligence tests than equally capable youngsters from culturally deprived homes. Conventional tests of mental ability are based on a pupil's facility with language and familiarity with the U.S. culture patterns. Most recently arrived Puerto Ricans are doomed automatically to low scores regardless of their actual potential. To a lesser but considerable extent this applies to Negroes who have moved from the South, and to whites from comparably underprivileged backgrounds.

The Demonstration Guidance Project sought to discover the abilities lying dormant beneath environmental poverty, to raise the students' and parents' aspirations and stimulate the most capable to seek higher education. In most cases the targets of this project were youngsters who normally would have quit high school at the age of 16 to seek employment. If successful the project would accomplish a vital mission—increase the Nation's pool of skilled manpower.

The project focused on two schools, Junior High School 43 and George Washington High School which enrolls most of its graduates.

Junior High School 43 is located at 129th Street and Amsterdam Avenue. With rare exceptions its student are from low-income families living in crowded, substandard housing. Only a small percentage live in the new low-cost apartments which tower above the tenements.

When the Demonstration Guidance Project began in 1956, a survey revealed that 48 percent of the school's 1,400 students were Negro, 38 percent were of Puerto Rican background, 2 percent of other Spanish-speaking origin, 11 percent were white and 1 percent were Orientals.

About one-third of the students' parents had been born in Puerto Rico, another third had migrated from the deep South. Of tragic consequence was the added fact that only half the children lived with both father and mother.

This environment had wreaked massive damage. Less than half of Forty-Three's graduates went on to complete high school. Fewer than 10 percent of the junior high school graduates continued their education beyond high school. This contrasts with the estimated 50 percent of U.S. high school graduates who receive some form of higher education.

There were other grim facts. The Junior High School 43 students attending George Washington High School presented disciplinary problems in disproportion to their numbers. They lagged far behind classmates from other neighborhoods in reading and arithmetic.

Today these figures have been reversed. A new picture of the potential of depressed populations has emerged from the experiment.

The dropout rate of project students attending George Washington High School has been cut in half. It is less than the rate for the school as a whole. The percentage of these graduates eligible for college has leaped from about 9 percent to 36 percent. IQ scores of the project youngsters have risen sharply. In an era of sensational journalism during which residents of the area have been charged with crimes of the most extreme brutality, discipline problems at school have virtually disappeared.

How did it happen?

When the Board of Education gave Junior High School 43 the go-ahead, Principal Dan Schreiber and Guidance Counselor Ethel Flanagan mobilized their forces for the attack on apathy. Three full-time counselors were hired reducing the ratio to 375 students per counselor in contrast to New York City's usual 2,000 to 1 ratio. A psychologist and social worker joined the staff part-time and two full-time remedial mathematics teachers were added to the remedial reading teachers already employed. Another teacher was recruited to supervise a large-scale cultural enrichment program.

Then the entire student body was tested. An intelligence test prepared by Science Research Associates, relying on pictures rather than words, sought to overcome the students' verbal handicaps. The results were encouraging. Slightly more than half the students scored 100 or more, a notable improvement over their conventional IQ scores. This, in combination with the verbal IQ and Stanford achievement tests in reading and arithmetic, past records and teacher evaluations furnished a profile of each student. Counselors combed these records to select the largest number of experimental students to be included in the project. Anyone who showed remote potential for college was to be chosen. Seven hundred seventeen seventh, eighth and ninth graders, more than half of the student body, were finally selected.

By traditional U.S. standards this was an unorthodox group of high potential students. Three hundred twenty-nine were retarded 1.3 years or more in reading; 341 lagged by 1.3 years or more in mathematics.

Disregarding these formidable odds a massive assault was launched simultaneously on all fronts to lift the level of the experimental 717.

Two remedial reading teachers met groups of six students for four periods a week. In addition the reading experts initiated a training program for teachers of language arts, social studies, mathematics and science. One day each month these teachers attended inservice training classes during unassigned periods. They were treated as pupils and during each session they learned a basic reading skill.

When they returned to their classes they spread the gospel by devoting 10 minutes of each period for 2 weeks to the development of that skill as it related to their own subject matter. In this manner a new basic reading skill was handed down to all classes every month. This supplemented the reading lessons for small groups of students which met four times each week.

Twenty-eight teachers enrolled in a speech improvement course and led another attack on an acute student problem. This paid immediate dividends among youngsters struggling to replace Spanish inflections with the New York version of the English language.

Seven months after the beginning of the Demonstration Guidance Project the effects of these programs were measured. Tests revealed that students receiving remedial reading assistance had registered a gain of 1.4 years in reading during the seven-month period. In one year *all* students gained more than a year and a half.

In mathematics the same procedure was followed. Two remedial mathematics teachers working with groups of six students four times a week also registered substantial gains.

Inseparably linked to this academic spurt was a guidance program which gave the students of Junior High School 43 a new look at themselves, their families and their career opportunities.

Each grade had its own counselor who met youngsters in individual sessions and in weekly group meetings. Concentrating on careers and career planning, the counselors shattered the students' belief that they were limited automatically by the occupations of their parents, by color and by the boundaries of neighborhood.

One of the counselors, Mrs. Susan Blakey, developed an effective technique to stimulate ambition. On charts listing requirements for professions and skilled occupations, she placed pictures of Negroes and Puerto Ricans as well as whites who had distinguished themselves in these fields. When a child indicated that a parent had discouraged him from pursuing a career because of color Mrs. Blakey, herself a Negro, would pack up her chart and visit the youngster's home.

In the beginning parents were somewhat loath to meet the counselors. For every 10 interviews requested by counselors during the first year there was only 1 proposed by a parent. Two years later 10 parents would request meetings for every 1 summoned by a counselor.

If parents could not meet counselors during working hours the appointments would be scheduled early in the morning or at night. One counselor had meetings with parents on 14 successive Sundays.

During the first year of the project counselors conducted over 2,000 individual interviews with the experimental students in addition to the weekly group guidance sessions. During this period there were over 800 contacts with parents.

The cultural enrichment program worked hand-in-hand with guidance. Many students of Forty-Three had never seen the world beyond their own drab, crowded streets. Suddenly that world was opened to them.

They visited art galleries, saw Broadway plays, heard symphony orchestras, were welcomed by great universities, attended performances at the Metropolitan Opera, were exposed to college spirit at football games and during campus visits.

And how did these youngsters from culturally barren homes respond?

Of a painting at the Museum of Modern Art: "When I looked at it, it made me feel warm and wonderful. It sort of picked me up and made me feel glad that I was living."

A symphony brought these comments: "I was very excited to hear a real symphony orchestra play for me . . . I thought it was going to be corny but it turned out to be fun . . . I don't think it's fair for a person to call someone a 'square' just because they like classical music . . . some of us didn't realize how much we liked this kind of music because we don't hear it often. I think he [the conductor] is a very nice and friendly and learned man."

Reporting on visits to Carnegie Hall one youngster wrote: "I like rock-n-roll but went to all [concerts]. Once I took my six-year-old cousin to Carnegie Hall with the school group. I had to watch her. She nudged me during the performance and said, 'Pretty, isn't it.' I have become interested in operas. I never went to an opera before, but now I will continue to go. Now, my parents, who have never gone to opera or concerts, have made plans to go."

In 1958, Junior High School 43 purchased 100 subscriptions to concerts of the New York Philharmonic, the largest number of tickets bought by a single school in the history of the orchestra. Although students who wished to attend could get free tickets by applying privately to their teachers, many paid a substantial share of the price.

This enrichment program was integrated with curriculum. One hundred seventh grade social studies students visited the Roosevelt Library and home at Hyde Park. For many it was the first trip outside the city. Ninth grade social studies classes attended the World Trade Fair at the New York Coliseum.

Top students interested in science and engineering toured the Sloan-Kettering Institute for Cancer Research and atomic energy facilities at the Brookhaven National Laboratory. Youngsters who had once felt unwelcome anywhere but in the back alleys of Harlem stood alongside engineering students in a Manhattan College laboratory and carried out experiments successfully.

Before each trip parents received a letter from Principal Schreiber explaining its purpose, outlining the preparatory work at school and the intended followup.

The cultural program within the school itself was expanded.

Films of 14 classics of English literature were rented and made available to all classes. Representatives of 10 foreign consulates presented songs, dances and travelogs at ninth grade assemblies. Capacity audiences watched professional theater groups perform in the school auditorium.

As the program unfolded and new horizons opened to the boys and girls of 129th Street, guidance counselors began to feel the full impact of their youngsters' problems.

There was a 12-year-old girl who cooked, cleaned, washed and ironed for her family and cared for three younger brothers and sisters. Tests revealed her as a student of high potential but worn out from her labors at home she was unable to do homework, barely stayed awake during class, failed in some courses. Guidance counselors described her capabilities to her working mother and helped to make arrangements lightening the child's burdens at home. Her scholastic average soared into the eighties.

Some problems seemed insurmountable. One father hurled his ambitious son's books out of the window when the boy brought them home for study. Junior High School 43 kept one classroom open after school so this youngster and others without privacy at home could work quietly.

Counselors made arrangements with parents in crowded apartments to turn television sets off between certain hours so students could complete homework and hammered out agreements with younger brothers and sisters to permit budding scholars to work without interruption.

The parents of these children were, for the most part, people of limited education struggling for survival in a strange environment. Yet with few exceptions they cooperated fully in the drive to lift the level of their children's aspirations.

In May 1957, eight months after the project began, 66.3 percent of the parents returned a questionnaire asking for their opinion of its effectiveness. Of these, 59.2 percent said it had helped their children but only 38.7 percent expressed an interest in seeing their youngster's counselor.

One year later the survey was repeated. This time 70.6 percent replied. Now 82.6 percent of the respondents said the project had helped their children and 84 percent were now interested in talking to the counselor.

This willingness to work with the school was reflected by attendance at parent meetings. Throughout New York City only 10 percent of junior high school parents attend daytime meetings but 23 percent of Forty-Three's parents met throughout the year to learn how they could contribute to the project's success.

The intellectual ferment at Forty-Three showed up in many ways. For one thing there was a 300 percent increase in the use of library books. In a "Readers Are Leaders" program, 118 students received buttons for completing at least 6 recommended books, 49 read at least 12. Pupils *purchased* more than 1,000 volumes through a school discount plan and each buyer received a personalized book plate to encourage the building of a personal library. An additional 800 volumes were sold at the annual Book Fair.

During the summer before the first experimental group moved up to George Washington High School, 36 students attended special classes in reading. In six weeks they gained seven months in average growth.

But the great test was still ahead. The high school had a proud tradition of scholarship and its Principal, Henry T. Hillson, did not intend to jeopardize its reputation. Hillson, a six-foot, five-and-a-half inch graduate of Dartmouth, was determined to give project students every possible opportunity but they were to make their way on achievement rather than sympathy. He was all for the cultural enrichment program but he believed that a solid academic groundwork was the essential prerequisite for college.

In September 1957, he looked at the records of the 148 experimental pupils from Forty-Three who had entered his school and he wondered if they could survive.

They had come a long way in that year at Forty-Three but they still had far to go. Eighty-nine percent were still below grade level in reading; 88 percent lagged in arithmetic. Tests revealed that they trailed their classmates from other neighborhoods in social studies background, correctness in writing, general vocabulary and quantitative thinking.

"Utterly ridiculous!" said some of the George Washington teachers, contemplating the newcomers. "They can't read, they can't write and they can't spell!"

Could one expect them to succeed in such a short time? They had been in the project only from September to June and now were to be thrust into high school. Perhaps future graduates of Forty-Three, bolstered by one and two extra years of the project, would make the grade but could one really expect success from the group entering in September 1957?

Having considered every reason why the experiment might fail Hillson hurled all the resources of his school into its success.

Project pupils were given double periods in English to narrow the greatest gap between themselves and more fortunate classmates.

Project classes were kept small. In mathematics and languages they were limited to 10–15 students. Students who showed potential but needed extra help were tutored in groups of three and four.

A psychiatric social worker and psychologist joined a team of guidance counselors intensifying the program begun at the junior high school. Weekly group guidance sessions focused on high school life, on college and on future occupations.

Results were so dramatic that they amazed even the counselors. One boy, of obvious high intelligence, concealed a desperate home situation by rebelliousness and erratic classwork. The joint efforts of teachers and counselors channeled the boy's energies into creative writing. One of his works has been selected for a national anthology, he has a better understanding of his home situation and his behavior has improved. In addition to passing all subjects he completed two advanced courses during the summer.

Trips to colleges continued to unlock hidden talents and unexpected enthusiasms. The dean of admissions of Amherst College invited high-ranking project boys to the college for a weekend. One of the boys, though a gifted student, had been withdrawn and uncommunicative. At Amherst, welcomed by students and faculty, shown about the lovely grounds, introduced to a wonderful world suddenly within reach, the boy began to talk freely. He still does!

In the 1958–59 term, project students at George Washington attended eight Broadway plays, the New York City Ballet, eight Philharmonic concerts and the Metropolitan Museum of Art. They toured the United States Military Academy and the Brookhaven National Laboratory. Perhaps the highlight of the year was the visit of 198 students to a performance of "A Midsummer Night's Dream" at the American Shakespeare Festival in Stratford, Conn.

The intensity of the counseling program had far-reaching effects. More than two-thirds of the students were interviewed 4 times or more during the first year, some as many as 20 times. Counselors acted as liaison between students and teachers. The teachers, fortified by information about the youngsters and their families, were better equipped to handle problems arising in class.

One boy, the youngest of 14 children, was inarticulate, withdrawn, forgotten at home. Buoyed by the counselors' interest in their son, proud of his newly discovered abilities, parental attitudes were changed. The boy ended the year with an 89 percent average and a brighter outlook on life.

At the end of the year, Principal Hillson added up the results. Of the 148 experimental pupils who had entered his school, 133 remained.

The number of students passing all academic courses was five times greater than among the group sent by Forty-Three the year before the project began. Eighteen project students averaged over 80 percent in all courses. Fourteen averaged 85 percent or over in English; 10 in mathematics; 14 in science and 23 in foreign languages. There was nothing comparable in the records of the earlier group.

Discipline problems of a serious nature had ended, a reversal of past history when graduates of Forty-Three had caused a disproportionate amount of trouble at George Washington.

A study of the social acceptance of project students at the high school conducted by the Board of Education's Bureau of Educational Research concluded that "after one year in high school, pupils involved in the Demonstration Guidance Project received general acceptance from other project students and from nonproject students. In no class were the project pupils, as a group, rejected."

The report went on to state that the pupils' images of themselves were no different than the self-images of the other youngsters.

As had been expected the project classes which entered George Washington in 1958 and 1959 are exceeding the performance of the original group. Even so, as many as 40 members of the original group may be eligible for college entrance in September 1960.

In May 1959, 105 project students took an advanced form of the same verbal IQ test they had taken in February 1956 (Pintner Test of General Ability). To those who cling to the belief that mental ability scores are unchanging the results are a revelation. Seventy-eight pupils showed an increase, 64 gaining more than 5 points; 25 showed a drop, 2 were identical.

Gains in reading ability were equally dramatic. When the project began, the experimental students lagged about 1½ years behind the national norm. *In 2½ years they had gained a full four years in reading growth* bringing them up to the national level.

Dropouts were cut in half.

As the senior class at George Washington approaches graduation its leadership includes several project students. Among contenders for top scholastic honors are three boys with averages of 95.3 percent, 94.7 percent and 93.4 percent.

An exhibit prepared by two of these youngsters won third prize in the New York City Science Fair. One of the winners, a shy boy who had not expected to go to college, was invited to participate in Columbia University's Science Honors Program. Other project students take part in athletics, social committeees and help to staff the school newspaper.

"The most dramatic fact about this project," says Henry Hillson, the realist who insisted on academic performance, "is that we can salvage a great number of boys and girls who would otherwise be lost. Many of these youngsters will not be able to attend college but if we make it possible for them to finish high school successfully they'll be on the way to becoming self-respecting citizens and assets to this community."

ROBERT J. HAVIGHURST and BERNICE J. NEUGARTEN

The School as a Sorting and Selecting Agency

Havighurst and Neugarten present evidence of how the life of the school, its groupings, honors, social life, favor the upper- and middle-class students. The authors believe that no innate intellectual differences exist (on the average) among social classes and races, but plans for grouping tend to discriminate against students from poorer homes. How can such knowledge as is presented here help the teacher to work with students from different backgrounds?

Since the landing of the pilgrims in Massachusetts more than three hundred years ago, America has been a land of opportunity. The people who came to these shores were poor; many had been victims of political oppression or religious persecution in the countries of their birth. What they wanted was freedom to live according to their personal convictions and opportunity to build a good life. "In the United States you can raise yourself up," they said. So the oppressed and the poor from the countries of Europe came to America, and later similar people came from East Asia and Latin America.

Their faith in the new country was justified. During the eighteenth and nineteenth centuries there was good land to be had at low prices, and there were jobs available in the expanding economy. New cities were being built and new industries were being established, providing work for these newcomers. A young man could start with no capital and become a wealthy merchant, banker, factory owner, or farmer.

Then the good free land gave out and the frontier society disappeared. Since 1900 the areas of economic opportunity in America have shifted to expanding industry and to the expanding technical and service professions.

Today we no longer witness the amassing of great private fortunes, as in the nineteenth century. Yet the evidence points to the over-all existence of as much economic opportunity in this country today as there was a century ago. Opportunities now lie in different areas and are fulfilled by different means. In the technical and service professions there has been an enormous increase in numbers since 1900, an increase that far exceeds the increase in population. For instance, the number of engineers doubled in just the ten years from 1940 to 1950, while the numbers of industrial research workers and chemists increased by 50 per cent during the same period.

Robert J. Havighurst and Bernice J. Neugarten, "The School as a Sorting and Selecting Agency," Chapter 9 in *Society and Education,* 2nd ed. (Boston: Allyn and Bacon, 1962), pp. 227–48. Reprinted with permission.

These increases continued during the 1950 to 1960 decade, a period in which the demand for teachers increased tremendously due to the rapid rise in school enrollments. Industry and trade have also expanded more rapidly than the population, thus creating a greater proportion of executive positions than existed in earlier generations. These are middle-class occupations, and children of middle-class families tend to enter them. At the same time, the numbers of these positions have increased so rapidly that there are not

The educational system as a selecting agency

enough children born in middle-class families to fill them. Consequently some of these positions must be filled by youth from lower-status levels.

These occupations require higher education. The professions all require at least a college degree, and executive positions in business and industry are awarded more and more to young men and women who have graduated from college. One recent study showed, for instance, that 57 per cent of business executives were college graduates in 1952, as compared with 32 per cent in 1928 (Warner and Abegglen, 1955).

A recent study by Anderson (1961) demonstrates the need for caution in assuming that upward mobility is closely dependent upon formal schooling. Comparisons based on educational levels and occupational levels attained by fathers and their sons showed that mobility independent of schooling occurred at a high rate in recent decades in Sweden, England, and the United States. The implication is that intelligence and motivation are also important factors which, to some extent at least, operate independently of formal schooling. Nevertheless, education is probably more closely related to mobility in the United States than in other countries; and on the whole, it is probably true that the school provides the best single channel through which ability and motivation can be demonstrated across the population of boys and girls. Thus education has become the principal avenue of opportunity in twentieth-century America: college education for upper-middle-class occupations, and high-school education for such lower-middle-class occupations as clerical work, sales work, and skilled technical work. Realizing that the avenue of opportunity is provided by the educational system, parents have encouraged their children to go further and further in school and college. Since 1890 the proportion of young people attending high school has multiplied elevenfold, while the proportion attending college has multiplied sevenfold. Table 1 (page 169) shows the increase in high school and college attendance since 1910.

Amount of education has now become a good indicator of socioeconomic status, from lower-lower up through upper-middle class, for education leads to economic opportunity. Young people, through education, secure higher-status jobs than their fathers had. With greater incomes, young adults from lower-status families tend to associate with persons of higher status and learn and adopt their ways. We may conclude, consequently, that education provides the channel not only to better socioeconomic status, but also to social mobility in the broader sense.

The American educational system provides opportunity for social and economic mobility by selecting and training the most able and industrious youth for the higher-status positions in society. Insofar as the school system does this job efficiently and fairly, it equips youth to be qualified for career opportunity and contributes to the success of democracy.

The degree of selection can be observed in Table 1, which shows the number of boys and girls out of a thousand born in a given year who reach various levels of the educational ladder. It will be seen that the high school is much less selective than it was forty or fifty years ago, but that the college, while graduating increasing numbers, still operates as a highly selective agency. The process of selection is not carried on in a formal sense by the school alone. Several factors determine how far a boy or girl goes in school: the parents' wishes, the individual's aspirations and ability, the financial status of the family, as well as the school's system of encouraging some students and discouraging others. The end result, however, is selection, with the school playing a major part in the process.

One may ask whether or not the educational system does an efficient and fair job of selecting able and industrious youth. This is not an easy question to answer, because it is not easy to determine who are the ablest and most industrious youth. The ablest in terms of intellectual ability (at least in terms of IQ) can be discovered more easily than the most industrious. Intelligence tests are fairly good measures of intellectual ability, even though they do not measure artistic, musical, or social leadership ability. Furthermore, the ordinary "paper-and-pencil" test of intelligence probably underestimates the abilities of lower-class youth, a point we shall return to presently.

TABLE 1

Change in the American educational system as a selecting agency

Number out of every thousand of a given age who reach a given educational level	YEAR *1910*	*1938*	*1960 (estimates)*
First year high school (age 14)	310	800	930
Third year high school (age 16)	160	580	760
Graduation from high school (age 18)	93	450	630
Entrance to college or a similar educational institution	67	150	340
Graduation from college (Bachelor's degree)	22	70	170
Master's degree	1.5	9	34
Doctor of Philosophy degree	0.2	1.3	4.3

With these qualifications, we may consider the question, How well does the educational system select and carry along the ablest youth? The answer is that the abler youth in general go farther in school and college, but a considerable proportion of able youth do not enter college, and some do not even finish high school.

INTELLECTUAL ABILITY

Most of the boys and girls who drop out of school are below average in academic ability, but a considerable proportion are above average. Table 2 shows the IQ distribution of those who dropped out of school before high school graduation in the class of 1958 in River City, a midwestern city of 45,000 population. About 5 per cent of the dropouts were in the top quarter of intelligence, while 40 per cent were in the bottom quarter. These data, although they come from one particular city, confirm the findings from earlier studies of school dropouts made by Hecker (1953) and by Dillon (1949) in several north central states. These studies showed that about 5 per cent of the dropouts were in the top fifth in intelligence, while about 33 per cent were in the bottom fifth.

Table 2 also illustrates the general tendency for youth of higher ability to stay longest in school and college. However, many youth of average ability also finish high school and enter college, as is seen in Table 3. The

TABLE 2

Intelligence and social class in relation to progress through school in River City

	BOYS			GIRLS		
	College and post-high school	*High school graduation only*	*High school dropout*	*College and post-high school*	*High school graduation only*	*High school dropout*
INTELLIGENCE QUOTIENT:						
IV (high)	27	13	4	36	23	3
III	22	17	18	18	24	12
II	7	25	25	3	26	27
I	3	15	37	4	17	26
SOCIAL CLASS:						
Upper and upper-middle	15	4	1	18	2	1
Lower-middle	27	22	9	22	28	10
Upper-lower	15	25	38	20	46	23
Lower-lower	2	19	36	1	14	34
Total number	59	70	84	61	90	68

TABLE 3

Amount of education in relation to intelligence

	Percentage in each IQ group achieving a given educational level in the U.S.A. (1955)			
Intelligence quotient	*Enter high school*	*Graduate from high school*	*Enter college*	*Graduate from college*
125+	99	97	50	44
115–124	98	91	40	29
105–114	94	81	30	17
95–104	85	61	18	6
85–94	70	38	8	1
84–	45	14	2	0

SOURCE: Wolfle, 1954, pp. 312–13 (adapted).

percentages given in Table 3 are estimates based upon findings from a number of studies made in various parts of the country (Wolfle, 1954).

A more recent set of estimates is that published by the National Science Foundation (1961): In terms of intellectual ability, presumably the top 30 per cent of young men and women are qualified for college work. Of young *men* in this ability range, 45 of every 100 now graduate from college.

Of the remaining 55, 22 enter college but do not finish; 22 finish high school, but do not enter college; and 11 do not even finish high school.

These proportions are considerably different for women. Of young women in the top 30 per cent of ability, 30 graduate from college. Of the remaining 70, 20 enter college but do not finish; 40 finish high school but do not enter college; and 10 do not even finish high school.

For the two sexes combined, then, approximately 60 per cent in this ability range enter college, and close to 40 per cent earn B.A. degrees or more.

INTELLECTUAL ABILITY AND SOCIAL STATUS

Although ability alone is a major factor in determining level of education, the general picture is greatly modified when we consider the additional factor of social status. Youth from upper-middle-class families are likely to go to college even though they have only average ability, while youth from lower-class families have less chance of entering college, even when they have high ability. It is clear that social class as well as intelligence determines who shall finish high school and who shall go to college.

Table 4 is based on information from a number of different studies concerning the educational experience and social status of boys and girls who are in the upper quarter of the population in intellectual ability, those with IQ's of 110 or above. Under the conditions existing in 1960, about 45 per cent of the ablest quarter of youth completed a four-year college program,[1] while about five per cent of these able youth did not finish high school.

It is clear that the educational system selects and carries along most of the ablest youth of upper and upper-middle status, but that able youth of working-class status (upper-lower and lower-lower classes) tend to stop their formal education at the end of high school. The reasons for this lie partly in the inability of most lower-class youth to pay for a college education, and partly in the lack of motivation of most lower-class youth for higher education. This lack of motivation is illustrated in the following statement made in an interview by Kenneth Walters, a filling station attendant. Kenneth was doing quite well in school when, a few months before his sixteenth birthday, he quit school and went to work. Ten years later, he was asked by an interviewer why he had not continued. He answered:

> Well, there was quite a few of us. At the time I quit school there was five of us children at home. My mother and father never got along very well. They broke up and, well, my brother and I quit school and went to work. We kept our two sisters going to school. But at that time—I'll be honest with you—it didn't make me very mad, because I didn't like school very well anyway. I was kind of fickle about the whole thing. 'Course now being a little older, I wouldn't mind going a little further. One funny thing—the same year I quit school I went to work up at the mill and that summer my grammar-school principal—he was a very nice fellow—well, he worked up at the mill too. So there was

[1] This estimate is consistent with that of the National Science Foundation; of the upper *30 per cent* in ability, approximately 40 per cent complete college.

me, the dumbbell, and him just as high as you can go, I guess, in education—both of us working at the mill. As a matter of fact I think I was makin' a little more than he was. He was just up there for the summer months you know. So he gets all that education—all filled up—and for what?

TABLE 4

Level of education in relation to social status of youth in the upper quarter of intellectual ability

Social status	*Composition of group* %	*Do not finish high school* %	*High school graduate; do not enter college* %	*Enter college but do not finish* %	*Complete a 4-year college program* %
Upper and Upper-middle	20	0	2	3	15
Lower-middle	40	2	14	5	19
Upper-lower and Lower-lower	40	4	20	5	11
Totals	100	6	36	13	45

Not all lower-class youth share Kenneth's attitudes, of course. Donald Borgeson, for instance, son of a janitor, was a boy who took readily to school. He was a favorite of his teachers because of his earnestness and his obvious gratitude for what the school gave him. While Donald was in high school, he and his classmates answered a question which read as follows, "What is the best thing that could happen to you?" Donald wrote: "The best thing is that somehow I should be able to go to college and to enter the profession I have in mind." After his military service Donald obtained a scholarship to go through college, and by his good work in college he won a sizable fellowship for graduate study.

. . . At this point in summarizing the facts it is clear that the educational system does tend to select and retain the more able pupils, but that it operates much less effectively in this respect with children from the lower social classes than with children from the upper-middle and upper classes.

INTELLIGENCE IN RELATION TO SOCIAL CLASS AND COLOR

The function of the school as a sorting and selecting agency would be easier to carry out if there were a close relationship between intellectual ability and social status, or between intellectual ability and ethnicity or skin color. Until recently some social scientists believed that there was an inborn intellectual inferiority in people of lower-class status and in people of non-white skin color. White people developed the idea that whites had the highest innate intelligence and that other races followed in the order of their departure from white color, with the blackest-skinned Negroes lowest in the scale of intelligence. This idea was supported by some of the earlier intelligence test studies, in which it was found that American Negro children scored lower than American white children, with children of mixed white and Negro parentage scoring between the two groups.

However, more critical studies of intelligence testing (Eells *et al.*, 1951) have shown that the ordinary intelligence tests favor children whose parents are of middle- or upper-class status. The problems in the tests are ones for which life in an upper-class or middle-class home give superior preparation. For example, in the following test item,

> A symphony is to a composer as a book is to what?
> ( ) paper ( ) sculptor ( ) author ( ) musician ( ) man

the problem is probably easier for middle-class children. They are more likely to have heard their parents talking about symphonies than are working-class children.

On the other hand, the following item is probably as difficult for high- as for low-status children:

> A baker goes with bread the same way as a carpenter goes with what?
> ( ) a saw ( ) a house ( ) a spoon ( ) a nail ( ) a man

The ordinary intelligence test contains many items of the first type. As a consequence, the test, by bringing in words that are less familiar to lower-class than to middle-class children, tends to penalize the lower-class child.

Furthermore, children of upper- and middle-class families are more often pushed by their families to do good work in school than are the children of lower-class families. School training itself helps one to do well in most intelligence tests. Therefore it is now thought that the differences in intelligence test performance between Negro and white children are mainly due to the fact that more Negro children are lower-class. When middle-class Negro children are given intelligence tests, they do about as well as middle-class white children.

Most anthropologists and psychologists now believe that there is no innate difference in intelligence between racial or ethnic or religious groups. There are innate differences between individuals within these groups, but the average intelligence of the groups is the same, it is thought, if the groups have equal opportunity and similar training in solving the ordinary problems of life. These conclusions are summed up in a statement issued in 1950 on behalf of UNESCO (the United Nations Educational, Scientific and Cultural Organization) by a committee of psychologists and anthropologists from seven countries, entitled "The Scientific Basis for Human Unity." One paragraph of their summary reads as follows:

> According to present knowledge, there is no proof that the groups of mankind differ in their innate mental characteristics, whether in respect of intelligence or temperament. The scientific evidence indicates that the range of mental capacities in all ethnic groups is much the same (*UNESCO Courier,* 1950, p. 1).

Such group differences as are actually found in studies based on intelligence tests are believed to result from several factors—differences in experience with the particular types of problems that make up the tests, differences in motivation to do one's best on the tests, and possibly differences in experience during the pre-school years.

SOCIAL CLASS AND THE SCHOOL PROGRAM

When the school system is viewed as a selecting and sorting agency, it becomes apparent that the sorting is done with respect to two quite different characteristics: (1) the child's ability and (2) his social class background. The educational system tends to treat children of high ability differently from those of low ability and keeps those of high ability in school for a longer period. At the same time, the system tends to keep children of higher social status in school for a longer period of time while allowing many of lower status, including some of high ability, to drop out early. This differential treatment in relation to social class is not intentional on the part of most school systems, but results primarily from the cultural differences between social classes.

The actual operation of these two selective factors is seen more clearly by looking at the school curriculum and the methods used by schools in grouping children.

In many elementary schools where there is more than one classroom per grade there is a sectioning system known as "homogeneous grouping," whereby pupils of the same general academic level are supposed to be grouped together. This is aimed at facilitating the work of the teacher, who can then expect all her pupils to do work at about the same level. Whenever there is "homogeneous grouping" in a school that draws from a socially diverse population, however, the groups tend to become homogeneous for social class as well as homogeneous for mental ability. In Old City, a small city in the Deep South, such a system is operative. Each grade is divided into three sections: A, B, and C.

> This division into sections pervades the whole school system but of necessity it has less formal characteristics in the later years of high school. The junior high-school principal says of these sections:
>
> "When a child enters school he is put into one of three sections according to what the teacher thinks his ability is. When you have dealt with children much you soon find that you can pretty well separate them into three groups according to ability. Then if a child shows more ability he may be shifted into a higher group or if he fails he may be moved into a lower group."
>
> Sometime later when this same principal was asked whether there seemed to be any class distinctions between the sections, he answered:
>
> "There is to some extent. You generally find that children from the best families do the best work. That is not always true but usually it is so. The children from the lower class seem to be not as capable as the others. I think it is to some extent inheritance. The others come from people who are capable and educated, and also the environment probably has a great effect. They come to school with a lot of knowledge already that the others lack."
>
> Whatever one may think of this principal's theory in explanation of the correlation between social position and school section, this correlation holds true.

There is a strong relationship between social status and rank in school. An analysis of the classes of three years (in the junior high school for white children) in which the social position of 103 girls was known, shows that

(1) of the ten upper-class girls eight were in section A, one in B, and one in C

(2) of the seven upper-middle-class girls, six were in section A and one in B

(3) of the thirty-three girls from lower-middle and indeterminate middle class, twenty-one were in section A, ten in section B, and two in section C

(4) of the fifty-three lower-class girls, only six were in section A, twenty-eight in section B, and nineteen in section C.

A teacher in junior high school was willing and able to talk more explicitly about these sections than was the principal quoted above. This teacher was asked if there was "much class feeling in the school" and she said:

"Oh, yes, there is a lot of that. We try not to have it as much as we can but of course we can't help it. Now, for instance, even in the sections we have, it is evident. Sections are supposed to be made up just on the basis of records in school, but it isn't and everybody knows it isn't. I know right in my own A section I have children who ought to be in B section, but they are little socialites and so they stay in A. I don't say there are children in B who should be in A but in the A section there are some who shouldn't be there. We have discussed it in faculty meetings but nothing is ever done."

Later on, she said,

"Of course, we do some shifting around. There are some borderliners who were shifted up to make the sections more nearly even. But the socialities who aren't keeping up their standard in the A section were never taken into B or C section and they never will. They don't belong there socially. Of course, there are some girls in A section who don't belong there socially, but almost everyone of the socialites is in A.[2]

This procedure of taking social status informally into account when grouping children according to intellectual ability is not limited to any one section of the country. The school staff is often under pressure from upper- and upper-middle-class parents to keep their children out of the slower-learning sections, and the school personnel, in the example just quoted, are often in agreement with parents on such points. On the other hand, many school principals and teachers are very careful to avoid favoring children of higher-status families.

The pattern of grouping children varies from community to community. Small schools with only one classroom per grade do not, of course, group children except by age. In some schools, ability groups are formed only in particular subject-matter areas, as when those children in a grade who are poor in reading, or those who are particularly good in science, are given special instruction as a group. In such schools, the child may spend only one period a day with a "special" group; the rest of the time, with his

[2] From *Who Shall Be Educated?*, pp. 73–74, by W. Lloyd Warner *et al.* Copyright 1944 by Harper & Brothers. Reprinted by permission of Harper & Row, Publishers, Incorporated.

regular and heterogeneous grade group. This modification of "homogeneous grouping" tends to counteract the possible social-class biases that may operate in school systems, such as Old City.

To take another example, schools in homogeneous parts of a large city, where the school population is drawn from one or two social classes, may use a scheme of sectioning by ability that brings together those children with the most motivation for education. The children who consistently work hard often seem to teachers to be the abler ones and will tend to be grouped together.

In a large city (while there are many exceptions) there is a tendency for boys and girls of a given social level to be found together in elementary school because the area around the school tends to be homogeneous as to social class. The districts from which the city high school draws students, on the other hand, are likely to be quite heterogeneous in population.

In the 1960's, with increasing national attention being given to the identification and utilization of talent, there is probably an over-all decrease in the extent to which social status influences homogeneous groupings in school. Teachers and administrators are increasingly sensitive to the need for selecting able students, no matter what their social backgrounds may be, and of placing them in "accelerated" or "honors" sections. Nevertheless, it continues to be true that by far the highest proportions of children and adolescents in such accelerated groups are from middle- rather than working-class families.

SCHOOL CURRICULA

In the high school there appears a new basis for grouping pupils: by type of curriculum. The typical American high school is of the "comprehensive" type, with several different curricula or courses of study. There is the college preparatory curriculum; the commercial; the vocational, which may include agricultural and home-economics programs; and the "general" curriculum for those whose vocational aim is not clear and whose ability is not high enough to warrant entrance to the college preparatory program. (The general curriculum does not usually include mathematics or a foreign language, and thus differs from the college preparatory.)

The several curricula tend to draw differentially from the social classes, with the college preparatory curriculum enrolling higher-status pupils and the general and vocational curricula those of lower status. For example, Table 5 shows how social class was related to curriculum in two midwestern high schools, Elmtown and Rivertown (Hollingshead, 1949; Dupre, 1958). This table shows that the college preparatory curriculum is chosen by boys and girls of all the social classes with the possible exception of the lower-lower. The comercial and general curricula, on the other hand, enroll very few youth of upper and upper-middle classes.

It is likely that the college preparatory curriculum is selected by lower-status youth who are headed for upward social mobility, since completion of this curriculum leads, typically, to college attendance and preparation for a middle-class occupation. The commercial curriculum is also good mobility preparation for certain lower-class youth and many use it for that purpose. Similarly, the vocational curriculum may provide a lower-class boy with an entry into a skilled trade that will later gain him lower-middle status.

TABLE 5

Choice of high school curriculum in relation to social class (shown in per cent)

	Type of curriculum					
	COLLEGE PREPARATORY		COMMERCIAL		GENERAL	
Social class	*Elm-town* [a]	*River-town* [b]	*Elm-town*	*River-town*	*Elm-town*	*River-town*
Upper and Upper-middle	6	13	0.3	0	3	1
Lower-middle	10	16	8	11	19	13
Upper-lower	4	10	15	11	27	14
Lower-lower	0.5	7	3	2	4	2
Total	20.5	46	26.3	24	53	30

[a] The Elmtown sample, studied in 1941, consists of all four high school grades, 390 pupils in all. The designations of the social classes of Elmtown as "upper," "upper-middle," and so on, are those of the present authors.

[b] The Rivertown sample, studied in 1951, includes 88 cases and consists of Juniors and Seniors only. Most lower-lower pupils have dropped out of school, leaving only the ones who are likely to be upwardly mobile.

SOURCE: Hollingshead, 1949, p. 462, Table X (adapted); and Dupre, 1958 (adapted).

The way the several curricula are viewed by students is illustrated by the following passage taken from *Elmtown's Youth,* in which "Class I" refers to the class of highest status in Elmtown, and "Class V," to the class of lowest status.

> A senior girl summarized the prevailing views of the college preparatory students when she said:
>
> "If you take a college preparatory course, you're better than those who take a general course. Those who take a general course are neither here nor there. If you take a commercial course, you don't rate. It's a funny thing, those who take college preparatory set themselves up as better than the other kids. Those that take the college preparatory course run the place. I remember when I was a freshman, my mother wanted me to take home economics, but I didn't want to. I knew I couldn't rate. You could take typing and shorthand and still rate, but if you took a straight commercial course, you couldn't rate. You see, you're rated by the teachers according to the course you take. They rate you in the first 6 weeks. The teachers type you in a small school and you're made in classes before you get there. College preparatory kids get good grades and the others take what's left. The teachers get together and talk, and if you are not in college preparatory you haven't got a chance."

The students may reflect the attitudes held generally by the teachers, but we believe that the favorable prestige assigned to the college preparatory course is connected functionally with the fact that the majority of Class II youngsters were enrolled in it. If a person wants to "rate," especially among the girls, it is wise to enroll in the college preparatory course. The following interview materials indicate how the process works.

Alice White (Class III) and Nellie Anderson (Class IV) were clique mates in Central School during the seventh and eighth grades. During the summer following their graduation from grammar school, they informally planned their high school years. Alice's father and mother expected her to go to high school, then on to college, so she had no other idea than to enter the college preparatory course. Nellie's father had deserted the family the spring she finished the seventh grade, leaving her mother with Nellie and two smaller children. Although Mrs. Anderson did not consider it necessary for Nellie to attend high school, she did not wish to violate the law; so she started her, telling Nellie many times of sacrifices necessary to send her to school "now that Daddy has run away." Nellie's mother wanted her to take the secretarial course so she could "get a job" when she was old enough to quit school.

On the first day of the fall semester, Nellie went to Alice's house and the two girls started to school together. On the way, they met Anne Parker (Class III), a third clique mate, whose mother had told her to be sure to take home economics. Anne, however, wanted to enroll in college preparatory because most of her girl friends intended to. The three girls discussed the situation on the way to school and decided that all three would enroll in the college preparatory course.

That evening Alice reported to her parents what she had done and her father commented, "Fine! Now I expect you to work hard on Latin and algebra. The rest will be easy." Her mother was happy until Alice told about the girls' discussion on the way to school. Then she exclaimed:

"I don't think Anne's mother realizes the girls in the home economics course are looked down upon by the girls from the better families. Alice, you did wrong in getting Nellie to sign up for the college preparatory course. Her mother can't send her to college, and the poor girl will be snubbed by the other girls in there. Why can't you ever learn you can't manage the lives of other people? Water will seek its level. Let Nellie take the secretarial course and go her way."

Anne's mother objected to her enrollment in the college preparatory course, but let her continue it with the comment, "If you do real well in your studies, your father may help you go to college, but it will be hard for us."

Nellie's mother was explosively angry with Nellie and with the high school authorities for allowing Nellie to enroll in the college preparatory course. She immediately told Nellie that she must change to the secretarial course. Nellie cried most of the night, but her mother went to school the next morning and changed Nellie's course herself. Nellie continued in school for a year and a half, but dropped out of her old clique, and then left school to work in the "dime" store.

Because the academic teachers believe that college preparatory students have more ability, are more interested, and do better work than those in the general course, they prefer to teach the former group. Although these contentions may be true, more probably teachers of the college preparatory group satisfy their desire to see the students reflect the academic values they hold. These teachers look upon students in the general course as persons who have nothing better to do with their time, are mediocre in ability, lack motivation and interest.[3]

CHOICE OF SECONDARY SCHOOL

In large city school systems, high schools themselves are often of various types (as differentiated from comprehensive high schools in which several curricula are offered within the same school building). Usually there are the "academic" or "general" high schools, and the "trade" or technical schools, each of which in turn may be public, parochial, or private.

A recent study of white eighth-grade graduates in St. Louis concerned the relationships between choice of secondary school, academic ability, and socioeconomic status of the child's family. Increases were found in both average socioeconomic and ability scores for both boys and girls, starting with those who did not attend any high school, and followed in order by those who attended public technical, public and parochial general, private parochial, and other private high schools. For both sexes, socioeconomic status was found to be a more important factor in the choice of secondary school than was academic ability. The author concludes:

> In view of the fact that the several types of secondary schools in St. Louis place a varying emphasis on college preparation and tend to direct their pupils into certain occupational levels, the findings of this study are significant in that they indicate a definite limitation on the role of education in promoting social mobility. Although it is not possible to generalize from the findings in one community, and although the specific pattern of school types may vary for other cities, there is reason to believe that similar relationships exist elsewhere (Pohlmann, 1956, pp. 396–397).

SCHOOL REWARDS

The grades or marks secured by pupils also reflect social class differences, as has been found in a number of studies in Elmtown and elsewhere. For example, a study of six junior high schools in eastern states is reported in Table 6, where it is seen that the grades awarded to pupils are closely related to their social class positions (Abrahamson, 1952). Similarly, in a study of eight different high schools in California, a much higher proportion of students in the middle-class schools obtained "A's" and "B's" than did those in the working-class schools (Wilson, 1959). This is not to say that teachers necessarily show favoritism to upper-status pupils. The study habits, the educational motivation, and the scholastic intelligence of the higher-status pupils are likely to be superior to those of lower-status pupils,

[3] Reprinted with permission from A. B. Hollingshead, *Elmtown's Youth*, 1949, John Wiley & Sons, Inc.

on the average. Neither does the relationship between school grades and social class position hold true equally in all communities. As Udry (1960) found, this relationship is less likely to appear in a new community where social class lines are less recognizable or have had less chance to crystallize; or in a school where teachers are particularly sensitive to social class differences and have learned how to minimize their own biases in this respect in evaluating students' performance.

TABLE 6

Academic marks received by junior high school students according to social class

Social class	Academic marks A	B	C	D	E
Upper-middle					
Received	135	208	84	17	2
Expected [a]	59	157	155	62	13
Lower-middle					
Received	206	444	330	103	15
Expected	145	386	382	153	32
Upper-lower					
Received	54	370	519	202	34
Expected	156	414	410	164	34
Lower-lower					
Received	6	42	121	99	37
Expected	40	107	106	42	9

[a] This number is the one that would be expected if the grades were distributed proportionately to the numbers of pupils in each social class.
SOURCE: Abrahamson, 1952 (adapted).

School grades themselves may be seen as a form of reward and punishment, but lower-status youth also get more direct forms of punishment, as is indicated in Table 7. The teachers in Elmtown were required to file a report in the principal's office every time they had a discussion with parents, and to say whether the parents were counseled about the work or about discipline of the child. This table shows that most of the counseling about discipline was with parents of lower-status children (Hollingshead, 1949, p. 179).

EXTRACURRICULAR ACTIVITIES

The extracurricular activities of the school provide opportunity for boys and girls to learn social skills, to practice leadership, and to develop a competence in music, dramatics, and speech. These activities, which are especially valuable for lower-status youth who are upwardly mobile, also provide good training for careers and interests that characterize the pursuits of the middle class.

There are large social-class differences in participation in extracurricular activities. For example, in the previously mentioned study of six junior high schools in eastern states it was found that middle-class boys and girls held many more offices and participated more often in extracurricular activities than did working-class boys and girls. In three of the schools where American Legion awards were made, fourteen out of eight winners were upper-middle class and the remaining four were lower-middle.

TABLE 7

Nature of counseling by teacher with parents in Elmtown high school

Social class	*Number of times parents were counseled about:* *Pupil's work*	*Discipline problem*
I, II [a]	5	2
III	16	4
IV	11	28
V	2	9
Total	34	43

[a] The designation "I" refers to the social class of highest status in Elmtown; "V," to the class of lowest status.
SOURCE: Hollingshead, 1949, p. 179.

Similar results have been found at the high-school level (Smith, 1945; and Hollingshead, 1949). In Elmtown, when 23 extracurricular activities were studied, it was found that the percentages of students participating in one or more activities were 100, 75, 57, and 27 respectively from highest- to lowest-status groups. There was a similar tendency for upper-status pupils to participate more frequently in school parties and dances. No boy from the lowest-status group attended a single dance within the period of time studied. There were two boys from the lowest social class who were members of the baseball team, but they did not even attend the party given for the team. Attendance at the athletic events of the high school was also closely related to social class, with upper-status pupils attending almost always, and lower-status pupils attending rarely or never (Hollingshead, 1949).

VARIATIONS AMONG DIFFERENT TYPES OF SCHOOLS

What has been reported about the relationship between social class and the school program probably applies best to schools in small cities, where boys and girls of all social classes are thrown together in the high school.

Schools in small towns and villages show less differentiation of program for the different social classes. Since these schools tend to be small, homogeneous grouping is impossible, and there is a minimum degree of variation in the high school curriculum. Youth of the several social classes associate much more closely in both regular classroom work and in extracurricular activities.

Schools in large cities are likely to be fairly homogeneous in terms of social class at the elementary, but not at the secondary, level. High schools are generally very heterogeneous in structure, and choice of curriculum (or type of secondary school) probably follows social class lines fairly closely. Some cities have specialized high schools, such as the School of Science and the School of Music and Art in New York City. In these schools there is a predominance of middle-class students, but for the minority of lower-class students who attend, there is probably excellent opportunity provided for upward mobility. On the other hand, a vocational high school in a city is generally regarded as leading only to a working-class occupation, although, as we have already indicated, such a school may provide lower-status boys and girls opportunities for mobility.

PRIVATE SCHOOLS

The parochial type of private school is usually quite similar to a public school in its relation to social class. Most parochial schools are Roman Catholic, and the Catholic Church in most communities is fairly representative of the populations as regards social class. In a large city the Catholic parishes are likely to be differentiated along social class as well as along ethnic lines, thus resulting in variation from one elementary school to the next. The parochial high schools are generally of the comprehensive type, and draw from all social groups.

The "independent" private schools cater to families of upper and upper-middle class and perform special functions in relation to the social structure. Boys and girls of upper-middle-class families may learn social skills and may make friendships that will help them later to rise to upper-class positions. The social and academic atmosphere in most private schools is rather different from that of a public school, even when the public school draws pupils from an upper-middle-class area of a city. A study of the personalities of boys in public and in private schools supports this statement (MacArthur, 1954). It was noted that public school boys are "Doing" boys, while those in private school are "Being" boys. The latter do not strive so hard to get ahead with vocational plans.

CONCLUSIONS

We have seen that the school system fits the American social structure in two ways. For most children, it enforces the status quo. At the same time, it marks some children for upward social mobility.

The school preserves the status quo by placing children of similar social status together, which is carried out by way of "homogeneous grouping" in some schools; others, such as elementary schools in big cities, draw their pupils from rather homogeneous neighborhoods. Thus the school may actually reinforce social class differences by virtue of the fact that it often keeps together children of similar social status. On the other hand, the school promotes upward social mobility of a minority of lower-status children by grouping them with children of high social status and by starting them on the avenue of educational opportunity.

As a sorting and selecting agency, the school system is not fully successful in sorting out the ablest children and in helping them achieve what they are capable of, even though the over-all results are in that direction. The most serious shortcoming of the school in this connection is the present difficulty in finding ways to motivate able lower-class youth for further education and for mobility. Those who are so motivated learn their motives from parents, friends, and teachers. But many other able children are not so motivated. For them, the school system should find ways to encourage education beyond the level of high school.

REFERENCES

Abrahamson, Stephen (1952), "School Rewards and Social Class Status," *Educational Research Bulletin,* 31, 8–15.

Anderson, C. Arnold (1961), "A Skeptical Note on the Relation of Vertical Mobility to Education," *American Journal of Sociology,* LXVI, 560–570.

Dillon, H. J. (1949), *Early School Leavers—A Major Education Problem.* New York: National Child Labor Committee.

Dupre, Vladimir (1958), "The Social Assimilation of Adolescents into the Adult Work Society." Unpublished Ph.D. dissertation, Committee on Human Development, University of Chicago.

Eells, Kenneth, *et al.* (1951), *Intelligence and Cultural Differences.* Chicago: University of Chicago Press.

Hecker, Stanley (1953), "Early School Leavers," *Bulletin of the Bureau of School Service,* Vol. 25, No. 4. College of Education, University of Kentucky.

Hollingshead, August B. (1949), *Elmtown's Youth.* New York: John Wiley & Sons.

McArthur, Charles (1954), "Personalities of Public and Private School Boys," *Harvard Educational Review,* 24, 256–262.

National Science Foundation (1961), *The Duration of Formal Education for High-ability Youth: A Study of Retention in the Educational System.* NSF 61–36. Washington, D.C.: National Science Foundation.

Pohlmann, Vernon C. (1956), "Relationship Between Ability, Socio-economic Status, and Choice of Secondary School," *Journal of Educational Sociology,* 29, 392–397.

Smith, Henry P. (1945), "Extra-Curricular Activities and Social Status in High School," *Journal of Educational Psychology,* 36, 229–246.

Udry, J. Richard (1960), "The Importance of Social Class in a Suburban School," *Journal of Educational Sociology,* 33, 307–310.

UNESCO Courier, 3, No. 6–7 (1950). Quotation occurs also in the *United Nations Bulletin,* 9, 105.

Warner, W. Lloyd, and James C. Abegglen (1955), *Big Business Leaders in America.* New York: Harper & Brothers.

Wilson, Alan B. (1959), "Residential Segregation of Social Classes and Aspirations of High School Boys," *American Sociological Review,* 24, 836–845.

Wolfle, Dael (1954), *America's Resources of Specialized Talent.* New York: Harper & Brothers.

Chapter 9

Skills

9-1

ROBERT M. GAGNÉ

Training and the Principles of Learning

9-2

ROY E. PRIEBE

AND WILLIAM H. BURTON

The Slow-Motion Picture as a Coaching Device

ROBERT M. GAGNÉ

Training and the Principles of Learning

The teaching of skills in school has much in common with training in other settings. Yet most educators have paid little attention to effective recent developments in training research. Here Gagné writes of techniques and principles found useful in training servicemen to do certain jobs. From his technical article, you may learn much of how a skillful experimental psychologist studies a new situation. What is the meaning of "task analysis," "intratask transfer," and "sequencing"? Could such concepts be useful for education?

. . . Suppose that I were a learning psychologist fresh out of an academic laboratory, who was to take a new job in charge of a program of research on some type of military training. What principles of learning would I look for to bring to bear on training problems? What kinds of generalizations from laboratory studies of learning would I search for and attempt to make use of in training situations? The answers I shall suggest for these questions require first a consideration of what kinds of principles have been tried, and how they have fared.

SOME REPRESENTATIVE MILITARY TASKS

First, we need to have in mind certain representative military tasks for which training either is or has been given, in order that we can consider in detail the kinds of learning principles that are applicable. Here are three which will serve well as examples: (1) flexible gunnery; (2) putting a radar set into operation; (3) finding malfunctions in an electronic system.

Flexible gunnery. The gunner of a now obsolete type of bomber aircraft was typically located in the waist or the tail of the plane, and aimed and fired a gun at fighter aircraft attacking on what was called a "pursuit course." To do this he looked at the attacking fighter through a reticle

Robert M. Gagné, "Military Training and Principles of Learning," *American Psychologist,* 17 (1962), 83–91. Reprinted with permission of the American Psychological Association, Inc.

Presidential address delivered at the annual meeting of the Division of Military Psychology, 69th Annual Convention of the American Psychological Association, New York, N. Y., September 5, 1961.

Supported in part by Contract AF 49(638)–975, with the Office of Scientific Research, U. S. Air Force. The opinions expressed are those of the author.

containing a central dot, which he lined up with the target by rotating his gunsight horizontally and vertically. At the same time, he had to "frame" the aircraft within a set of dots arranged in a circle whose circumference could be varied by rotating the round hand-grip by means of which he grasped the gunsight. This is the kind of task the psychologist calls "tracking," on which a great many laboratory studies have been carried out. It was, of course, tracking simultaneously in the three dimensions of azimuth, elevation, and range. To perform this task, the individual had to learn a motor skill.

Putting a radar set in operation. This kind of task is typically what is called a "fixed procedure." That is, the individual is required to push buttons, turn switches, and so on, in a particular sequence. Here, for example, is a set of steps in a procedure used by radar operators to check the transmitter power and frequency of an airborne radar (Briggs & Morrison, 1956):

1. Turn the radar set to "Stand-by" operation
2. Connect power cord of the TS-147
3. Turn power switch on
4. Turn the test switch to transmit position
5. Turn DBM dial fully counter-clockwise
6. Connect an RF cable to the RF jack on the TS-147

There are 14 more steps in this procedure. Notice that each of the steps by itself is easy enough; the individual is quite capable of turning a switch or connecting a cable. What he must learn to do, however, is to perform each step in the proper sequence. The sequence is important, and doing step 5 before step 4 may be not only an error, it may be dangerous. What must be learned, then, is a sequence of acts in the proper order.

Finding malfunctions in complex equipment. This is in many respects a most complex kind of behavior. There are of course some very simple kinds of equipment in which this activity can be reduced to a procedure; and when this is true, the task is one that can be learned from that point of view. But the major job, for complex equipment, is one of troubleshooting, a problem-solving activity that has considerable formal resemblance to medical as well as other kinds of diagnosis. Suppose this is a radar set, again, and that the initial difficulty (symptom) is that no "range sweep" appears on the oscilloscope tube face. Beginning at this point, the troubleshooter must track down a malfunctioning component. He does this first by making a decision as to how he will check the operation of subordinate parts of the system, next by carrying out the check and noting the information it yields, next by making another decision about a next check, and so on through a whole series of stages until he finds the malfunctioning unit. In each of these stages, he presumably must be formulating hypotheses which affect his actions at the next stage, in the typical and classically described manner of problem solving. What does the individual have to learn in order to solve such problems? This is indeed a difficult question to answer, but the best guess seems to be that he must acquire concepts, principles, rules, or something of that nature which he can arouse within himself at the proper moment and which guide his behavior in diagnosing malfunctions.

Here are, then, three types of activities that are not untypical of military jobs, and which are aimed at in military training: a motor skill like flexible gunnery; a procedure like putting a radar set into operation; and trouble-shooting, the diagnosing of malfunctions in complex electronic equipment. Each one of these tasks has been examined more or less intensively by military psychologists and learning specialists. Among other things, each of these tasks can be shown to be not entirely unique, but to represent a rather broad class of tasks, in its formal characteristics, which cuts across particular content or occupational areas. For example, flexible gunnery is a tracking skill, which formally resembles many others, like maneuvering an airplane, sewing a seam on a sewing machine, hovering a helicopter, and many others. As for procedures, these are common indeed, and may be found in jobs such as that of a clerk in filling in or filing forms, a cook preparing food, or a pilot preflighting an airplane. Diagnosing difficulties is certainly a widely occurring kind of activity, which may be engaged in by the leader of a group who detects the symptom of low morale, as well as by a variety of mechanics who "fix" equipment of all sorts. Accordingly, one should probably not consider these particular examples as peculiar ones; instead, they appear to be representative of a wide variety of human activities.

LEARNING

How are these three kinds of tasks learned? What is it that the learning psychologist can say about them which will enable anyone (the teacher, the curriculum builder, the training manager) to undertake to arrange the external conditions in such a way that the desired performances will be acquired with the minimal expenditure of time, money, and wasted effort?

Suppose that you were, in fact, a psychologist who had studied learning, both animal and human, from the standpoint of experiment and theory, and that you were faced with this problem. How can scientific knowledge of learning be used to improve the process of training? Notice how I have stated this question. I am not asking, how can a scientific approach be applied to the study of training? Nor am I asking, how can experimental methodology be applied to the study of training? There are certainly answers to these questions, which have been provided by several people, notably Crawford (1962). The question is, rather, how can what you know about learning *as an event,* or *as a process,* be put to use in designing training so that it will be maximally effective?

The psychologist who is confronted with this question is likely to appeal, first, to a basic point of view towards learning which is so highly ingrained it may be called an *assumption.* Beyond this, and secondly, he looks for certain *principles* which have been well established by experiment. These are principles which relate certain variables in the learning situation, like time intervals between trials, sequence of trials, kind of feedback after each trial, and so on, to such dependent variables as rate of learning or goodness of performance. Let us try to see what can be done both with the basic assumption and with some of the more important of the principles.

The assumption. The assumption that many learning psychologists would bring to the problem of designing training is something like this: "The best way to learn a performance is to practice that performance." I should like to show, later on, that this assumption is by no means a good one. But before I do that, I want to consider the question, where does this assumption come from, anyhow? First, it seems to have a cultural basis, by derivation from the writings of John Dewey, preserved in the educational catchphrase "learning by doing." Second, it appears to come by unwarranted generalization from laboratory prototypes of learning such as the conditioned response. In conditioning, classical or otherwise, one observes learning only *after* the animal has made the first *response.* Thus, performance comes first, and learning is often considered to result from practice of this performance. Third, the assumption comes from theory which deals with conditioning, and which conceives of what is learned as either a response or an association terminating in a response, in either case established by *practicing the response* (with reinforcement). Without going into the matter further at the moment, the basic reason that generalization of this notion to the learning of the human tasks I have mentioned seems questionable is simply that the responses required (turning switches, inserting plugs, moving handles) do not have to be learned at all—they are already there in the human's repertoire.

PRINCIPLES

Beyond this assumption that learning comes about when performances are practiced, what *principles* can the learning psychologist depend on? What kinds of conditions have been found to affect the rate of learning? What findings can he bring to bear on the problem of designing training to be maximally effective?

Let me mention some of the best-known of these principles, not necessarily all of them, using various sources. In part, I shall depend on an excellent article by Underwood (1959). First of all, there is *reinforcement,* the principle that learning will be more rapid the greater the amount of reinforcement given during practice. Other principles include *distribution of practice, meaningfulness,* increasing the *distinctiveness* of the elements of a task, and *response availability.*

These principles would appear to provide the learning psychologist with a fairly adequate bag of tricks with which he can approach the job of designing effective training. There is much evidence in the experimental literature that one can in fact alter the rate of learning by manipulating these variables in the learning situation, whether one is working with single conditioned responses or with verbal material having a somewhat more complex organization. Each of these variables, so far as is known, can be manipulated to make a dependable difference on learning, in the direction of increased as well as decreased effectiveness.

USING THESE ASSUMPTIONS AND PRINCIPLES IN TRAINING DESIGN

How does one fare if he seriously attempts to use this basic assumption and these principles to design effective training situations? *Not particularly well.* The assumption that the most effective learning is provided by practice on the final task leads one astray on many occasions. As for the principles, sometimes they can clearly not be applied, that is, there is no way to manipulate the training situation in the manner suggested by the principle. In other instances, the evidence simply fails to support the principle. When this happens, there may be good theoretical reasons for the event, but this still does not restore one's faith in the usefulness of the principle.

It will be possible here only to give a few examples of military training situations in which these assumptions and principles failed to work, but I have chosen them to be as representative as possible. Let me emphasize again that I do not maintain that these examples demonstrate that the principles are invalid. I simply want to show that they are strikingly inadequate to handle the job of designing effective training situations.

Motor skill. First let's consider what is perhaps the most difficult case, the learning of a motor skill like gunnery. What happens if we try to employ the assumption that the best way to learn gunnery is to practice gunnery? Using the kind of task required of a flexible gunner, a number of studies were made of the conditions of learning for this performance. One of the earliest ones, during World War II, reported by Melton (1947), showed that different amounts of practice in firing at sleeve targets during one through ten gun-camera missions made no significant difference in the measured proficiency of gunners. A number of other studies of gunnery also indicate the very small and often insignificant effects of practice continued beyond the first three trials or so (Rittenhouse & Goldstein, 1954). Furthermore, several such studies confirm the finding that the major improvement in this performance comes as a result of informing the learners of the correct picture to be achieved in ranging (i.e., so that the dots just touch the wing tips of the target aircraft) (Goldstein & Ellis, 1956). In other words, to summarize the finding very briefly, the evidence is that simple practice on the gunnery task is not a particularly effective training method; instruction about the correct sighting picture for ranging is much more effective in bringing about improved performance. Perhaps there are good theoretical reasons for this. But the fact remains that practicing the performance is *not* the best way to learn.

What about the principles of learning? Well, let's consider the one which a learning psychologist might be inclined to think of first—reinforcement, or the introduction of knowledge of results during practice. Translated into a form applicable to motor skills learning, the principle is that the more adequate are the knowledge of results, the more rapid the learning. This variable, too, has been tried out in a number of studies. Typically what was done was to augment the knowledge of results that come to the gunner through his observing his own tracking performance on a screen, by providing an extra cue, such as a buzzer, which sounded whenever the gunner was exactly on target in all three dimensions. The effect of this extra cue, it was found, was to improve the performance during learning. But did this mean that the learning itself was more effective, or simply that the buzzer "propped up" the performance? One seeks the answer to this question by comparing the performance of buzzer-trained and non-buzzer-trained groups on a standard criterion task without the buzzer. When this was done, the findings in several studies were negative (cf. Goldstein & Ellis, 1956), and one (Goldstein & Rittenhouse, 1954) actually showed that learners who had the advantage of augmented knowledge of results (reinforcement) exhibited a lower performance on a second gunnery task.

Other learning principles were unconfirmed in training situations. For example, a carefully executed study could find no evidence for changes in learning as a result of alterations in conditions of practice and rest periods (Rittenhouse & Goldstein, 1954). Still other variables simply cannot be used in the training situation. For example, the meaningfulness of the task is set by the task itself, and cannot be altered by changing the conditions of training. Similarly, the internal similarity of the elements of the task are fixed by the task; one cannot, for example, change the degree of resemblance of the aircraft or of the tracks they follow by simply redesigning the training, without setting about to change the nature of the task itself. (I omit here a discussion of the transfer effects of training with an easy discrimination to performance on a hard discrimination, and vice versa. This is a different principle than the one under discussion, and the evidence about it is not clear-cut.) What about response availability or familiarity? From the evidence on practice previously cited, as well as studies on part-training (cf. Goldstein & Ellis, 1956) it seems fairly clear that the responses in this task (turning knobs, moving the gunsight up and down with a handle) were highly familiar in the first place. No one, so far as I know, ever seriously proposed that they were not.

Perhaps these examples are sufficient to at least raise doubts about the usefulness of the learning psychologist's assumptions and principles, when he attempts to apply them to the practical job of designing training for motor skills. On the whole, it may fairly be said, I think, that the assumption was often wrong and the principles were seldom useful in bringing about training improvement. I caution you again that I am not saying the learning psychologist was unsuccessful in improving training. In many instances, he was very successful. What I am trying to answer is the question, when he was successful, what knowledge or set of principles was he using?

Procedures. There are not many analytical studies of the learning of procedures. Perhaps the reason for this is that learning procedures is relatively such an easy matter, and the methods used to train them seem relatively so obvious, that little work was done on them. Consequently, I shall have to base my arguments primarily on these obvious features, rather than on a great deal of experimental evidence.

Suppose one is faced with the task of training someone to "turn on" a radar set by turning and pushing a series of fifteen switches in a particular sequence. (This is taken to be a simplified version of a representative procedural task.) How does one go about it? If one proposes to conduct training simply by "practicing the task" it becomes obvious almost immediately that this is an inefficient method to use. What is usually done is this: the learner is provided with a *list,* which states, in effect, "First, turn on power switch; second, depress voltage switch; third, set voltage knob to reading 10; etc." (e.g., Briggs & Morrison, 1956). Now the individual may be required to commit the list to memory first, and then proceed to the task; or, he may be allowed to use the list while he practices going through the sequence. The important thing is, however, that it is the *learning of the list* that contributes most to the performance of the task, not the practice of the switch-pressing responses, another example contrary to the principle that the best way to learn is to practice the required performance. I do not say that the performance should never be practiced, simply that something other than direct practice of the final task is more effective for learning procedures, just as is true for motor skills in the example previously described.

Learning principles applied to the training of procedures do not fare very well, either, although again I must note the absence of experimental evidence. One cannot alter meaningfulness, and in most cases the responses required are highly familiar. When they are not, as may be the case when a single step requires the use of an unfamiliar tool, this principle may actually have some limited usefulness. Sometimes the principle of increasing the distinctiveness of the elements of the task can be used, and one would indeed expect it to work. For example, one could put distinctive cues or labels on each of the switches in the 15-switch procedure, and this might be expected to speed up the rate of learning. However, it may be noted that this becomes a matter of changing the task (i.e., the equipment), rather than of changing the conditions of learning. From evidence on the learning of nonsense-syllable lists, one would not expect a variable like distribution of practice to make much difference as a training variable, as Underwood (1959) has noted. Again a review of learning assumptions and principles has indicated limited usefulness.

Diagnosing malfunctions. When we turn to a consideration of troubleshooting complex equipment, even the most theoretically-dedicated learning psychologist is forced to recognize, almost from the start, that the idea of learning to troubleshoot by simply practicing troubleshooting verges on the ridiculous. The most obvious reason is that one cannot identify a single *task* to be practiced. The troubleshooter is faced with a great variety of initial problem situations, each of which may have a great variety of causes. He cannot possibly practice solving all of them. In fact, it is clear that he must learn not a single task, but a *class of tasks,* or perhaps even several classes of tasks. Yet people do learn to do them, quite successfully, without ever doing anything that can legitimately be called "practicing the final performance."

What they do learn, among other things, is an elaborate set of rules pertaining to the flow of signals through a complex circuit. To a large extent, they learn these rules by looking at and responding to a circuit diagram which is a representation of the equipment rather than the equipment itself. And they use the rules in thinking about the signal flow, that is to say, in making successive decisions leading to a solution of the problem (finding the malfuction).

Since, as I have said, it is impossible to define a single task to be practiced in learning troubleshooting, it is just about equally difficult to apply the principles of reinforcement, meaningfulness, internal differentiation, and so on, to the design of training. If one accepts the task of "learning the rules" as what must be done, it is of course possible to ask the question as to whether such learning variables would apply to that task. This is a job that may some day be done by those interested in research on "learning programing." But it has not been done as yet. The evidence to date (such as it is) has not indicated strong effects, or even significant ones, for the variable of reinforcement in connection with learning programs (Goldbeck & Briggs, 1960). Other variables have not yet been investigated in relation to the learning of rules and principles.

WHAT IS APPLICABLE TO THE DESIGN OF TRAINING?

Does this mean that the psychologist has virtually nothing to offer to the problem of designing effective training? Have the results of psychologists' efforts to improve training been entirely negative? Quite to the contrary, it seems to me that efforts can be identified which were quite effective in producing significant improvements in training, and which led to some demonstrably useful designs for training. But the principles which were found to be effective for such purposes were not those that have been mentioned.

Here are the psychological principles that seem to me to be useful in training:

1. Any human task may be analyzed into a set of component tasks which are quite distinct from each other in terms of the experimental operations needed to produce them.

2. These task components are mediators of the final task performance; that is, their presence insures positive transfer to a final performance, and their absence reduces such transfer to near zero.

3. The basic principles of training design consist of: (*a*) identifying the component tasks of a final performance; (*b*) insuring that each of these component tasks is fully achieved; and (*c*) arranging the total learning situation in a sequence which will insure optimal mediational effects from one component to another.

These statements certainly imply a set of principles which would have very different names from those we are now most familiar with. They are concerned with such things as *task analysis, intratask transfer, component task achievement,* and *sequencing* as important variables in learning, and consequently in training. These principles are not set in opposition to the traditional principles of learning, such as reinforcement, differentiation of task elements, familiarity, and so on, and do not deny their relevance, only their *relative importance.* They are, however, in complete opposition to the previously mentioned assumption "the best way to learn a task is to practice the task."

It should also be pointed out here that I am unable to refer to any well-organized body of experimental evidence for these newly proposed principles. They come instead by inference and generalization from a wide variety of instances of learning and military training. I do not claim more for them than this. But they have to be stated before any systematic experimental work can be done on them.

Let me try now to illustrate a definite meaning for these principles with some examples. Consider first the procedural task described previously. "1. Turn radar set to 'standby' operation; 2. Connect power cord of the TS-147; 3. Turn power switch on; 4. Turn test switch to transmit position; etc." The first step to be undertaken here is to analyze this task; and (with certain minor assumptions on our part), this is seen to be, first, the learning of an order series of responses to things; and second and subordinate to this, the locating of these things. These two *component tasks* have a hierarchical relationship to each other, and immediately suggest the proper *sequencing* for the arrangement of the learning (or training) situation. That is to say, what must first be undertaken is that the learner learn what and where the "things" are (the "standby operation" switch, the "TS-147," the power switch, the test switch, and so forth). This is a matter of identification learning, which has considerable resemblance to the paired-associate learning of the psychological laboratory. Having achieved this subordinate task, it is then possible for the learner to undertake the second, or "serial order of things" task. According to the principle proposed here, maximal positive transfer to this task would be predicted following completely adequate performance on the subordinate task of identifying the "things."

Laboratory experiments which have undertaken to test such a hypothesis seem to be scarce. It is possible, however, to make reference to two studies (Primoff, 1938; Young, 1959) which have some suggestive findings. Generally speaking, when one learns a set of paired associates first, and then undertakes the learning of these units serially, there is high positive transfer; but when one learns units serially first, the amount of transfer to paired associate learning is very low indeed. These results strongly suggest that there is a *more efficient* and a *less efficient* sequence which can be arranged for the learning of a procedural task, and that this sequence involves learning one subtask before the total task is undertaken. A procedure is a task that can be analyzed into at least two component tasks, one of identification, and the other of serial ordering. The first is subordinate to the second in the sense that it meditates positive transfer to the second, provided it is first completely mastered.

Can this kind of analysis be applied to a more complex task like troubleshooting? Indeed it can, and those psychologists who thought about the problem of training troubleshooting came close to the kind of analysis I have suggested. Generally speaking, they recognized that troubleshooting some particular equipment as a final performance was supported by two broad classes of subordinate tasks. First, there was knowledge of the rules of signal flow in the system, and second, the proper use of test instruments in making checks. The rules of signal flow themselves constitute an elaborate hierarchy of subordinate tasks, if one wants to look at it that way. For example, if the signal with which the mechanic is concerned is the output of an amplifier, then it may be necessary that he know some of the rules about data flow through an amplifier. Thus the task may be progressively analyzed into subordinate components which support each other in the sense that they are predicted to mediate positive transfer.

The task of using test instruments in making checks provides an even clearer example, perhaps. Obviously, one subordinate task is "choosing the proper check to make" (presumably a matter of knowing some "rules"); another is "selecting the proper test instrument" (an identification task); still another is "setting up the test instrument" (a procedural task, which in its turn has components like those previously described); and another is "interpreting the instrument reading" (another task involving a "rule"). Even identifying these component tasks brings to troubleshooting a vast clarification of the requirements for training. If one is able to take another step of arranging the proper sequencing of these tasks in a training program, the difference which results is remarkable. This is the interpretation I should be inclined to make of the studies which have demonstrated significant improvements in troubleshooting training, such as those of Briggs and Besnard (1956); of Highland, Newman, and Waller (1956); and of French, Crowder, and Tucker (1956). In providing training which was demonstrably successful, these investigators were giving instruction on a carefully analyzed set of subordinate tasks, arranged in a sequence which, so far as they could tell, would best insure positive transfer to the variety of problem situations encountered in troubleshooting. It was *the identification of these tasks and this sequence* which I believe was the key to training improvement.

A good deal of other work also proceeded along these lines, although not always with a terminal phase of measured training effectiveness. For example, a whole series of studies by Miller and Folley, and their associates, were concerned with what was called *task analysis*. They had such titles as these: Line maintenance of the A-3A fire control system: III. Training characteristics (Folley & Miller, 1955); Job anticipation procedures applied to the K-1 system (Miller, Folley, & Smith, 1953); A comparison of job requirements for the line maintenance of two sets of electronic equipment (Miller, Folley, & Smith, 1954). What was all this talk about task analysis? Did it have anything to do with training? My answer is that it had to do with training more than with anything else. These were thoroughgoing and highly successful attempts to identify the variety of tasks contained in a job, and the variety of subtasks which contributed to each task. There was in fact explicit recognition of the idea that successful final performance must be a matter of attaining competence on these subtasks. So here again was the notion that effective training somehow depended on the identification of these subordinate tasks, as well as on their arrangement into a suitable sequence to insure positive transfer to the final performance.

A third source of these ideas in military training research should be mentioned. This was the development of training devices applicable to such jobs as electronic maintenance. It came to be recognized that these devices were in some respects very different from the traditional trainers such as those for developing skill in aircraft maneuvers. They were called "concept trainers," and this, as Briggs' (1959) discussion of them implies, was another name for "teaching machines." As such, they were developed independently of Skinner's ideas, and they were in fact based upon an entirely different set of principles, as is clear from the accounts provided by Briggs (1956), Crowder (1957), and French (1956). Each of these training devices (or teaching machines), aside from its hardware engineering, was developed on the basis of a painstaking task analysis, which identified the subordinate tasks involved in a total task like troubleshooting a particular electronic system. The subordinate tasks thus identified were then incorporated into a sequence designed to insure maximal positive transfer to the final task. There were certainly some programing principles, but they bore little resemblance to those which are most frequently mentioned in recent literature; in my opinion, they were much more important than these.

Still a fourth area of effort in training research was related to these ideas. This was the development of techniques to provide behavioral guides, or "jobs aids" in support of performance in various technical jobs (Hoehn, Newman, Saltz, & Wulff, 1957). In order to do this, it was found necessary to distinguish between those kinds of capabilities which could best be established by thorough training, and those kinds which could be established by minimal training plus the provision of a check list or handbook. Obviously, here again there had to be a detailed task analysis. Subordinate tasks had to be identified which would mediate transfer either to the kind of performance required without a handbook, or the kind required with a handbook. Besides the initial task analysis, it is again evident that this line of work was making use of ideas about component task achievement and intratask transfer.

SUMMARY

Now that I have conveyed the message, my summary can be quite brief. If I were faced with the problem of improving training, I should not look for much help from the well-known learning principles like reinforcement, distribution of practice, response familiarity, and so on. I should look instead at the technique of task analysis, and at the principles of component task achievement, intratask transfer, and the sequencing of subtask learning to find those ideas of greatest usefulness in the design of effective training. Someday, I hope, even the laboratory learning psychologist will know more about these principles.

REFERENCES

Briggs, L. J. A troubleshooting trainer for the E-4 Fire Control System. *USAF Personnel Train. Res. Cent. Tech. Note,* 1956, No. 56–94.

Briggs, L. J. Teaching machines for training of military personnel in maintenance of electronic equipment. In E. Galanter (Ed.), *Automatic teaching: the state of the art*. New York: Wiley, 1959. Ch. 12.

Briggs, L. J., & Besnard, G. G. Experimental procedures for increasing reinforced practice in training Air Force mechanics for an electronic system. In G. Finch & F. Cameron (Eds.), *Research symposium on Air Force human engineering, personnel, and training research.* Washington, D.C.: National Academy of Sciences—National Research Council, 1956. Pp. 48–58.

Briggs, L. J., & Morrison, E. J. An assessment of the performance capabilities of fire control system mechanics. *USAF Personnel Train. Res. Cent. Tech. Memo.,* 1956, No. ML–56–19.

Crawford, M. P. Concepts of training. In R. M. Gagné (Ed.), *Psychological principles in system development.* New York: Holt, Rinehart, & Winston, 1962. Ch. 9.

Crowder, N. A. A part-task trainer for troubleshooting. *USAF Personnel Train. Res. Cent. Tech. Note,* 1957, No. 57–71.

Folley, J. D., Jr., & Miller, R. B. Line maintenance of the A-3A Fire Control System: III. Training characteristics. *USAF Personnel Train. Res. Cent. Tech. Memo.,* 1955, No. 55–5.

French, R. S. The K-System MAC-1 troubleshooting trainer: I. Development, design, and use. *USAF Personnel Train. Res. Cent. Tech. Note,* 1956, No. 56–119.

French, R. S., Crowder, N. A., & Tucker, J. A., Jr. The K-System MAC-1 troubleshooting trainer: II. Effectiveness in an experimental training course. *USAF Personnel Train. Res. Cent. Tech. Note,* 1956, No. 56–120.

Goldbeck, R. A., & Briggs, L. J. An analysis of response mode and feedback factors in automated instruction. Santa Barbara, Calif.: American Institute for Research, 1960. (AIR tech. Rep. No. 2)

Goldstein, M., & Rittenhouse, C. H. Knowledge of results in the acquisition and transfer of a gunnery skill. *J. Exp. Psychol.,* 1954, 48, 187–196.

Goldstein, M., & Ellis, D. S. Pedestal sight gunnery skills: a review of research. *USAF Personnel Train. Res. Cent. Tech. Note,* 1956, No. 56–31.

Highland, R. W., Newman, S. E., & Waller, H. S. A descriptive study of electronic troubleshooting. In G. Finch & F. Cameron (Eds.), *Research symposium on Air Force human engineering, personnel, and training research.* Washington, D.C.: National Academy of Sciences—National Research Council, 1956. Pp. 48–58.

Hoehn, A. J., Newman, S. E., Saltz, E., & Wulff, J. J. A program for providing maintenance capability. *USAF Personnel Train. Res. Cent. Tech. Memo.,* 1957, No. ML-57-10.

Melton, A. W. (Ed.) Apparatus tests. *USAAF Aviat. Psychol. Program Res. Rep.,* 1947, No. 4, pp. 917–921.

Miller, R. B., Folley, J. D., Jr., & Smith, P. R. Job anticipation procedures applied to the K-1 system. *USAF Hum. Resources Res. Cent. Tech. Rep.,* 1953, No. 53–20.

Miller, R. B., Folley, J. D., Jr., & Smith, P. R. A comparison of job requirements for line maintenance of two sets of electronics equipment. *USAF Personnel Train. Res. Cent. Tech. Rep.,* 1954, No. 54–83.

Primoff, E. Backward and forward association as an organizing act in serial and in paired associate learning. *J. Psychol.*, 1938, 5, 375–395.

Rittenhouse, C. H., & Goldstein, M. The role of practice schedule in pedestal sight gunnery performance. *USAF Personnel Train. Res. Cent. Tech. Rep.*, 1954, No. 54–97.

Underwood, B. J. Verbal learning in the educative processes. *Harvard Educ. Rev.*, 1959, 29, 107–117.

Young, R. K. A comparison of two methods of learning serial associations. *Amer. J. Psychol.*, 1959, 72, 554–559.

ROY E. PRIEBE and WILLIAM H. BURTON

The Slow-Motion Picture as a Coaching Device

One important field of skill training is physical education. In this selection, Priebe and Burton discuss the role of conscious analysis and imitation in the learning of a fundamental athletic performance: the high jump. The conclusions presented by the authors are the result of a six-week experiment conducted at a California high school. How are their results related to the principles set forth by Gagné in the preceding selection? Does this experiment indicate that practice is *not* important?

CURRENT USE OF SLOW-MOTION PICTURES IN COACHING

The importance of visual aids in instruction is increasingly recognized. Every day new visual devices are being purchased by school administrators and are being used by teachers who have little or no know knowledge of the actual value of the specific aids selected.

Motion pictures are being used by athletic coaches more extensively every year. The leading high schools, preparatory schools, and colleges spend thousands of dollars annually in the taking of motion pictures of athletic contests. Coaches are of the opinion that the showing of these films to the athletes who participated will bring about an improvement in individual or team performance. Coaches have observational evidence of the truth of this opinion but practically no objective evidence.

NATURE AND CONDUCT OF THE INVESTIGATION

The investigation here reported was designed to secure evidence of the value or the lack of value of slow-motion pictures as a coaching device,

Reprinted from Roy E. Priebe and William H. Burton, "The Slow-Motion Picture as a Coaching Device," *School Review*, 47 (1939), 192–98, by permission of The University of Chicago Press.

with particular reference to the high jump. Attention was given to the use of these pictures in presenting a new form of jumping, in diagnosing and correcting errors, and in stimulating practice. The high jump was selected because it contains factors of fundamental importance in various other athletic events. Timing, coordination, natural ability, facility in given skills, and other factors are involved. Hence it may be hoped that evidence derived here will apply to other forms of athletic performance.

The human eye is not sensitive enough nor quick enough to catch even a small portion of what actually takes place in an athletic event. Actions which look to be easily executed turn out, upon analysis, to be exceedingly complex. It is at this point that slow-motion pictures may bring about a revolutionary change in coaching methods.

A number of leading track coaches were interviewed with regard to various forms of high jumping, the form favored, methods of teaching, provision for individual differences, and the like. Standard books and articles on coaching the high jump were analyzed. Slow-motion pictures of three champions [1] were available and were analytically studied.

Forty pupils at Polytechnic High School, Los Angeles, responded to a call for volunteers for the experiment. Fourteen were eliminated because of irregular attendance, excessive weight, lack of physical ability, and other causes. The remaining twenty-six, all Sophomores, were matched into thirteen pairs equated as nearly as possible on age, height, weight, leg spring,[2] previous athletic experience, and natural ability in jumping as shown by scissors-style jumping.[3] The data for these pairings are given in Table 1. The averages show the groups to be identical in age. The control group was superior in height by 0.35 of an inch, in leg spring by 0.40 of an inch, and in first scissors jump by 0.65 of an inch. The experimental group was superior in weight by 0.6 of a pound and in intelligence quotient by 1.4. All differences were statistically insignificant.

The experiment covered six weeks of the regular track season. The groups came at nine and ten o'clock but were so divided that half of each group was handled in each hour so that no advantage in time of day could accrue.

For determining the average jump of each pupil, the first week was given over to jumping in scissors style for height. In addition, instruction was given in the standard terminology used in coaching the high jump. In the second week instruction began in the western-roll form, new to all boys participating. This instruction included detailed explanations, demonstration of the whole movement and of selected parts, and initial attempts by all boys, followed by individual criticism and assistance. This procedure was continued for the remaining five weeks.

[1] Robert Van Osdel, of the University of Southern California, former champion of the Intercollegiate Association of Amateur Athletes of America; Walter Marty, Fresno (California) State College, former holder of the world's record; and Simon Toribio, record-holder of the Philippine Islands.

[2] Leg spring is a jump straight up without take-off.

[3] Scissors style is the natural form of untrained jumpers and may be seen wherever boys are practicing jumping. The legs go over the bar one after the other in "scissors" style. The western-roll form is much more complicated and involves throwing the body over the bar horizontally and approximately at full length.

TABLE 1

Comparison of boys in control and experimental groups

Boy	Age	Height (inches)	Weight	Intelligence quotient	Previous athletic experience	Leg spring (inches)	First scissors jump (inches)
PAIR 1							
Control	16	71.50	140	96	Basketball	16.00	54.0
Experimental	16	70.50	133	100	Basketball	15.50	52.0
PAIR 2							
Control	16	69.50	134	98	None	20.00	54.5
Experimental	16	69.50	132	101	None	17.00	54.0
PAIR 3							
Control	16	71.75	167	107	None	22.25	55.0
Experimental	16	70.00	165	90	None	24.00	53.0
PAIR 4							
Control	16	69.00	145	96	None	19.13	54.0
Experimental	17	69.25	149	99	None	22.25	55.0
PAIR 5							
Control	17	66.25	142	97	Soccer	26.00	57.0
Experimental	17	67.00	148	90	None	21.75	54.0
PAIR 6							
Control	17	63.50	117	97	None	20.50	55.0
Experimental	18	65.00	120	88	None	16.50	54.0
PAIR 7							
Control	16	65.50	115	100	None	15.50	51.0
Experimental	15	65.00	118	96	None	19.50	50.0
PAIR 8							
Control	16	66.00	107	97	None	22.00	52.0
Experimental	16	63.50	105	95	None	22.13	53.0
PAIR 9							
Control	17	66.00	146	78	None	19.00	52.0
Experimental	18	68.00	149	84	None	21.25	51.0
PAIR 10							
Control	15	68.50	134	121	None	21.50	55.0
Experimental	15	68.00	137	120	None	21.50	53.0
PAIR 11							
Control	16	67.75	135	103	None	22.00	54.0
Experimental	15	67.00	133	122	None	18.00	56.0
PAIR 12							
Control	17	72.00	139	97	None	18.50	56.0
Experimental	17	71.50	141	101	None	18.00	54.0
PAIR 13							
Control	17	68.00	130	102	None	14.25	52.0
Experimental	16	66.50	129	122	None	14.00	54.0
AVERAGE:							
Control	16.3	68.10	134.7	99.2		19.74	53.96
Experimental	16.3	67.75	135.3	100.6		19.34	53.31

In addition to the foregoing procedure, which was identical for both groups, the pictures of the champion jumpers were shown to the experimental group in the second week. These films were run, re-run, and discussed. Both slow and normal speeds were used. The film was stopped at crucial points. Continuous discussion and questioning from the boys accompanied this showing. During the third week slow-motion pictures of the boys in the experimental group were taken during the regular practice period and were shown to that group. Again detailed analytic discussion of good form, defects, and co-ordination took place. During the fifth and sixth weeks the experimental group saw its own pictures and also those of the champions again and engaged in further discussion.

THE RESULTS OF EXPERIMENTATION

The rate of progress and the final results are shown in Table 2. Examination of the figures reveals some interesting items. It must be noted here, before the results are discussed, that this experiment involved only twenty-six subjects and six weeks' time. At best, therefore, the results are only suggestive. It is hoped that other more extensive studies may be carried on.

It will be noted that the groups were practically equal on the original scissors-style jump. Marked differences appeared, however, as soon as the different methods of instruction took effect. After three weeks of instruction and practice, the experimental group, having the advantage of seeing and discussing pictures of champions and pictures of their own initial performances, outjumped the control group by 5.39 inches on the average jump. At the end of the fourth week the superiority of the experimental group became 5.96 inches. During the fifth week the experimental group outjumped the control group by 5.16 inches per jump. The control group then began to hold its own in improvement. Their rate of progress was somewhat faster than it had previously been. At the end of the sixth week the superiority of the experimental group was reduced to 3.69 inches on the average jump.

It is interesting to note that the experimental group made their best record during the fourth and the fifth weeks and did not improve thereafter. The control group, in contrast, was just reaching its maximum during the sixth week. A valuable extension of this study would discover whether the control group would eventaully match, fall short of, or exceed, the records of the experimental group.

Comparison of the original scissors jump with the best performance on the western-roll style shows that the experimental group had increased the height of their jumps by 4.62 inches on the average. The control group after six weeks of instruction and practice had been able to add an average of only 0.04 of an inch.

However, when the poorest and the best performances on the western-roll style are compared, it is seen that the control group made progress but that they had a handicap which was eliminated for the experimental group by the pictures. The average of the differences between the poorest and the best western-roll jump for the control group was 4.77 inches; for the experi-

TABLE 2

Height of jumps (in inches) of paired groups of boys during progress of experiment

Boy	Original scissors jump	Western-roll jump: Test 1 (third week)	Test 2 (fourth week)	Test 3 (fifth week)	Test 4 (sixth week)	Gain of best western roll over scissors jump	Difference between poorest and best western roll
PAIR 1							
Control	54.0	48.0	49.0	49.0	51.0	−3.0	3.0
Experimental	52.0	52.0	55.5	55.0	54.0	3.5	3.5
PAIR 2							
Control	54.5	52.0	51.0	52.0	53.0	−1.5	2.0
Experimental	54.0	54.0	55.0	56.0	54.0	2.0	2.0
PAIR 3							
Control	55.0	51.0	54.0	56.0	58.0	3.0	7.0
Experimental	53.0	25.0	55.0	57.0	56.0	4.0	5.0
PAIR 4							
Control	54.0	55.0	56.0	57.0	57.0	3.0	2.0
Experimental	55.0	58.0	60.0	59.0	60.0	5.0	2.0
PAIR 5							
Control	57.0	58.0	60.0	59.0	61.0	4.0	3.0
Experimental	54.0	56.0	59.0	60.0	60.0	6.0	4.0
PAIR 6							
Control	55.0	50.0	54.0	58.0	56.0	3.0	8.0
Experimental	54.0	53.0	56.0	57.0	57.0	3.0	4.0
PAIR 7							
Control	51.0	48.0	47.0	50.0	52.0	1.0	5.0
Experimental	50.0	52.0	55.5	55.0	55.5	5.5	3.5
PAIR 8							
Control	52.0	40.0	42.0	42.0	44.0	−8.0	4.0
Experimental	53.0	53.0	56.0	57.0	58.0	5.0	5.0
PAIR 9							
Control	52.0	50.0	52.0	53.0	54.0	2.0	4.0
Experimental	51.0	57.0	59.0	61.0	61.5	10.5	4.5
PAIR 10							
Control	55.0	50.0	52.0	55.0	57.0	2.0	7.0
Experimental	53.0	54.0	57.0	57.0	57.0	4.0	3.0
PAIR 11							
Control	54.0	48.0	54.0	54.0	55.0	1.0	7.0
Experimental	56.0	57.0	59.5	59.0	59.0	3.5	2.5
PAIR 12							
Control	56.0	52.0	53.0	54.0	55.0	−1.0	3.0
Experimental	54.0	56.0	56.0	57.0	57.0	3.0	1.0
PAIR 13							
Control	52.0	40.0	40.0	43.0	47.0	−5.0	7.0
Experimental	54.0	58.0	58.0	59.0	59.0	5.0	1.0
AVERAGE:							
Control	53.96	49.38	51.08	52.46	53.85	0.04	4.77
Experimental	53.31	54.77	57.04	57.62	57.54	4.62	3.15

mental group, 3.15 inches. This difference is explained by the fact that the first performances by the control group on the western-roll style were far below their original marks on the scissors jump. The experimental group, on the other hand, were at once able to use the western-roll style about as well as they had the scissors style. The motion pictures evidently cut down greatly the initial trial-and-error period. After the control group had learned the fundamentals of the new style, they progressed as rapidly as did the experimental group. It would be of interest to discover how long it would take the control group to overtake the experimental group. Thus far the evidence indicates that slow-motion pictures are of great value in initial learning but nearly on a par with directions, demonstrations, and verbal analyses of faults as the learning period progresses. This finding presents a further problem for study, namely, the diversification of the use of pictures for different periods of learning. The experiment might also be extended to test the limits of the boys' abilities and to see what, if any, differences would appear in the later stages of learning.

CONCLUSIONS

The following conclusions seem justified: (1) The use of slow-motion pictures in coaching the high jump made for faster progress and better achievement. (2) The use of slow-motion pictures in coaching the high jump eliminated, to a large extent, the initial period of trial and error. (3) Illustrations of good form in slow-motion pictures seem definitely superior to verbal directions and physical demonstration of good form, particularly during the initial period of learning. (4) The use of slow-motion pictures in coaching the high jump was of definite assistance in aiding performers to change from a familiar form of skill to a new, superior, but unfamiliar form. (5) The use of slow-motion pictures enabled the coach to handle effectively a larger number of boys. The average amount of instructional time for the individual was significantly cut down. (6) The use of slow-motion pictures in coaching the high jump contributed definitely to the interest and the attention of the boys. There was marked interest in analyzing individual errors and in improving pictured defects. (7) The general conclusions derived from this experiment seem to be in agreement with those derived from investigations of the use of motion pictures in other forms of learning.

Chapter 10

Intellectual Development as Transfer of Learning

10-1

JEROME S. BRUNER

Readiness for Learning

10-2

LLOYD G. HUMPHREYS

Transfer of Training in General Education

JEROME S. BRUNER

Readiness for Learning

Many persons believe that at some given mental age a child is "ready" to learn reading, or long division, or some other intellectual skill. They hold to the theory that before such "readiness" occurs, most teaching effort will be wasted. Bruner holds to a contrary view and claims that, in some sense, almost anything may be taught to almost anyone at almost any age. What arguments does he use to support this revolutionary hypothesis? How may the teacher of the primary grades, for example, most intelligently apply this view of readiness?

We begin with the hypothesis that any subject can be taught effectively in some intellectually honest form to any child at any stage of development. It is a bold hypothesis and an essential one in thinking about the nature of a curriculum. No evidence exists to contradict it; considerable evidence is being amassed that supports it.

To make clear what is implied, let us examine three general ideas. The first has to do with the process of intellectual development in children, the second with the act of learning, and the third with the notion of the "spiral curriculum" introduced earlier.

Intellectual development. Research on the intellectual development of the child highlights the fact that at each stage of development the child has a characteristic way of viewing the world and explaining it to himself. The task of teaching a subject to a child at any particular age is one of representing the structure of that subject in terms of the child's way of viewing things. The task can be thought of as one of translation. The general hypothesis that has just been stated is premised on the considered judgment that any idea can be represented honestly and usefully in the thought forms of children of school age, and that these first representations can later be made more powerful and precise the more easily by virtue of this early learning. To illustrate and support this view, we present here a somewhat detailed picture of the course of intellectual development, along with some suggestions about teaching at different stages of it.

The work of Piaget and others suggests that, roughly speaking, one may distinguish three stages in the intellectual development of the child. The first stage need not concern us in detail, for it is characteristic principally of the pre-school child. In this stage, which ends (at least for Swiss school children) around the fifth or sixth year, the child's mental work consists principally in establishing relationships between experience and action; his concern is with manipulating the world through action. This stage corresponds roughly to the period from the first development of language to the point at which the child learns to manipulate symbols. In this so-called preoperational stage, the principal symbolic achievement is that the child learns how to represent the external world through symbols established by simple generalization; things are represented as equivalent in terms of sharing some common property. But the child's symbolic world does not make a clear separation between internal motives and feelings on the one hand and external reality on the other. The sun moves because God pushes it, and the stars, like himself, have to go to bed. The child is little able to separate his own goals from the means for achieving them, and when he has to make corrections in his activity after unsuccessful attempts at manipulating reality, he does so by what are called intuitive regulations rather than by symbolic operations, the former being of a crude trial-and-error nature rather than the result of taking thought.

What is principally lacking at this stage of development is what the Geneva school has called the concept of reversibility. When the shape of an object is changed, as when one changes the shape of a ball of plasticene, the preoperational child cannot grasp the idea that it can be brought back readily to its original state. Because of this fundamental lack the child cannot understand certain fundamental ideas that lie at the basis of mathematics and physics—the mathematical idea that one conserves quantity even when one partitions a set of things into subgroups, or the physical idea that one conserves mass and weight even though one transforms the shape of an object. It goes without saying that teachers are severely limited in transmitting concepts to a child at this stage, even in a highly intuitive manner.

The second stage of development—and now the child is in school—is called the stage of concrete operations. This stage is operational in contrast to the preceding stage, which is merely active. An operation is a type of action: it can be carried out rather directly by the manipulation of objects, or internally, as when one manipulates the symbols that represent things and relations in one's mind. Roughly, an operation is a means of getting data about the real world into the mind and there transforming them so that they can be organized and used selectively in the solution of problems. Assume a child is presented with a pinball machine which bounces a ball off a wall at an angle. Let us find out what he appreciates about the relation between the angle of incidence and the angle of reflection. The young child sees no problem: for him, the ball travels in an arc, touching the wall on the way. The somewhat older child, say age ten, sees the two angles as roughly related—as one changes so does the other. The still older child begins to grasp that there is a fixed relation between the two, and usually says it is a right angle. Finally, the thirteen- or fourteen-year-old, often by pointing the ejector directly at the wall and seeing the ball come back at the ejector, gets the idea that the two angles are equal. Each way of looking at the phenomenon represents the result of an operation in this sense, and the child's thinking is constrained by his way of pulling his observations together.

An operation differs from simple action or goal-directed behavior in that it is internalized and reversible. "Internalized" means that the child does not have to go about his problem-solving any longer by overt trial and error, but can actually carry out trial and error in his head. Reversibility is present because operations are seen as characterized where appropriate by what is called "complete compensation"; that is to say, an operation can be compensated for by an inverse operation. If marbles, for example, are divided into subgroups, the child can grasp intuitively that the original collection of marbles can be restored by being added back together again. The child tips a balance scale too far with a weight and then searches systematically for a lighter weight or for something with which to get the scale rebalanced. He may carry reversibility too far by assuming that a piece of paper, once burned, can also be restored.

With the advent of concrete operations, the child develops an internalized structure with which to operate. In the example of the balance scale, the structure is a serial order of weights that the child has in his mind. Such internal structures are of the essence. They are the internalized symbolic systems by which the child represents the world, as in the example of the pinball machine and the angles of incidence and reflection. It is into the language of these internal structures that one must translate ideas if the child is to grasp them.

But concrete operations, though they are guided by the logic of classes and the logic of relations, are means for structuring only immediately present reality. The child is able to give structure to the things he encounters, but he is not yet readily able to deal with possibilities not directly before him or not already experienced. This is not to say that children operating concretely are not able to anticipate things that are not present. Rather, it is that they do not command the operations for conjuring up systematically the full range of alternative possibilities that could exist at any given time. They cannot go systematically beyond the information given them to a description of what else might occur. Somewhere between ten and fourteen years of age the child passes into a third stage, which is called the stage of "formal operations" by the Geneva school.

Now the child's intellectual activity seems to be based upon an ability to operate on hypothetical propositions rather than being constrained to what he has experienced or what is before him. The child can now think of possible variables and even deduce potential relationships that can later be verified by experiment or observation. Intellectual operations now appear to be predicated upon the same kinds of logical operations that are the stock in trade of the logician, the scientist, or the abstract thinker. It is at this point that the child is able to give formal or axiomatic expression to the concrete ideas that before guided his problem-solving but could not be described or formally understood.

Earlier, while the child is in the stage of concrete operations, he is capable of grasping intuitively and concretely a great many of the basic ideas of mathematics, the sciences, the humanities, and the social sciences. But he can do so only in terms of concrete operations. It can be demonstrated that fifth-grade children can play mathematical games with rules modeled on highly advanced mathematics; indeed, they can arrive at these rules inductively and learn how to work with them. They will flounder, however, if one attempts to force upon them a formal mathematical description of what they have been doing, though they are perfectly capable of guiding their behavior by these rules. At the Woods Hole Conference we were privileged to see a demonstration of teaching in which fifth-grade children very rapidly grasped central ideas from the theory of functions, although had the teacher attempted to explain to them what the theory of functions was, he would have drawn a blank. Later, at the appropriate stage of development and given a certain amount of practice in concrete operations, the time would be ripe for introducing them to the necessary formalism.

What is most important for teaching basic concepts is that the child be helped to pass progressively from concrete thinking to the utilization of more conceptually adequate modes of thought. But it is futile to attempt this by presenting formal explanations based on a logic that is distant from the child's manner of thinking and sterile in its implications for him. Much teaching in mathematics is of this sort. The child learns not to understand mathematical order but rather to apply certain devices or recipes without understanding their significance and connectedness. They are not translated into his way of thinking. Given this inappropriate start, he is easily led to believe that the important thing is for him to be "accurate"—though accuracy has less to do with mathematics than with computation. Perhaps the most striking example of this type of thing is to be found in the manner in which the high school student meets Euclidian geometry for the first time, as a set of axioms and theorems, without having had some experience with simple geometric configurations and the intuitive means whereby one deals with them. If the child were earlier given the concepts and strategies in the form of intuitive geometry at a level that he could easily follow, he might be far better able to grasp deeply the meaning of the theorems and axioms to which he is exposed later.

But the intellectual development of the child is no clockwork sequence of events; it also responds to influences from the environment, notably the school environment. Thus instruction in scientific ideas, even at the elementary level, need not follow slavishly the natural course of cognitive development in the child. It can also lead intellectual development by providing challenging but usable opportunities for the child to forge ahead in his development. Experience has shown that it is worth the effort to provide the growing child with problems that tempt him into next stages of development. As David Page, one of the most experienced teachers of elementary mathematics, has commented: "In teaching from kindergarten to graduate school, I have been amazed at the intellectual similarity of human beings at all ages, although children are perhaps more spontaneous, creative, and energetic than adults. As far as I am concerned young children learn almost anything faster than adults do if it can be given to them in terms they understand. Giving the material to them in terms they understand, interestingly enough, turns out to involve knowing the mathematics oneself, and the better one knows it, the better it can be taught. It is appropriate that we warn ourselves to be careful of assigning an absolute level of difficulty to any particular topic. When I tell mathematicians that fourth-grade students can go a long way into 'set theory' a few of them reply: 'Of course.' Most of them are startled. The latter ones are completely wrong in assuming that 'set theory' is intrinsically difficult. Of course it may be that nothing is intrinsically difficult. We just have to wait until the proper point of view and corresponding language for presenting it are revealed. Given particular subject matter or a particular concept, it is easy to ask trivial questions or to lead the child to ask trivial questions. It is also easy to ask impossibly difficult questions. The trick is to find the medium questions that can be answered and that take you somewhere. This is the big job of teachers and textbooks." One leads the child by the well-wrought "medium questions" to move more rapidly through the stages of intellectual development, to a deeper understanding of mathematical, physical, and historical principles. We must know far more about the ways in which this can be done.

Professor Inhelder of Geneva was asked to suggest ways in which the child could be moved along faster through the various stages of intellectual development in mathematics and physics. What follows is part of a memorandum she prepared for the Conference.

"The most elementary forms of reasoning—whether logical, arithmetical, geometrical, or physical—rest on the principle of the invariance of quantities: that the whole remains, whatever may be the arrangement of its parts, the change of its form, or its displacement in space or time. The principle of invariance is no a priori datum of the mind, nor is it the product of purely empirical observation. The child discovers invariance in a manner comparable to scientific discoveries generally. Grasping the idea of invariance is beset with difficulties for the child, often unsuspected by teachers. To the young child, numerical wholes, spatial dimensions, and physical quantities do not seem to remain constant but to dilate or contract as they are operated upon. The total number of beads in a box remains the same whether subdivided into two, three, or ten piles. It is this that is so hard for the child to understand. The young child perceives changes as operating in one direction without being able to grasp the idea that certain fundamental features of things remain constant over change, or that if they change the change is reversible.

"A few examples among many used in studying the child's concept of invariance will illustrate the kinds of materials one could use to help him to learn the concept more easily. The child transfers beads of a known quantity or liquids of a known volume from one receptacle to another, one receptacle being tall and narrow, the other flat and wide. The young child believes there is more in the tall receptacle than the flat one. Now the child can be confronted concretely with the nature of one-to-one correspondence between two versions of the same quantity. For there is an easy technique of checking: the beads can be counted or the liquid measured in some standard way. The same operations work for the conservation of spatial quantity if one uses a set of sticks for length or a set of tiles for surface, or by having the child transform the shape of volumes made up of the same number of blocks. In physics dissolving sugar or transforming the shapes of balls of plasticene while conserving volume provides comparable instruction. If teaching fails to bring the child properly from his perceptual, primitive notions to a proper intuition of the idea of invariance, the result is that he will count without having acquired the idea of the invariance of numerical quantities. Or he will use geometrical measures while remaining ignorant of the operation of transitivity—that if A includes B, and B includes C, then A also includes C. In physics he will apply calculations to imperfectly understood physical notions such as weight, volume, speed, and time. A teaching method that takes into account the natural thought processes will allow the child to discover such principles of invariance by giving him an opportunity to progress beyond his own primitive mode of thinking through confrontation by concrete data—as when he notes that liquid that looks greater in volume in a tall, thin receptacle is in fact the same as that quantity in a flat, low vessel. Concrete activity that becomes increasingly formal is what leads the child to the kind of mental mobility that approaches the naturally reversible operations of mathematics and logic. The child gradually comes to sense that any change may be mentally cancelled out by the reverse operation—addition by subtraction—or that a change may be counterbalanced by a reciprocal change.

"A child often focuses on only one aspect of a phenomenon at a time, and this interferes with his understanding. We can set up little teaching experiments in such a way that he is forced to pay attention to other aspects. Thus, children up to about age seven estimate the speed of two automobiles by assuming that the one that gets there first is the faster, or that if one passes the other it is faster. To overcome such errors, one can, by using toy automobiles, show that two objects starting at different distances from a finish line cannot be judged by which one arrives first, or show that one car can pass another by circling it and still not finish first. These are simple exercises, but they speed the child toward attending to several features of a situation at once.

"In view of all this it seems highly arbitrary and very likely incorrect to delay the teaching, for example, of Euclidian or metric geometry until the end of the primary grades, particularly when projective geometry has not been given earlier. So too with the teaching of physics, which has much in it that can be profitably taught at an inductive or intuitive level much earlier. Basic notions in these fields are perfectly accessible to children of seven to ten years of age, *provided that they are divorced from their mathematical expression and studied through materials that the child can handle himself.*

"Another matter relates particularly to the ordering of a mathematics curriculum. Often the sequence of psychological development follows more closely the axiomatic order of a subject matter than it does the historical order of development of concepts within the field. One observes, for instance, that certain topological notions, such as connection, separation, being interior to, and so forth, precede the formation of Euclidian and projective notions in geometry, though the former ideas are newer in their formalism in the history of mathematics than the latter. If any special justification were needed for teaching the structure of a subject in its proper logical or axiomatic order rather than its order of historical development, this should provide it. This is not to say that there may not be situations where the historical order is important from the point of view of its cultural or pedagogical relevance.

"As for teaching geometrical notions of perspective and projection, again there is much that can be done by the use of experiments and demonstrations that rest on the child's operational capacity to analyze concrete experience. We have watched children work with an apparatus in which rings of different diameter are placed at different positions between a candle and a screen with a fixed distance between them so that the rings cast shadows of varying sizes on the screen. The child learns how the cast shadow changes size as a function of the distance of the ring from the light source. By bringing to the child such concrete experience of light in revealing situations, we teach him maneuvers that in the end permit him to understand the general ideas underlying projective geometry.

"These examples lead us to think that it is possible to draw up methods of teaching the basic ideas in science and mathematics to children considerably younger than the traditional age. It is at this earlier age that systematic instruction can lay a groundwork in the fundamentals that can be used later and with great profit at the secondary level.

"The teaching of probabilistic reasoning, so very common and important a feature of modern science, is hardly developed in our educational system before college. The omission is probably due to the fact that school syllabi in nearly all countries follow scientific progress with a near-disastrous time lag. But it may also be due to the widespread belief that the understanding of random phenomena depends on the learner's grasp of the meaning of the rarity or commonness of events. And admittedly, such ideas are hard to get across to the young. Our research indicates that the understanding of random phenomena requires, rather, the use of certain concrete logical operations well within the grasp of the young child—provided these operations are free of awkward mathematical expression. Principal among these logical operations are disjunction ('either A *or* B is true') and combination. Games in which lots are drawn, games of roulette, and games involving a gaussian distribution of outcomes are all ideal for giving the child a basic grasp of the logical operation needed for thinking about probability. In such games, children first discover an entirely qualitative notion of chance defined as an uncertain event, contrasted with deductive certainty. The notion of probability as a fraction of certainty is discovered only later. Each of these discoveries can be made before the child ever learns the techniques of the calculus of probabilities or the formal expressions that normally go with probability theory. Interest in problems of a probabilistic nature could easily be awakened and developed before the introduction of any statistical processes or computation. Statistical manipulation and computation are only tools to be used *after* intuitive understanding has been established. If the array of computational paraphernalia is introduced first, then more likely than not it will inhibit or kill the development of probabilistic reasoning.

"One wonders in the light of all this whether it might not be interesting to devote the first two years of school to a series of exercises in manipulating, classifying, and ordering objects in ways that highlight basic operations of logical addition, multiplication, inclusion, serial ordering, and the like. For surely these logical operations are the basis of more specific operations and concepts of all mathematics and science. It may indeed be the case that such an early science and mathematics 'pre-curriculum' might go a long way toward building up in the child the kind of intuitive and more inductive understanding that could be given embodiment later in formal courses in mathematics and science. The effect of such an approach would be, we think, to put more continuity into science and mathematics and also to give the child a much better and firmer comprehension of the concepts which, unless he has this early foundation, he will mouth later without being able to use them in any effective way."

A comparable approach can surely be taken to the teaching of social studies and literature. There has been little research done on the kinds of concepts that a child brings to these subjects, although there is a wealth of observation and anecdote. Can one teach the structure of literary forms by presenting the child with the first part of a story and then having him complete it in the form of a comedy, a tragedy, or a farce—without ever using such words? When, for example, does the idea of "historical trend" develop, and what are its precursors in the child? How does one make a child aware of literary style? Perhaps the child can discover the idea of style through the presentation of the same content written in drastically different styles, in the manner of Beerbohm's *Christmas Garland*. Again, there is no reason to believe that any subject cannot be taught to any child at virtually any age in some form.

Here one is immediately faced with the question of the economy of teaching. One can argue that it might be better to wait until the child is thirteen or fourteen before beginning geometry so that the projective and intuitive first steps can immediately be followed up by a full formal presentation of the subject. Is it worth while to train the young inductively so that they may discover the basic order of knowledge before they can appreciate its formalism? In Professor Inhelder's memorandum, it was suggested that the first two grades might be given over to training the child in the basic logical operations that underlie instruction in mathematics and science. There is evidence to indicate that such rigorous and relevant early training has the effect of making later learning easier. Indeed the experiments on "learning set" seem to indicate just that—that one not only learns specifics but in so doing learns how to learn. So important is training per se that monkeys who have been given extensive training in problem-solving suffer considerably less loss and recover more quickly after induced brain damage than animals who had not been previously thus educated. But the danger of such early training may be that it has the effect of training out original but deviant ideas. There is no evidence available on the subject, and much is needed.

The act of learning. Learning a subject seems to involve three almost simultaneous processes. First there is *acquisition* of new information—often information that runs counter to or is a replacement for what the person has previously known implicitly or explicitly. At the very least it is a refinement of previous knowledge. Thus one teaches a student Newton's laws of motion, which violate the testimony of the senses. Or in teaching a student about wave mechanics, one violates the student's belief in mechanical impact as the sole source of real energy transfer. Or one bucks the language and its built-in way of thinking in terms of "wasting energy" by introducing the student to the conservation theorem in physics which asserts that no energy is lost. More often the situation is less drastic, as when one teaches the details of the circulatory system to a student who already knows vaguely or intuitively that blood circulates.

A second aspect of learning may be called *transformation*—the process of manipulating knowledge to make it fit new tasks. We learn to "unmask" or analyze information, to order it in a way that permits extrapolation or interpolation or conversion into another form. Transformation comprises the ways we deal with information in order to go beyond it.

A third aspect of learning is *evaluation:* checking whether the way we have manipulated information is adequate to the task. Is the generalization fitting, have we extrapolated appropriately, are we operating properly? Often a teacher is crucial in helping with evaluation, but much of it takes place by judgments of plausibility without our actually being able to check rigorously whether we are correct in our efforts.

In the learning of any subject matter, there is usually a series of episodes, each episode involving the three processes. Photosynthesis might reasonably comprise material for a learning episode in biology, fitted into a more comprehensive learning experience such as learning about the conversion of energy generally. At its best a learning episode reflects what has gone before it and permits one to generalize beyond it.

A learning episode can be brief or long, contain many ideas or a few. How sustained an episode a learner is willing to undergo depends upon what the person expects to get from his efforts, in the sense of such external things as grades but also in the sense of a gain in understanding.

We usually tailor material to the capacities and needs of students by manipulating learning episodes in several ways: by shortening or lengthening the episode, by piling on extrinsic rewards in the form of praise and gold stars, or by dramatizing the shock of recognition of what the material means when fully understood. The unit in a curriculum is meant to be a recognition of the importance of learning episodes, though many units drag on with no climax in understanding. There is a surprising lack of research on how one most wisely devises adequate learning episodes for children at different ages and in different subject matters. There are many questions that need answers based on careful research, and to some of these we turn now.

There is, to begin with, the question of the balance between extrinsic rewards and intrinsic ones. There has been much written on the role of reward and punishment in learning, but very little indeed on the role of interest and curiosity and the lure of discovery. If it is our intention as teachers to inure the child to longer and longer episodes of learning, it may well be that intrinsic rewards in the form of quickened awareness and understanding will have to be emphasized far more in the detailed design of curricula. One of the least discussed ways of carrying a student through a hard unit of material is to challenge him with a chance to exercise his full powers, so that he may discover the pleasure of full and effective functioning. Good teachers know the power of this lure. Students should know what it feels like to be completely absorbed in a problem. They seldom experience this feeling in school. Given enough absorption in class, some students may be able to carry over the feeling to work done on their own.

There is a range of problems that have to do with how much emphasis should be placed on acquisition, transformation, and evaluation in a learning episode—getting facts, manipulating them, and checking one's ideas. Is it the case, for example, that it is best to give the young child a minimum set of facts first and then encourage him to draw the fullest set of implications possible from this knowledge? In short, should an episode for a young child contain little new information but emphasize what can be done to go beyond that bit on one's own? One teacher of social studies has had great success with fouth-graders through this approach: he begins, for example, with the fact that civilizations have most often begun in fertile river valleys —the only "fact." The students are encouraged in class discussion to figure out why this is the case and why it would be less likely for civilizations to start in mountainous country. The effect of this approach, essentially the technique of discovery, is that the child generates information on his own, which he can then check or evaluate against the sources, getting more new information in the process. This obviously is one kind of learning episode, and doubtless it has limited applicability. What other kinds are there, and are some more appropriate to certain topics and ages than others? It is not the case that "to learn is to learn is to learn," yet in the research literature there appears to be little recognition of differences in learning episodes.

With respect to the optimum length of a learning episode, there are a few commonsense things one can say about it, and these are perhaps interesting enough to suggest fruitful research possibilities. It seems fairly obvious, for example, that the longer and more packed the episode, the greater the pay-off must be in terms of increased power and understanding if the person is to be encouraged to move to a next episode with zest. Where grades are used as a substitute for the reward of understanding, it may well be that learning will cease as soon as grades are no longer given—at graduation.

It also seems reasonable that the more one has a sense of the structure of a subject, the more densely packed and longer a learning episode one can get through without fatigue. Indeed, the amount of new information in any learning episode is really the amount that we cannot quite fit into place at once. And there is a severe limit, as we have already noted, on how much of such unassimilated information we can keep in mind. The estimate is that adults can handle about seven independent items of information at a time. No norms are available for children—a deplorable lack.

There are many details one can discuss concerning the shaping of learning episodes for children, but the problems that have been mentioned will suffice to give their flavor. Inasmuch as the topic is central to an understanding of how one arranges a curriculum, it seems obvious that here is an area of research that is of the first importance.

The "spiral curriculum." If one respects the ways of thought of the growing child, if one is courteous enough to translate material into his logical forms and challenging enough to tempt him to advance, then it is possible to introduce him at an early age to the ideas and styles that in later life make an educated man. We might ask, as a criterion for any subject taught in primary school, whether, when fully developed, it is worth an adult's knowing, and whether having known it as a child makes a person a better adult. If the answer to both questions is negative or ambiguous, then the material is cluttering the curriculum.

If the hypothesis with which this section was introduced is true—that any subject can be taught to any child in some honest form—then it should follow that a curriculum ought to be built around the great issues, principles, and values that a society deems worthy of the continual concern of its members. Consider two examples—the teaching of literature and of science. If it is granted, for example, that it is desirable to give children an awareness of the meaning of human tragedy and a sense of compassion for it, is it not possible at the earliest appropriate age to teach the literature of tragedy in a manner that illuminates but does not threaten? There are many possible ways to begin: through a retelling of the great myths, through the use of children's classics, through presentation of and commentary on selected films that have proved themselves. Precisely what kinds of materials should be used at what age with what effect is a subject for research—research of several kinds. We may ask first about the child's conception of the tragic, and here one might proceed in much the same way that Piaget and his colleagues have proceeded in studying the child's conception of physical causality, of morality, of number, and the rest. It is only when we are equipped with such knowledge that we will be in a position to know how the child will translate whatever we present to him into his own subjective terms. Nor need we wait for all the research findings to be in before proceeding, for a skillful teacher can also experiment by attempting to teach what seems to be intuitively right for children of different ages, correcting as he goes. In time, one goes beyond to more complex versions of the same kind of literature or simply revisits some of the same books used earlier. What matters is that later teaching build upon earlier reactions to literature, that it seek to create an ever more explicit and mature understanding of the literature of tragedy. Any of the great literary forms can be handled in the same way, or any of the great themes—be it the form of comedy or the theme of identity, personal loyalty, or what not.

So too in science. If the understanding of number, measure, and probability is judged crucial in the pursuit of science, then instruction in these subjects should begin as intellectually honestly and as early as possible in a manner consistent with the child's forms of thought. Let the topics be developed and redeveloped in later grades. Thus, if most children are to take a tenth-grade unit in biology, need they approach the subject cold? Is it not possible, with a minimum of formal laboratory work if necessary, to introduce them to some of the major biological ideas earlier, in a spirit perhaps less exact and more intuitive?

Many curricula are originally planned with a guiding idea much like the one set forth here. But as curricula are actually executed, as they grow and change, they often lose their original form and suffer a relapse into a certain shapelessness. It is not amiss to urge that actual curricula be reexamined with an eye to the issues of continuity and development referred to in the preceding pages. One cannot predict the exact forms that revision might take; indeed, it is plain that there is now available too little research to provide adequate answers. One can only propose that appropriate research be undertaken with the greatest vigor and as soon as possible.

LLOYD G. HUMPHREYS

Transfer of Training in General Education

There is an intimate connection between a philosophy of education and a theory of transfer, and this selection places the connection in historical perspective. Humphreys uses the term "training" to refer not to skills alone, as did the previous articles, but to the total problem of learning. He describes theories of transfer underlying certain educational beliefs. Are all questions of "educational philosophy" really philosophical? Or are some psychological hypotheses, which may be experimentally studied?

The expected outcomes of education do not always materialize. Time spent in training seems wasted when students are asked to use their learning in new situations. A group of children are taught multiplication combinations by rote alone. They later have great difficulty in utilizing their multiplication skills in long division. The graduates of a course in English literature, supposedly designed to promote literary appreciations, show no increase in either the quantity or the quality of their reading in comparison with their pre-course status. A Sunday-school teacher believes that she is engaged in moral training. Her charges acquire a great deal of biblical information, but there is no observable effect on their moral behavior. The information is also rather quickly forgotten. An instructor believes that his language course sharpens the intellect, but no generalized intellectual advantage can be observed in comparing his students with those of initially comparable ability who have had no language training. The claimed function of a laboratory course in physical science is to teach the scientific method. Not only

Reprinted from Lloyd G. Humphreys, "Transfer of Training in General Education," *Journal of General Education,* 5 (1951), 210–16, by permission of The University of Chicago Press.

does there seem to be no carry-over by the students to biological science or social science, but the skills and attitudes acquired are more those of the technician than of the scientist. It is claimed that geometry increases logical reasoning ability. The only measurable outcome of a traditional geometry course, however, is an increase in the ability to solve problems in geometry.

These problems are known in psychology as "transfer-of-training" problems;[1] they were selected to dramatize the issue, since in each case someone expected transfer that did not occur. All of us make similar assumptions, either implicitly or explicitly, concerning possible transfer effects from our courses. Few of us attempt to check the validity of those assumptions. We need to know, first, whether transfer is possible in situations such as those described. Second, if transfer is possible, we need to know how to maximize it.

Questions such as the following pose similar problems: Does the usual music-appreciation course actually produce a change in the student's appreciation of music? If not, what can be done in the course to produce the desired change in student behavior? Do foreign-language courses promote international understanding? What are the transfer effects to later civilian status of compulsory military training for eighteen-year-olds? If these effects are undesirable, how can we change military training to promote desirable democratic objectives and still maintain our national security? How can we teach the graduates of our schools, as citizens of a democracy, to make intelligent choices concerning control of atomic energy, antivivisection legislation, protective tariffs, treatment of minorities, etc.?

Definitions and assumptions. Before attempting to state the principles, derived from experimental data, which would be used to explain why the expected transfer did not take place in the first group of illustrations or which would be used to predict outcomes where answers are not presently known, it will be useful to state important definitions and assumptions. Psychology has a technical terminology that has largely been borrowed from popular usage. As a consequence, misunderstandings easily result.

Psychologists use the term "training" in the transfer literature as synonymous with "learning." The latter term includes the changes in skills, attitudes, feelings, emotions, knowledge, perceptions, ideas, etc., that are the relatively stable result of experience.[2] Many psychologists today might include all these different kinds of learning in the phrase "changes in behavior," but in so doing they would not restrict themselves to the Watsonian

[1] The writer has not attempted to document each point made in this paper, but, rather, has presented his interpretation of a fifty-year literature of many titles. The interested reader is referred to the following general sources: E. R. Hilgard, "The Relation of Schools of Psychology to Educational Practices," *California Journal of Elementary Education,* VIII (1939), 17–26; J. A. McGeoch, *The Psychology of Human Learning* (New York: Longmans, Green & Co., 1942); A. I. Gates and others, *Educational Psychology* (New York: Macmillan Co., 1949); and National Society for the Study of Education, *Forty-first Yearbook,* Part II: *The Psychology of Learning* (Chicago: University of Chicago Press, 1942).

[2] Temporary changes such as those due to fatigue, boredom, and warming up are, of course, excluded from learned changes.

behaviorism of the twenties. The term "behavior" includes all the psychological functions of the organism.

Other definitions of training are possible. For some educators, training means narrow, vocationally directed learning. These individuals use "education" as a broader term which includes much more than vocational training. Psychologically, however, "training" has developed into a broader term than "education," including both the latter and the informal, incidental learning that takes place, for example, in the neighborhood, school, and office. A "training situation" is one in which learning takes place.

By "transfer of training" we mean the influence of past training in a new situation which differs from the original training situation. The situation in which the influence of past training is to be tested can be called the "transfer" or "test situation." Differences between training and transfer situations vary from great to small. The direction of the influence of past training can be either negative or positive, either inhibitory or facilitory. The influence of past training in the new situation, or the "transfer effect," can vary in amount from zero to a positive amount equivalent to the effects of direct training on the transfer task. A maximum amount for negative transfer is more difficult to specify.

An interest in transfer of training is not synonymous with an interest in vocational education. The personal or social desirability of the behavior in transfer situations is an educational and social, but not a psychological, problem. Determination of the facts concerning transfer, for example, how much and under what circumstances, is a psychological problem. The development of generalizations to fit these facts and the prediction of new facts from these generalizations is also a psychological problem. Transfer is an issue whether the objectives of training are vocational or liberal, specific or general, attitudinal or informational. Given a set of objectives for education, the development of techniques of training, including both method and curriculum, that will produce the desired behavior to the highest degree and with the broadest transfer possibilities is a problem that can best be solved by the co-operation of the specialist in subject matter and the psychologist.

While educational objectives are not an issue in the science of psychology, individual psychologists have the right of any faculty member, or citizen, to favor certain objectives. The present writer, for example, is seriously concerned about general or liberal education. He believes that both students and the general public typically overstress vocational goals. He further believes, however, that much of the curriculum that was important several hundred years ago in promoting a liberal education is perhaps outmoded. We should consider the problems of liberal education from the point of view both of modern needs and of knowledge of learning and transfer principles.

HISTORY OF THE TRANSFER PROBLEM

Formal discipline. The history of the transfer problem usually starts with the doctrine of formal discipline. This doctrine is unusual, since the facts of transfer that the theory was supposed to explain did not exist. Under the circumstances it would hardly seem to warrant attention. Discussion is indicated, however, because at one time the theory was so strongly intrenched and because remnants of it are still with us today.

Mind was considered to be composed of many faculties, of which reasoning and memory are appropriate examples. Faculties were strengthened by exercise, as muscles are strengthened by exercise. Since the most difficult subjects provided most exercise, Latin, Greek, and mathematics were, therefore, the most desirable subjects in the curriculum and could be used for both vocational and liberal-arts training. Some of the more biologically oriented theorists suggested that these faculties were localized in the cerebral hemispheres. Furthermore, if a given faculty were a prominent aspect of an individual's personality, the corresponding brain area would be found to be enlarged. A few individuals took the additional step of assuming that these enlargements would affect the cranium. Thus we find a tie between the doctrine of formal discipline and the pseudo-science of phrenology.

Educators such as Eliot and psychologists such as William James had begun to suspect the validity of the formal-discipline doctrine before the end of the nineteenth century. The hypothesized faculties were suspect, and the physiological basis of the faculties had been completely overthrown. Then, around the turn of the century, Thorndike and his co-workers began making the direct measures of transfer effect that have proved to be most damaging to formal-discipline notions. In general, it has been found that no learning activity has any widespread mental disciplining power. In a typical experiment two groups of subjects are matched in terms of initial ability; both groups are trained similarly except for the experimental variable, e.g., Latin is taught one group, shop is taught the other; both groups are given a reasoning (or memory) test at the conclusion of training; little, if any, difference in final ability is discovered.

Experiments similar to the one described above have brought to light an important function served by the classical curriculum that undoubtedly confused early thinkers about transfer. If students are not carefully matched for initial ability, a difference in both initial and final ability is typically discovered. The initial difference in aptitude between those who have taken Latin and those who have taken shop is explained in terms of the self-selection that goes on in the choice of a curriculum and in terms of the greater elimination rate of students in classics who have low reasoning ability. All difficult academic subjects serve as valid selection devices for later educational or occupational placement, though this function is served quite inefficiently today in comparison with the results obtained in a few hours from the use of available aptitude tests.

Identical elements. Thorndike, after showing the lack of disciplining effect of traditional academic subjects, was still able to demonstrate the existence of transfer in limited areas. He suggested that transfer took place when there were identical elements between the training and the transfer situations. More recently this statement of the basis for transfer has been called the "identical-components theory" in order to avoid criticism directed at the atomistic, specific stimulus-response connotations of the original expression. Since there is no compulsion to consider the problem atomistically, the change in terminology is valid. At the same time, the major emphasis of the theory remains the same.

Thorndike's contribution led to educational conclusions similar to the following: If you need accounting in your occupation, study accounting during your training and preferably the type of accounting you will need. If you want to read Cicero in Latin, by all means study Latin. If, however, you want to learn French, do not spend several years in the study of Latin, since you will be farther ahead if you concentrate on French. If you want to learn to solve social problems, spend your time in the social sciences, not in the study of geometry. If classroom activities resemble the work of a laboratory technician, the habits acquired will be those of a technician. It is sufficiently difficult to teach scientific methodology in a single science that to attempt to teach it in a physics class as a behavioral trait is hardly feasible.

Examples such as the above could be continued indefinitely. The indicated transfer is narrow in scope but, in terms of predictable outcomes, is still a sound basis for curriculum planning and instruction. More recent research has indicated that certain modifications have to be introduced, modifications that lead to a little more generality in transfer, but thinking about transfer problems in terms of identical elements should not be discarded. The argument that Thorndike's theorizing contributed to the utilitarian movement in American education is not critical. This was not a necessary consequence of the theory but resulted, instead, from the increasing importance attached by the public and certain educators to vocational objectives. The above examples indicate that the theory applies equally well to other educational objectives. Specifically, if literary appreciations constitute a desired out-of-class outcome of the educational process, then the in-class activities must involve similar behaviors.

Generalization. Increasing dissatisfaction with the identical-elements theory as more transfer data became available led to the development of additional principles to account for the results. At times, particularly in the realm of attitudes, more widespread transfer was obtained than might have been expected from the limited, original interpretation of the identical-components theory. At other times—e.g., the failure of multiplication skills to transfer to the solution of long-division problems—less transfer was observed than might have been expected from an objective analysis of the identical components involved.

A widely quoted experiment by Judd is pertinent here. One group of subjects was given instruction concerning the refraction of light. A second comparable group, serving as controls, had no theoretical instruction. Both groups were given practice in aiming a dart at an underwater target. Neither group exhibited any superiority in original learning. Then the depth of the target was changed. The group given the principle of refraction was now clearly superior to the control group on the transfer test. Judd reasoned that an analysis in terms of identical perceptual-motor components was inadequate. He stated that transfer took place when appropriate generalizations had been formed.

The Gestalt psychologists have talked about what is essentially the same phenomenon as that studied by Judd in terms of the meaningful organization of learning. Such learning, in their terminology, transposes or transfers more readily than material learned in meaningless, rote fashion. When multiplication is taught by methods that stress the meaningful order of the arithmetic processes, considerable transfer results. The introduction of principles in the teaching of spelling results in better spelling, including greater transfer to the spelling of new words than can be obtained following the use of the rote methods.

Other general factors that promote transfer are habits of work, methods of attacking problems, and motivation to find transfer possibilities. All involve more than identical components as originally used and defined by Thorndike, but they supplement rather than supplant the earlier theory. Transfer possibilities for specific subject-matter learning are broadened by taking into account this more recent theorizing, and the problem of curriculum selection is lessened by the decreased emphasis on specificity, but observed transfer effects are still small in comparison with the unsubstantiated beliefs of the adherents of formal discipline.

Common elements in current theories. Psychologists of all points of view reject transfer claims that represent formal-discipline notions. The latter beliefs frequently show up today, at times using the same terms that were popular a hundred years ago, at times disguising the formal disciplinary claims in new terms, but no evidence has been presented to back the beliefs. Psychologists feel that, while some matters are properly in the sphere of belief, principles of learning and transfer are just as properly the subject of quantitative, scientific inquiry.

All theories of transfer also require sound initial learning. There is nothing in the transfer literature to suggest that schools should ease up or that instructors should require less work. Objections to a curriculum composed primarily of Latin, Greek, and mathematics are not based on the difficulty of the subjects or the high standards of teachers of these subjects. The important objection is that the supposed benefits are not obtained by the students.

APPLICATIONS TO EDUCATIONAL PROBLEMS

The study of language. Two statements can be made dogmatically about the study of any language. First, there will be no sharpening of intellect, no increase in reasoning ability, no increase in memory ability. Second, if a student needs to know the language, he must, of course, study the language. The position of language instruction in special education is secure. For possible outcomes of interest in general education, the amount of transfer is less certain, particularly when the cost in time is considered.

To take an example, analysis of the Latin and English languages indicates that there are identical elements in vocabulary and grammar. There are also possible elements in common between Latin and ancient history. Can we expect transfer in these areas? In answering this question, we recall the multiplication—long-division example. The expected transfer will not take place unless the identical components as seen by the instructor are made meaningful to the students. The teacher, in other words, has to teach English vocabulary, English grammar, and ancient history along with Caesar and Cicero.

Practice in translating any language into English may well have an appreciable effect on the student's skill in English composition. We would expect more transfer from translation in the indicated direction than from translation of English into the foreign language. We would also expect more transfer in this area if stress is placed on idiomatic English translations.

The skeptic may ask at this point whether perhaps greater gains for the majority of students in these areas can be made by the use of some more direct medium than a second language. After all, the mere demonstration of desirable transfer in some amount does not furnish conclusive evidence for keeping a particular subject in the curriculum. The criticism is undoubtedly valid in the present instance, since there are ways of manipulating English alone to achieve the same ends more efficiently. If there are other reasons for the student to learn the language, however, he might as well obtain maximum benefit from his endeavor.

The claim that study of a modern foreign language increases international understanding is heard increasingly today. It has been conclusively demonstrated that attitudes toward a specific country can be changed in a favorable direction by *proper* study of the language. One suspects also that it would not be difficult to find language courses taught somewhat differently that produce the opposite effect, but data are not available. When the time spent by the average student in learning the language is balanced against the gain in attitude toward a single country, one is tempted to seek again for a more direct approach to international good will. Language training is best justified when the student needs to know the language, whether his need is for business or aesthetic reasons.

Aesthetic appreciations. There are specific problems in the teaching of aesthetic appreciations in music, art, and literature, but only common problems will be considered here. It should also be noted that transfer of appreciations from one area to another will not take place automatically, i.e., aesthetic appreciation cannot be trained as a whole by working in any one medium. If the instructor in music wishes to have the students relate his subject to art or literature, classroom activities must include such relationships.

In training for appreciations, we frequently run afoul of the grading system. Grades based on proficiency are essential in professional courses, but we should consider the possibility that the problems may not be the same in general education. If we are interested in increasing reading and enjoyment in reading, why should we construct tests and grade our students solely in terms of their intellectual grasp of the subject? Is the ability to memorize the names of Shakespeare's characters related to the main objective of instruction? Grades are not easy to assign in the learning of appreciations, but undesirable practices should not be continued, even though there is no easy substitute.

General education in all fields is frequently in conflict with the interests of special education. We sometimes confuse what an advanced graduate student should know about Shakespeare, for example, with the needs of lower-division students, most of whom will major in other fields. This confusion frequently leads also to stress on information and analysis at the expense of appreciations.

Aesthetic appreciation is not solely an emotional experience. Intellectual competence is necessary; e.g., ability to read the English language with understanding is basic to literary appreciation. Historical information may also be important. Principles of psychology, including symptoms of abnormal behavior and of unconscious motivation, may at times be involved. These can be organized to increase the appreciation of the novel, or they can be taught as ends in themselves. The sort of organization intended here can frequently be obtained in good films or plays better than by the usual classroom procedures. Visual aids must be carefully selected and used, however, if they are to make the desired contribution.

The great-books approach. The contribution of the so-called "great-books" approach to general education is sometimes assessed in terms of the need to acquaint students with the wisdom of the past. The problem becomes of more interest from the transfer point of view if something is added about the need to use the past wisdom in the present. Isolated information about the past is easy to teach but is difficult for the student to retain and use. Use of the wisdom of the past in considering present problems does not take place automatically, even with the brightest of students. The student must have the opportunity in the classroom to try out ideas obtained from his study if his knowledge is going to transfer to new situations. In attempting to make history meaningful to secondary students, for example, teachers have successfully taught history "backward." This does not mean that we must always start with the present, but, if we want effects in the present, we must teach for that objective.

Social scientists frequently find themselves at odds with the enthusiasts for the great-books program on an issue that is less clearly related to the transfer problem. These enthusiasts sometimes imply that study of the great books is a sufficient basis for deciding present social problems and problems of human interrelationships. The social scientist does not believe that such problems can be solved by anyone, even with optimum teaching, from the study of our classics alone. He argues that the essential content simply is not there. In addition to the wisdom of the ages, we need to obtain reliable information about human problems by the application of scientific methods to those problems. Since the content is considered inadequate, the advocate of an extreme position with regard to the value of the great-books approach to general education is only, so it is reasoned, rationalizing his position on grounds of formal discipline.

Science. During the last fifty years many institutions have required students to have one laboratory course in science in the lower division. Typical reasons offered are to train students in the disciplined habits of scientists and to give students an understanding and appreciation of the scientific method. Since any laboratory course can fill the requirement in most institutions, it is obvious that claims for considerable transfer are involved.

There are several reasonable predictions that can be made concerning this procedure. In the first place, the training in the physics laboratory will probably extend only to the subject matter of physics. If greater breadth than that is required, the course must be broadened. Second, the techniques taught in the usual laboratory are only in small part the techniques of the scientist. The techniques learned have been characterized in an earlier section as those of the technician, not of the scientist. The major omission from the laboratory of techniques essential to the scientist are his problem-solving activities. If problem-solving is desired, problem-solving must be an essential part of the laboratory procedure.

Also omitted from the usual laboratory course is any attention to attitudes toward science. There is little profit in required courses in science that may increase the student's dislike of science and scientists. Desirable changes in attitudes in this area can no more be taken for granted than they can in the area of aesthetic appreciations. Changes in attitudes can be measured with some success. Techniques for changing attitudes in specific courses must be developed.

The writer has attempted to interpret the transfer-of-training literature in psychology as it pertains to the problems of general education. In doing this, the history of the thinking and experimentation with regard to transfer problems has been traced up to the present, and an evaluation of present status has been given. A highly personal interpretation of the implications of the transfer theory to a number of educational problems has also been attempted.

The first step in analyzing an educational problem in terms of transfer possibilities is to decide on the ends to be accomplished. The second step is to select the classroom (or course) content that seems most suitable for the achievement of the objectives. This selection is made primarily in terms of the identical-components basis for transfer, that is, the content of the training situation should correspond as closely as possible to the content of the prospective transfer situation. The third step is to decide how this content should be presented or to determine the techniques of instruction that will be most effective. Here the contributions of Judd and the Gestalt psychologists are most appropriate: the teaching must stress general principles, organization of the learning, etc. The fourth step, and perhaps more important than either the second or the third, is to attempt to measure the extent to which the predicted transfer takes place.[3]

[3] Any reader can disagree with conclusions reached by the writer and still be respectable in psychological circles. The reader who disagrees is under compulsion, however, to do something about his disagreement. One does not need to be a psychologist in order to participate in the measurement of educational outcomes.

Chapter **11**

Improving Understanding and Thinking

11-1

ELLEN FROGNER

Grammar Approach Versus Thought Approach in Teaching Sentence Structure

11-2

GERTRUDE HILDRETH

The Difficulty Reduction Tendency in Perception and Problem Solving

ELLEN FROGNER

Grammar Approach Versus Thought Approach in Teaching Sentence Structure

Most people agree that good English composition is important, but they do not agree on how it should be taught. Ellen Frogner tells of one experiment designed to test two approaches to better sentence structure. What do her results prove about the usefulness of each method? Is the fact that one group apparently spent more time studying nomenclature perhaps the source of handicap for the "grammatical" approach? Analyze the conditions, and decide how you would let the results modify your own practice if you were an English teacher.

He knows neither Ablative, Conjunctive, Substantive, nor Grammar, no more than doth his Lackey, nor any Oyster-wife about the streets, and yet if you have a mind to it, he will entertaine you your bill, and peradventure stumble as little and as seldom against the rules of his tongue, as the best Master of Arts in France.—*The Essayes of Michael, Lord of Montaigne.*

Teachers of English are challenged today to justify the amount of time spent on grammar. The language program as a whole aims to develop accuracy and power in oral and written expression, to make pupils conscious of the joy of expressing ideas and sharing experience, to foster ability in evaluating ideas and experience in terms of interest to others, and to ensure competence in meeting with ease the social situations involving the use of language. The present large emphasis given to the teaching of grammar indicates a belief that such instruction must be of the utmost importance in accomplishing the aims of the language program.

Particularly has the contribution of grammar to ability in sentence structure been emphasized. A survey of the literature on the subject from the beginning of the century up to the present time reveals a decided tendency to think of sentence mastery as the primary purpose in the study of grammatical principles. The importance of submitting the assumption to investigation is evident, especially in consideration of the fact that the structure of sentences is recognized as contributing in a notable measure to the total effect of the composition.

In order to lend some clarification to the problem the writer carried out

Ellen Frogner, "Grammar Approach Versus Thought Approach in Teaching Sentence Structure," *English Journal,* 28 (1939), 518–26. Reprinted with permission of the National Council of Teachers of English and Ellen Frogner.

an extended study of the relative effectiveness of a grammatical and a thought method in the teaching of sentence structure.[1] The experiment was conducted for one semester in Minneapolis and in Bemidji, Minnesota, with forty-seven pairs in Grade IX and sixty pairs in Grade XI. The aim was to compare the improvement made by pupils who were directed to approach problems of sentence structure entirely from the standpoint of the adequate expression of thought with the improvement made by pupils who, besides having their attention directed to the clear expression of thought, were also given the drill needed to ensure an understanding of the grammatical construction of the sentence. In other words, the important point is that while some of the thought approach was included in the grammar classes, no grammar was used in the classes taught according to the thought method, where the underlying principle was the clear, effective expression of ideas.

ILLUSTRATIONS OF THE TWO METHODS

Examples from the units taught during the course of the experiment will bring out more specifically the differences between the two methods.

UNIT I. CO-ORDINATION AND SUBORDINATION OF IDEAS IN CLAUSES

A primary aim in the first unit was to make pupils conscious of the fact that a mature speaker or writer reveals the exact relationship between ideas. Pupils using the thought method began by noting that a sentence like "Mary plays a good game of tennis, and she makes excellent cake" is not good because the two statements about Mary are hardly related in thought. The class suggested a second idea which would be related to the first, as, for instance, "Mary plays a good game of tennis, and she is also a true sportsman." It was noticed that "and" was used correctly here, since one idea was added to another, both of the ideas being closely related and equal in importance. The next step was to have the pupils volunteer with similar sentences, noting words suitable as substitutes for "and." During the procedure a faulty sentence like the following was suggested: "Betty carefully explained her plan to the chairman, and he was not interested." The sentence, of course, is not an exact expression of the thought, as here the purpose is to contrast two ideas. "But" would bring out accurately the relationship between the thoughts. From suggested sentences containing one idea in contrast to another, a list was made of words to use in place of "but" for the sake of variety.

The classes taught according to the thought method continued by going from the problem of expressing related ideas of equal importance in the same sentence to the problem of subordinating one idea to another. The pupils noted how for variety the thought in the sentence just used for purposes of illustration could also be stated: "Although Betty explained her plan carefully, the chairman was not interested." They found that combining ideas from short, choppy sentences or from those that were long and

[1] "A Study of the Relative Efficiency of a Grammatical and a Thought Approach to the Improvement of Sentence Structure in Grades Nine and Eleven" (Doctor's thesis, University of Minnesota, 1938).

rambling made not only for sentence variety but also for greater accuracy of statement and for a more mature expression of the thought.

The pupils went on to study common types of errors in the coordination and subordination of ideas. One example is found in the following sentence: "I gave my brother a copy of *Smoky*, and which he read many times." The explanation of the error according to the thought method was that "and," which connects ideas of equal importance, should not be used in joining a subordinate idea to one of greater importance. Another common error occurs in the use of "is when" and "is where" in definitions: "To portage is when you carry canoes and provisions from one lake to another." Instead of pointing out the mistake of an adverbial clause used as a noun (as was done in the grammar classes), pupils taught by the thought method reasoned that "to portage" is not "when" or time, but "to portage" is "to carry." They noted also the parallelism and balance of the second part of the sentence with the first.

Pupils in the grammar classes likewise directed their attention to stating ideas accurately and effectively. The distinguishing difference lay in the approach through knowledge of grammar. From illustrative sentences pupils came to the conclusion that ideas of equal importance are expressed in independent clauses, while subordinate ideas are expressed in dependent clauses. Grammatical terminology was used also in the discussion of errors. Necessarily, any terms used should be understood. What, for instance, would seem to be required for a thorough understanding of subordinate clauses? Clearly, a knowledge of subject and predicate, the distinction between independent and dependent or subordinate clauses, the recognition of subordinate conjunctions, and a clear conception of adjectives, adverbs, and nouns, in order to explain the various uses of the clauses. Consequently, in order that the understanding desired might be effected, the pupils in the grammar classes not only practiced subordinating ideas in clauses but also analyzed sentences by selecting clauses and explaining their use.

UNIT II. SUBORDINATION OF IDEAS IN PHRASES

The classes in which the grammar method was used began Unit II with examples of subordinating ideas by means of different kinds of phrases: prepositional, appositive, participial, gerund, and infinitive. Pupils differentiated phrases according to their kind and their use in the sentence. Ideas from short, choppy sentences were combined into a more effective expression of the thought by means of phrases. In all probability if this last step had been omitted, the procedure would have been more typical of grammar teaching today. With the inclusion of this step, however, grammar should contribute to the acquiring of more effective sentence structure, if knowledge of grammar is essential to accuracy and clarity of expression. The pupils then proceeded to the discussion and correction of errors in the use of phrases, such as the misplaced prepositional phrase or the dangling participle.

The thought approach was less involved. Pupils started out by noticing the various ways of subordinating ideas. Illustrative sentences were written on the board, and in combining ideas pupils were urged to try as many of these sentence patterns as possible. There was, however, no pointing out that certain kinds of phrases had been used. For instance, a composition contained such statements as the following: "Mr. White is our class adviser. He grasped the seriousness of the situation. He immediately called a meeting of the officers." How could the ideas be combined to avoid the monotonous childish sentences? Several possibilities were suggested, one of which was: "Having grasped the seriousness of the situation, Mr. White, our class adviser, immediately called a meeting of the officers." Pupils improved the expression of the thought by means of subordinating ideas in a participial and an appositive phrase; yet they were not drilled in the recognition of the grammatical constructions used. The classes taught according to the thought method also went on to the correction of errors in the use of phrases, but from the standpoint of meaning only. In a sentence like "Waiting on the corner for a bus, the accident occurred," there was no labeling of "waiting" as a dangling participle. The test was: Did the writer say what he evidently meant to say?

UNIT III. RECOGNITION OF THE SENTENCE

Unit III dealt with a problem constantly facing every teacher of English, namely, the development of sentence sense. The teaching of grammar is often justified on the ground that knowledge of subject and predicate is essential to the recognition of the sentence. The approach to sentence completeness in the grammar classes was through recognition of subject and predicate and, in addition, through the test of the completeness of the idea expressed.

On the other hand, pupils in the classes using the thought method attacked both fragmentary and run-on sentences from the single test of clear, complete expression of ideas. Such questions as the following were asked in approaching the many types of sentence fragments: Is the idea immediately clear? Do the words leave you "up in the air," as if something else belonged with them? What seems to be left unstated? What is the main statement to which these words add something as a contributing or subordinate idea? How can the subordinate idea be expressed in proper relationship to the main idea of which it is a part? Thus the pupil was led to consider the expression of the whole thought rather than to search for the grammatical elements of subject and predicate.

The thought approach in the matter of run-on sentences can be illustrated by a typical situation: Assume that a boy in the ninth grade has written: "We went to a deserted house on Nineteenth Avenue six of us went there were two small boys and four big boys." If the writer is confronted with his own sentences some time after he has written them and if he is asked to read them aloud, he will usually come to the conclusion that they seem "mixed up." Examining his work, he will see that there are no signals along the way to let a person know when one idea ends and another begins; in other words, the reader has to be considered. What is the first idea that the writer wants to get across? "We went to a deserted house on Nineteenth Avenue." What are the other main points to be left with the reader? "Six of us went. There were two small boys and four big boys." The three ideas are now perfectly clear, but with most pupils we can go a step beyond mere correctness and ask whether or not there are other possibilities for improvement. A pupil who has already had his attention directed toward combining ideas will in all probability suggest in this case: "Six of us, two small boys and four big boys, went to a deserted house on Nineteenth Avenue."

If the ninth-grade boy hesitates about the punctuation in writing this last sentence, how can he be helped according to the thought approach? The principle to which his attention should be called is that information subordinate to the main thought of the sentence and inserted simply as an additional or explanatory idea is set off by commas. The illustration shows how closely punctuation is connected with work in sentence structure. Dealing with problems of punctuation as the need arises in the expression of ideas provides well-motivated drill. While the results of the experiment carried out by the writer were directed toward a comparison of the two methods in the teaching of sentence structure only, the study nevertheless made clear the importance of submitting to investigation questions similar to the following: Which is more helpful to the pupil—to approach punctuation through a knowledge of appositive modifiers, nonrestrictive phrases, and nonrestrictive clauses or through simply an understanding of the general principle that information inserted as additional or explanatory and subordinate to the main thought of the sentence is set off by commas?

The essential difference between the two methods appeared also in the other units in sentence structure taught during the course of the experiment: reference of the pronoun, sequence of tenses, parallel construction, and omissions. The unit dealing with parallel structure, for instance, provided an excellent opportunity to test the contribution of grammar to style, in which proper parallelism is an important factor. The fundamental principle in the grammar method was that ideas parallel in thought should also be parallel in grammatical construction; in the thought method, that ideas parallel in thought should also be parallel in statement. In a sentence like "Swimming is more strenuous exercise than to walk" pupils in the grammar classes pointed out that "swimming" and "to walk," both parallel in thought and parallel as subjects of the verb "is" (expressed or understood), should also be stated in parallel grammatical form; that is, both should be either gerunds or infinitives. Pupils using the thought approach noted the parallel ideas in "swimming" and "to walk," two kinds of exercise being compared. Since the two are parallel in thought, they should also be so in statement. Means used to further the recognition of parallelism in statement were the listing of ideas under one another on the board to discover whether any were not stated in comparable manner and also the repeating of sentences orally to develop a recognition of the rhythm of proper parallelism.

RESULTS OF THE EXPERIMENT

The effectiveness of the two methods was compared in results for three general tests of sentence structure, tests for each of the seven units, and two tests of knowledge of technical grammar. Following are the major conclusions based on many specific comparisons for one hundred and seven pairs of pupils in Grades IX and XI:

1. The pupils in the grammar classes definitely learned more grammar than did those in the group using the thought method. All of the differences in gains, for instance, made on the two tests of grammar were in favor of the grammar classes. Five of the twelve possible differences satisfied the upper level of statistical significance. Other comparisons evidenced a like superiority on the part of the pupils in the grammar classes.

2. In spite of this fact, the thought method brought about superior results in sentence structure, as measured by general tests covering the work of the semester. All of the eighteen possible differences in gains favored the classes taught according to the thought method. Three of these differences satisfied the upper level of statistical significance.

A comparison of the thirty-three pairs in the ninth grade in Bemidji illustrates the fact that knowledge of grammar is evidently not essential to improvement in sentence structure: In gains made on the general test in sentence structure especially constructed for the experiment seventeen pupils in the grammar class surpassed their mates by a total of 148 points, while sixteen pupils taught according to the thought method surpassed by a total of 217 points. Yet in gains made on the test measuring knowledge of the grammar involved in the items of sentence structure, thirty-one pupils in the grammar class surpassed their mates by a total of 1,489 points, compared with two pupils in the thought class exceeding their mates by a total of only 10 points.

3. Results of the unit tests in individual elements of sentence structure given immediately at the close of each unit did not, in general, favor either group. Comparison of these figures with those for the long-time tests at the end of the experiment suggests that when a test calls for the application of grammatical rules recently learned and practiced, little difference is evident between the grammar and thought methods, but that the thought approach makes for longer retention of the fundamental abilities involved.

4. The thought method in both Grades IX and XI was definitely superior to the grammar approach for all pupils with an I.Q. below 105. Evidence for the statement is found in the fact that all of the differences in gains made by the pupils of average and below average intelligence favored the thought method, and in every instance the difference more than satisfied the lower level of statistical significance. There was little difference between the two methods among superior pupils, except for a tendency on the part of those of the highest range of intelligence (I.Q. from 114–129) to profit more from the thought than from the grammar method.

5. The thought approach required approximately 80 per cent of the time required by the grammar method; thus a saving of the equivalent of one day out of five could be effected.

6. A study of the reasoning used by the pupils revealed that those in the thought classes made use of the thought method predominantly. In the grammar classes more pupils used thought aids along with grammatical reasoning than confined themselves to a strictly grammatical approach.

Results of the study, therefore, lend no support to the claims made for grammar as being essential to improvement in sentence structure. On the contrary, since the experiment demonstrates that an emphasis upon thought is effective in improving details of usage and style, it makes evident the value of such an approach in the whole problem of fostering ability in speaking and writing—an approach wherein the major emphasis in the improvement of ability in language coincides with the inherent purpose of language as a means of expressing ideas.

GERTRUDE HILDRETH

The Difficulty Reduction Tendency in Perception and Problem Solving

What we call a "mistake" may often be, to the child, a perfectly plausible response. Indeed, from the child's point of view, his "error" may be quite in keeping with good sense. Gertrude Hildreth reports a varied and sometimes amusing catalogue of logical boners. She shows that instead of being random errors, these actions are patterned and predictable from the prior experience of the student. Although her explanation is not the only one possible, most of us will agree with her inferences for better teaching.

When children or adults are confronted with problems too difficult for them to solve, or situations beyond their understanding and experience, they tend to substitute simpler mental responses for the appropriate ones. For a required goal which is too difficult, an intermediate goal is set up. The natural tendency is to reach a solution that fits a simpler problem or situation, that allies the new problem to a familiar one, or that fits the person's insight, knowledge and experience. The problem is solved, not by straining to meet the difficulty, but rather by dropping it down to a simpler level. Piaget [1] observed that to understand certain notions and concepts the child has to deform and assimilate them according to a mental structure of his own.

The reduction process may be entirely automatic; ordinarily it is quite unconscious. A person's limited resources for dealing with the problem may prevent him from grasping the real problem in all its implications, and from seeing that his response is erroneous.

If people were less influenced by this principle in problem-solving they

[1] Piaget, J.: *The Child's Conception of the World.* New York: Harcourt, Brace & World, 1929.

Gertrude Hildreth, "The Difficulty Reduction Tendency in Perception and Problem Solving," *Journal of Educational Psychology,* 32 (1941), 305–13. Reprinted with permission of Abrahams Magazine Service, Inc.

would more frequently respond in random fashion or give up all attempt at solution; but the fact is that random responses or "giving up" in ordinary daily life situations is infrequent as contrasted with simplifying the problems. The child in his normal daily activities, or the typical adult going about his routines, responding largely on a habit level, reveals in countless instances the operation of this principle, if solutions on different levels of insight and maturity are possible.

Psychologists are familiar with the principle of apperception early formulated by Herbert and elaborated by his followers. According to this principle, a person's mental responses are influenced by his experience and background. Herbert called this assimilative function of the mind "apperception." According to this doctrine, environmental influences determine which presentations the mind receives and also their manner of combining into higher mental processes. Acquisitions of new experiences are affected by those already acquired. Young children show the influence of apperception in many situations. One baby who was given some Phenolax asked for more "pink candy." The child who calls all animals "dogs" or all men "daddy" is responding in harmony with the "apperceptive mass."

The distinctive feature of the Difficulty Reduction Tendency as contrasted with apperception or "mind set" is the unconscious tendency to simplify the problem. This is not necessarily true in all responses affected by apperception or "mind set."

Errors and distortions are frequent when this tendency operates. These errors and distortions, though absurd, are not random nor chance. The response made to the simplified problem is a genuine, usually a meaningful, coherent solution. In fact, the tendency toward reducing the problem usually represents an effort to make the problem more meaningful. The movement is always in the direction from the less to the more meaningful.

Too frequently an individual's responses are rated as right or wrong with little attempt on the part of the rater to understand the significance of the particular response made. We obtain an excellent clue to the child's maturity in language development through studying his substitution errors in reading or speaking. The "boners" that cause teachers and parents endless amusement and that furnish the substance for our "humor" magazines are all first-hand data for the psychologist who would understand the operation of the Difficulty Reduction Principle. The errors that school children make provide analytic material for evaluating the child's mental development, understanding his thought processes and diagnosing teaching and learning situations. Through studying such errors we would be less prone to attribute errors to chance, or to be baffled by mistakes children make. Instead, we would have more sympathetic understanding of each child's learning difficulties.

These Difficulty Reduction Tendencies are shown in auditory and visual perception, in word meanings, in reasoning and thinking. The resulting errors are nowhere more commonly shown than in verbal responses due to the insecurity of auditory and visual perception. We say the individual misunderstood the verbal stimulus, that his hearing or vision was defective; the truer explanation is that he interpreted the question or problem in terms of his own mental grasp and insight which may have been inadequate for the problem. The chance that this type of error will appear in puzzle-solving or running a maze is less frequent.

Illustrations of the Difficulty Reduction Tendency are found in responses that involve reading, understanding spoken language, drawing or copying figures, and in broader thinking and reasoning problems.

ILLUSTRATIONS

ERRORS IN READING

The person who makes an error while reading is seldom making a purely mechanical error. He is generally attempting to make sense out of what he is reading and in so doing he may perceive word symbols incorrectly. In his effort to make sense from symbols that are meaningless to him he may substitute his own preferred word symbols.

A schoolmaster in Virginia always called on one boy each morning to read a passage from the Scripture. One boy read: "Then shall the Kingdom of Heaven be likened unto ten Virginians . . . and five of them were wise and five were foolish." The schoolmaster stopped the boy and asked him to repeat the passage. He read exactly as before. "Well," commented the schoolmaster, "if the Bible says so, it must be true. But I never would have believed there were five foolish Virginians."

A young gifted child who had more zeal than ability made the following substitutions in her reading efforts, as noted by W. F. Dearborn:

"Ping" was read as "pink" or "pig"; "Forever" as "father"; "Organize" was read as "orange"; "Basket" for "breakfast"; "Tumble" for "theatre"; "Paints" then "Plants" for "parents"; "Business" as "Bess"; "Pleasant" as "plant"; "Friendship" as "friends." Another child read "large" for "lapse"; "purse" for "puree"; "ten fingers" for "ten figures." These were all easier substitutions for unfamiliar or difficult words.

A doctor's son read: "The children took off their stockings to wade," as "to get weighed." An adult read the book title "M Day" as "My Day," and was surprised not to see Mrs. Roosevelt's name on the title page.

ERRORS IN AUDITORY PERCEPTION SHOWN IN VOCABULARY AND NAMING ERRORS

It is a common tendency to interpret what we hear in terms of what we know or what we wish to hear. This makes what we hear easier to comprehend. We reduce auditory stimuli to our understanding level just as we tend to simplify visual percepts. The most frequent illustrations of these errors are found in the auditory perception of words and names. Many of our misunderstandings and slips of the tongue fall under this heading. We say, "I didn't hear"; we mean, "I did not understand the words used."

Anyone who has asked children to respond with definitions to the words of the Standford-Binet Vocabulary lists has frequently met this type of error, particularly in the young or dull child who quickly "gets beyond his depth." Since the words are given out of context, errors are inevitable.

A child of eight responded: "Guitar—you spread it on the streets";

"Muzzle—your arm is strong"; "Ochre—what you put in soup." "Roar" is confused with "raw" and "row," no matter how carefully it is pronounced.

A young child at church heard the clergyman read, "The *zeal* of thy house hath eaten me up," and asked his mother if he could see the animal after church. "My Country is a tree," one child sang lustily. Third-grade children reciting the Lord's Prayer in unison were heard to say, "Forgive us our trashbaskets and give them their trashbaskets."

High-school students made the following errors in themes.[2] The Crusades were fought in *Plasticine.* In a simple ceremony George Green, the president, handed over the *gravel* to the new encumbent. The fellows were cheered on to victory for our Alma *Martyr.* A new course prepares the student for the *vacations* for which he is fitted.

Children who labeled drawings of trains wrote most frequently on the coal car, "Cold" or "cool" car. A preacher reported that he was going to *officiate* elsewhere next Sunday afternoon, hence there would be no service. A child in the audience reported to his parents that the preacher was going fishing next Sunday afternoon and so there would be no Sunday School. One teacher repeatedly told the beginning first-grade class: "Sit erect, sit erect." The children reported at home that she said, "Cigarette, cigarette," to them repeatedly. Parents complained that the teacher did not enunciate distinctly enough.

At the Chicago World's Fair the artistically illiterate, eager to see the widely advertised and famous picture of Whistler's mother, asked to see the "Whistling Woman." Students in statistics class referred to the "medium" of a group rather than "median."

In 1818 Beethoven received a Broadwood piano from London, but a recent New York newspaper article referred to the instrument as a "Broadway." An article in the French press devoted to American customs observed that "After dinner some Americans play *three-robbers* bridge."

Word Etymology is illustrated in the following instances: Soubresault (French) from Latin "supre-saltus," "leap over" has become *Somer sault* and *Summer set.* We associate it with summertime and landing on the grass. "Breukelen" became "Brooklyn" to English-speaking people. Paul Dreiser became "Dresser"; "Izzy" Baline is now Irving Berlin; "Pumpkins" were originally "pompions"; "Kind" became Anglicized as "Kid."

ERRORS IN VISUAL PERCEPTION AND DRAWING

The Difficulty Reduction Tendency is illustrated when children and adults attempt to copy or draw from memory figures that either are meaningless to them, which are difficult to draw, or for which the time exposure is too short to enable them to study the figure sufficiently to reproduce it correctly. Children show to a marked extent a tendency to simplify intricacies in ambiguous figures by drawing substitute objects that are meaningful to them or easier to draw for any reason. A tendency toward integration and unification is shown in drawings of both adults and children, apparently in an effort to simplify the percept. Rhythm, symmetry and proportion

[2] Salisbury, R. and Leonard, J. P.: *Making sense; how to say what you mean and understand what you say.* Chicago: Scott, Foresman, 1936.

may be introduced where it was originally lacking, because these tendencies help to organize and consequently to simplify the figures. The tendencies also represent more "primitive" and habituated responses. In children's drawings this tendency suggests a trend toward mental economy and least effort.

In drawing, young children tend to substitute a circle for anything suggesting roundness. The tendency is to "square" anything with angles. Apparently the square is simpler than the rectangle because all sides are equal. The rectangle is usually shortened. In copying a diamond, the child of four makes a rough triangle. A still younger child, instead of drawing a square or diamond as directed, will say, "I'll make a bed," or "It's a windmill," and draws a crude cross. A boy of three persistently made drawings of locomotives and trains of freight cars, but invariably made sausage shaped units instead of cylinders or rectangles. This tendency persisted in his drawings for over a year.

When young children before school age are asked to write their names, a task that is generally unpracticed and too difficult for them, they tend to scribble in imitation of adult cursive writing or essay a few large capital letters, such as they have seen on their blocks. In response to the request to write his name one child of three years and a half made the cross he had made many times previously in response to other items in the Binet test.

ERRORS IN THINKING AND REASONING

The illustrations cited in the foregoing sections suggest what we may expect to find when we watch for the operation of the Difficulty Reduction Principle in problem-solving, thinking and reasoning. The typical response when the individual meets a problem beyond his powers of thinking or comprehension is to reinterpret the problem through simplifying it until it falls into familiar grooves. Laurence Shaffer found this tendency in children's responses to cartoons. The subjects could usually give a response to the cartoons shown them, but the response given by duller or younger subjects was on an inferior level, mere description rather than interpretation. Only the most mature and brightest subjects saw the full meaning in certain cartoons, *e.g.*, those having political significance, though others could interpret the pictures in general terms.

A four-year-old was asked to do the "Patience" test of the Binet Series, which involves putting two right-angled triangles together to make a rectangle. This child, after listening to the directions, said, "Our teacher taught us that. I can make the Trylon," and proceeded to make an isosceles triangle of the two pieces.

A child seven years, five months of age with an IQ of 100, when asked, "Who discovered the North Pole?," answered "Oh yes, who discovered America?" The examiner said again, "North Pole." He responded, "Oh yes, who discovered America? Why, Columbus."

A four-year-old at the beach was told: "It's low tide." "Who tied it?," he promptly asked. A school boy, viewing for the first time the statue of Lorenzo de Medici, exclaimed "Oh look at the mounted cop." A child telling of his experience in watching a carpenter for the first time, exclaimed to his mother: "The carpenter was busy taking curls off a board." A child in a garden after a heavy rain inquired: "Mother, why are the flowers leaking?"

A child observed his grandfather at morning and evening prayers and asked, "Mama, what does Grandfather say to the chair when he gets down on his legs?" A child who had been irregular in school attendance finally refused to go at all. She told her mother that the teacher had threatened to "drop her from the register." She interpreted this as the furnace register.

A high school boy heard about "major powers encircling Europe" and wished to know more about *Major Powers,* whether he resembled Major Bowes, etc. A student reading *Hamlet* reported: "Then Hamlet took the body of Polonius and cut it up in pieces." Seeing the shocked surprise from the teacher he said, "Right here it is. I'll read it to you." "He hath drawn apart the body he hath slain."

Professor Muse tells of the impatient surgeon who stuck his head out of the patient's room and called sharply to a passing nurse, "Bring me a probe, —quick." The nurse, who had just that day received her cap, answered, "There is no Probe (probationer) on this ward, doctor, won't I do?" A secretary advised her employer that all zeros must hereafter be omitted from Western Union messages to countries at war. When the employer asked where she got that idea she showed him the instructions: "Not accepting cipher in messages to countries at war."

Children's attempts to solve arithmetic problems too difficult for them show the "reduction" tendency. They tend to respond habitwise, using the processes that are most familiar to them in ways that have become habitual. This tendency gives the impression that the results were obtained by chance. Addition and multiplication processes are used more frequently than any others.

Illustration: Question: If two pencils cost five cents, how many can you buy for twenty cents? Answer: one hundred.

Illustration from Piaget: Question: How much is five times faster than fifty minutes? Answer: Forty-five. Question: How did you get it? Answer: I took ten and ten, then ten and ten, then added five.

INTERPRETATION AND CONCLUSIONS

The errors and mistakes cited in the foregoing sections are not random, mechanical or attributable to chance, but may be ascribed to the tendency to reduce a problem to simpler terms more or less unconsciously when it is too difficult in its original form. In this sense the answers given are not even "wrong," though in an absolute or a standard sense they are. The reductions tend to be meaningful transcriptions. Only as a last resort does the subject fail or give up. So long as he can respond meaningfully, he makes some response. The human mind abhors the meaningless. The responses to stimuli tend to be dynamic, not mechanical. The subject remakes the problem so that it will be a meaningful whole for him.

This reduction tendency is not wholly intellectual. It is also emotional and involves feeling tone as well. The reduction is a comfort-seeking device.

The unpleasant situation is avoided. Blocked or thwarted efforts have little pleasure tone; quite the contrary, and that fact motivates the reduction.

Whether or not the illustrations given reflect clever or stupid errors cannot be determined directly from the nature of the response. This depends chiefly on who the individual is, and how adequate are his background and mental maturity for dealing with the problem. Most of the illustrations cited for children under seven were responses of normal or bright children to problems obviously too difficult for them. Bright as well as dull persons make these errors, but the more glaring illustrations occur with children responding to adult situations, and dull illiterate adults.

Do these illustrations suggest mental inertia on the part of the subjects, a tendency to respond with least effort, a retreat to an easier level? Unquestionably many of them do. Mental inertia appears to be as true a concept as physical inertia. Any given mental state of rest tends to persist. Habit binds people to lower level mental responses than they are actually capable of making. People respond in the way they have become habituated. Some of this response adults will not readily outgrow. The child has more chance for habit modification since he is in the unfinished evolutionary growth process and will be subjected to training for a period of years.

The Difficulty Reduction Principle operates universally. The phenomenon appears at all levels of mental maturity. It pervades varied types of response, materials and situations. It appears at all levels of perception and reasoning. It is particularly common in verbal responses.

These findings have significance for education. Teachers should pay more attention to these errors as clues to children's thought processes, degree of maturity, and background. Many Reduction errors are natural but immature responses that will be eradicated when the individual attains better mastery or understanding. The need for ascertaining the levels on which the individual who is instructed thinks and reasons is obvious. The principle illustrates the need for adopting a rational attitude toward the child's errors. Teachers commonly misunderstand this type of error. They caution students: "If you were careful and always pronounced syllables clearly and took pains to distinguish similar spellings that are easily confused, you wouldn't make such mistakes." We should put the proper interpretation on pupils' errors. Calling the pupil's attention to the error or suggesting in general the need for more precision, better attention, will not necessarily take care of the problem.

The phenomenon indicates the futility of talking to people over their heads, particularly children, without sufficient background and explanation. It suggests the need for keeping requirements of reading, spelling, and arithmetic, as well as material in the content subjects, at the child's experience and maturity level. Children should not be given new concepts, words to master, problems to solve before having the necessary background and meaning. When presenting new concepts we should not take for granted that children will assimilate the idea without explanation and illustration.

Chapter 12

Communicating Knowledge

12-1

B. F. SKINNER

The Science of Learning and the Art of Teaching

12-2

HERBERT A. THELEN

Programmed Materials Today: Critique and Proposal

B. F. SKINNER

The Science of Learning and the Art of Teaching

This article is one of the most influential in the history of educational psychology. Partly because of it, much money and talent have been recently poured into educational technology, and more information has been gathered about planned instruction than in any prior period. Skinner boldly sets forth—for all the educational world to test—his beliefs about learning gained from laboratory experimentation. What principles useful in school learning has he ignored?

Some promising advances have recently been made in the field of learning. Special techniques have been designed to arrange what are called "contingencies of reinforcement"—the relations which prevail between behavior on the one hand and the consequences of that behavior on the other—with the result that a much more effective control of behavior has been achieved. It has long been argued that an organism learns mainly by producing changes in its environment, but it is only recently that these changes have been carefully manipulated. In traditional devices for the study of learning —in the serial maze, for example, or in the T-maze, the problem box, or the familiar discrimination apparatus—the effects produced by the organism's behavior are left to many fluctuating circumstances. There is many a slip between the turn-to-the-right and the food-cup at the end of the alley. It is not surprising that techniques of this sort have yielded only very rough data from which the uniformities demanded by an experimental science can be extracted only by averaging many cases. In none of this work has the behavior of the individual organism been predicted in more than a statistical sense. The learning processes which are the presumed object of such research are reached only through a series of inferences. Current preoccupation with deductive systems reflects this state of the science.

Recent improvements in the conditions which control behavior in the field of learning are of two principal sorts. The Law of Effect has been taken seriously; we have made sure that effects *do* occur and that they occur under conditions which are optimal for producing the changes called learning. Once we have arranged the particular type of consequence called a

B. F. Skinner, "The Science of Learning and the Art of Teaching," *Harvard Educational Review*, 25 (1954), 86–97. Reprinted in B. F. Skinner, *Cumulative Record*, Enlarged Edition (New York: Appleton-Century-Crofts, 1961). Reprinted with permission.

Paper presented at a conference on Current Trends in Psychology and the Behavioral Sciences at the University of Pittsburgh, March 12, 1954.

reinforcement, our techniques permit us to shape up the behavior of an organism almost at will. It has become a routine exercise to demonstrate this in classes in elementary psychology by conditioning such an organism as a pigeon. Simply by presenting food to a hungry pigeon at the right time, it is possible to shape up three or four well-defined responses in a single demonstration period—such responses as turning around, pacing the floor in the pattern of a figure-8, standing still in a corner of the demonstration apparatus, stretching the neck, or stamping the foot. Extremely complex performances may be reached through successive stages in the shaping process, the contingencies of reinforcement being changed progressively in the direction of the required behavior. The results are often quite dramatic. In such a demonstration one can *see* learning take place. A significant change in behavior is often obvious as the result of a single reinforcement.

A second important advance in technique permits us to maintain behavior in given states of strength for long periods of time. Reinforcements continue to be important, of course, long after an organism has learned *how* to do something, long after it has acquired behavior. They are necessary to maintain the behavior in strength. Of special interest is the effect of various schedules of intermittent reinforcement. Charles B. Ferster and the author are currently preparing an extensive report of a five-year research program, sponsored by the Office of Naval Research, in which most of the important types of schedules have been investigated and in which the effects of schedules in general have been reduced to a few principles. On the theoretical side we now have a fairly good idea of why a given schedule produces its appropriate performance. On the practical side we have learned how to maintain any given level of activity for daily periods limited only by the physical exhaustion of the organism and from day to day without substantial change throughout its life. Many of these effects would be traditionally assigned to the field of motivation, although the principal operation is simply the arrangement of contingencies of reinforcement.[1]

These new methods of shaping behavior and of maintaining it in strength are a great improvement over the traditional practices of professional animal trainers, and it is not surprising that our laboratory results are already being applied to the production of performing animals for commercial purposes. In a more academic environment they have been used for demonstration purposes which extend far beyond an interest in learning as such. For example, it is not too difficult to arrange the complex contingencies which produce many types of social behavior. Competition is exemplified by two pigeons playing a modified game of ping-pong. The pigeons drive the ball back and forth across a small table by pecking at it. When the ball gets by one pigeon, the other is reinforced. The task of constructing such a "social relation" is probably completely out of reach of the traditional animal trainer. It requires a carefully designed program of gradually changing contingencies and the skillful use of schedules to maintain the behavior in strength. Each pigeon is separately prepared for its part in the total

[1] The reader may wish to review Dr. Skinner's article, "Some Contributions of an Experimental Analysis of Behavior to Psychology as a Whole," *The American Psychologist*, 1953, 8, 69–78. Ed.

performance, and the "social relation" is then arbitrarily constructed. The sequence of events leading up to this stable state are excellent material for the study of the factors important in nonsynthetic social behavior. It is instructive to consider how a similar series of contingencies could arise in the case of the human organism through the evolution of cultural patterns.

Cooperation can also be set up, perhaps more easily than competition. We have trained two pigeons to coordinate their behavior in a cooperative endeavor with a precision which equals that of the most skillful human dancers. In a more serious vein these techniques have permitted us to explore the complexities of the individual organism and to analyze some of the serial or coordinate behaviors involved in attention, problem solving, various types of self-control, and the subsidiary systems of responses within a single organism called "personalities." Some of these are exemplified in what we call multiple schedules of reinforcement. In general a given schedule has an effect upon the rate at which a response is emitted. Changes in the rate from moment to moment show a pattern typical of the schedule. The pattern may be as simple as a constant rate of responding at a given value, it may be a gradually accelerating rate between certain extremes, it may be an abrupt change from not responding at all to a given stable high rate, and so on. It has been shown that the performance characteristic of a given schedule can be brought under the control of a particular stimulus and that different performances can be brought under the control of different stimuli in the same organism. At a recent meeting of the American Psychological Association, Dr. Ferster and the author demonstrated a pigeon whose behavior showed the pattern typical of "fixed-interval" reinforcement in the presence of one stimulus and, alternately, the pattern typical of the very different schedule called "fixed ratio" in the presence of a second stimulus. In the laboratory we have been able to obtain performances appropriate to *nine* different schedules in the presence of appropriate stimuli in random alternation. When Stimulus 1 is present, the pigeon executes the performance appropriate to Schedule 1. When Stimulus 2 is present, the pigeon executes the performance appropriate to Schedule 2. And so on. This result is important because it makes the extrapolation of our laboratory results to daily life much more plausible. We are all constantly shifting from schedule to schedule as our immediate environment changes, but the dynamics of the control exercised by reinforcement remain essentially unchanged.

It is also possible to construct very complex *sequences* of schedules. It is not easy to describe these in a few words, but two or three examples may be mentioned. In one experiment the pigeon generates a performance appropriate to Schedule A where the reinforcement is simply the production of the stimulus characteristic of Schedule B, to which the pigeon then responds appropriately. Under a third stimulus, the bird yields a performance appropriate to Schedule C where the reinforcement in this case is simply the production of the stimulus characteristic of Schedule D, to which the bird then responds appropriately. In a special case, first investigated by L. B. Wyckoff, Jr., the organism responds to one stimulus where the reinforcement consists of the *clarification* of the stimulus controlling another response. The first response becomes, so to speak, an objective form of "paying attention" to the second stimulus. In one important version of this experiment, as yet unpublished, we could say that the pigeon is telling us whether it is "paying attention" to the *shape* of a spot of light or to its *color.*

One of the most dramatic applications of these techniques has recently been made in the Harvard Psychological Laboratories by Floyd Ratliff and Donald S. Blough, who have skillfully used multiple and serial schedules of reinforcement to study complex perceptual processes in the infrahuman organism. They have achieved a sort of psycho-physics without verbal instruction. In a recent experiment by Blough, for example, a pigeon draws a detailed dark-adaptation curve showing the characteristic breaks of rod and cone vision. The curve is recorded continuously in a single experimental period and is quite comparable with the curves of human subjects. The pigeon behaves in a way which, in the human case, we would not hesitate to describe by saying that it adjusts a very faint patch of light until it can just be seen.

In all this work, the species of the organism has made surprisingly little difference. It is true that the organisms studied have all been vertebrates, but they still cover a wide range. Comparable results have been obtained with pigeons, rats, dogs, monkeys, human children, and most recently, by the author in collaboration with Ogden R. Lindsley, human psychotic subjects. In spite of great phylogenetic differences, all these organisms show amazingly similar properties of the learning process. It should be emphasized that this has been achieved by analyzing the effects of reinforcement and by designing techniques which manipulate reinforcement with considerable precision. Only in this way can the behavior of the individual organism be brought under such precise control. It is also important to note that through a gradual advance to complex interrelations among responses, the same degree of rigor is being extended to behavior which would usually be assigned to such fields as perception, thinking, and personality dynamics.

From this exciting prospect of an advancing science of learning, it is a great shock to turn to that branch of technology which is most directly concerned with the learning process—education. Let us consider, for example, the teaching of arithmetic in the lower grades. The school is concerned with imparting to the child a large number of responses of a special sort. The responses are all verbal. They consist of speaking and writing certain words, figures, and signs which, to put it roughly, refer to numbers and to arithmetic operations. The first task is to shape up these responses—to get the child to pronounce and to write responses correctly, but the principal task is to bring this behavior under many sorts of stimulus control. This is what happens when the child learns to count, to recite tables, to count while ticking off the items in an assemblage of objects, to respond to spoken or written numbers by saying "odd," "even," "prime," and so on. Over and above this elaborate repertoire of numerical behavior, most of which is often dismissed as the product of rote learning, the teaching of arithmetic looks forward to those complex serial arrangements of responses involved in original mathematical thinking. The child must acquire responses of transposing, clearing fractions, and so on, which modify the order or pattern of the original material so that the response called a solution is eventually made possible.

Now, how is this extremely complicated verbal repertoire set up? In the first place, what reinforcements are used? Fifty years ago the answer would have been clear. At that time educational control was still frankly aversive. The child read numbers, copied numbers, memorized tables, and performed operations upon numbers to escape the threat of the birch rod or cane. Some positive reinforcements were perhaps eventually derived from the increased efficiency of the child in the field of arithmetic and in rare cases some automatic reinforcement may have resulted from the sheer manipulation of the medium—from the solution of problems or the discovery of the intricacies of the number system. But for the immediate purposes of education the child acted to avoid or escape punishment. It was part of the reform movement known as progressive education to make the positive consequences more immediately effective, but any one who visits the lower grades of the average school today will observe that a change has been made, not from aversive to positive control, but from one form of aversive stimulation to another. The child at his desk, filling in his workbook, is behaving primarily to escape from the threat of a series of minor aversive events—the teacher's displeasure, the criticism or ridicule of his classmates, an ignominious showing in a competition, low marks, a trip to the office "to be talked to" by the principal, or a word to the parent who may still resort to the birch rod. In this welter of aversive consequences, getting the right answer is in itself an insignificant event, any effect of which is lost amid the anxieties, the boredom, and the aggressions which are the inevitable by-products of aversive control.[2]

Secondly, we have to ask how the contingencies of reinforcement are arranged. When is a numerical operation reinforced as "right"? Eventually, of course, the pupil may be able to check his own answers and achieve some sort of automatic reinforcement, but in the early stages the reinforcement of being right is usually accorded by the teacher. The contingencies she provides are far from optimal. It can easily be demonstrated that, unless explicit mediating behavior has been set up, the lapse of only a few seconds between response and reinforcement destroys most of the effect. In a typical classroom, nevertheless, long periods of time customarily elapse. The teacher may walk up and down the aisle, for example, while the class is working on a sheet of problems, pausing here and there to say right or wrong. Many seconds or minutes intervene between the child's response and the teacher's reinforcement. In many cases—for example, when papers are taken home to be corrected—as much as 24 hours may intervene. It is surprising that this system has any effect whatsoever.

A third notable shortcoming is the lack of a skillful program which moves forward through a series of progressive approximations to the final complex behavior desired. A long series of contingencies is necessary to bring the organism into the possession of mathematical behavior most efficiently. But the teacher is seldom able to reinforce at each step in such a series because

[2] Skinner, B. F. *Science and Human Behavior*. New York: Macmillan, 1953.

she cannot deal with the pupil's responses one at a time. It is usually necessary to reinforce the behavior in blocks of responses—as in correcting a work sheet or page from a workbook. The responses within such a block must not be interrelated. The answer to one problem must not depend upon the answer to another. The number of stages through which one may progressively approach a complex pattern of behavior is therefore small, and the task so much the more difficult. Even the most modern workbook in beginning arithmetic is far from exemplifying an efficient program for shaping up mathematical behavior.

Perhaps the most serious criticism of the current classroom is the relative infrequency of reinforcement. Since the pupil is usually dependent upon the teacher for being right, and since many pupils are usually dependent upon the same teacher, the total number of contingencies which may be arranged during, say, the first four years, is of the order of only a few thousand. But a very rough estimate suggests that efficient mathematical behavior at this level requires something of the order of 25,000 contingencies. We may suppose that even in the brighter student a given contingency must be arranged several times to place the behavior well in hand. The responses to be set up are not simply the various items in tables of addition, subtraction, multiplication, and division; we have also to consider the alternative forms in which each item may be stated. To the learning of such material we should add hundreds of responses concerned with factoring, identifying primes, memorizing series, using short-cut techniques of calculation, constructing and using geometric representations or number forms, and so on. Over and above all this, the whole mathematical repertoire must be brought under the control of concrete problems of considerable variety. Perhaps 50,000 contingencies is a more conservative estimate. In this frame of reference the daily assignment in arithmetic seems pitifully meagre.

The result of all this is, of course, well known. Even our best schools are under criticism for their inefficiency in the teaching of drill subjects such as arithmetic. The condition in the average school is a matter of widespread national concern. Modern children simply do not learn arithmetic quickly or well. Nor is the result simply incompetence. The very subjects in which modern techniques are weakest are those in which failure is most conspicuous, and in the wake of an ever-growing incompetence come the anxieties, uncertainties, and aggressions which in their turn present other problems to the school. Most pupils soon claim the asylum of not being "ready" for arithmetic at a given level or, eventually, of not having a mathematical mind. Such explanations are readily seized upon by defensive teachers and parents. Few pupils ever reach the stage at which automatic reinforcements follow as the natural consequences of mathematical behavior. On the contrary, the figures and symbols of mathematics have become standard emotional stimuli. The glimpse of a column of figures, not to say an algebraic symbol or an integral sign, is likely to set off—not mathematical behavior—but a reaction of anxiety, guilt, or fear.

The teacher is usually no happier about this than the pupil. Denied the opportunity to control via the birch rod, quite at sea as to the mode of operation of the few techniques at her disposal, she spends as little time as possible on drill subjects and eagerly subscribes to philosophies of education which emphasize material of greater inherent interest. A confession of weakness is her extraordinary concern lest the child be taught something unnecessary. The repertoire to be imparted is carefully reduced to an essential minimum. In the field of spelling, for example, a great deal of time and energy has gone into discovering just those words which the young child is going to use, as if it were a crime to waste one's educational power in teaching an unnecessary word. Eventually, weakness of technique emerges in the disguise of a reformulation of the aims of education. Skills are minimized in favor of vague achievements—educating for democracy, educating the whole child, educating for life, and so on. And there the matter ends; for, unfortunately, these philosophies do not in turn suggest improvements in techniques. They offer little or no help in the design of better classroom practices.

There would be no point in urging these objections if improvement were impossible. But the advances which have recently been made in our control of the learning process suggest a thorough revision of classroom practices and, fortunately, they tell us how the revision can be brought about. This is not, of course, the first time that the results of an experimental science have been brought to bear upon the practical problems of education. The modern classroom does not, however, offer much evidence that research in the field of learning has been respected or used. This condition is no doubt partly due to the limitations of earlier research. But it has been encouraged by a too hasty conclusion that the laboratory study of learning is inherently limited because it cannot take into account the realities of the classroom. In the light of our increasing knowledge of the learning process we should, instead, insist upon dealing with those realities and forcing a substantial change in them. Education is perhaps the most important branch of scientific technology. It deeply affects the lives of all of us. We can no longer allow the exigencies of a practical situation to suppress the tremendous improvements which are within reach. The practical situation must be changed.

There are certain questions which have to be answered in turning to the study of any new organism. What behavior is to be set up? What reinforcers are at hand? What responses are available in embarking upon a program of progressive approximation which will lead to the final form of the behavior? How can reinforcements be most efficiently scheduled to maintain the behavior in strength? These questions are all relevant in considering the problem of the child in the lower grades.

In the first place, what reinforcements are available? What does the school have in its possession which will reinforce a child? We may look first to the material to be learned, for it is possible that this will provide considerable automatic reinforcement. Children play for hours with mechanical toys, paints, scissors and paper, noise-makers, puzzles—in short, with almost anything which feeds back significant changes in the environment and is reasonably free of aversive properties. The sheer control of nature is itself reinforcing. This effect is not evident in the modern school because it is masked by the emotional responses generated by aversive control. It is true that automatic reinforcement from the manipulation of the environment is probably only a mild reinforcer and may need to be carefully husbanded, but one of the most striking principles to emerge from recent research is that the *net* amount of reinforcement is of little significance. A very slight reinforcement may be tremendously effective in controlling behavior if it is wisely used.

If the natural reinforcement inherent in the subject matter is not enough, other reinforcers must be employed. Even in school the child is occasionally permitted to do "what he wants to do," and access to reinforcements of many sorts may be made contingent upon the more immediate consequences of the behavior to be established. Those who advocate competition as a useful social motive may wish to use the reinforcements which follow from excelling others, although there is the difficulty that in this case the reinforcement of one child is necessarily aversive to another. Next in order we might place the good will and affection of the teacher, and only when that has failed need we turn to the use of aversive stimulation.

In the second place, how are these reinforcements to be made contingent upon the desired behavior? There are two considerations here—the gradual elaboration of extremely complex patterns of behavior and the maintenance of the behavior in strength at each stage. The whole process of becoming competent in any field must be divided into a very large number of very small steps, and reinforcement must be contingent upon the accomplishment of each step. This solution to the problem of creating a complex repertoire of behavior also solves the problem of maintaining the behavior in strength. We could, of course, resort to the techniques of scheduling already developed in the study of other organisms but in the present state of our knowledge of educational practices, scheduling appears to be most effectively arranged through the design of the material to be learned. By making each successive step as small as possible, the frequency of reinforcement can be raised to a maximum, while the possibly aversive consequences of being wrong are reduced to a minimum. Other ways of designing material would yield other programs of reinforcement. Any supplementary reinforcement would probably have to be scheduled in the more traditional way.

These requirements are not excessive, but they are probably incompatible with the current realities of the classroom. In the experimental study of learning it has been found that the contingencies of reinforcement which are most efficient in controlling the organism cannot be arranged through the personal mediation of the experimenter. An organism is affected by subtle details of contingencies which are beyond the capacity of the human organism to arrange. Mechanical and electrical devices must be used. Mechanical help is also demanded by the sheer number of contingencies which may be used efficiently in a single experimental session. We have recorded many millions of responses from a single organism during thousands of experimental hours. Personal arrangement of the contingencies and personal observation of the results are quite unthinkable. Now, the human organism is, if anything, more sensitive to precise contingencies than the other organisms we have studied. We have every reason to expect, therefore, that the most effective control of human learning will require instrumental aid. The simple fact is that, as a mere reinforcing mechanism, the teacher is out of date. This would be true even if a single teacher devoted all her time to a single child, but her inadequacy is multiplied many-fold when she must serve as a reinforcing device to many children at once. If the teacher is to take advantage of recent advances in the study of learning, she must have the help of mechanical devices.

The technical problem of providing the necessary instrumental aid is not particularly difficult. There are many ways in which the necessary contingencies may be arranged, either mechanically or electrically. An inexpensive device which solves most of the principal problems has already been constructed. It is still in the experimental stage, but a description will suggest the kind of instrument which seems to be required. The device consists of a small box about the size of a small record player. On the top surface is a window through which a question or problem printed on a paper tape may be seen. The child answers the question by moving one or more sliders upon which the digits 0 through 9 are printed. The answer appears in square holes punched in the paper upon which the question is printed. When the answer has been set, the child turns a knob. The operation is as simple as adjusting a television set. If the answer is right, the knob turns freely and can be made to ring a bell or provide some other conditioned reinforcement. If the answer is wrong, the knob will not turn. A counter may be added to tally wrong answers. The knob must then be reversed slightly and a second attempt at a right answer made. (Unlike the flash-card, the device reports a wrong answer without giving the right answer.) When the answer is right, a further turn of the knob engages a clutch which moves the next problem into place in the window. This movement cannot be completed, however, until the sliders have been returned to zero.

The important features of the device are these: Reinforcement for the right answer is immediate. The mere manipulation of the device will probably be reinforcing enough to keep the average pupil at work for a suitable period each day, provided traces of earlier aversive control can be wiped out. A teacher may supervise an entire class at work on such devices at the same time, yet each child may progress at his own rate, completing as many problems as possible within the class period. If forced to be away from school, he may return to pick up where he left off. The gifted child will advance rapidly, but can be kept from getting too far ahead either by being excused from arithmetic for a time or by being given special sets of problems which take him into some of the interesting bypaths of mathematics.

The device makes it possible to present carefully designed material in which one problem can depend upon the answer to the preceding and where, therefore, the most efficient progress to an eventually complex repertoire can be made. Provision has been made for recording the commonest mistakes so that the tapes can be modified as experience dictates. Additional steps can be inserted where pupils tend to have trouble, and ultimately the material will reach a point at which the answers of the average child will almost always be right.

If the material itself proves not to be sufficiently reinforcing, other reinforcers in the possession of the teacher or school may be made contingent upon the operation of the device or upon progress through a series of problems. Supplemental reinforcement would not sacrifice the advantages gained from immediate reinforcement and from the possibility of constructing an optimal series of steps which approach the complex repertoire of mathematical behavior most efficiently.

A similar device in which the sliders carry the letters of the alphabet has been designed to teach spelling. In addition to the advantages which can be gained from precise reinforcement and careful programming, the device will teach reading at the same time. It can also be used to establish the large and important repertoire of verbal relationships encountered in logic and science. In short, it can teach verbal thinking. As to content instruction, the device can be operated as a multiple-choice self-rater.

Some objections to the use of such devices in the classroom can easily be foreseen. The cry will be raised that the child is being treated as a mere animal and that an essentially human intellectual achievement is being analyzed in unduly mechanistic terms. Mathematical behavior is usually regarded, not as a repertoire of responses involving numbers and numerical operations, but as evidences of mathematical ability or the exercise of the power of reason. It is true that the techniques which are emerging from the experimental study of learning are not designed to "develop the mind" or to further some vague "understanding" of mathematical relationships. They are designed, on the contrary, to establish the very behaviors which are taken to be the evidences of such mental states or processes. This is only a special case of the general change which is under way in the interpretation of human affairs. An advancing science continues to offer more and more convincing alternatives to traditional formulations. The behavior in terms of which human thinking must eventually be defined is worth treating in its own right as the substantial goal of education.

Of course the teacher has a more important function than to say right or wrong. The changes proposed would free her for the effective exercise of that function. Marking a set of papers in arithmetic—"Yes, nine and six *are* fifteen; no, nine and seven *are not* eighteen"—is beneath the dignity of any intelligent individual. There is more important work to be done—in which the teacher's relations to the pupil cannot be duplicated by a mechanical device. Instrumental help would merely improve these relations. One might say that the main trouble with education in the lower grades today is that the child is obviously not competent and *knows it* and that the teacher is unable to do anything about it and *knows that too*. If the advances which have recently been made in our control of behavior can give the child a genuine competence in reading, writing, spelling, and arithmetic, then the teacher may begin to function, not in lieu of a cheap machine, but through intellectual, cultural, and emotional contacts of that distinctive sort which testify to her status as a human being.

Another possible objection is that mechanized instruction will mean technological unemployment. We need not worry about this until there are enough teachers to go around and until the hours and energy demanded of the teacher are comparable to those in other fields of employment.

Mechanical devices will eliminate the more tiresome labors of the teacher but they will not necessarily shorten the time during which she remains in contact with the pupil.

A more practical objection: Can we afford to mechanize our schools? The answer is clearly yes. The device I have just described could be produced as cheaply as a small radio or phonograph. There would need to be fewer devices than pupils, for they could be used in rotation. But even if we suppose that the instrument eventually found to be most effective would cost several hundred dollars and that large numbers of them would be required, our economy should be able to stand the strain. Once we have accepted the possibility and the necessity of mechanical help in the classroom, the economic problem can easily be surmounted. There is no reason why the school room should be any less mechanized than, for example, the kitchen. A country which annually produces millions of refrigerators, dishwashers, automatic washing-machines, automatic clothes-driers, and automatic garbage disposers can certainly afford the equipment necessary to educate its citizens to high standards of competence in the most effective way.

There is a simple job to be done. The task can be stated in concrete terms. The necessary techniques are known. The equipment needed can easily be provided. Nothing stands in the way but cultural inertia. But what is more characteristic of America than an unwillingness to accept the traditional as inevitable? We are on the threshold of an exciting and revolutionary period, in which the scientific study of man will be put to work in man's best interests. Education must play its part. It must accept the fact that a sweeping revision of educational practices is possible and inevitable. When it has done this, we may look forward with confidence to a school system which is aware of the nature of its tasks, secure in its methods, and generously supported by the informed and effective citizens whom education itself will create.

HERBERT A. THELEN

Programmed Materials Today: Critique and Proposal

The present article was written eight years after the proposal by Skinner. Thelen describes his view of the current status of programmed materials. Many of the early theories, he says, have been discredited, but rich discoveries have been made and promising avenues opened for exploration. As a comparison of this selection with Skinner's article will reveal, in educational psychology a "truth" is neither unitary nor permanent; rather, it is tentatively held, pending further clarification and amendment. These two articles taken together should convey this spirit well.

What I am about to describe is both a reaction away from the recently developed neo-orthodoxy of the teaching machine and programmed materials and a movement toward the positive goal of improved educational practice.

Since the Skinner-Crowder concepts of teaching machines and programmed materials are fairly familiar to the people who will read this article, it might be well to start by pointing out what we are moving away from.

We are moving away from a set of dubious concepts about self-learning materials. They seem to me to be on the wrong track, and I shall briefly list my doubts and criticisms.

First, the notion that the learner must be rewarded at each step is by no means proved. Experiments similar to Skinner's studies on rats have shown that latent learning, unguided and unrewarded, does take place.

Second, if we assume that reward is necessary at each step, the question becomes one of deciding how to give this reward. The present answer is to have steps so easy that the student makes very few errors: he is almost continuously successful. The doubt is that continuous success is in fact rewarding. In theory, it should not be, and reports that boredom sets in after the first few hours of programmed instruction seem to be practical evidence.

Third, the criterion of a good linear program so far used is that it be error free; but the relationship between this criterion and any educational criterion remains completely unestablished.

Herbert A. Thelen, "Programmed Materials Today: Critique and Proposal." Reprinted from *Elementary School Journal,* 64 (1963), 189–96, by permission of The University of Chicago Press.

Fourth, while the art of programming is very much concerned with developing an effective sequence of items, two experiments have already revealed that the students learned just as much when the items were presented in random order as when they were presented in the sequence designed by the programmers. In other words, the programs were regarded simply as collections of discrete, independent bits of information. This finding suggests that if the purpose of the program is to give information, then sequence does not matter. If the purpose is to teach principles that must be developed over a set of items, then it appears unlikely that principles will be learned through present types of sequences.

Fifth, the role of the teacher is unspecified. Basically it appears to be that of doing whatever has to be done to make the program work. But discussions of this problem merely emphasize the notion of relieving the teacher from drudgery and freeing his time so that he can talk with individuals. The relationship between experience with the materials and the nature of class discussion remains unspecified, and therefore the place of the materials in teaching remains undefined.

Sixth, the talk of individual differences is misleading. The only individual differences the programs can cater to are differences in speed of going through the program and differences in the size of step or in the number of steps. The same program is used with all the students, the mental skills required of all the students are the same, and the content is covered in the same way.

Seventh, the notion that learning is better when it is active and that the machine requires activity is uncertain in its application to present programs. A number of experiments show no differences in learning when the student actually makes the responses as compared with when he merely reads the items.

Eighth, there is no control over student purposes or motives. It is assumed that the student wants to be successful and that the continual feedback of knowledge of success will keep him going. For the most part, the student has little idea where the program is headed, and he therefore has little opportunity to find means-ends relationships between each item and some clear-cut purpose for his immediate activity. His posture is to be extraordinarily docile, and he is not expected to participate in goal-setting.

Finally, present programs are designed to be teacher-proof and self-contained. By definition, then, they cannot deal with unanticipated or emergent purposes, feelings, or ideas: they are limited to the alternatives and ideas that were thought up by the authors before publication of the programs. The emergent aspect of learning, which is the creative part and the stock in trade of the inquiry-oriented teacher, is relegated to helping the individual student.

All in all, I conclude that the validity of programming of the Skinner and Crowder types remains unestablished and is theoretically questionable. The conditioning principles on which it is said to be based are questionable in this application, and at least one leader in the movement says that the only principle involved is that once a person has been enticed into making a response, he will be more likely to make the same response if the situation comes up again. The educational principles are badly defined beyond the notion that a body of content must be selected before it can be presented. The one viable idea incorporated in programs of today is the notion of feedback, but the meaning and the facilitative effect of the feedback are completely undemonstrated.

The sorts of concepts we seek can be developed from two lines of reasoning. One can look at all the objections listed here and see how they could be overcome and thus arrive at a new definition of what programming should accomplish and how it can be used. Or one can start with an educational theory and simply deduce from it the specifications to be met by programmed materials. My own preference is for the latter approach, but since I have started by raising questions about existing programs, it might be most useful here to see how my objections could be countered and to visualize the sort of programming ideas that would be involved. I will consider my nine points in order.

First, reward should be available only during or after effort, and should be commensurate with effort. The "step" is not a unit of effort and, in any case, is supposed to require a minimum of effort. For rewards to be possible, a program must be purposive; it must have possibilities of risk (and frustration).

Second, the criterion of continuous success needs to be replaced by the criterion of visible progress toward a goal. In this view, "wrong" responses are highly useful if they eliminate unproductive pathways or help define what needs to be done next. The required program will make little use of the concept of "right" and "wrong"; it will employ at various times a large number of bases of judgment: relevant-irrelevant, consistent-inconsistent, central-peripheral, certain-doubtful, to name several.

Third, the educational criterion to be used is progress toward reaching a conclusion, toward formulating a hypothesis, toward summarizing an argument, or toward accomplishing other meaningful intellectual tasks.

Fourth, the idea of learning through a fixed sequence of small discrete steps must be discarded. For all learning not confined to nonsense syllables, the requirement is for seeing relationships within a pattern of elements; and this pattern must be visible as a whole. The pattern may be built up through a sequence of small operations, but it must accumulate and remain before the student. The required program will enable the student to search out a pattern from a number of elements; and it will then require him to make interpretations from this pattern. The sequence of operations will be unspecified; the student must seek his own path; and the quality and character of this path are themselves of great concern; it most certainly must not be specified and controlled by the programmer.

With regard to the role of the teacher, the fifth point, he is, of course, the over-all supervisor of all the activities in his course. He determines which activity to set up next through diagnosis of the imperatives for further experience that have been generated in preceding activities. In some activities—for example, lecturing, leading discussion—the teacher plays a central role. In other activities—for example, setting up subgroups and committees, advising, locating resources and making them available to students—he plays a facilitative or consulting role. Each activity is seen as a part of a whole, and each activity has a unique flavor because of the way it fits into the whole of a subunit or macroscopic period of instruction. Within the sequence of activities, there will be some that can best be done by the student alone in a situation structured through previous activities; there will be others that require the interaction of the teacher and of other persons. These solitary and interactive activities will have an integral relationship: the student is alone with materials so that he can prepare himself for a high-level discussion; in the discussion the student must deal with the different points of view of his teacher and classmates in such a way that a sense of problem develops. The problems thus identified are then to be tackled by the student in his own way. Thus the idea of completely self-contained programmed materials is rejected in favor of the notion of fairly substantial programmed task-problems that emerge through discussion of experiences with preceding problems. This conception of the relationship between solitary and interactive activities leads, among other things, to the notion that the mechanics of the materials ought to be so simple that teachers and students can devise some of their own programmed materials.

Individual differences, point six, should not be something to ameliorate or to sweep under the rug by mechanical means. The fact that individuals have different needs, different reactions, and different points of view is the basic strength of democracy; and this fact plays a major role in inquiry within the community of scholars. Programs should give students maximum practical freedom to find their own paths; and the teacher should capitalize on the differences among these paths to illustrate various approaches that might be taken. At the same time, similarities among paths point to universals. If all the students think the same and take the same paths through tasks, then there is no difference or conflict among them and hence no stimulus or justification for class discussion.

The concept of activity is meaningless and empty unless it is linked to the concept of purpose (points seven and eight). Activity can be judged only as having some degree of appropriateness to a purpose; the means-ends relationship is central. If the student can achieve his purpose better by not taking the time to write responses, then either he should not be expected to write responses or the purpose should be redefined in such a way that making responses is essential.

In the materials we seek, two kinds of responses will have to be made. First, the student will have to discover a pattern among elements, and initially (for example, in inductive tasks) he may have no clues except feedback from the machine to guide him. Second, the student will have to formulate some testimony as a result of his experiences because this testimony is to be used later by the class. No item within the material is ever to be an end in itself. If the student fails to give it attention when he first encounters it, he will have to go back to it later as part of the basis for further interpretation and conclusion. It will be for him to discover just what responses, in what order and according to what plan, are most useful to him to meet the demands of the inquiry situation.

Finally, the emergent aspect of the learning situation consists of the ideas and discoveries made by the students. The materials must be designed to stimulate a wide array of such discoveries. Some of these discoveries can, of course, be anticipated from the internal logic of the situation; but there is always a unique flavoring, an affective element, which gives a logical possibility its own meaning to the individual. The teacher is concerned, not with the logical possibility alone, but also with the context of assumptions and purposes in which it is imbedded in the thinking of the student; it is these underlying apprehensions which, in conflict, produce the sense of a problem and which constitute readiness for new learning through discovery and inquiry.

The notion of feedback enters in two ways. In general, perception of consequences of behavior is a natural kind of feedback; in this sense, discussion in the class gives feedback about certain dimensions of the preceding discovery periods. Feedback may also be immediate and specific. During the individual discovery period, the student needs feedback as he searches out patterns among the elements structured into the situation through the materials. Such feedback should enable the student to be confident of the arrangement of elements in the pattern and should then enable him to proceed to make interpretations freely from the established pattern.

In inductive thinking, the central theme of the pattern emerges in the student's mind as he discovers through feedback which elements constitute the pattern; by the time he has searched out the pattern he is likely to have the generalization already implicit in his mind. The elements, incidentally, may range in abstraction from direct sense impression and data to any array of general assumptions; the pattern may be arrived at inductively or deductively; and it may be designed to satisfy any of a wide variety of possible criteria: consistency, progression, classification, demonstration, and others.

As we consider the objections and how to overcome them, we become aware of what the programmed materials would look like. They would be guide sheets for inquiry activities. They would be resource materials to draw on as needed. They would be filed and cross-indexed, and the same sheets might be used in different ways in different units or courses. Each student would accumulate these sheets during a course, and, together with other materials such as bibliographies and reports, they would constitute a self-made reference manual on the subject.

The sheets themselves would require many responses and many choices which, taken together, would encompass a single experiment or problem. For some responses (those involving the search for a pattern), the student would get immediate feedback; for other responses (those involving interpretations and speculation), machine feedback is impossible, and the student would get his feedback during the subsequent discussion. The formats of items would be extremely varied, as required by the nature of the mental processes demanded by the task.

The source of the required items is to be thoughtful teaching experience, not studies of infrahuman learning. The items are to challenge the higher mental processes of all students, not to reduce all learning to what can be accomplished with the lowest-level mental processes that human beings have in common with rats, apes, pigeons. For the purpose is the education of human beings, not the efficient transmission of information. One learns information more effectively by trying to satisfy human purposes than by simply trying to learn information.

It is hoped that items based on teaching experience will provide much the same sort of mental activity that a good teacher produces when he can give his full attention to the student. The teacher would point to facts, would be quiet while the student formulated his opinion, would question the bases of opinion, would speculate on what would follow if the opinion is correct. He would give the students many choices and would insist that at least some choices be made after careful examination of alternatives. The model in the teacher's mind would be that of a student actively inquiring—beginning with vagueness and impression, moving to efforts to clarify the problem, finding rational means for dealing with the problem, making a choice, and taking action. The teacher would tailor his role in such a way as to maximize the student's participation along these lines. The guide sheet should require the same behaviors the teacher does.

In general, teaching-learning activities alternate between two modes. One is private study by the individual, in which he discovers, and to some extent formulates, ideas and develops awareness of feelings. The other is interactive discussion in which the spoken or written testimony of classmates, teacher, and authors can be analyzed, compared, and brought into dynamic interplay. The private experience is the discovery of personal knowledge, which may be subjective, unwarranted, unconsolidated, impressionistic; the interactive experience is the socialization of personal knowledge through the use of established knowledge and discipline of the field of study. The first I call *discovery;* the second, *dialogue.* In crass terms, properly designed materials can provide the core structure for dialogue, and dialogue develops the set for discovery. Neither structure can be assessed apart from its causal and consequential relations to the other.

This basic alternation is almost universally found when human beings interact in common purpose. In therapy, the individual dreams, reflects, observes his own reactions, and then deals with his thoughts and feelings in the therapy session. In the boss-employee relationship, the boss structures tasks and standards, and the employee reacts to the structure as he attempts to live with it; his reactions are then used to help structure the demands more appropriately. The parent instructs the child, but when the matter at hand is important, he also asks the child to think it over and report back later. The facilitation of discovery and personal knowledge is what we ask for when we speak of respect for the individual; the examination of testimony in the light of established knowledge is what we ask for when we speak of respect for the facts. The educated man respects both the individual and the facts, for either one alone has no adequate basis for correction.

A firm conception of teaching is required to guide the creation of materials and activities. But the conception by itself remains merely one of several possible conceptions until it is legitimized by proper authority. Much of the present conception of teaching is legitimized by the authority of tradition, of college-entrance examinations, of popular teachers, of the generally accepted. But these are inadequate and improper bases, and therefore the teaching concepts they legitimize, being based on false authority, are bad concepts. And no amount of so-called research can make up for the error.

There are two kinds of authority that legitimize the conception of teaching offered here. One is the authority of the subject field as a discipline—an organized body of propositions about the part of the world the knowledge treats and an organized body of ideas about how this knowledge is to be arrived at, extended, and appraised for its content of truth or validity. Some demands on the student come legitmately from the discipline, and he acts in accordance with it. The second kind of authority is the human nature of learners. A teaching method that calls on this nature, respects it and works with it, is sound; a teaching method that denies the facts of human nature is self-defeating and has to settle for the mundane and the superficial.

These two authorities are reconciled in the concept of learning as inquiry and in the concept of inquiry as a spontaneous mode of productive behavior when the situation is sufficiently meaningful to the learner to be worth mobilizing his full resources to deal with it. The concept of teaching method then develops through asking two questions: At what points in inquiry (or purposive learning) must the student discover or formulate notions by himself? At what points and for what specific purposes must the student have what sorts of interactions with his peers and with the teacher? It is as we answer these questions that we shall begin to be able to specify what part of these kinds of situations can be structured by materials; and it will be as we test the usefulness of such materials that we shall also have the grounds for revising and correcting our conceptual model.

As we view the job ahead, we can see several interrelated foci. One of these has to do with cognitive pathways, that is, with establishing that each item in fact typically engenders thought processes through which inquiry can progress. The investigation of this question calls for empirical study of students as they perform with items.

A second focus, related to the first, places these kinds of thought processes in an educational setting. What is the course of development of these processes? What qualities characterize sophisticated and productive inquiry? What factors of temperament, background, opportunity, and demand influence the development of these qualities?

The third focus has to do with teaching method. Does experience with the materials have the hoped-for consequences on the subsequent activities? What characteristics of the dialogue lead to development of readiness to use the materials as part of inquiry rather than as a hurdle to jump over?

The fourth focus is the program art itself, a body of policy and suggestion to be continually revised in the light of the preceding questions, but, nonetheless, a stimulus to thinking about materials in the only practical way: constructing them and trying them out.

A fifth focus, more diffuse than the others, has to do with the promulgation of ideas, skills, and concepts throughout the field. We shall have to learn to define a variety of roles through which large numbers of teachers and others can identify with the purposes, assimilate some of the ideas, and develop skills that will contribute directly or indirectly to the proposed and needed reconstruction of education.

Chapter 13

Identification and the Learning of Attitudes

13-1

IRVING L. JANIS
AND BERT T. KING

The Influence of Role Playing on Opinion Change

13-2

ALBERT BANDURA

Social Learning Through Imitation

IRVING L. JANIS and BERT T. KING

The Influence of Role Playing on Opinion Change

What is the best way to mold student opinion about an issue? Janis and King instructed some students to pretend publicly to hold certain views and instructed others to act as audience. Following this experiment, they compared the opinions of the students engaged in the role playing with the opinions of the students who were not active participants. What experimental controls make this study a particularly good one? How might a teacher use the findings to develop proper attitudes in a student?

In many everyday situations, people are induced to play social roles in which they express ideas that are not necessarily in accord with their private convictions. That certain types of role-playing experiences can facilitate changes in personal opinions has been suggested by various impressionistic observations (e.g., Myers [8]). In recent years, psychodramatic techniques which involve role playing have been developed for use in adult education programs, leadership training, employee counseling, and psychotherapy (1, 5, 6, 7, 9). The usual procedure consists of having persons in a group play specified roles in a simulated life situation. One of the main values of this role-playing device, according to its proponents, is that it has a corrective influence on various beliefs and attitudes which underlie chronic difficulties in human relations (cf. Maier [6]).

As yet little is known about the conditions under which role playing leads to actual changes in personal opinions. The present experiment was designed to investigate the effects of one type of demand that is frequently made upon a person when he is induced to play a social role, namely, the requirement that he overtly verbalize to others various opinions which may not correspond to his inner convictions.

As a preliminary step in exploring the effects of role playing, one of the present authors interviewed a group of collegiate debaters who, as members of an organized team, repeatedly were required to play a role in which they publicly expressed views that did not correspond to their personal

Irving L. Janis and Bert T. King, "The Influence of Role Playing on Opinion Change," *Journal of Abnormal and Social Psychology,* 49 (1954), 211–18. Reprinted with permission of the American Psychological Association, Inc.

This study was conducted at Yale University as part of a program of research on factors influencing changes in attitude and opinion. The research program is supported by a grant from the Rockefeller Foundation and is under the general direction of Professor Carl I. Hovland, to whom the authors wish to express appreciation for helpful suggestions and criticisms. The authors also wish to thank Professor Fred D. Sheffield for valuable suggestions during discussions preparatory to designing the experiment.

opinions. Most of the debaters reported that they frequently ended up by accepting the conclusions which they had been arbitrarily assigned to defend. Myers' (8) impressionistic account of the improvement in morale attitudes produced by participation in an Army public-speaking course points to the same phenomenon and suggests that attitude changes may occur even when role playing is artificially induced. If true, it would appear that "saying is believing"—that overtly expressing an opinion in conformity to social demands will influence the individual's private opinion. Consequently, it seemed worth while to attempt to investigate the effects of this type of role playing in a more controlled laboratory situation where, if the alleged gain from role playing occurs, it might be possible to isolate the critical factors and to explore systematically the mediating mechanisms.

The role-playing effects described above have not as yet been verified by systematic research. If verified, they would still remain open to a variety of alternative explanations. For instance, inducing the individual to play a role in which he must advocate publicly a given position might guarantee exposure to one set of arguments to the exclusion of others. An alternative possibility, however, is that even when exposed to the same persuasive communications, people who are required to verbalize the content to others will tend to be more influenced than those who are only passively exposed. In order to test this hypothesis, the present experiment was designed so that communication exposure would be held constant by comparing the opinion changes of active participants and passive controls who were exposed to the same communications.

METHOD AND PROCEDURES

An initial questionnaire, which was administered as an opinion survey in a large classroom of male college students, contained a series of questions concerning expectations about the future. Included in this "before" questionnaire were the following key opinion items, which dealt with the subject matter of the three communications to which the experimental groups were subsequently exposed:

Item A: During the past year a number of movie theaters were forced to go out of business as result of television competition and other recent developments. At the present time there are about *18,000* movie theaters remaining. How many commercial movie theaters do you think will be in business three years from now?

Item B: What is your personal estimate about the *total supply of meat that will be available for the civilian population* of the United States during the year 1953? (. . . —per cent of what it is at present.)

Item C: How many years do you think it will be before a *completely effective* cure for the common cold is discovered?

The experimental sessions were held approximately four weeks after the initial questionnaire had been filled out, and were represented as being part of a research project designed to develop a new aptitude test for assessing oral speaking ability. The subjects (*Ss*) were asked to give an informal talk based on an outline prepared by the experimenters (*Es*) which stated the conclusion and summarized the main arguments to be presented. The arguments were logically relevant but highly biased in that they played up and interpreted "evidence" supporting only one side of the issue. Each active participant was instructed to play the role of a sincere advocate of the given point of view, while two others, who were present at the same experimental session, listened to his talk and read the prepared outline. Each S delivered one of the communications and was passively exposed to the other two. In order to prevent selective attention effects, the active participant was not told what the topic of his talk would be until his turn came to present it. He was given about three minutes to look over the prepared outline, during which time the others (passive controls) also were requested to study duplicate copies of the same outline so as to be prepared for judging the adequacy of the speaker's performance. After the first talk was over, another S was selected to present the second communication, and then the remaining S presented the third communication, the same procedures being followed in each case.

TABLE 1

Schema of the experimental conditions

	Group A (N = *31*)	*Group B* (N = *29*)	*Group C* (N = *30*)
Communication A: movie theaters	active participants	passive controls	passive controls
Communication B: meat supply	passive controls	active participants	passive controls
Communication C: cold cure	passive controls	passive controls	active participants

Immediately after the last talk was finished, Ss were given the "after" questionnaire, much of which was devoted to rating the performance of each speaker. The key opinion items were included among numerous filler items, all of which were introduced as questions designed to provide information about the student's interests and opinions concerning the three topics so as to enable the investigators to select the most appropriate topic for future applications of the oral speaking test.

In all three communications, the conclusion specified an opinion estimate which was numerically *lower* than that given by any of the students on the "before" test. Thus, all active participants were required to argue in favor of an extreme position which differed from their initial beliefs. The influence of each communication could readily be observed by noting the degree to which the students in each group *lowered* their opinion estimates on the "after" test.

The basic schema of the experiment is shown in Table 1. In each row of the table which represents exposure to a given communication, there is one group of active participants and two contrasting groups which, when combined, form the group of passive controls. In effect, the experimental treatments were repeated with different communication contents, providing three separate instances of active versus passive exposure, although the same Ss were used throughout.

In order to obtain some information for checking on selective attention effects, a variation of the passive control condition (not represented in the table) was introduced into the experiment by using a small supplementary group who listened and took notes on all three talks. In addition, base-line data for assessing the effectiveness of the communications were obtained from a comparable group of "pure" controls who were not exposed to any of the communications.

RESULTS AND DISCUSSION

Effects of active participation. Initially, on each of the three key items in the precommunication questionnaire, the difference between the active participation group and the passive control group was nonsignificant. The opinion changes observed after exposure to the three communications are shown in Table 2.[1] The results indicate that in the case of two of the three communications (A and B), the active participants were more influenced than the passive controls. For both communications, the differences in net sizable change are statistically reliable, and the differences in net (slight or sizable) change, although nonreliable, are in the expected direction.

In the case of the third communication (C), the two groups showed approximately the same amount of opinion change. But additional findings (based on confidence ratings given by each S immediately after answering the key opinion questions) indicate that the active participants who presented Communication C, like those who presented the other two communications, expressed a higher level of *confidence* in their postcommunication estimates than did the corresponding passive controls. Table 3 shows the net changes in confidence ratings for each of the three communications in terms of a breakdown that takes account of the direction and magnitude of opinion change. The breakdown was necessary inasmuch as a successful communication would be expected to increase the confidence only of those who changed their opinions in the direction advocated by the communication. The net change in confidence shown for each subgroup is based on a comparison of pre- and postcommunication ratings given by each S, and was computed by subtracting the percentage who showed a decrease in confidence from the percentage who showed an increase in confidence. In general, the findings in Table 3 reveal a consistent pattern for all three

[1] The table does not include the data on the "pure" (unexposed) control group. The net changes for this group were approximately zero in the case of all three key items, and the corresponding net changes for the active participants and the passive controls (shown in the last rows of the table) were significantly greater (p's range from .10 down to $<.01$). Hence, all three communications had a significant effect on the opinions of those who were either actively or passively exposed to them.

The probability values reported throughout this paper are based on one tail of the theoretical distribution. Whenever intergroup comparisons were made with respect to the net percentage who changed by a given amount, the reliability of the difference was tested by the formula presented in Hovland, Lumsdaine, and Sheffield (3, p. 321).

TABLE 2

Comparison of active participants with passive controls on amount of change in opinion estimates

Changes in opinion estimates [b]	Communication A: (movie theaters) Active participants (N = 31)	Communication A: Passive controls (N = 57) [a]	Communication B: (meat shortage) Active participants (N = 29)	Communication B: Passive controls (N = 57)	Communication C: (cold cure) Active participants (N = 30)	Communication C: Passive controls (N = 53)
Sizable increase	0%	2%	0%	2%	7%	6%
Slight increase	3%	9%	7%	14%	10%	9%
No change	23%	20%	24%	16%	13%	19%
Slight decrease	29%	46%	27½%	49%	23%	15%
Sizable decrease	45%	23%	41½%	19%	47%	51%
Total	100%	100%	100%	100%	100%	100%
Net change (% increase minus % decrease)						
Slight or sizable change	−71%	−58%	−62%	−52%	−53%	−51%
Sizable change	−45%	−21%	−41½%	−17%	−40%	−45%
p	.01		.01		>.30	

[a] The number of cases in each passive control group is slightly smaller than expected from the *N*'s shown in Table 1 because the data from a few cases were inadequate and hence were eliminated from the analysis (e.g., the individual failed to give an answer to the particular question).

[b] The "net change (slight or sizable)" is defined as the percentage changing in the direction advocated by the communication minus the percentage changing in the opposite direction. The "net sizable change" in the case of Communication A refers to the difference in the percentages who lowered and raised their estimate by 5,000 (movie theaters) or more. For Communication B, a sizable change was 25 (per cent) or more; for Communication C it was 5 (years) or more.

communications: in every instance, active participation tended to have at least a slight positive effect with respect to increasing the confidence of those whose opinion estimates were influenced by the communication. The results indicate that active participation resulted in a significant gain in confidence, particularly among those students whose opinion estimates were markedly influenced by Communication C.[2] This finding is especially strik-

[2] For the entire group of active participants who were exposed to Communication C, there was a net increase in confidence of 37 per cent; the corresponding net increase for the entire group of passive controls was only 13½ per cent. This difference was due entirely to the marked gain in confidence manifested by those students in the active group who had changed their opinion estimates in the direction advocated by the communication. The results in the first row of the table indicate that, among the students whose opinion estimates were uninfluenced by Communication C, the active participants showed a small net decrease in confidence which was equal to that shown by the passive controls. The next row of Table 3 indicates that, among those students who decreased their opinion estimates by at least one-half year or more after exposure to Communication C, the active participants showed a greater net increase in confidence than the passive controls; the difference of 31 per cent approaches statistical significance ($p = .07$). Finally, the last row of the table shows that an even greater difference in confi-

ing in view of the fact that the opinion change results for Communication C (Table 2) failed to show any gain from active participation.

Insofar as confidence ratings can be regarded as indicators of the degree of conviction with which the new opinions are held, the positive findings based on the opinion change data for Communications A and B are partially confirmed by the confidence change data based on Communication C. Thus, the data based on all three communications contribute evidence that the effectiveness of the communications (as manifested by opinion changes or by confidence changes) tended to be augmented by active participation.

TABLE 3

Comparison of active participants with passive controls on amount of change in confidence

Subgroup breakdown according to changes in opinion estimates	*Net change in confidence (per cent increase minus per cent decrease)*					
	Communication A		*Communication B*		*Communication C*	
	Active participants	*Passive controls*	*Active participants*	*Passive controls*	*Active participants*	*Passive controls*
1. *Uninfluenced:* opinion estimates increased or unchanged	−12% ($N = 8$)	−5% ($N = 18$)	0% ($N = 9$)	+6% ($N = 18$)	−11% ($N = 9$)	−11% ($N = 18$)
2. *Influenced:* opinion estimates slightly or sizably decreased	+9% ($N = 23$)	−10% ($N = 39$)	+20% ($N = 20$)	+5% ($N = 39$)	+57% ($N = 21$)	+26% ($N = 35$)
Gain from active participation	+19%		+15%		+31%	
3. *Highly influenced:* opinion estimates sizably decreased	−7% ($N = 14$)	−38% ($N = 13$)	+25% ($N = 12$)	0% ($N = 11$)	+64½% ($N = 14$)	+15% ($N = 27$)
Gain from active participation	+31%		+25%		+49½%	

Although Ss were not told what their topic would be until they were about to begin giving the talk, it is possible that the ego-involving task of presenting one of the talks may have given rise to emotional excitement or other interfering reactions which could have had the effect of reducing the Ss' responsiveness when passively exposed to the other two communications.

dence changes emerges when the comparison is limited to those students who decreased their opinion estimates by five years or more. (The 49½ per cent difference is reliable at beyond the .05 confidence level.) Further analysis of the subgroup data indicated that the differences shown in this table could not be attributed to statistical artifacts arising from initial differences between the various subgroups.

This possibility appears extremely improbable, however, in the light of supplementary control observations:

1. Some of the passive controls had been exposed to the communications *before* giving their own talk, while others were passively exposed *after* having given their own talk. Nonsignificant differences were found in the amount of opinion change shown under these two conditions.

2. The results from the passive controls were "replicated" by the results from an independent group of 16 students who did not give an oral presentation, but who were asked to follow the prepared outline carefully and to note down the main arguments given by each of the three speakers. Despite the fact that their notes were fairly complete and indicated a relatively high degree of attention to the content of all three communications, these supplementary controls displayed approximately the same amount of opinion change as the original group of passive controls.[3]

Observations pertinent to explanatory hypotheses. Many different types of speculative hypotheses could be put forth to account for the facilitating effects of active participation, postulating a gain in attention and learning from overtly rehearsing the communication, or a gain in comprehension from reformulating the arguments in one's own words, or a gain in motivation from playing the role of communicator, etc. Some supplementary observations were made for the purpose of exploring various factors which might provide leads to the key mediating mechanisms. Although far from conclusive, the evidence derived from these observations provides a preliminary basis for selecting explanatory hypotheses which warrant further experimental analysis.

The findings based on the supplementary controls (who were required to take notes on the three talks) suggest that variation in attention level probably was not a crucial factor that could explain the participation effects observed in the present experiment. More promising clues were discovered by taking account of differences in the types of reactions evoked by the three communications. We have seen that in the case of Communications A and B, a clear-cut gain from active participation was manifested by changes in opinion estimates; but, in the case of Communication C, opinion estimates were unaffected, the gain being manifested only in the form of increased confidence. With a view to discovering some differentiating factor, we examined the available evidence bearing on the question of why active participation might be more effective under certain stimulus conditions (represented by Communications A and B) than under other conditions (represented by Communication C).

The first step in this inquiry was to examine *E*'s notes on: (*a*) the active

[3] It is conceivable, of course, that the activity of taking notes on the talks might have interfered with responsiveness to the persuasive content of the communications. While this possibility cannot be excluded, it seems implausible inasmuch as our Ss were college students who had had considerable practice in taking notes during lectures. Educational research on the effects of note taking indicates that this form of activity generally has a beneficial rather than a detrimental effect on the student's ability to absorb the content of an oral communication (2).

Ss' behavior while giving their talks, and (*b*) Ss' statements in the informal interviews conducted at the end of each experimental session. These observations provide two suggestive leads:

1. The active participants who presented Communication C seemed to engage in *less improvisation* than those who presented the other two communications. The Communication C group appeared to adhere much more closely to the prepared outline, making little attempt to reformulate the main points, to insert illustrative examples, or to invent additional arguments.
2. Active participants in the Communication C group seemed to experience much more difficulty than the other groups in presenting their talks. During their performance they appeared to be more hesitant and tense. Afterwards, they expressed many more complaints about the task, claiming that their topic was more difficult to present than either of the other two. In general, these subjects seemed *less satisfied* with their performance than those who presented the other two topics.

The first observation suggests that mere repetition of a persuasive communication may have little or no effect as compared with an improvised restatement. This observation is in line with some suggestive findings from an opinion change study by Kelman (4) in which seventh-grade students were given a communication, and, immediately afterwards, were offered various incentives to write essays in support of the communicator's position. Kelman observed that the essays written by the group which showed the greatest amount of opinion change tended to be longer, to include more improvisation, and to be of better over-all quality (as rated by several judges) than the essays written by the other experimental groups.

Reformulating and elaborating on the communication might be a critical factor in producing the gain from active participation, perhaps because the communicatee is stimulated to think of the kinds of arguments, illustrations, and motivating appeals that he regards as most convincing. The importance of the improvisation factor in relation to participation effects could not be investigated further with the data at hand from the present experiment, but is currently being studied by the present authors in another experiment that is specifically designed to compare the effects of different types of active participation.

With respect to the second observation, it should be noted that there may have been an objective basis for the greater dissatisfaction experienced on Communication C because of the greater amount of unfamiliar technical material it contained. The "cold cure" outline referred to a great many technical details concerning the cold virus, antibiotics, allergic reactions, and antihistamines. Many of these details were probably unfamiliar to Ss, and consequently it may have been difficult for them to "spell out" the implications of the arguments. In contrast, the outlines for the other two topics contained very little technical material, relying mainly on arguments that were likely to be quite familiar to college students.

Systematic evidence relevant to Ss' *perception* of the difficulty of presenting each communication was obtained by making use of the self-rating schedule which each student filled out after exposure to the three communications. Table 4 shows the percentage in each experimental group who rated their own performance as adequate or satisfactory on each of six self-appraisal items.

The most comprehensive question was the following: "What is your over-all rating of the informal talk given by this speaker—how good a job do you think he did in presenting his material? ____ Excellent; ____ Very Good; ____ Satisfactory; ____ Poor; ____ Very Poor."

TABLE 4

Self-ratings of active participants in each experimental group

	Experimental groups (active participants)		
Self-rating response	*Communication A: (movie theaters)* (N = 31)	*Communication B: (meat supply)* (N = 29)	*Communication C: (cold cure)* (N = 30)
1. *Over-all performance* was at least "satisfactory"	94%	83%	63%
2. Rarely or never spoke in a *monotonous* tone of voice	64%	76%	53%
3. Rarely or never *incoherent* in presenting arguments	74%	83%	57%
4. No *distortions* or *misinterpretations* of arguments in the prepared outline	32%	52%	13%
5. No *omissions* of any of the main arguments	74%	72%	70%
6. Succeeded in giving the impression of being "*sincere*"	52%	52%	43%
Combined ratings on all six items: five or more favorable self-ratings	39%	52%	13%

The percentage who rated themselves as "satisfactory" or better (shown in the first row of the table) was significantly lower for the group who presented Communication C than for the groups who presented Communications A and B ($p = .002$ and .04, respectively). On the remaining five items, each of which dealt with a specific aspect of the speaker's performance, the Communication C group also tended to rate themselves lower than did the other two groups. (On the combined rating, based on all six items, the percentage differences are statistically significant at beyond the .05 confidence level.) The findings consistently indicate that the students in the Communication C group felt less satisfied with their oral speaking performance than did those in the other two groups. Since the group differences in self-ratings tend to parallel the group differences in amount of gain from active participation, the results suggest that *satisfaction with one's own performance* may be a critical factor that determines the magnitude of participation effects.

Further evidence which supports this hypothesis was obtained from an analysis of individual opinion changes, comparing active participants with high and low self-ratings for each of the three communications. For example, among the active participants who presented Communication C, there were 18 students whose self-ratings were comparatively "high" (three to six favorable responses) and 12 cases whose self-ratings were predominantly "low" (zero, one, or two favorable responses); 55 per cent of the "highs" as against only 17 per cent of the "lows" showed a sizable net opinion change in the direction advocated by the communications ($p = .05$). In general, the comparisons based on all three communications consistently indicate that a greater amount of opinion change occurred among those active participants who rated their oral speaking performance as satisfactory or better. Active participants who felt that they performed poorly, on the other hand, failed to show any more opinion change than the passive controls, and, in the case of Communication C, showed markedly less change than the passive controls ($p = .07$).

During the experimental sessions there were no apparent sources of external social rewards from the environment. Since the others present remained silent, the active participant had no opportunity to know how they were reacting to his talk, except possibly by subtle signs from their facial expressions or from their bodily movements. But even in the absence of any external cues to social approval, it seems probable that *anticipations* concerning such approval would occur if the individual felt that he was performing well, as expressed in his self-ratings. Thus, expectations of favorable audience reactions may have occurred less frequently among Ss who were required to perform the relatively difficult task of presenting the unfamiliar technical material in Communication C than among those who were required to perform the less difficult task of presenting Communication A or B. The increase in opinion change produced by role playing might be mediated by the individual's sense of achievement or his elated feelings about the adequacy of his oral performance. One hypothesis that would follow from this assumption is that when a person conforms outwardly to social demands by playing a role which requires him to advocate a given opinion, he will begin to believe what he is saying if he is made to feel that he says it well.

Although the above hypothesis is suggested by the supplementary correlational findings, it will obviously remain open to question until tested by more precise methods. One cannot be certain that the responses used to assess "satisfaction" represent a separate variable which is causally related to opinion changes. Acceptance of the communication might be a common factor which inclines those who are most influenced to perceive themselves as having performed well, in which case the self-ratings might merely reflect the same thing as the measures of opinion change. Moreover, even if the two variables can be varied and measured independently, the possibility remains that the observed relationship may be due to some third variable, such as amount of improvisation.

As was noted earlier, the group of active participants who showed the least amount of opinion change not only expressed a low degree of satisfaction but also displayed a relative absence of improvisation in their oral performances. Either the "satisfaction" factor or the "improvisation" factor might prove to be a critical mediating variable. Before drawing a definite conclusion, it is necessary to investigate each factor experimentally—for instance, by giving the Ss "expert" performance ratings which raise or lower their feelings of satisfaction, and by using instructions which increase or decrease the amount of improvisation. These methods are currently being employed in our further research on the effects of role playing.

There is another important problem which arises from the findings in the present experiment and which also requires systematic investigation: Does social role playing facilitate the internalization of externally imposed value judgments, mores, and taboos? The persuasive communications used in this study dealt with relatively impersonal beliefs about the future, and the main findings show that acceptance of opinions of this sort was markedly increased by experimentally induced role playing. It remains problematical, however, whether active participation also influences the acceptance of opinions and attitudes that are more directly tied up with daily life activities, interpersonal relationships, and emotionally charged dilemmas.

Obviously, it is unsafe to generalize widely from a single exploratory study based on the opinion changes of college students produced in a somewhat artificial test situation. Nevertheless, the present experiment provides preliminary evidence indicating that verbal conformity elicited by role playing can significantly influence the acceptance of new beliefs. Under certain specifiable conditions which await further investigation, it seems to be true that "saying is believing."

SUMMARY AND CONCLUSIONS

The experiment was designed to determine whether or not overt verbalization, induced by role playing, facilitates opinion change. Male college students were assigned at random to two main experimental groups: (*a*) active participants, who, with the aid of a prepared outline, played the role of a sincere advocate of the given point of view, and (*b*) passive controls, who silently read and listened to the same communication. In the experimental sessions, three different communications were used, each of which argued in favor of a specific conclusion concerning expected future events and was presented by a different active participant. Opinion measures obtained at the end of the session were compared with the "before" measures obtained about one month earlier.

In general, the active participants tended to be more influenced by the communications than were the passive controls. In the case of two of the communications the active participants showed significantly more opinion change than the passive controls. In the case of the third communication, both groups showed approximately the same amount of opinion change, but active participation, nevertheless, tended to increase the level of confidence of those whose opinion estimates were influenced by the communication. The main findings, together with various methodological checks, support the hypothesis that overt verbalization induced by role playing tends to augment the effectiveness of a persuasive communication.

Additional observations were analyzed in order to explore possible mediating factors underlying the gain in opinion change due to active participation. From behavioral records and interviews, two suggestive leads emerged. In those cases where role playing produced a marked increase in opinion change: (*a*) the individual displayed a relatively great amount of improvisation in his talk, and (*b*) he felt comparatively well satisfied with his oral speaking performance. The first factor suggests that the gain from role playing may occur primarily because the active participant tends to be impressed by his own cogent arguments, clarifying illustrations, and convincing appeals which he is stimulated to think up in order to do a good job of "selling" the idea to others. The second factor suggests an alternative explanation in terms of the rewarding effects of the individual's sense of achievement or feelings of satisfaction with his performance in the role of active participant. Additional evidence pertinent to the second factor, based on a self-rating questionnaire which the Ss filled out immediately after giving the talk, consistently indicated that the greatest amount of opinion change occurred among those active participants who felt that their oral speaking performance was satisfactory. Both the "improvisation" factor and the "satisfaction" factor warrant further investigation.

REFERENCES

1. Bavelas, A. Role-playing and management training. *Sociatry,* 1947, 1, 183–191.
2. Crawford, C. E. Some experimental studies of the results of college note taking. *J. Educ. Res.,* 1925, 12, 379–386.
3. Hovland, C. I., Lumsdaine, A. A., & Sheffield, F. D. *Experiments on mass communication.* Princeton: Princeton Univer. Press, 1949.
4. Kelman, H. C. Attitude change as a function of response restriction. *Hum. Relat.,* in press.
5. Lippitt, R. The psychodrama in leadership training. *Sociometry,* 1943, 6, 286–292.
6. Maier, N. R. F. *Principles of human relations.* New York: Wiley, 1952.
7. Moreno, J. L. *Psychodrama.* Vol. 1. New York: Beacon House, 1946.
8. Myers, G. C. Control of conduct by suggestion: an experiment in americanization. *J. Appl. Psychol.,* 1921, 5, 26–31.
9. Zander, A., & Lippitt, R. Reality-practice as educational method. *Sociometry,* 1944, 7, 129–151.

ALBERT BANDURA

Social Learning Through Imitation

While reinforcement learning theory has been very helpful, it has not adequately explained all major types of human learning. Bandura illustrates the inadequacy of simple reinforcement to predict one sort of learning, and explores the importance of imitation and models. To teachers, who consciously or not serve as models for much youthful behavior, the importance can hardly be exaggerated.

Despite the considerable attention devoted to theoretical analyses of the learning process, an adequate theory of *social learning* has been remarkably slow in developing. Prevailing theorizing and experimentation appear to be limited to a relatively narrow range of learning principles encompassing some of the most tedious and inefficient procedures for promoting learning in human organisms. I am referring here primarily to the principle of operant or instrumental conditioning around which most of the current empirical research in learning is centered.

It is generally assumed that responses which are absent from the behavioral repertoire of an organism are acquired through the method of successive approximation (Skinner, 1953). This process involves the positive reinforcement of elements in available responses which resemble the terminal form of the new behavior, while component responses which have little or no similarity to it go unrewarded. By gradually raising the criterion of reinforcement in the direction of the final form the behavior is to take, the available behavior can be shaped into novel response patterns, as frequently illustrated by Skinner's ping-pong pigeons.

In spite of the widespread acceptance and application of the method of successive approximation to human learning, it is doubtful that many social responses would ever be acquired if social training proceeded solely by this method. This is particularly true of behavior for which there is no reliable eliciting stimulus apart from the cues provided by others as they exhibit

From Albert Bandura, "Social Learning Through Imitation," *Nebraska Symposium on Motivation,* 1962 (Lincoln: University of Nebraska Press, 1962), pp. 211–69. Reprinted with permission.

The experiments reported in this paper were supported in part by Research Grants M-1734, M-4398, and M-5316, from the National Institute of Health, Public Health Service, and the Lewis S. Haas Child Development Research Fund, Stanford University.

The author wishes to express his appreciation to Dorothea Ross, Sheila Ross, Aletha Huston Stein, Ted Rosenthal, and to John Steinbruner for their assistance in various phases of this research. I am also grateful to Edith Dowley, Director, Marilyn Haley and Patricia Rowe, Head Teachers, Stanford University Nursery Schools, for their aid in arranging the research facilities.

the behavior. If a child had no occasion to hear speech, for example, or in the case of a deaf-blind person (Keller, 1927), no opportunity to match the mouth and laryngeal muscular responses of a verbalizing model (Young and Hawk, 1955), it would probably be impossible to teach him the kind of verbal responses that constitute a language.[1]

Even in cases where some stimulus is known to be capable of eliciting an approximation to the desired behavior, the process of learning can be considerably shortened and accelerated by the provision of social models.

As a way of illustrating the gross inefficiency of operant conditioning procedures in human learning let us imagine an automobile driver training program based on the principle of successive approximation through differential reinforcement.

As a first step our trainer, who has been carefully programed to produce head nods, resonant hm-hms, and other verbal reinforcers, loads up with an ample supply of candy, chewing gum, and filter-tip cigarettes. A semi-willing subject who has never observed a person drive an automobile, and a parked car complete the picture. Our trainer might have to wait a long time before the subject emits an orienting response toward the vehicle. At the moment the subject does look even in the general direction of the car, this response is immediately reinforced and gradually he begins to gaze longingly at the stationary automobile. Similarly, approach responses in the desired direction are promptly reinforced in order to bring the subject in proximity to the car. Eventually, through the skillful use of differential reinforcement, the trainer will teach the subject to open and to close the car door. With perseverance he will move the subject from the back seat or any other inappropriate location chosen in this trial-and-error ramble until at length the subject is shaped up behind the steering wheel. It is unnecessary to depict the remainder of the training procedure beyond noting that it will likely prove an exceedingly tedious, not to mention an expensive and hazardous enterprise.

In actual training programs, of course, some of the relevant responses are elicited by appropriate verbal stimuli, a fact that is generally ignored in descriptions of the application of successive approximation procedures to human learning. It is important to bear in mind, however, that verbal cues expedite learning to the extent that they present modeling behavior symbolically (*i.e.*, the trainer describes rather than demonstrates the necessary responses and their serial order), and the corresponding responses are already present in the learner's behavioral repertoire. Little would be gained by simply instructing the subject to drive the automobile. The role of symbolic models in facilitating learning will be considered in greater detail later.

[1] It might be argued that if one engaged in a process of successive regression of learners, one would eventually end up with a single person with no model for imitation and consequently our lonesome survivor could never develop linguistic responses. This hypothetical example, however, poses no problems for language learning since any sound can be selected arbitrarily to symbolize a particular object. A symposium, for example, could be labeled arbitrarily a "tonkawazurp." The language learning problem arises, however, when one is assigned the delightful task of teaching a second person to say "tonkawazurp" without the aid of a verbalizing model.

Let us now contrast the process of social learning described above with a program of driver training based upon modeling procedures. First, the model performs the necessary orienting and approach responses toward the automobile, opens the car door, and sits behind the steering wheel. A single demonstration along with a verbal description of the sequence of responses necessary to start, to accelerate, to stop, and to control the movement of the automobile will greatly curtail unnecessary and dangerous experimentation. This substantially increases the probability that both the subject and the trainer will survive the learning process. The subject, in turn, will have acquired a substantial portion of the repertoire of responses essential for successful motoring simply by observing the behavior of the model without performing any overt responses or experiencing any response-consequences. By contrast, the process of shaping motoring behavior by means of differential reinforcement is very likely to unshape the driver, the trainer, the automobile and the surrounding environment.

This example does not represent an atypical learning situation. Informal observation of the process of social learning as it occurs in naturalistic situations reveals that the behavior of models in one form or another is utilized to some degree in facilitating learning regardless of whether the subject is being taught the responses necessary for playing golf, swimming, performing surgical operations, flying an airplane, or for conducting psychotherapeutic interviews. Indeed, as Reichard has pointed out, in many cultures "the word for 'teach' is the same as the word for 'show,' and the synonymity is literal" (1938, p. 471).

In one Guatemalan sub-culture, for example, the acquisition of complex vocational skills often proceeds entirely on the basis of imitation (Nash, 1958). In learning to operate a cotton textile machine, the young Cantelense apprentice stands beside the machine and observes the operator perform the set of responses necessary for running the loom, and for getting it in motion whenever it stops or snags. During the training period the learner asks no questions, is given no verbal instructions or practice in operating the textile machine. As soon as the apprentice feels that she has mastered the necessary sequence of responses through observation, the machine is turned over to her. Typically, on the first trial she performs almost as skillfully as did the model operator.

Adult role behavior is transmitted to young children in a similar manner. The young Cantelense girl is provided with a miniature water jar, a small broom, and a tiny grinding stone modeled after the mother's domestic utensils. The child constantly observes and imitates the mother's behavior with little or no direct tuition. While parents in our culture generally do not provide their young daughters with miniature stainless steel kitchens, they do supply them with a varied array of play materials—toy kitchen ensembles, dolls with complete nursery equipment and wardrobes, cooking utensils, food-mix sets, and other junior-size homemaker kits—that serve much the same purpose. In games utilizing such stimulus material, children frequently reproduce the entire parental role behavior including the appropriate mannerisms, voice inflections, and attitudes which the parents have never directly attempted to teach. This example illustrates the efficacy of imitative learning since children acquire numerous classes of complex interrelated responses *in toto,* apparently without proceeding through a laborious process of response differentiation and extinction.

This type of learning is generally labeled "imitation" in behavior theory, and "identification" in most theories of personality. These concepts, however, are treated in the present paper as synonymous since both encompass the same behavioral phenomenon, *i.e.*, the tendency for a person to match the behavior or attitudes as exhibited by actual or symbolized models. Numerous distinctions have been proposed, of course, at one time or another. Some writers, for example, reserve the term "identification" for matching behavior falling within a class of responses defined as "meanings," and "imitation" for highly specific acts (Lazowick, 1955). Similarly, Parsons (1955) contrasts imitation with identification in terms of specificity and diffuseness of learning with the additional qualification that a "generalized cathectic attachment" is an essential antecedent of identification but unnecessary or absent in the case of imitation. Others define imitation as matching behavior occurring in the presence of the model, whereas identification involves the performances of the model's behavior in the latter's absence (Mowrer, 1950).

The diversity in the definitions of imitation and indentification also stems in part from the fact that some writers are applying these terms primarily to response-defined variables; others are referring to antecedent or process variables which are stimulus-defined, while still others are assigning to imitation the status of a dependent variable and treating identification as an independent variable, and vice versa.

It is possible to draw distinctions between these and other related terms (*e.g.*, introjection, incorporation, etc.) based on certain stimulus, mediating, or terminal response variables. However, one might question whether it is meaningful to do so since essentially the same learning process is involved regardless of the content of what is learned, the object from whom it is learned, or the stimulus situations in which the relevant behavior is emitted. Therefore, in the interests of clarity, precision, and parsimony I shall employ a single concept, *i.e.*, imitation, to refer to the occurrence of matching responses.

The concept of imitation in psychological theory has had a long history dating back to Tarde (1903) and McDougall (1908), who considered imitativeness an innate or instinctive tendency. It was not until the publication of *Social Learning and Imitation* in 1941 by Miller and Dollard, that the concept was integrated into behavior theory and conceptualized systematically as a problem in learning.

The experiments reported by Miller and Dollard in the imitation monograph involved a series of discrimination problems in which a trained leader responded to discriminative environmental cues of which the subject was unaware; consequently the subject was dependent upon the cues provided by the leader's behavior. The responses performed by the leader were consistently rewarded and the subject was similarly reinforced whenever he matched the choice responses of the imitatee. This form of imitation was labeled by the authors "matched-dependent behavior" because subjects relied on the leaders for relevant cues and matched their responses. Under these conditions, both rats and children readily learned to follow their respective models and generalized imitative responses to new stimulus situations, new models, and different motivational states.

While these experiments have been widely accepted as demonstrations of learning by means of imitation, they in fact represent a special case of discrimination place-learning in which the actions of others serve as discriminative stimuli for responses that already exist as part of the subject's behavioral repertoire. Had the relevant environmental cues been made more distinctive, the presence of the models would have been quite irrelevant, and perhaps even a hindrance, in the acquisition process. In contrast, most forms of imitation involve *response* rather than *place* learning in which subjects combine fractional responses into relatively complex novel patterns solely by observing the performance of social models, often without any opportunity to perform the model's behavior in the exposure setting, and without any reinforcers delivered immediately either to the models or to the observers. Here, clearly, social cues constitute an indispensable aspect of the learning process.

According to the Miller-Dollard theory, the necessary conditions for learning through imitation include a motivated subject who secures reinforcement while accidentally matching the correct responses of a model. These conditions, while meaningful for place learning, pose some serious problems when applied to response learning. As Mowrer has cogently pointed out (1950; 1960), the theory requires the subject to perform a close approximation of the response before he can learn it. Continuing with our example of language learning, in order for a child to learn the word "symposium" imitatively, he would first have to emit the word "symposium" in the course of random vocalization, match it accidentally with the model's verbal response, and secure a positive reinforcement.

Miller and Dollard's conceptualization of imitation as simply a case of instrumental conditioning, together with their focus on place learning perhaps accounts for the paucity of research generated by the publication of *Social Learning and Imitation.* The few experiments that have been reported almost without exception employ simple two-choice discrimination problems and constitute essentially replications rather than extensions of the original studies.

New patterns of behavior cannot be learned imitatively unless the necessary fractional responses are available to the organism. Undoubtedly, many of the behavioral elements that enter into the formation of more complex responses are provided in the unlearned repertoire. The theory that most adequately accounts for the acquisition of additional component responses and their integration into novel patterns of behavior is the two-factor theory of imitation proposed by Mowrer (1950). According to this view, the responses in an organism's repertoire are initially developed through a process of classical conditioning. As a model mediates rewards for a child the behavioral attributes of the model are paired repeatedly with positive reinforcement. Through this process of classical conditioning the model's behavior acquires secondary reinforcing properties. On the basis of stimulus generalization, such responses are also rewarding, in proportion to their similarity to those exhibited by the model, when they are reproduced by the child himself. Thus, once the model's behavior has attained positive valence, the child can self-administer secondary reinforcers simply by reproducing the desirable responses.

This process of imitation is well illustrated by Mowrer's description of the acquisition of language responses (1950; 1958). In the first step of training a bird to talk, for example, the trainer emits words in conjunction with the presentation of food, water, physical contact, and other primary reinforcers. As the formerly neutral word stimuli take on secondary reward value for the bird, it will be predisposed to reproduce the positively conditioned words.

The sensory feedback theory of imitation accounted for the process of response selection and facilitation, but the underlying mechanisms whereby observational experiences are translated into equivalent motor responses were unspecified. In a recent revision of this theory, therefore, Mowrer (1960) has introduced additional explanatory mediating constructs. It is assumed that sensory experiences not only classically condition positive or negative emotions, but also produce conditioned sensations or images which provide the necessary sensory-motor linkage.

Initially, responses are acquired and maintained, according to Mowrer, not because of their instrumental value, but because of their self-rewarding properties. Nor is it necessary, in this phase of imitative learning, for the subject to perform a response before he can learn it.

Once imitative responses are learned, however, they are apt to be highly effective in eliciting positive reinforcement from external agents and thus come to function as instrumental responses as well. The extrinsic rewards may take several forms. In the first place, parents and other models are likely to express pleasure and approval whenever children exhibit their attitudes or emulate their behavior. Secondly, matching the behavior of successful models is likely to be rewarding because it provides the imitator with correct responses to the same or related stimulus situations. Through the repeated association of matching responses with reinforcement, imitative habits can become strongly established and generalized to a wide range of social models.

In Mowrer's recent revised theory of habit formation (1960) instrumental learning simply involves the conditioning of positive and negative emotions to response-correlated stimuli and thus all learning is reduced to classical conditioning. A theory of imitation based primarily on sensory feedback, however, poses some theoretical problems. . . .

[Editorial Comment: In the original article there were thirty pages of detailed experimental results, inappropriate to this anthology. What follows are Bandura's concluding remarks.]

. . . Even a casual examination of the manner in which behavior is acquired, reveals that the learning process receiving the most intensive laboratory investigation is not at all representative of the natural process of social learning; consequently, present day social learning theories fail to fit the facts of response acquisition in at least two important respects.

In the first place, the available learning theories are remarkably "culture-free," and social agents are typically considered little more than inefficiently programed reinforcer-dispensing devices. Social transmission of behavior, however, is governed not only by the particular patterns of response-reinforcement contingencies adopted by the cultural agents, but also by the behavioral examples they provide. Nevertheless, the importance of social agents as a *source of patterns of behavior* continues to be essentially ignored, despite evidence from informal observation and laboratory experimentation that the provision of models in actual or in symbolic form is an exceedingly effective procedure for transmitting and for controlling behavior. This relative neglect of the *social aspects* of the learning process cannot be attributed entirely to the fact that much of the learning experimentation has been confined to infrahuman organisms. Numerous studies, spanning several decades, have demonstrated that learning even in animals can be considerably accelerated by the provision of animal models who exhibit the desired behavior.

In studies of simultaneous imitation, for example, Warden and his associates (Warden & Jackson, 1935; Warden, Fjeld, & Koch, 1940) utilized the duplicate-cage method in which naive monkeys watched from an adjacent cage a trained demonstrator monkey successfully solve a series of relatively novel puzzle tasks and multiple discrimination problems in order to secure food rewards. While the training of the monkeys who were to serve as models required considerable time and effort even with careful guidance, the vast majority of the observing monkeys solved identical sets of problems almost instantaneously simply by viewing the model's performances.

Hayes and Hayes (1952a; 1952b), reporting on cross-species imitation, demonstrated considerable precise imitation by a domesticated monkey of complex social and problem-solving behavior performed by human models.

The speed and accuracy with which the primates in the Warden and Hayes experiments reproduced relatively complicated series of matching responses is illustrative of how models may serve as sources of entire patterns of behavior even in the case of animals.

In order for imitative responses to occur, the model's behavior must be within the perceptual and motor capacity of the observing organism. If the relevant cues are not observed, or if the component responses required for reproducing the model's behavior are not available to the imitator, exposure to modeling behavior will have little or no influence on rate of learning. Perhaps for this reason, animal experiments utilizing primates as subjects have been most successful in demonstrating the efficacy of imitative learning. The occurrence of imitation in subprimates, however, has also been shown, particularly when the learning tasks are within the animals' perceptual-motor capability (Bayroff & Lard, 1944; Church, 1957; Herbert & Harsh, 1944; Miller & Dollard, 1941; Solomon & Coles, 1954).

In light of the substantial evidence for the efficacy of imitative learning in both animal and human subjects, it is surprising, indeed, to find that the tedious and comparatively inefficient instrumental conditioning procedures are assigned considerable prominance in behavior theory to the relative neglect of more powerful learning principles. This finding is in itself, perhaps, interpretable as a modeling phenomenon. In many experiments of human learning the responses selected for study (*e.g.*, manipulating plungers, pressing bars, levers, buttons, etc.) are modeled on the fractional responses elicited in experimentation with infrahuman organisms, and bear little or no relationship to the classes of behavior considered to be of importance in social learning. Similarly, the learning procedures singled out for study are largely confined to the narrow range of principles given special prominence by the current leading experimenter models.

A second way in which current social learning theories depart from reality has to do with the *unit of response acquisition.* From the research cited in this paper, it is evident that responses are typically acquired by means of imitation in large segments or in their entirety rather than through a slow, gradual process of response differentiation based on differential reinforcement. Following actual demonstrations by a model or verbal descriptions of the desired behavior, the learner generally reproduces more or less the entire pattern of behavior which can then be further refined, and maintained by the application of reinforcement procedures. Clearly, the acquisition process is not as piecemeal as depicted in our current learning theories. While this is most evident in human learning, it is also apparently true to some extent for animal response acquisition. The quotation given below illustrates a monkey's extensive delayed spontaneous imitation of human grooming behavior in the absence of any trial and error learning.

> At about 16 months of age she began to imitate such bits of household routine as dusting furniture and washing clothes and dishes. Her early efforts were quite crude and could perhaps be ascribed to stimlus enhancement. Before she was two years old, however, some of her play was much too complex and precise to be so explained. For instance, she appropriated a lipstick, stood on a washbasin, looked in the mirror, and applied the cosmetic—not at random, but to her mouth. She then pressed her lips together and smoothed the color with her finger, just as she had seen the act performed. A similar performance occurred involving face powder (Hayes and Hayes, 1952a, p. 451).

In a recent theoretical account of learning from demonstration, Sheffield (1961) has proposed several possible explanations for the speed and accuracy of this form of learning. According to this theory, during the course of a demonstration a subject acquires appropriate perceptual and symbolic responses possessing cue properties which are capable of eliciting, at a later time, the corresponding overt responses. Since the acquisition of a perceptual-symbolic pattern or sequence of responses requires no physical manipulations it is less subject to the physiological limitations imposed on motor execution of the corresponding behavior. This would be particularly true in the learning of lengthy or complex response patterns requiring considerable expenditure of time and effort. Secondly, on the basis of relevant prior learning the perceptual response sequence representing the overt sequence can be reduced to fewer units and consequently expedite the acquisition process.

The theory of observational learning proposed by Sheffield is congruent with Mowrer's theory of imitation in several important respects. Both views consider this form of learning to be based upon the principle of contiguity. In addition, both theories assume that matching behavior is mediated by essentially similar cue-producing cognitive or imaginal responses. Sheffield, however, makes no assumptions about mediating conditioned emotional responses. This difference may be due to the fact that Sheffield has addressed himself primarily to the learning of perceptual motor tasks from filmed demonstrations which do not contain strong positive or aversive stimuli essential for conditioning emotional responses.

Whether or not imitative behavior is in fact mediated by perceptual "blueprints" as suggested by Sheffield, by images and emotional responses as propounded by Mowrer, or by other cue-producing mediating responses, can be demonstrated only through study of imitative learning as a function of systematic manipulation of these various mediational reactions.

The theory of imitation that emerges from the material presented in this paper strongly suggests that the process of response acquisition is based upon contiguity of sensory events, and that instrumental conditioning and reinforcement should perhaps be regarded as response-selection rather than response-acquisition or response-strengthening procedures. This last point can be well illustrated by reference to verbal conditioning studies.

In countless laboratories throughout the country, experimenters are nodding their heads and hm-hming in order to demonstrate that whenever these subtle cues are made contingent upon the emission of personal pronouns or other specified classes of behavior, these responses gradually increase in frequency of occurrence and presumably acquire response strength. The inclusion of a relevant control group in these investigations, however, in which the experimenter is less ambiguous in communicating his wishes to the subjects, would reveal the questionable value of many of these experiments for understanding the process of response acquisition.

If the experimenter simply asked subjects politely to emit personal pronouns, it is a safe prediction that these responses would reach asymptotic level almost instantaneously. Based on these findings and the generally accepted definition of reinforcement as any stimulus that increases the probability of preceding responses, one would be forced to conclude that a polite request is an exceedingly powerful reinforcer, and that the responses in question acquired massive strength on the basis of a single reinforcement. Similarly, by asking subjects to discontinue emitting the relevant behavior, the experimenter would produce instantaneous 'extinction.' Finally, if subjects were requested to emit responses in a different response class, these behavior would suddenly emerge with dominant strength in the habit hierarchy.

In like manner, the procedure of shaping behavior by 'differential reinforcement' simply involves a succession of communications to the subject concerning the responses that he should select from his available repertoire and the order in which they must be sequenced. In the example of training motoring behavior, the subject may engage in considerable trial and error before he accidentally places the key in the ignition switch. The experimenter then 'reinforces' (informs) the subject that he has emitted one of several appropriate responses. This process is repeated until eventually the subject narrows his response output to those required for successful driving. He must then engage in considerable trial-and-error behavior to discover the required serial order of responses. This whole tedious process can, of course, be avoided by simple demonstration or verbal description.

Results yielded by operant conditioning studies, while highly relevant for a theory of action, probably have little bearing on the acquisition or 'conditioning' process.

A theoretical conceptualization of imitation as a form of learning which takes place through mere contiguity of sensory stimulation independently of motivation, reinforcement and other factors would be of questionable validity. A group of automobile passengers, for example, who are provided with ample opportunities to observe the behavior of a skillful driver would in all probability exhibit varying degrees of imitative learning ranging from a few fragmentary responses to a complete mastery of the entire motoring sequence. Obviously, learning by imitation is not a passive observational matter but rather an active process in which other factors operate in conjunction with sensory stimulation in determining the level of imitative learning. Exposure of a person to a complex set of stimuli, therefore, is no guarantee that he will attend to the whole range of stimuli, that he will necessarily select and learn the relevant cues and disregard the irrelevant ones, or that he will even perceive the cues accurately.

The selectivity of modeling stimuli may be partly a function of their inherent physical characteristics based on intensity, size, and vividness. Certain model attributes will have acquired distinctiveness on the basis of the subject's earlier social conditioning. Models who are attractive, rewarding (Bandura & Huston, 1961), prestigeful (Asch, 1948; Miller & Dollard, 1941; Mausner, 1953), competent (Kanareff & Lanzetta, 1960; Mausner, 1954a; 1954b; Mausner & Bloch, 1957) high status (Lefkowitz, Blake, & Mouton, 1955), and powerful (Bandura, Ross, & Ross, 1962b; Bandura, Ross, & Ross, 1962c; Lippitt, Polansky, Redl, & Rosen, 1952) are likely to command more attention and therefore elicit more imitation than models who lack these qualities.

Similarly, subject characteristics may serve as determinants of observational response dispositions. Persons who are dependent (Jakubczak & Walters, 1959; Kagan & Mussen, 1956; Ross, 1962), lacking in self-esteem (deCharms & Rosenbaum, 1960; Gelfand, 1961; Lesser & Abelson, 1959), incompetent (Kanareff & Lanzetta, 1960) and who have been frequently rewarded for displaying matching responses (Lanzetta & Kanareff, 1959; Miller & Dollard, 1941; Schein, 1954) are apt to be highly attentive to the cues produced by the behavior of others. Difference between sex of model and sex of subject may also influence the extent to which modeling behavior will be observed and imitated (Bandura, Ross, & Ross, 1961; Maccoby & Wilson, 1957; Rosenblith, 1959; Rosenblith, 1961).

Motivational variables can alter perceptual threshholds and in other ways facilitate, impede and channel observing responses (Easterbrook, 1959; Kausler & Trapp, 1960).

Finally, the induction of incentive-oriented sets or the anticipation of positive reinforcement for reproducing behavior resembling that of a model will greatly enhance and focus the viewer's observing responses. According to the theory adopted in this paper, however, the anticipation of reinforcement probably exerts its greatest influence in the acquisition process on the receptor rather than on the effector systems. A hot-blooded teenager, for example, who anticipates an increase in the number and attractiveness of dates contingent upon his learning to drive an automobile, will be considerably more vigilant of the modeling behavior exhibited by a driver than will an elderly spinster plagued with a freeway phobia. In other words, reinforcement may function as a causal agent in *learning* primarily by augmenting or reducing the arousal and maintenance of observing reactions.

Imitative learning will be influenced not only by attention-directing variables but also by the rate and mode of stimulus presentation. If modeling stimuli are presented at a rate that exceeds the observer's receptive capabilities, imitation will necessarily be limited and fragmentary. Under such conditions repeated exposure to the modeling behavior would therefore be required in order to produce accurate matching responses.

In the acquisition of patterned responses for which the components are both readily observable and available to the subject, contiguity is probably a sufficient condition for learning the appropriate cognitive responses and their motor equivalents. This is most clearly illustrated in the aggression imitation experiments reviewed earlier. It is evident, however, that exposure to modeling behavior is insufficient for learning certain classes of motor skills, and that varying amounts of overt practice are generally required (Maccoby, 1959).

In the first place, a subject may fail to produce accurate matching motor responses following repeated observation simply because the crucial motor elements are unobservable. An aspiring operatic singer may benefit considerably from observing an accomplished voice instructor; nevertheless, imitative voice learning may be limited by the fact that the model's laryngeal and respiratory muscular responses are neither readily observable nor easily described verbally. Consequently the voice pupil must engage in considerable trial-and-error practice in order to bring the necessary motor responses under proprioceptive stimulus control.

Secondly, even though a subject can observe all the relevant elements of the modeling responses, he may still fail to reproduce the pattern precisely in his own behavior due to physical limitations. Young boys or even a vast majority of adults could never accurately match a Wilt Chamberlain regardless of their vigilance and the frequency of model presentations.

Many of the problems encountered in the transmission of perceptual motor skills, however, may be primarily ones of programing rather than of overt practice and proprioception. Thus, Sheffield and Maccoby (1961) found that college undergraduates achieved approximately 90 per cent proficiency in assembling an airplane waste-gate engine containing 64 assembly operations, after two viewings of a carefully programed filmed demonstration, interspersed with two brief practice sequences.

The necessity for a subject to make overt responses during the acquisition process is further questioned by evidence from recent studies of programed learning. Subjects who are presented information in small units and simply observe the correct responses usually perform on a criterion test as well as subjects who are required to emit the relevant overt responses in one form or another (Krumboltz, 1961).

It should be mentioned in passing that I am not advocating an anti-practice theory of imitation. Under some conditions with certain tasks overt practice has been shown to enhance learning from response demonstration. The learning increments contributed by practice may be attributable, however, to factors other than proprioceptive conditioning and response-strengthing effects. Performance of overt or covert responses provide the subject an opportunity to identify the response elements that he has failed to learn and thus direct his attention to relevant modeling cues during subsequent exposures (McGuire, 1961a). The interpolation of practice in a response demonstration sequence may serve to distribute the learning and to reduce serial order effects that inevitably arise in exposure to a lengthy uninterrupted sequence of behavior (McGuire, 1961b). Overt participation procedures may also increase the subject's motivation and thereby heighten generalized attending responses (Hovland, Lumsdaine, & Sheffield, 1948; Maccoby, Michael, & Levine, 1961).

In conclusion, the theory of imitative learning which I have described places primary emphasis on contiguous sensory stimulation as a sufficient condition for the acquisition of most forms of matching responses. To the extent that subject and model characteristics, stimulus programing, rate and mode of presentation, motivational variables, reinforcement, and set-inducing operations create conditions which enhance and channel an organism's observing responses, these factors will determine in part the level of imitative learning achieved and the types of models who will be selected as sources of behavior. These latter variables, however, are regarded as facilitative rather than as necessary preconditions for the occurrence of imitative learning.

REFERENCES

Asch, S. E. The doctrine of suggestion, prestige, and imitation in social psychology. *Psychol. Rev.*, 1948, 55, 250–277.

Bandura, A., & Huston, Aletha C. Identification as a process of incidental learning. *J. Abnorm. Soc. Psychol.*, 1961, 63, 311–318.

Bandura, A., Ross, Dorothea, & Ross, Sheila A. Transmission of aggression through imitation of aggressive models. *J. Abnorm. Soc. Psychol.*, 1961, 63, 575–582.

———. 'Vicarious' reinforcement and imitation. Unpublished MS, Stanford Univer., 1962. (b)

———. An experimental test of the status envy, social power, and the secondary reinforcement theories of identificatory learning. Unpublished MS, Stanford Univer., 1962. (c)

Bayroff, A. G., & Lard, K. E. Experimental social behavior of animals: III. Imitational learning of white rats. *J. Comp. Physiol. Psychol.*, 1944, 37, 165–171.

Church, R. M. Transmission of learned behavior between rats. *J. Abnorm. Soc. Psychol.*, 1957, 54, 163–165.

deCharms, R., & Rosenbaum, M. E. Status variables and matching behavior. *J. Pers.*, 1960, 28, 492–502.

Easterbrook, J. A. The effect of emotion on cue utilization and the organization of behavior. *Psychol. Rev.*, 1959, 66, 183–201.

Gelfand, Donna M. The influence of self-esteem on rate of conditioning and social matching behavior. Unpublished doctoral dissertation, Stanford Univer., 1961.

Hayes, K. J., & Hayes, Catherine. Imitation in a home-raised chimpanzee. *J. Comp. Physiol. Psychol.*, 1952, 45, 450–459. (a)

———. *Imitation in a home-raised chimpanzee.* (16 mm. silent film.) State College, Pa., Psychological cinema Register, 1952. (b)

Herbert, J. J., & Harsh, C. M. Observational learning by cats. *J. Comp. Physiol. Psychol.*, 1944, 17, 81–95.

Hovland, C. I., Lumsdaine, A. A., & Sheffield, F. D. *Experiments on mass communication.* Princeton: Princeton Univer. Press, 1949.

Jakubczak, L. F., & Walters, R. H. Suggestibility as dependency behavior. *J. Abnorm. Soc. Psychol.*, 1959, 59, 102–107.

Kagan, J., & Mussen, P. H. Dependency themes on the TAT and group conformity. *J. Consult. Psychol.*, 1956, 20, 29–32.

Kanareff, V. T., & Lanzetta, J. Effects of success-failure experiences and probability of reinforcement upon the acquisition and extinction of an imitative response. *Psychol. Rev.*, 1960, 7, 151–166.

Kausler, D. H., & Trapp, E. P. Motivation and cue utilization in intentional and incidental learning. *Psychol. Rev.*, 1960, 67, 373–379.

Keller, Helen. *The story of my life.* New York: Doubleday, 1927.

Krumboltz, J. D. Meaningful learning and retention: practice and reinforcement variables. *Rev. Educ. Res.*, 1961, 31, 535–546.

Lanzetta, J. T., & Kanareff, V. T. The effects of a monetary reward on the acquisition of an imitative response. *J. Abnorm. Soc. Psychol.*, 1959, 59, 120–127.

Lazowick, L. On the nature of identification. *J. Abnorm. Soc. Psychol.*, 1955, 51, 175–183.

Lefkowitz, M., Blake, R. R., & Mouton, Jane S. Status factors in pedestrian violation of traffic signals. *J. Abnorm. Soc. Psychol.*, 1955, 51, 704–705.

Lesser, G. S., & Abelson, R. P. Personality correlates of persuasibility in children. In I. L. Janis & C. I. Hovland (Eds.), *Personality and persuasibility.* New Haven: Yale Univer. Press, 1959.

Lippitt, R., Polansky, N., Redl, F., & Rosen, S. The dynamics of power. *Hum. Relat.*, 1952, 5, 37–64.

Maccoby, Eleanor E. Role-taking in childhood and its consequences for social learning. *Child Develpm.*, 1959, 30, 239–252.

Maccoby, Eleanor E., & Wilson, W. C. Identification and observational learning from films. *J. Abnorm. Soc. Psychol.*, 1957, 55, 76–87.

Maccoby, N., Michael, D. N., & Levine, S. Further studies of the use of "audience participation" procedures in film instruction. In A. A. Lumsdaine (Ed.), *Student response in programmed instruction: A symposium.* Washington, D.C.: National Academy of Sciences—National Research Council, 1961, in press.

McDougall, W. *An introduction to social psychology.* London: Methuen, 1908.

McGuire, W. J. Audience participation and audio-visual instruction. In A. A. Lumsdaine (Ed.), *Student response in programmed instruction: A symposium.* Washington, D.C.: National Academy of Sciences—National Research Council, 1961, in press. (a)

———. Interpolated motivational statements within a programmed series of instructions as a distribution of practice factor. In A. A. Lumsdaine (Ed.), *Student response in programmed instruction: A symposium.* Washington, D.C.: National Academy of Sciences—National Research Council, 1961, in press. (b)

Mausner, B. Studies in social interaction: III. Effect of variation in one partner's prestige on the interaction of observer pairs. *J. Appl. Psychol.*, 1953, 37, 391–393.

———. The effect of prior reinforcement on the interaction of observer pairs. *J. Abnorm. Soc. Psychol.*, 1954, 49, 65–68. (a)

———. The effect of one partner's success in a relevant task on the interaction of observer pairs. *J. Abnorm. Soc. Psychol.*, 1954, 49, 557–560. (b)

Mausner, B., & Bloch, B. L. A study of the additivity of variables affecting social interaction. *J. Abnorm. Soc. Psychol.*, 1957, 54, 250–256.

Miller, N. E., & Dollard, J. *Social learning and imitation.* New Haven: Yale Univer. Press, 1941.

Mowrer, O. H. *Learning theory and personality dynamics.* New York: Ronald, 1950.

———. Hearing and speaking. An analysis of language learning. *J. Speech & Hearing Dis.*, 1958, 23, 143–152.

———. *Learning theory and the symbolic processes.* New York: Wiley, 1960.

Nash, M. *Machine age Maya. The industrialization of a Guatemalan community.* Amer. Anthrop. Assn., 1958, 60 (2).

Parsons, T. Family structure and the socialization of the child. In T. Parsons & R. F. Bales, *Family, socialization, and interaction process.* Glencoe, Ill.: Free Press, 1955. Pp. 35–131.

Reichard, Gladys A. Social life. In F. Boas (Ed.), *General anthropology.* Madison, Wisc.: C. D. Heath, 1938. Pp. 409–486.

Rosenblith, Judy F. Learning by imitation in kindergarten children. *Child Develpm.*, 1959, 30, 69–80.

———. Imitative color choices in kindergarten children. *Child Develpm.*, 1961, 32, 211–223.

Ross, Dorothea. The relationship between dependency, intentional learning and incidental learning in preschool children. Unpublished doctoral dissertation, Stanford Univer., 1962.

Schein, E. H. The effect of reward on adult imitative behavior. *J. Abnorm. Soc. Psychol.*, 1954, 49, 389–395.

Sheffield, F. D. Theoretical considerations in the learning of complex sequential tasks from demonstration and practice. In A. A. Lumsdaine (Ed.), *Student response in programmed instruction: A symposium.* Washington, D.C.: National Academy of Sciences—National Research Council, 1961, in press.

Sheffield, F. D., & Maccoby, N. Summary and interpretation of research on organizational principles in constructing filmed demonstrations. In A. A.

Lumsdaine (Ed.), *Student response in programmed instruction: A Symposium.* Washington, D.C.: National Academy of Sciences—National Research Council, 1961, in press.

Skinner, B. F. *Science and human behavior.* New York: Macmillan, 1953.

Solomon, R. L., & Coles, M. R. A case of failure of generalization of imitation across drives and across situations. *J. Abnorm. Soc. Psychol.,* 1954, 49, 7–13.

Tarde, G. *The laws of imitation.* New York: Holt, 1903.

Warden, C. J., Fjeld, H. A., & Koch, A. M. Imitative behavior in the Cebus and Rhesus monkeys. *J. Genet. Psychol.,* 1940, 56, 311–322.

Warden, C. J., & Jackson, T. A. Imitative behavior in the Rhesus monkey. *J. Genet. Psychol.,* 1935, 46, 103–125.

Young, Edna H., & Hawk, Sara S. *Moto-kinesthetic speech training.* Stanford, Calif.: Stanford Univer. Press, 1955.

Chapter 14

Purposes and Aspirations

14-1

PERCIVAL M. SYMONDS

Classroom Discipline

14-2

EVAN R. KEISLAR

A Descriptive Approach to Classroom Motivation

PERCIVAL M. SYMONDS

Classroom Discipline

The motivation of good student conduct is sometimes the largest concern of the beginning teacher. It is also one of the areas most neglected by research. Symonds' article, a classic position on discipline, has great popularity among educators. What sorts of evidence does he muster to support his position? Is his reasoning persuasive?

Recently I received a letter from a member of the Woman's City Club Education Committee in a Midwestern city, asking for suggestions with regard to a situation which had developed in the local school system. She states that the committee "plans a meeting in the fall on physical punishment in the schools, known here as paddling for it is applied with a wooden paddle commonly, though steel-edged rulers have been used. . . . I have spent the last six months inquiring about this form of punishment and find it widespread, sadistically applied in many cases, used daily for minor offenses or no offenses at all. That it is used in a school system is a great shock to me."

Unfortunately this situation is not rare, and classroom discipline is viewed as a problem in schools in countless communities. Not only does it give concern to the citizens and school administrators, but teachers themselves view it as one of their most difficult problems. In graduate classes of teachers there is continuous interest in matters concerning the curriculum and teaching methods, but the greatest interest centers around problems of teacher-pupil relationships and classroom discipline.

Classroom discipline is important, not only because it is an ever-present concern of teachers but also because methods of classroom control are closely related to the whole problem of training for democratic living and action. David Levy, who had an opportunity to study the mentality of anti-Nazis in Germany following the war, reports that the typical Nazi was one who was brought up under strict authoritarian discipline whereas the childhood of the anti-Nazi departed from this typical German pattern. Levy says, "The typical German father is dominating in the family and uses corporal punishment in the discipline of his children. The child is in awe of the father and does not talk to him freely. At the table during mealtime

Percival M. Symonds, "Classroom Discipline," *Teachers College Record,* 51 (1949), 147–58. Reprinted with permission of the estate of Percival M. Symonds.

This paper was read in part at an All-College Conference held in the Horace Mann Auditorium August 2, 1949.

conversation is discouraged."[1] Methods of control in the classroom as well as in the home exert an influence on the growing personality of the children and democratic attitudes formed by them are determined in no small part by the kind of relations set up between teachers and pupils in the classroom.

We are frequently told that the term "discipline" is used in two senses —one referring to repressive and punitive discipline in the interests of control by the teacher, and the other to self-discipline, which is exercised by pupils. There is a widespread belief that the aim in education should be the acquisition of self-discipline and self-control and the assumption of self-responsibility on the part of the pupils. Even though this is a final goal to be achieved, the problem of control by the teacher continues as a real problem at all stages of the process.

THE PROBLEM OF CONTROL

Control in and of itself is not an educational aim. Control serves primarily the needs of the teacher. A teacher may attempt to justify his efforts to secure and retain control on the grounds that it is in the interests of education. The statement is frequently made that one must have an orderly classroom if effective learning is to take place, but it has never been demonstrated that learning requires the high degree of order and restraint that is the ideal of many teachers, and the fact remains that effort to secure quiet orderliness serves primarily the need of the teacher to feel secure in his work.

PUNISHMENT

The problem of this discussion, therefore, will be restated as: What forms of teacher-pupil relationships are most conducive to good personality development? Let us get to the heart of the problem and look at the matter of punishment. Is punishment necessary and desirable as a way of gaining and keeping classroom control? Is punishment necessary in order to guide behavior of children into acceptable channels? This is a question for psychology to answer. Thorndike originally stated that when a response is followed by an annoying state of affairs the connection between this response and the stimulus which preceded it tends to be weakened.[2] This original statement of the negative law of effect served as a guide for educators for many years. In later experimentation, however, Thorndike discovered that punishment is by no means the opposite of reward and the effect of punishment is by no means so significant in weakening learning as reward is in strengthening learning. In 1932 he stated, "A satisfying after-effect which belongs to a connection can be relied on to strengthen the connection. An annoying after-effect under the same conditions has no such uniform weakening effect. . . . There is no evidence that an annoying after-effect takes away strength from the physiological basis of the connection in any way compa-

[1] D. M. Levy, "Anti-Nazi: Criteria of Differentiation." *Psychiatry,* 11:125–67, 1948.

[2] E. L. Thorndike, *The Original Nature of Man,* p. 172. Bureau of Publications, Teachers College, Columbia University, 1913.

rable to the way in which a satisfying after-effect adds strength to it." [3] In another place he is even more emphatic: "Rewarding a connection always strengthened it substantially; punishing it weakened it little or not at all." [4]

More recently, Estes, working under the direction of Skinner, carried out a thoroughgoing experimental study of punishment in which he concludes, "No evidence has been forthcoming to indicate that punishment exerts a direct weakening effect upon a response comparable to the strenthening produced by a reward." [5]

Many persons find it difficult to accept this conclusion which apparently goes in the face of common sense and everyday observation. The question may well be asked: What does punishment do if it does not result in a decrease of learning?

Perhaps the effect of punishment can best be seen by resorting to a homely illustration. A mother has forbidden her son to play in the street because of the danger of passing automobiles. On one occasion when she sees him run into the street to recover a ball, she speaks sharply to him and gives him a few sharp thwacks. It was noted that after this the boy stayed on the sidewalk and refrained from running into the street. Could it be that the punishment had taught him not to run into the street? The question, however, concerns the strength of the learning. One would have to admit that after the punishment the boy was just as able to run into the street as he was before, and that the inclination to do so when he wished to recover his ball was as strong after the punishment as before. After the punishment, however, he *repressed* his tendency to run into the street and refrained from doing it. In other words, the effect of punishment is to produce an inhibition of behavior, which is quite different from weakening the response or the tendency to make it.

IS PUNISHMENT EDUCATIVE?

It is true that punishment, if properly administered, can stop a child from committing any act. The question, however, is: Is this education? One would have to reconsider the fundamental goals of education. Properly speaking, education is primarily concerned with helping children to form desirable habits, skills, attitudes, interests, and appreciations. It is a debatable question whether the formation of inhibitions can be considered a worthy goal of education. It would seem as though the proper and worthy *direction* of energies and impulses is more desirable than the *repression* of them. Instead of teaching children not to run into the street, education would do better to teach them to exercise proper precaution in the interests of safety. This may seem like hairsplitting, but the emphasis on the positive attitudes and direction of conduct is entirely different from the repression

[3] E. L. Thorndike, *The Fundamentals of Learning*, pp. 311 and 313. Bureau of Publications, Teachers College, Columbia University, 1932.

[4] E. L. Thorndike, *Reward and Punishment in Animal Learning*. Comparative Psychology Monographs 8, No. 4, p. 58. Serial No. 39, 1932.

[5] W. K. Estes, *An Experimental Study of Punishment*. Psychological Monographs 57, No. 3, p. 36. Whole No. 263, 1944.

of impulses and the inhibition of behavior. Repressions serve the needs of the parent and the teacher but do not help the child to become more self-directing, which should be the primary goal of education.

There is a certain futility to punishment that is a corollary to the discoveries of Thorndike and Estes. Every inhibition requires a reinforcement in the guise of the repetition of the punishment in order that it may be maintained. The strength of the desire to run into the street, evoked by the ball game, may constantly be reinforced by the needs of the game, and the strength of the inhibition may periodically weaken. Eventually, when punishment becomes accepted by the individual as a necessary and expected outcome of wrongdoing, the result may be conflict of the forces within. An individual's desires may be blocked by his inner conscience, which tells him that the act is wrong or inadvisable. This conflict leads inevitably to guilt, and continuing pressure of the urge may result in one form or another of neurotic behavior.

CONCOMITANTS TO PUNISHMENT

Punishment carries with it many undesirable concomitants. For one thing, anxiety may be aroused by the threat of punishment which may cause the effect of punishment to spread to other situations. As Estes says, "An emotional state such as 'anxiety' or 'dread' which has become conditioned to the incipient movements of making the response will be aroused by any stimuli which formerly acted as occasions for the occurrence of the response." [6]

Second, the emotional response and the inhibition may spread to objects or individuals in the neighboring field. It is common knowledge that punishment arouses hate of the punisher and what the punisher stands for, possibly school and learning. When a teacher punishes a child in order to control his behavior he is at the same time fostering feelings of hate and revenge toward himself and possible dislike toward the school and everything connected with it.

Third, since punishment is frequently administered in a spirit of anger, it may arouse in the child who is its recipient tendencies toward counter-aggression. Many children respond to punishment by becoming sulky, revengeful, or obstinate. Punishment may provoke in a child a tendency to struggle and challenge the authority of the person who has administered it.

Fourth, since punishment leads to guilt for the repressed tendencies which on the one hand struggle for expression and on the other hand are blocked from acceptable expression, it eventually leads to a need for punishment to expiate the guilt. This phenomenon explains the tendency which children often show to provoke punishment as a way of paying the penalty for and being absolved from the guilt which they feel for unexpressed tendencies for which on previous occasions they have been punished.

Fifth, the punished child frequently finds it necessary to test the environment in order to discover the extent and severity of punishment to which he is liable and whether this punishment can be tolerated. Frequently,

[6] Estes, *op. cit.*, p. 37.

neurotic children, because of their insecurity and their fear of dire consequences of bad behavior, have a need to test the limits of the situation to see whether they can bear the punishment which they will receive. This testing the limits challenges the teacher's patience and self-control where both firmness and restraint of the emotions (but not punishment) are called for. This child needs to know that he is understood.

Perhaps the most devastating effect of punishment is the lowering of self-esteem and the arousal of feelings of inferiority that follow in its wake. The punished child feels that he has fallen from the good graces of the punishing person and that as a result he is a person of less value. Snygg and Combs [7] bring out clearly the point that an individual acts in accordance with his conception of himself. If he is made to think of himself as bad, incompetent, worthless, an outcast (as punishment helps him to think of himself), then he will tend to act in accordance with his concept of himself.

In my first year of teaching in the Punchard High School in Andover, Massachusetts, there was the practice of afternoon detention for whatever misdemeanors in the classroom a teacher felt should be corrected. Detention slips were distributed freely for even minor infractions of the rules, but they apparently had little influence in improving classroom conditions, for the numbers who appeared for these afternoon sessions did not diminish during the year. The next year the school became so crowded that it was necessary to hold afternoon sessions, and consequently not only was there no room available for a detention period but teachers were not free to take charge of it. As I recall it we did not feel the need for these detention periods when it was no longer possible to arrange for them, and in some way it was possible to manage without them. In fact, if my memory serves me correctly, there was less need for them in general throughout the school the second year than the first.

I have been told that the incidence of crime is less in London than in New York City, although London policemen carry only their billies, whereas New York policemen are equipped with side arms. Certainly one cannot attribute the respective incidence of crime in the two cities to these facts. It is obvious, however, that the carrying of a revolver does not reduce the occurrence of crime.

NEGLECT AS DISCIPLINE

Neglect is another method of discipline which is sometimes advocated. Dr. Hohman, professor of neuropsychiatry at Duke University, makes a strong case for this method. The psychological principle involved he describes as follows: [8] "If the reinforcement, which for practical purposes can be called 'rewards' or 'punishment' does not *follow* the desired conditioned response, either the conditioned response is not established or else it is promptly extinguished or abolished. In animals, as well as children, as soon

[7] D. Snygg and A. W. Combs, *Individual Behavior.* Harper and Brothers, New York, 1949.

[8] L. B. Hohman, "Directive vs Permissive Techniques in Counseling Children." *Marriage and Family Living,* 11:66, 67, Spring, 1949.

as a conditioned response is not reinforced or rewarded, the pattern begins to disappear. After several trials without reward, there is no longer any conditioned response." Applying Dr. Hohman's point of view, teachers who wish to suppress show-off behavior in the classroom could achieve the results that they desire by ignoring this behavior.

Dr. Hohman is correct in the psychological principle which he adduces and his interpretation of it. He overlooks certain factors, however, which illustrate how dangerous it may be to interpret psychological laws derived from experimentation with animals as applying to human situations. For one thing, the neglect may be looked upon and interpreted by the child as a punishment, and the child may be responding as much to what he considers to be a punishment as to the psychological condition of lack of response. For instance, children are quite frequently punished by being confined alone in a closet, a cellar, or an empty room. Furthermore, this form of control may also have its undesirable concomitants and the resulting insecurity that the child experiences through the parents' failure to respond may be even more traumatic in its consequence than severe punishment. A child may become panic-stricken when he finds himself alone and realizes that his parents will not respond to his cries. Instead of reducing in intensity his behavior may become frenzied.

Both punishment and failure to respond overlook the meaning of the child's original behavior. There is an instructive case in a book by Foster and Anderson [9] which illustrates the point to be made.

Mabel was referred to a clinic at the age of two years and seven months by her mother for a variety of complaints. On the first call to the clinic, the mother complains that the child wets the bed every night, that she refuses to take her nap, is obstinate, does not obey, eats mud, and runs away. Mrs. Miller is advised by the clinic to be more firm, to punish Mabel by isolating her in a room, to allow the child less water to drink in the late afternoon, and to have her wear long cardboard cuffs extending above the elbow so that she will be unable to put her hands in her mouth while playing outdoors.

On the second visit, the mother reports that these difficulties of Mabel's have cleared up but she now has trouble playing amicably with other children and tells small untruths. Again the mother is given suggestions, and by the next visit the fibbing has disappeared but the child's table manners have become atrocious. On still another visit, it is reported that the table manners have improved, but Mabel has developed show-off behavior. Her mother follows the clinician's advice to ignore the child when she refuses to eat, and to put her in a room by herself away from company when she persists in showing off, and at the next visit reports that these difficulties have been overcome but now Mabel whines continually when she cannot have her way. In short, each one of Mabel's problems could be eradicated by a suitable punishment or neglect, but Mabel still remained a problem child.

This case makes it clear that the behavior was a symptom of inner dis-

[9] J. C. Foster and J. E. Anderson, *The Young Child and His Parents.* Case 11, Mabel Miller, pp. 49–53. University of Minnesota Press, Minneapolis, 1930.

satisfaction of a fundamental sort, and when one symptom was stamped out another arose to take its place. In spite of the mother's attempts to control and guide the child, following the directions suggested at the clinic, the child's fundamental problems persisted. This case also illustrates very clearly the point which has been frequently made—that punishment does not get to the root of a child's difficulties and that while punishment may be successful in eradicating undesirable behavior, it does not do anything toward correcting the basic problems. Mabel was a child who needed to be understood. It was interesting in this case that when she went to kindergarten her teacher reported her as very obedient and as doing excellent work, and Mabel apparently enjoyed the kindergarten. Her earlier behavior was a response to the mother's basic rejection and was undoubtedly a persistent attempt on the part of the child to force the mother to pay attention to her and to be good to her. In addition, Mabel's guilt repeatedly forced her to test her mother's evaluation of her and to try out her belief that she was a bad child.

One cannot escape the basic fact that neither punishment nor neglect considers the underlying needs. Much of the undesirable behavior which a child exhibits in the classroom is neurotic—an unsatisfactory attempt to satisfy some underlying need—but neither punishment nor neglect gets to the root of this trouble. It is more important to solve the basic conflict that gives rise to the undesirable behavior than it is to attempt to suppress the behavior directly.

ADMINISTRATIVE PROBLEMS

One should not dismiss this topic of punishment without stopping to consider what discipline and punishment mean to the teacher. Unfortunately, many teachers who would like to adopt a more constructive attitude toward the problems of classroom discipline and control are prevented from doing so by the conditions under which they must teach and the attitude of their superior officers and the community. In the first place, control is a difficult matter at best when one has charge of a class of forty or more children, however high a teacher's ideals may be. In spite of various suggestions, most teachers are reduced to rather rigid and autocratic methods of management and control of large classes over a long period of time. Second, discipline in a school is a function of the administration. The principal sets the pattern for the social relations in a school by his philosophy and interpretation of the meaning of education. If he takes a positive and constructive point of view toward education he makes possible a constructive attitude for his teachers, but if he is a believer in authoritarian control and repression he makes the teacher's task difficult. If the principal places great emphasis on order, system, and quiet in the classroom, it is the unusual teacher who is able to achieve these standards by which he is to be evaluated without using methods that are in a degree repressive. The tone and morale of a school go back to the psychology of the principal and the principal, in so many cases, calls the turn for his teachers. It is true that each teacher in a school will reveal his individual personality in his relations with the class, but limits are set on what he can accomplish by the standards and expectations of the principal.

The atmosphere of the classrooms also reflects the expectations of the community. It is easy for the members of a community to resort to strict-control and repression because so many have never fully learned to control their own impulses. It is well known that teachers are expected to be paragons of excellence in the community, reflecting the ideals rather than the practice of the community.

THE INSECURE TEACHER

However, within the leeway afforded by the expectations of the principal and the community, variations in teacher–pupil relations in the classroom reflect the security of the individual teacher. An insecure teacher does not dare to relax control for fear that his authority will be irrevocably undermined. He is afraid that he will not be able to handle the hostilities of his pupils as well as his own anger, and he is also afraid of the criticism of his superior officers. The emotionally secure teacher, on the other hand, feeling confident in his own strength, dares to be more informal and natural, and if at the same time he is secure in his position or is above caring whether he is, he can afford to face possible criticism that he may invoke from his superiors.

The need for repressive discipline is often an indication of the otherwise unexpressed hostile impulses of the teacher. It is well known that many teachers use the classroom situation as an outlet for their sadistic impulses, and children are subjected to strict and punitive control in order to satisfy the teacher's unexpressed needs.

The insecure teacher does not dare to let an offense pass unnoticed, but feels that he must deal with it precipitately. The secure teacher, on the other hand, dares to wait. He does not feel the necessity for handling the situation immediately. The secure teacher, because he knows that he has the majority of his class with him, feels that when he must deal with some disciplinary situation he can deal with the individual concerned without undermining his relations with the class as a whole.

The insecure teacher is frequently given to projecting his weakness onto the situation with which he is unable to cope. One should be suspicious of a teacher who finds it necessary to be critical of the school, of the pupils, of the curriculum, of the principal, or of the community, for the chances are that this teacher finds himself inadequate in the situation. It is true that there are many situations with which a teacher is justified in being dissatisfied and in making complaints, but the secure teacher eventually either finds some way of meeting the situation or seeks another position where his efforts can be more effective.

In good teaching, problems of discipline seldom arise, because both teacher and pupils are interested in the activities of the class. Apparently the insecure teacher is consigned to being ineffective and the secure teacher, in spite of himself, is effective. Actually, classroom discipline cannot be reduced to a set of rules and principles; it is more a matter of attitude and feeling. The successful teacher concentrates on matters other than classroom order and control. He encourages the class to share his interest in the activities and subject matter with which they are concerned, and problems of order do not arise.

THE GOOD TEACHER

A good teacher is firm and active. It is important not to confuse firmness with punishment. The two are by no means identical. It is possible to be quietly yet insistently firm without threatening or practicing punishment. A good teacher avoids issuing commands, but he expresses his wishes and his expectations with considerable vigor and, if necessary, persistence. A good teacher does not fail to let his pupils know what he expects of them, and the very clarity with which he expresses his wishes helps to secure good relations.

A teacher cannot afford to take an entirely passive attitude toward a boy who is troublesome, noisy, and obstreperous. On the other hand, the teacher is lost if he gets angry or annoyed, for then perhaps the boy has achieved one of his purposes. It is most important that the teacher know why the boy is noisy or interfering, and it may safely be assumed that such behavior is not just pure thoughtlessness but arises from something that has happened before, either at school or at home. In such a situation a teacher might say, "You are interfering with what we are trying to do here. I don't like it and the class doesn't like it. I know you are angry with me for not accepting the paper you turned in to me this morning, but at the same time I can't permit you to continue to interrupt the class." A good teacher will take time to explain over and over again in considerable detail and in the clearest and simplest language what he expects and why. A good teacher refuses to be drawn into a contest of wills. I have seen some excellent teachers permit a child to spend a whole hour with head on desk or reading some book not connected with the lesson rather than to reach a deadlock with a child who is in a highly resistant mood. It is better to suffer a temporary defeat in order to win the child over by more persuasive methods at a later time. It is more important to show the child that he is understood than it is to force him into submission to authority.

A good teacher expects courtesy, chivalry, and fair play from his pupils, and most pupils feel ashamed not to live up to the expectations of their teacher if those expectations are reasonable and explicit and if the teacher shows that he cares very much what pupils do. A good teacher treats boys and girls with respect even to the point of showing restrained affection. A good teacher is sensitive to the feelings of boys and girls and takes pains to avoid belittling or humiliating any child. A good teacher holds pupils up to their best work. Not only does he make clear what he expects from them, but he shows pleasure when they meet his expectations and disappointment when they fail. A good teacher challenges his pupils; he makes them proud of their achievement or ashamed if their work is not up to their best. No teacher can expect to succeed with a pupil whom he dislikes, hence he must find something in every child to like. He must believe that each has possibilities in some direction; he must have faith that each will succeed in some way. A good teacher is patient and tolerant with his pupils; he recognizes that they are children and still have some way to travel to maturity and he is willing to overlook irregularities. But once an irregularity has been condoned, the teacher should not fail to make clear his expectations for them. A good teacher is as honest in telling his pupils when and in what way they please him as in telling them when and in what way they displease him.

Even the best teachers, however, find that disciplinary crises arise on some occasions, but every teacher should recognize that they may arise through no fault of his. Teachers should not expect to be successful with every pupil and it is no threat or defeat for a teacher to find that some pupils do not respond to every effort that he may make to help them succeed. Hostility directed toward a teacher or the classroom situation is in many instances a displacement of hostility which has been aroused in some other situation. The teacher should recognize this and refuse to be drawn into the relationship. The secure teacher does not feel that he must repay rudeness with rudeness or resistance with stubbornness. Some children simply are not ready to accept membership in certain classroom situations and need therapeutic help before they can become acceptable and tolerated members of a group.

DISCIPLINE IN THE NEW SITUATION

The problem of how to begin with a new and difficult situation is always troublesome. Members of my classes have told me repeatedly that they have handled new teaching situations by "treating 'em rough" and demonstrating physically that they are masters of the situation. Frequently it is the biggest and strongest boy in the class on whom this demonstration is made. I would very much distrust a relationship based on physical mastery and dominance, for I would fear that it might be at the same time a token of self-inadequacy. I would rather put my trust in a relationship based on the inner strength and security of the teacher, his objectivity, fairness, kindliness, and understanding. Physical force begets physical force, which is not particularly educational.

Every teacher must decide on the basis of the relationship which he expects to establish with his class. Is it to be a contest of wills or a show of physical superiority or is the relationship going to be pitched on a different level? A secure teacher in a new situation has to be strong enough to decide that the relationship is to be one of reasonableness and interest in the work and not based on dominance and submission. Teachers should be secure enough to be willing to adopt an attitude of take it or leave it with regard to the cooperation of individual pupils, but every teacher must always be ready and able to defend his own person and self-respect. It is one thing to tolerate rebellion and resistance that is expressed verbally and another to be helpless against physical attack and violence. Verbal criticism and attack are not fatal and may actually afford welcome release for a pupil. Any teacher should expect to defend himself from physical attack, but at the same time he should be sure that he has not precipitated such an attack by arbitrary exercise of his authority. A teacher at the beginning of a new relationship with a group should expound clearly the basis of the relationship by which he proposes to operate and his attitude and expectation toward the group.

If disciplinary problems arise, it is essential that the teacher recognize and permit the expression of feeling as Baruch[10] and Axline[11] have so clearly shown. To permit pupils to express their feelings in words need be no threat to the teacher's authority and prestige, and, in fact, may release a good deal of the pent-up emotion which was the occasion of the irregular behavior. When a disciplinary problem arises the successful teacher holds his own feelings in check and deals with the pupil on the basis of reason and an understanding of the motives that lie behind the act. He attempts to guide his pupils into more accepted and preferred modes of behavior with a minimum of emphasis on the mistakes that have been made in the past.

The problem of classroom discipline cannot and should not be thought of in terms of some immediate incident. It is difficult, if not impossible, to tell a teacher how to handle some isolated incident that may arise in the classroom. The problem of discipline is one that requires growth in relationship over a long period of time. Little can be done to help a teacher know how to manage in a given situation. Much can be done to help a teacher work out constructive and growth-producing relationships with his class over a period of weeks and months. Eventually a class must so trust and respect the teacher that he can deal with individuals as occasions arise without disturbing his relationship to the group as a whole.

The foregoing represents the kind of answer I would give to the lady in a Midwestern city who asked me for help with regard to a disciplinary situation in the local schools. In my letter to her I said, "If a school has a program which engages the interest and enthusiasm of teachers and pupils and if teachers are encouraged to put their attention on the positive side of growth and development, the problems of discipline usually disappear. Of course there are always individual children who present behavior and personality problems, but they can usually be dealt with on an individual basis and in a constructive manner."

[10] D. W. Baruch, *New Ways in Discipline*. McGraw-Hill Book Company, New York, 1949.

[11] V. M. Axline, *Play Therapy*. Houghton Mifflin Company, Boston, 1947.

EVAN R. KEISLAR

A Descriptive Approach to Classroom Motivation

This approach to studying motivation contrasts with Symonds' approach. Keislar is wary of verbal, circular explanations; he wants to pare away popular professional words, to leave only those with some physical, specifiable referent. He illustrates his method of evidence with a series of crisp experiments. A small but important number of psychologists believe that education needs this sort of parsimony.

In developing a useful conceptual structure for education, the topic of motivation appears to require a central position. And yet motivational terms are exceedingly difficult to clarify; in fact, in psychology itself the status of the word "motivation" is very unclear. Richard Littman [1] has given a definition for motivation which appears to comprise no more than what investigators have at one time or another included under this term; the definition, as Littman himself points out, unfortunately encompasses just about everything which psychologists study.

In this report it is proposed that, for certain kinds of problems in the classroom, motivation be discussed without recourse to the usual constructs such as "motive" or "interest." Some motivational phenomena might be treated profitably in purely descriptive terms, that is, with words which refer only to observable events and their mathematical relations. As an illustration of the application of this purely descriptive approach to motivation a series of experiments is briefly reviewed. This attack upon problems of motivation is to be evaluated in terms of its usefulness in providing hypotheses for the control of student behavior, a process important for teacher and experimenter alike. When the utility of other motivational words becomes more clearly established, this descriptive approach could at such times become easily enriched.

MOTIVATION AS STIMULUS CONTROL

Motivation is usually assessed in education by noting the kind and amount of behavior of the learner. When we say that a student is motivated,

[1] Richard A. Littman, "Motives, History, and Causes," in M. R. Jones, ed., *Nebraska Symposium on Motivation* (Lincoln, Nebraska: University of Nebraska Press, 1958), pp. 114–168.

Evan R. Keislar, "A Descriptive Approach to Classroom Motivation," *Journal of Teacher Education,* 11 (1960), 310–15. Reprinted with permission.

we generally mean that he is or probably will be active. Pupils who read a good deal are said to be "interested" in reading, those who are aggressive have a "need" for aggression, students who study many hours a week have a strong achievement "motive," and persons who answer a set of items in certain ways have a particular vocational "interest." If motivational terms such as interest, motive, desire, goal, level of aspiration are inferred entirely from behavior, they have little use in attempts to produce such behavior. Such circularity of reasoning is found, for example, when it is said, "You can tell that Bill is interested in reading, since he spends so much time at it! His interest in reading is what makes him read so much."

As descriptions of observable behavior, these motivational terms possess considerable value. In the first place they are useful in predicting other behavior. On the basis of correlational data we may be able to predict, better than chance at least, that a student with a particular interest score on some test will engage in certain other kinds of activities, or that a child who says he is interested in tractors will read books about tractors. Secondly, such information about the "motives" of students can be used to supply parameters in the statement of relationships dealing with control; this description of prior behavior is therefore useful in the same way that data are about the student's age, intelligence, and socio-economic status.

But when we infer, on the basis of observations alone, some internal motivational state, the usefulness of such language in education may well be questioned. Even from a practical point of view, a word like "interest" often adds little to the teacher's effectiveness. For example, it isn't very helpful for a teacher to make the hypothesis, "If I arouse my pupils' interest in arithmetic they will do their problems regularly," if such interest can be identified only by the way the pupils act. Since it is still necessary to clarify what must be done to "arouse" the interest, she might just as well formulate a hypothesis which suggests what she must do to get pupils to do their problems; she does not need to use the word "interest" at all.

Motivational terms will have far greater utility for education when they refer to antecedent as well as consequent conditions. In other words, we must identify the conditions which have to occur before the child is active or "motivated." The establishment of these conditions will then permit control of student behavior for teacher and experimenter alike; the conditions are then said to have "stimulus control." [2]

In the series of investigations being reported there was an attempt to distinguish "motivating" stimuli from other kinds of stimuli. Incentives, or "motivating" stimuli, control broad classes of behavior. General instructions may be regarded as stimuli which control behavior classes of intermediate breadth while cues are stimuli which control very narrow classes. While this concept of "breadth of class of behavior" is admittedly imprecise, it suggests that on occasion teachers might be helped by viewing their presentation in terms of incentives, instructions, and cues. This classification system may have "engineering" value in some school situations; in many others it may be quite adequate simply to describe the situations students face without regard to these categories.

[2] B. F. Skinner, *Science and Human Behavior* (New York: Macmillan, 1953).

Loosely speaking, an incentive may be regarded as a "promise" of a reinforcement. A grade of "A," social approval, or money are not incentives for a student; these are the reinforcements. The situations which "promise" these things are the incentives. Although a stimulus may become both an incentive and a reinforcement, when we refer to it as an incentive we are emphasizing its property of arousing a broad class of behavior subsequently. (Which particular responses in this class will be emitted depend upon the other stimuli, the instructions, and the cues which are present.) When we refer to a stimulus as a reinforcement we are talking about its usefulness in strengthening behavior which has just previously occurred. Parenthetically, it should be noted that the term "incentive" is here used with about the same functions as the term "drive-arousing stimulus" proposed by Dollard and Miller.[3]

DEVELOPMENT OF STIMULUS CONTROL OF PROBLEM-SOLVING BEHAVIOR

While it is valuable to continue normative studies of our pupils to find out what stimuli are effective incentives for them, it is even more important to find out how new incentives are developed. An attempt was made to conceptualize one such process in Experiment I. The hypothesis for this experiment was that if a neutral stimulus (a bell and light combination) is present when the child is reinforced for solving a variety of problems but is not present when he is not reinforced, then this stimulus will gain control of the problem-solving behavior; it will become an incentive.

Twenty-two second grade children were tested individually. When presented with a picture card, each child moved a knob along any of three grooves. Moving the knob in the correct groove was reinforced with marbles to be exchanged later for trinkets. For each of three different cards, the children learned to give the correct response a variable number of times only when a bell and light were presented with the card; responses to the card alone were never reinforced.

On the test, in which no responses were reinforced, each child was shown a new card for just one trial. Half the children were presented with the bell and light (the incentive) in addition; the other half were given no such stimulus pattern. The number of responses each child gave before stopping was then recorded. Ten of the group with the incentive present and one of the group without the incentive were above the median ($p < .01$). Since the children were clearly more active in this new problem when the incentive was present than in its absence, we may conclude that, under these conditions, by associating a neutral stimulus with reinforcement in a variety of problems, its presence in a new task will bring about problem-solving activity.

This descriptive approach to motivation may have some utility in suggesting hypotheses for researcher and teacher. For the researcher it means that particular attention must be given to the prior reinforcements his subjects

[3] J. Dollard and N. E. Miller, *Personality and Psychotherapy* (New York: McGraw-Hill, 1950).

have had with the stimuli present during the experiment. In Hurlock's classic study,[4] for example, pupils who had been praised for several days were found to do better on an arithmetic test than pupils who had been reproved. That this may reflect nothing about a general change of skill in arithmetic may easily be tested by changing the incentives (but not the instructions or cues); if, after the experiment, the same type of test had been given by the local Kiwanis club with a promise of bicycles for superior performance, both groups may have done equally well.

Many school children appear inactive in school situations although they act differently on the playground or in the shop. Instead of saying that these children are "disinterested" or "non-motivated," it may be more helpful to the teacher to say that the school setting is no incentive for such children. She might act upon a hypothesis which states that if such children are provided with a wealth of appropriately-administered reinforcements in the classroom setting, they will participate actively in school.

STIMULUS CONTROL AND THE ENERGIZING FUNCTION OF DRIVE

It will be objected that the illustration of "motivating stimulus" given in the previous experiment was inadequate, that the bell and light merely informed the child when it would be worth his effort, or that the "real motivators" were somewhere inside the child. But we do not yet have any way of determining the "real motivators." If these motive states are inferred entirely from behavior, they have little value for control. In the field of primary motivation such as hunger, the energizing function of drive is a respectable intervening variable, anchored between data on antecedent conditions such as hours of deprivation and data on consequent conditions like eating behavior. But even here Estes[5] has proposed a stimulus-response theory of drive which places the energizing function in a position subordinate to that of stimulus. When we come to secondary or learned motivation, the energizing function of drives is even more confused. In very few instances have we a way of using secondary drive as a true intervening variable. Most of the time it is simply a construct which offers no value for the purposes of control of behavior. By regarding the stimuli as the "motivators" we can move ahead with our research in certain areas of education without waiting for psychologists of motivation to clarify the nature of secondary drives.

LEARNING SETS

A central "motivational" problem in education is that of getting students to change their behavior as a result of being presented with information or a pattern of stimuli. For example, when students are given a lecture, shown a film, presented with printed material, or provided with a demonstration, it is hoped that they will learn (i.e., change their behavior) as

[4] Elizabeth Hurlock, "An Evaluation of Certain Incentives Used in School Work," *Journal of Educational Psychology*, 16:145–59; 1925.

[5] W. K. Estes, "Stimulus-Response Theory of Drive." In M. R. Jones, *ibid.*, pp. 35–68.

a result. This "motivational" problem has been frequently stated as one of teaching students to "pay attention," to "study hard," to "concentrate," or to "remember." With a descriptive approach to motivation, the above problem is regarded as one of developing stimulus control of a learning set. "Motivating students to study or to pay attention" is thus looked upon as a matter of presenting stimuli which control the appropriate learning sets.

A learning set was defined in this study as the relationship between a pattern of stimuli, which is not contingent upon the subject's responses, and a change in operant behavior. The distinctive feature of a learning set, as used in this study, is that learning results from sheer exposure to stimuli; there is apparently no three-term contingency (stimulus, response, and reinforcement) recognized generally as essential for operant learning. It is true that one can observe an orientation of sense receptors to the information; the student, for example, stops doing other things and looks directly at the material. But every teacher is familiar with the danger of assuming that students learn just because they appear attentive. The teacher (or experimenter) usually observes neither the response students ultimately learn to make nor the reinforcements contingent upon such responses. While one may explain such learning by assuming that students reinforce themselves for their covert responses or by discussing the phenomena in terms of some form of cognitive activity, the pressing problem, at the operational or practical level, is to find out under what conditions a set to learn is acquired and displayed. The position taken in this study is that a stimulus can acquire control of a learning set in exactly the same fashion as stimuli which control problem-solving behavior.

DEVELOPMENT OF STIMULUS-CONTROL OF A LEARNING SET

The general hypothesis of Experiments II and III was that a learning set (this relationship) is brought under the control of a stimulus through a reinforcement program. For example, if students exhibit this set in a variety of situations where a common distinctive stimulus is present and if they are reinforced for the appropriate learning in each case, this stimulus will acquire control of the learning set. In other words, students will learn if this stimulus is present, or, this stimulus will act as an incentive and will "motivate" them to learn. On the other hand, if subjects learn in a variety of situations where a distinctive stimulus is present but are not reinforced for this learning, this stimulus will lose control of the learning set; subjects will not learn when this stimulus is present, or, in this situation they will remain "apathetic" or "non-motivated."

In Experiment II twenty-two second grade children (not those used in Experiment I, of course) were tested individually. Each subject was shown, through a window in a panel board, a series of 48 "information" cards, each of which presented pictures and colors to be associated. After each information card was exposed, there followed randomly either a blank card or a set of question cards, one question card for each pair presented in the information card. If the pupil indicated the correct color he received a marble from the automatic dispenser.

For half the subjects a green light was turned on when the information card was exposed, if the pupil was to be questioned on this card; a white light with black stripes was on when no questions, just the blank card, were to follow. The functions of these two lights were reversed for the other half of the subjects.

Information Card 49 was presented with a "test" light and Information Card 50 with a "no-test" light but three questions followed each information card, one question for each pair on the card. To counterbalance item difficulty these two cards and their three questions were interchanged for half the group. Fourteen children learned more when the "test" light was on; two children learned more when the "no-test" light was on. This difference, when tested by the Wilcoxon matched-pairs signed-ranks method, is significant at the .01 level. It may be concluded that these children learned more from information accompanied by a light previously associated with a test than they did from information presented with a light with no such association. Assuming that the test provided opportunities for reinforcement, the principles of operant conditioning appear to apply to the development of stimulus control of a learning set.

EFFECT OF KNOWLEDGE OF RESULTS UPON A LEARNING SET

In Experiment III an attempt was made to assess the effect of giving knowledge of results upon the learning set. Knowledge of results usually includes both positive and negative reinforcements. The material, apparatus, and general procedure were identical with the previous experiment, but the experimental and control conditions both involved test questions; pupils were given questions following each information card. When one light (the "KR" light) was turned on with the information card, pupils were given marbles for each right answer to the test question on this information. When the other light (the "No-KR" light) was on with the information card, pupils were never informed in any way as to whether their answers were right or wrong.

The criterion consisted of the nine questions on the last three information cards for each light condition. The pupils obtained a score of 6.3 when the "KR" light was on, and 4.8 when the "No-KR" light was on. This difference is significant at the .05 level. (Using the last half of the cards, seven under each light condition, the difference was proportionately about the same but was significant at the .01 level.) It has been well known that knowledge of results is an important factor in the acquisition of specific behavior. But the findings of Experiment III point up the fact that knowledge of results can also strengthen a learning set.

SHAPING OF A LEARNING SET

In the previous two experiments, the emphasis was placed upon the development of stimulus control of a learning set. Although this set to learn may have been altered, the relationship between the stimuli presented on the information card and the kind of change of behavior was not deliberately modified. This relationship was brought under the control of one stimulus and not another. In other words, pupils were taught *when* to learn.

In Experiment IV an attempt was made to alter the relationship, to modify what students learned. Students were reinforced for learning certain kinds of things from the information and not other kinds. This process of shaping a learning set may be regarded as analogous to response differentiation. In this experiment, therefore, students were taught *what* to learn.

What most high school and college students learn from their study in a course is less likely to be influenced by the stated objectives of the course, objectives which are often expressed in "high sounding and broad" terms. Students are far more likely to learn those things for which they get reinforced on course examinations. The learning sets of students are shaped largely by the kind of reinforcements teachers actually provide. The specific hypothesis of Experiment IV was that pupils would learn better (1) the kind of information from a paragraph for which they had been previously tested than they would (2) the kind for which they had not been previously tested. Forty sixth- and seventh-grade children were tested individually. Each was presented with 22 paragraphs of pseudo-historical information containing a date, a name, and a place as well as three reasons for this event. Immediately after each paragraph was exposed, one half of the group was tested on the date, name, and place; the other half was tested on the reasons. Correct answers were immediately reinforced.

On Paragraph No. 23 both groups were asked questions on both kinds of material (order of presentation of the two sets of test items being counterbalanced). The mean score (1.5) made by the group on the questions about the information of the type on which they had previously been tested was higher, at the .05 level, than the mean score (1.0) on the questions of the other kind. It was concluded that, at this level of confidence, the learning set of these pupils in reading these paragraphs was altered by a program of differential reinforcement; the two groups of pupils had acquired different learning sets for this situation.

When students are shown the same film, given the same lecture, or taken on the same field trip, different students learn different things. This is often "explained" by saying that students differ in their "interests" and therefore "pay attention" to different things. But such language is of little value in making education more effective; it merely describes the phenomena we observe. It is far more fruitful, for purposes of controlling what students learn, to suggest that such learning sets have been shaped differently by virtue of different reinforcement histories. With appropriate reinforcement programs such learning sets might be altered and improved to make the students' educational experiences more effective.

CONCLUSION

This discussion of motivation has emphasized the stimuli in the presence of which the child is active or learns. But it has also stressed the fact that such stimuli function as they do because of prior reinforcements. The crucial aspects of motivation are therefore to be found in the systems of reinforcements which a school provides for pupils. Such a discussion of reinforcements already has been extensively presented by other writers, notably B. F. Skinner,[6] with implications for education. The descriptive approach presented in this paper may, however, bring many research problems in education more clearly within the framework of reinforcement theory.

[6] *Op. cit.*

Chapter 15

The Teacher as Classroom Leader

15-1

ELLIS B. PAGE

Teacher Comments and Student Performance

15-2

JULES HENRY

The Problem of Spontaneity, Initiative, and Creativity in Suburban Classrooms

ELLIS B. PAGE

Teacher Comments and Student Performance

One of the most common ways the classroom teacher influences the individual student is in marking his papers. The following study examines the effect of teacher's written comments upon the subsequent test performance of the students. Notice the criticisms of prior studies, and the steps taken here to improve the experimental design. Can you think of other subtle experiments to evaluate common practice of teachers in the classroom?

Each year teachers spend millions of hours writing comments upon papers being returned to students, apparently in the belief that their words will produce some result, in student performance, superior to that obtained without such words. Yet on this point solid experimental evidence, obtained under genuine classroom conditions, has been conspicuously absent. Consequently each teacher is free to do as he likes; one will comment copiously, another not at all. And each believes himself to be right.

The present experiment investigated the questions: 1. Do teacher comments cause a significant improvement in student performance? 2. If comments have an effect, which comments have more than others, and what are the conditions, in students and class, conducive to such effect? The questions are obviously important for secondary education, educational psychology, learning theory, and the pressing concern of how a teacher can most effectively spend his time.

PREVIOUS RELATED WORK

Previous investigations of "praise" and "blame," however fruitful for the general psychologist, have for the educator been encumbered by certain weaknesses: Treatments have been administered by persons who were extraneous to the normal class situation. Tests have been of a contrived nature in order to keep students (unrealistically) ignorant of the true comparative quality of their work. Comments of praise or blame have been administered on a random basis, unlike the classroom where their administration is not at all random. Subjects have often lacked any independent measures of their performance, unlike students in the classroom. Areas of training have often been those considered so fresh that the students would have little previous history of related success or failure, an assumption

Ellis B. Page, "Teacher Comments and Student Performance: A Seventy-Four Classroom Experiment in School Motivation," *Journal of Educational Psychology,* 49 (1958), 173–81. Reprinted with permission of the American Psychological Association, Inc.

impossible to make in the classroom. There have furthermore been certain statistical errors: tests of significance have been conducted as if students were totally independent of one another, when in truth they were interacting members of a small number of groups with, very probably, some group effects upon the experimental outcome.

For the educator such experimental deviations from ordinary classroom conditions have some grave implications, explored elsewhere by the present writer (5). Where the conditions are highly contrived, no matter how tight the *controls,* efforts to apply the findings to the ordinary teacher-pupil relationship are at best rather tenuous. This study was therefore intended to fill both a psychological and methodological lack by *leaving the total classroom procedures exactly what they would have been without the experiment,* except for the written comments themselves.

METHOD

Assigning the subjects. Seventy-four teachers, randomly selected from among the secondary teachers of three districts, followed detailed printed instructions in conducting the experiment. By random procedures each teacher chose one class to be subject from among his available classes.[1] As one might expect, these classes represented about equally all secondary grades from seventh through twelfth, and most of the secondary subject-matter fields. They contained 2,139 individual students.

First the teacher administered whatever objective test would ordinarily come next in his course of study; it might be arithmetic, spelling, civics, or whatever. He collected and marked these tests in his usual way, so that each paper exhibited a numerical score and, on the basis of the score, the appropriate letter grade A, B, C, D, or F, each teacher following his usual policy of grade distribution. Next, the teacher placed the papers in numerical rank order, with the best paper on top. He rolled a specially marked die to assign the top paper to the *No Comment, Free Comment,* or *Specified Comment* group. He rolled again, assigning the second-best paper to one of the two remaining groups. He automatically assigned the third-best paper to the one treatment group remaining. He then repeated the process of rolling and assigning with the next three papers in the class, and so on until all students were assigned.

Administering treatments. The teacher returned *all* test papers with the numerical score and letter grade, as earned. No Comment students received nothing else. Free Comment students received, in addition, whatever comment the teacher might feel it desirable to make. Teachers were instructed: "Write anything that occurs to you in the circumstances. There is not any 'right' or 'wrong' comment for this study. A comment is 'right' for the study if it conforms with your own feelings and practices." Specified Comment students, regardless of teacher or student differences, all received comments designated in advance for each letter grade, as follows:

[1] Certain classes, like certain teachers, would be ineligible for a priori reasons: giving no objective tests, etc.

A: Excellent! Keep it up.
B: Good work. Keep at it.
C: Perhaps try to do still better?
D: Let's bring this up.
F: Let's raise this grade!

Teachers were instructed to administer the comments "rapidly and automatically, trying not even to notice who the students are." This instruction was to prevent any extra attention to the Specified Comment students, in class or out, which might confound the experimental results. After the comments were written on each paper and recorded on the special sheet for the experimenter, the test papers were returned to the students in the teacher's customary way.

It is interesting to note that the student subjects were totally naive. In other psychological experiments, while often not aware of precisely what is being tested, subjects are almost always sure that something unusual is underway. In 69 of the present classes there was no discussion by teacher or student of the comments being returned. In the remaining five the teachers gave ordinary brief instructions to "notice comments" and "profit by them," or similar remarks. In none of the classes were students reported to seem aware or suspicious that they were experimental subjects.

Criterion. Comment effects were judged by the scores achieved on the very next objective test given in the class, regardless of the nature of that test. Since the 74 testing instruments would naturally differ sharply from each other in subject matter, length, difficulty, and every other testing variable, they obviously presented some rather unusual problems. When the tests were regarded primarily as *ranking* instruments, however, some of the difficulties disappeared.

TABLE 1

Illustration of ranked data

	PART A (*Raw scores on second test*)			PART B (*Ranks-within-levels on second test*)		
Level	*N*	*F*	*S*	*N*	*F*	*S*
1	33	31	34	2	1	3
2	30	25	32	2	1	3
3	29	33	23	2	3	1
.	.	.	.	.	.	.
10	14	25	21	1	3	2
Sum				19	21	20

NOTE: *N* is No Comment; *F* is Free Comment; *S* is Specified Comment.

A class with 30 useful students, for example, formed just 10 levels on the basis of scores from the first test. Each level consisted of three students, with each student receiving a different treatment: No Comment, Free Comment, or Specified Comment. Students then achieved new scores on the second (criterion) test, as might be illustrated in Table 1, Part A. On the basis of such scores, they were assigned rankings within levels, as illustrated in Table 1, Part B.

If the comments had no effects, the sums of ranks of Part B would not differ except by chance, and the two-way analysis of variance by ranks would be used to determine whether such differences exceeded chance. Then the *sums* of ranks themselves could be ranked. (In Part B the rankings would be 1, 3, and 2 for Groups N, F, and S; the highest score is ranked 3 throughout the study.) And a new test, of the same type, could be made of all such rankings from the 74 experimental classrooms. Such a test was for the present design the better alternative, since it allowed for the likelihood of "Type G errors" (3, pp. 9–10) in the experimental outcome. Still a third way remained to use these rankings. The summation of each column could be divided by the number of levels in the class, and the result was *a mean rank within treatment within class.* This score proved very useful, since it fulfilled certain requirements for parametric data.

RESULTS

Comment vs. no comment. The over-all significance of the comment effects, as measured by the analysis of variance by ranks, is indicated in Table 2. The first row shows results obtained when students were considered as matched independently from one common population. The second row shows results when treatment groups within classes were regarded as intact groups. In either case the conclusions were the same. The Specified Comment group, which received automatic impersonal comments according to the letter grade received, achieved higher scores than the No Comment group. The Free Comment group, which received individualized comments from the teachers, achieved the highest scores of all. Not once in a hundred times would such differences have occurred by chance if scores were drawn from a common population. Therefore it may be held that the comments had a real and beneficial effect upon the students' mastery of subject matter in the various experimental classes.

TABLE 2

The Friedman test of the over-all treatment effects

Units considered	*N*	*F*	*S*	*df*	χ_r^2	*p*
Individual Subjects	1363	1488	1427	2	10.9593	$<.01$
Class-group Subjects	129.5	170.0	144.5	2	11.3310	$<.01$

It was also possible, as indicated earlier, to use the mean ranks within treatments within classes as parametric scores. The resulting distributions, being normally distributed and fulfilling certain other assumptions underlying parametric tests, permitted other important comparisons to be made.[2] Table 3 shows the mean-ranks data necessary for such comparisons.

TABLE 3

Parametric data based upon mean ranks within treatments within classes

Source	*N*	*F*	*S*	*Total*
Number of Groups	74	74	74	222
Sum of Mean Ranks	140.99	154.42	148.59	444.00
Sum of Squares of Mean Ranks	273.50	327.50	304.01	905.01
Mean of Mean Ranks	1.905	2.087	2.008	2.000
S.D. of Mean Ranks	.259	.265	.276	
S.E. of Mean Ranks	.030	.031	.032	

The various tests are summarized in Tables 4 and 5. The over-all F test in Table 5 duplicated, as one would expect, the result of the Friedman test, with differences between treatment groups still significant beyond the .01 level. Comparisons between different pairs of treatments are shown in Table 5. All differences were significant except that between Free Comment and Specified Comment. It was plain that comments, especially the individualized comments, had a marked effect upon student performance.

TABLE 4

Analysis of variance of main treatment effects (based on mean ranks)

Source	*Sum of squares*	*df*	*Mean square*	*F*	*Probability*
Between Treatments: N, F, S	1.23	2	.615	5.69	<.01
Between Class-groups	0.00	73	.000	. . .	
Interaction: T × Class	15.78	146	.108		
Total	17.01	221			

NOTE: Modeled after Lindquist (3), p. 157 *et passim,* except for unusual conditions noted.

Comments and schools. One might question whether comment effects would vary from school to school, and even whether the school might not be the more appropriate unit of analysis. Since as it happened the study had 12 junior or senior high schools which had three or more experimental

[2] It may be noted that the analysis of variance based upon such mean ranks will require no calculation of sums of squares between levels or between classes. This is true because the mean for any class will be $(k + 1)/2$, or in the present study just 2.00. . . . An alternative to such scores would be the conversion of all scores to *T* scores based upon each class-group's distribution; but the mean ranks, while very slightly less sensitive, are much simpler to compute and therefore less subject to error.

TABLE 5

Differences between means of the treatment groups

Comparison	*Difference*	*S. E. of diff.*	*t*	*Probability*
Between N and F	.182	.052	3.500	<.001
Between N and S	.103	.054	1.907	<.05
Between F and S	.079	.056	1.411	<.10 (n.s.)

NOTE: The *t* tests presented are those for matched pairs, consisting of the paired mean ranks of the treatment groups within the different classes. Probabilities quoted assume that one-tailed tests were appropriate.

classes, these schools were arranged in a treatments-by-replications design. Results of the analysis are shown in Table 6. Schools apparently had little measurable influence over treatment effect.

TABLE 6

The influence of the school upon the treatment effect

Source	*Sum of squares*	*df*	*Mean square*	*F*	*Probability*
Between Treatments: N, F, S	.172	2	.086	. . .[a]	. . .
Between Schools	.000	11	.000		
Between Classes Within Schools (pooled)	.000	24	.000		
Interaction: T × Schools	1.937	22	.088	. . .	. . .
Interaction: T × Cl. W. Sch. (pooled)	4.781	48	.099		
Total	6.890	107			

NOTE: Modified for mean-rank data from Edwards (1, p. 295 *et passim*).

[a] Absence of an important main treatment effect is probably caused by necessary restriction of sample for school year (*N* is 36, as compared with Total *N* of 74), and by some chance biasing.

Comments and school years. It was conceivable that students, with increasing age and grade-placement, might become increasingly independent of comments and other personal attentions from their teachers. To test such a belief, 66 class-groups, drawn from the experimental classes, were stratified into six school years (Grades 7–12) with 11 class-groups in each school year. Still using mean ranks as data, summations of such scores were as shown in Table 7. Rather surprisingly, no uniform trend was apparent. When the data were tested for interaction of school year and comment effect (see Table 8), school year did not exhibit a significant influence upon comment effect.

Though Table 8 represents a comprehensive test of school-year effect, it was not supported by all available evidence. Certain other, more limited tests did show significant differences in school year, with possibly greater responsiveness in higher grades. The relevant data . . . are too cumbersome for the present report, and must be interpreted with caution. Apparently, however, comments do *not* lose effectiveness as students move through school. Rather they appear fairly important, especially when individualized, at all secondary levels.

TABLE 7

Sums of mean ranks for different school years

School year	*N*	*F*	*S*
12	21.08	22.92	22.00
11	19.06	23.91	23.03
10	20.08	23.32	22.60
9	22.34	22.06	21.60
8	21.21	22.39	22.40
7	22.04	22.98	20.98

NOTE: Number of groups is 11 in each cell.

TABLE 8

The influence of school year upon treatment effect

Source	*Sum of squares*	*df*	*Mean square*	*F*	*Probability*
Between Treatments: N, F, S	1.06	2	.530	5.25	<.01
Between School Years	0.00	5	.000		
Between Cl. Within Sch. Yr. (pooled)	0.00	60	.000		
Interaction: T × School Year	1.13	10	.113	1.12	(n.s.)
Interaction: T × Class (pooled)	12.11	120	.101		
Total	14.30	197			

NOTE: Modified for mean-rank data from Edwards (1, p. 295 *et passim*).

One must remember that, between the present class-groupings, there were many differences other than school year alone. Other teachers, other subject-matter fields, other class conditions could conceivably have been correlated beyond chance with school year. Such correlations would in some cases, possibly, tend to modify the *visible* school-year influence, so that illusions would be created. However possible, such a caution, at present, appears rather empty. In absence of contradictory evidence, it would seem reasonable to extrapolate the importance of comment to other years outside the secondary range. One might predict that comments would appear equally important if tested under comparable conditions in the early college years. Such a suggestion, in view of the large lecture halls and detached professors of higher education, would appear one of the more striking experimental results.

Comments and letter grades. In a questionnaire made out before the experiment, each teacher rated each student in his class with a number from 1 to 5, according to the student's *guessed responsiveness* to comments made by that teacher. Top rating, for example, was paired with the description: "Seems to respond quite unusually well to suggestions or comments made by the teacher of this class. Is quite apt to be influenced by praise, correction, etc." Bottom rating, on the other hand, implied: "Seems rather negativistic about suggestions made by the teacher. May be inclined more than most students to do the opposite from what the teacher urges." In daily practice, many teachers comment on some papers and not on others. Since teachers would presumably be more likely to comment on papers of those students they believed would respond positively, such ratings were an important experimental variable.

TABLE 9

Mean of mean ranks for different letter grades

Letter grade	*N*	*F*	*S*
A	1.93	2.04	2.03
B	1.91	2.11	1.98
C	1.90	2.06	2.04
D	2.05	1.99	1.96
F	1.57	2.55	1.88

NOTE: Each eligible class was assigned one mean rank for each cell of the table.

Whether teachers *were* able to predict responsiveness is a complicated question, not to be reported here. It was thought, however, that teachers might tend to believe their able students, their high achievers, were also their responsive students. A contingency table was therefore made, testing the relationship between *guessed* responsiveness and letter grade achieved on the first test. The results were as predicted. More "A" students were regarded as highly responsive to comments than were other letter grades; more "F" students were regarded as negativistic and unresponsive to comments than were other letter grades; and grades in between followed the same trend. The over-all C coefficient was .36, significant beyond the .001 level.[3] Plainly teachers believed that their *better* students were also their more *responsive* students.

If teachers were correct in their belief, one would expect in the present experiment greater comment effect for the better students than for the poorer ones. In fact, one might not be surprised if, among the "F" students, the No Comment group were even superior to the two comment groups.

[3] In a 5×5 table, a perfect correlation expressed as C would be only about .9 (McNemar [4], p. 205).

The various letter grades achieved mean scores as shown in Table 9, and the analysis of variance resulted as shown in Table 10. There was considerable interaction between letter grade and treatment effect, but it was caused almost entirely by the remarkable effect which comments appeared to have *on the "F" students.* None of the other differences, including the partial reversal of the "D" students, exceeded chance expectation.

TABLE 10

The relation between letter grade and treatment effect

Source	*Sum of squares*	*df*	*Mean square*	*F*	*Probability*
Between Treatments: N, F, S	2.77	2	1.385	5.41	$<.01$
Between Letter Grades	0.00	4	0.000		
Bet. Blocks Within L. Gr. (pooled)	0.00	65	0.000		
Interaction: T × Letter Grades	4.88	8	.610	2.40	$.05 > p > .01$
Residual (error term)	32.99	130	.254		
Total	40.64	209			

NOTE: Modified for mean-rank data from Lindquist (3, p. 269). Because sampling was irregular (see text) all eligible classes were randomly assigned to 14 groupings. This was done arbitrarily to prevent vacant cells.

These data do not, however, represent the total sample previously used, since the analysis could use only those student levels in which all three students received the same letter grade on Test One.[4] Therefore many class-groups were not represented at all in certain letter grades. For example, although over 10% of all letter grades were "F," only 28 class-groups had even one level consisting entirely of "F" grades, and most of these classes had *only* one such level. Such circumstances might cause a somewhat unstable or biased estimate of effect.

Within such limitations, the experiment provided strong evidence against the teacher-myth about responsiveness and letter grades. The experimental teachers appeared plainly mistaken in their faith that their "A" students responded relatively brightly, and their "F" students only sluggishly or negatively to whatever encouragement they administer.

SUMMARY

Seventy-four randomly selected secondary teachers, using 2,139 unknowing students in their daily classes, performed the following experiment: They administered to all students whatever objective test would occur in

[4] When levels consisted of both "A" and "B" students, for example, "A" students would tend to receive the higher scores on the second test, regardless of treatment; thus those Free Comment "A" students drawn from mixed levels would tend to appear (falsely) more responsive than the Free Comment "B" students drawn from mixed levels, etc. Therefore the total sample was considerably reduced for the letter-grade analysis.

the usual course of instruction. After scoring and grading the test papers in their customary way, and matching the students by performance, they randomly assigned the papers to one of three treatment groups. The No Comment group received no marks beyond those for grading. The Free Comment group received whatever comments the teachers felt were appropriate for the particular students and test concerned. The Specified Comment group received certain uniform comments designated beforehand by the experimenter for all similar letter grades, and thought to be generally "encouraging." Teachers returned tests to students without any unusual attention. Then teachers reported scores achieved on the next objective test given in the class, and these scores became the criterion of comment effect, with the following results:

1. Free Comment students achieved higher scores than Specified Comment students, and Specified Comments did better than No Comments. All differences were significant except that between Free Comments and Specified Comments.
2. When samplings from 12 different schools were compared, no significant differences of comment effect appeared between schools.
3. When the class-groups from six different school years (grades 7–12) were compared, no *conclusive* differences of comment effect appeared between the years, but if anything senior high was more responsive than junior high. It would appear logical to generalize the experimental results, concerning the effectiveness of comment, at least to the early college years.
4. Although teachers believed that their better students were also much more responsive to teacher comments than their poorer students, there was no experimental support for this belief.

When the average secondary teacher takes the time and trouble to write comments (believed to be "encouraging") on student papers, these apparently have a measurable and potent effect upon student effort, or attention, or attitude, or whatever it is which causes learning to improve and this effect does not appear dependent on school building, school year, or student ability. Such a finding would seem very important for the studies of classroom learning and teaching method.

REFERENCES

1. Edwards, A. *Experimental design in psychological research.* New York: Rinehart, 1950.
2. Friedman, M. The use of ranks to avoid the assumption of normality implicit in the analysis of variance. *J. Amer. Statist. Ass.*, 1937, 32, 675–701.
3. Lindquist, E. F. *Design and analysis of experiments in psychology and education.* Boston: Houghton Mifflin, 1953.
4. McNemar, Q. *Psychological statistics.* (2nd ed.) New York: Wiley, 1955.
5. Page, E. B. Educational research: replicable *or* generalizable? *Phi Delta Kappan,* 1958, 39, 302–304.

JULES HENRY

The Problem of Spontaneity, Initiative, and Creativity in Suburban Classrooms

Although the over-all objective of this research report is related to that of the preceding article—both are studies of teacher-student relations in the classroom—the methods employed by the anthropologist Henry are wholly different. Henry summarizes anecdotal material gathered by directly observing student behavior in a number of classrooms. From such materials, he derives interesting interpretations of a teacher's role in society. Henry is particularly concerned with "impulse," which he calls the "root of life." If you observed the same actions as Henry, would your interpretations necessarily agree with his?

Nowadays much of the preoccupation with creativity seems to stem not so much from interest in artistic and scientific originality as from anxiety about preserving any human impulse toward spontaneity and initiative. Fundamentally, our contemporary concern about creativity is a culturally acceptable rationalization of our own fear of loss of Self. In our expressed anxiety over creativity in our children, we are really saying that we are frightened that our culture has wrested our Selves from us and is selling them down the river. The present paper, reflecting the current fear, deals, therefore, with factors affecting initiative and spontaneity in elementary public school classrooms in middle-class suburbs.

This paper is based on direct observations by my students and me over a three-year period.[1] We owe a debt of deepest gratitude to the teachers who voluntarily put up with our intrusions into their classrooms. There is no doubt that an objective description of anyone's behavior in our culture would have in it much that might appear on superficial examination to be strange or bizarre. Our observations show teachers as normal and dedicated human beings struggling with massive problems the culture has dropped in their lap, and if anything in these studies of them were to be construed as absurd or bizarre, it would be a gross injustice.

[1] Other publications on this research are: J. Henry, "Culture, Education, and Communications Theory," in George D. Spindler (Ed.), *Education and Anthropology* (Stanford, Calif.: Stanford Univ. Press, 1955); J. Henry, *Docility, or Giving Teacher What She Wants*, J. Soc. Issues, 11:No. 2, 33–41, 1955; J. Henry, *Attitude Organization in Elementary School Classrooms*, Am. J. Orthopsychiatry, 27:117–133, 1957; J. Henry, *Working Paper on Creativity*, Harvard Educ. Rev., 27:148–155, 1957.

DIRECT OBSERVATIONS

The root of life is impulse; and its release in the proper amounts, at the proper time and place, and in culturally approved forms, is one of the primary concerns of culture. Day after day in the classroom, the public school teacher faces the surging impulses of the children and she resists them in order not to be overwhelmed; in order to do her duty as a cultural surrogate; and in order that the whelming impulse life of her charges—normal as well as sick—may not get in the way of their learning the materials prescribed in the curriculum. The contemporary public school teacher is thus faced with the following paradox: in line with current educational philosophy she must foster initiative and spontaneity in her children and at the same time maintain order and teach according to school requirements. In the middle-class suburban classrooms we have studied, however, the emphasis on initiative and spontaneity fosters a "permissiveness" which, in some rooms, sweeps the class to the brink of chaos. In these circumstances it became an empirical requirement of our research to develop a rough rating for noise; and it is still an unsolved problem as to whether such classrooms can be said at certain times to have any social structure at all. Indeed, it would almost appear as if the pivot of order were no longer, as under more traditional discipline, the teacher, but rather had become lodged in the egos of the children; as if responsibility for the maintenance of order had been shifted from the teacher to the children. Meanwhile, it is important to bear in mind that these are not delinquent children, tearing the social structure from its hinges by brute force, but nice, clean middle-class suburban boys and girls who are merely given their heads.

The impulses of the children are always a serious matter to teachers, and one of the most important problems of our day is to discover the variety of devices they use to control or evade them. Since, quite without our requesting it, principals have selected for us classrooms having what they consider outstanding teachers, the examples I give here of classroom control represent forms considered best by the principals. The first example is from a second-grade classroom in school A, with 37 children. Rather full excerpts are taken from one typical day, and very brief materials from one day a month later.

> The Observer arrives in the classroom at 12:45 and remarks, "As has been the case in past observations, the noise rating was 2."
>
> There are about seven children walking around, apparently doing nothing. There are about nine children sitting on the floor on the left side of the teacher's desk. Teacher is passing back some papers the children worked on yesterday. She says, "If you missed more than one of the questions on the board, it means that you either aren't reading carefully or that you aren't thinking enough. Betty, will you sit over here, please. Thank you."

This teacher, like most of the teachers in the area, uses "honey" and "dear" a great deal in interaction with the children. Some of the examples recorded on this day are:

1. Could you talk a little louder, Johnny dear?
2. I'll have to ask you to go to your seat, honey.
3. Honey, where were you supposed to go if you didn't have your paper?
4. Bill, I think George can do that by himself, honey.
5. Susie, honey, what's the name of it?
6. It's up here, dear.

The record continues:

1:10. The reading period is over. Children return to their seats. Teacher begins to write four words on the board. As she does this the talking and moving around the room increase to a mild uproar. Noise rating 3. Teacher says, "May I have your eyes this way, please? Bill, will you and Tommy please watch?"

1:20. "May I suggest that the people in John Burns' group, instead of doing this work with the vowels, read in *The Family Village*."

1:40. Teacher is sitting at desk. Children seem to be busy at work. Everyone seems to be doing something different. Noise rating has dropped to 2. Fifteen out of 34 of the children present are not doing the assigned work. Most of the children in this group are doing absolutely nothing in the line of schoolwork. Some are merely staring into space; some are playing with rubber bands, hankies, etc.

1:56. Presently there are ten children out of their regular seats and seated in the rockers at the bookcase, at the library table, or just aimlessly walking around the room. Two little girls in the back of the room are showing each other their scarves. There is a great deal of foot shuffling; everyone looks as if he is preparing to go home. Teacher comments, "Boys and girls, we do not go home at two o'clock, so please continue with your work. Doug, may I talk to you a minute?" Doug goes up to Teacher, who says, "We're going to let you stay five minutes after school because of this talking."

A month later the record reads as follows:

12:40. When the teacher reprimands the children, her voice in all instances is soft, almost hesitant. She informed me (the Observer) later that when she scolds she wants the children to feel she is disappointed in them. I can see how the sad tone of her voice would convey this message.

12:50. Teacher says, "May I have you in your seats, please." During the collection of papers the noise rate had increased to 2, and 12 people were out of their seats.

A few minutes later the teacher left the room and the noise rate approached 3. Six children were walking around the room, most of them chatting with their neighbors. Roger says to Observer, "Kind of noisy, isn't it?"

1:04. Teacher returns and says, "Annie, would you sit down, honey, and get busy. Whose feet are making so much noise?" One child says, "Pam's!" and the teacher says, "Pam, that's very annoying, please don't." Observer remarks, "It's odd that this small noise should bother Mrs. Olan. I didn't even hear it." Teacher says, "Doug, will you turn around, please? Billy, do you understand the process—how to do it? I thought maybe Jimmy was helping you. Stephen, are you finished? Murray and Mickey! Boys and girls, let's tend to our own work, please."

> 1:55. Five minutes before recess. Teacher says, "Put your work away quietly." She sits back and with a completely expressionless face waits for the five minutes to pass. The number of children out of their seats increased to 17. Three boys were bouncing balls on the floor; one was throwing his against the wall of the cloakroom; three children were killing each other with imaginary guns.

Regardless of their age, our observers became tired and irritated by the noise in this type of classroom. During any 1½-hour observation period, Mrs. Olan was in and out of the classroom several times, sometimes for as long as 10 minutes. It will be observed that at one point she merely sat and stared into space. Meanwhile, her repeated withdrawal results in an intensification of the noise, which mounts toward the third level when she leaves, so that when she returns, an effort must be made to re-establish the previous lower noise level. Probably the reason why the social structure of the room does not disintegrate is that the teacher warms the atmosphere with "honey" and "dear" and by occasionally fondling a child; and because by saying she is "disappointed" in them she makes the children afraid of loss of love. Actually, Mrs. Olan plays the role of the tired, overburdened, entreating mother, who attempts to control her children by making them feel guilty. Her sweetness and elaborate politeness—she even says "honey" and "dear" when she reprimands a child—are really saying to the children, "Look how sweet and courteous *I* am; how could you be otherwise?"

In all of this the children's egos seem remarkably firm, and Mrs. Olan's capacity to do an all-but-impossible job is striking. Although the noise rating is never zero in this room, it is sometimes recorded as 1 or approaching 2, which suggests that the children have inner resources of control which are skillfully mobilized by the teacher. When one understands, however, the pressure toward "permissiveness" in these schools, the fact that the children do learn something is a tribute to Mrs. Olan's fortitude and to her dedication to teaching, as well as to the ego strength of the children.

The contemporary American idea that good elementary school teachers should be accepting, giving parents has resulted, as we have seen, in the teachers' using affection as a defense against other impulses of the children: the teacher stimulates their love by calling them "honey" and "dear" and by fondling, while at the same time she awakens fear of loss of her love if they get out of line. Though in our sample caressing is common, its full possibilities in the classroom can be evaluated best by studying minutely the behavior of one teacher who obtains deep pleasure from fondling the children. Mrs. Thorndyke is affectionate, sensitive, and alert, and, as usual, is considered one of the best by her principal. In the observation record we are present at a reading lesson in her third-grade class on a day when the children are asking each other questions about the story instead of being asked questions by her. There are 25 children in the class, but the group to be described is made up of the dozen or so best readers, and they are sitting facing each other in two rows of little chairs placed in front of the room. The rest of the children are working at their desks on their exercise books. This paper picks up the lesson when it has been in progress about

15 minutes, during which excitement has mounted and the children tend to erupt in noisy argument. At 10:27 Mrs. Thorndyke is standing behind one row:

> She pats Alfred to restrain him and he shows a slight tendency to withdraw. There is a loud burst of noise. Mrs. Thorndyke's hand is on Alfred and he seems to wish to get out. Now her hand is on Arty, who makes no move. Teacher pats and strokes Matty, who also makes no move to withdraw. Now Teacher is standing behind Arty, lightly passing her finger tips over his neck. She goes back to Arty, puts a hand on Alfred to restrain him. He makes withdrawal signs. Alfred and Arty are now interlocking their hands in the air and Alfred is talking to Arty. At 10:32, Teacher stops behind Otto to restrain him. Her hands are on his cheeks; his tongue goes in the direction of his right cheek and pushes it out as he closes his eyes. When Mrs. Thorndyke withdraws her hands, his eyes pop open as if he had suddenly awakened. Mary, who previously was holding onto Mrs. Thorndyke as the teacher stroked the child's arm, has now slumped in her seat. Teacher goes to her, puts her arms around her and pulls her back. Mary takes Teacher's hand. Alfred is talking and Mrs. Thorndyke pats and strokes him. He does not withdraw this time. Alfred is now talking to Arty and Teacher is stroking Alfred. Again he does not withdraw. Now Alfred caresses Otto and Arty caresses Alfred. Malcolm asks questions now (10:38) and all the children say his questions have been asked. Mrs. Thorndyke says, "My only objection to that question is that it can be answered by either yes or no." She strokes Matty. All this time the questions are being asked and there is great excitement among the children. Sherry asks questions and Teacher says, "We've gone over that." She strokes Matty and he does not resist. She touches Mary flutteringly with her finger tips.
>
> Now Mrs. Thorndyke terminates the lesson, and the papers with the questions are collected. Suddenly she becomes very grave and silent. She later told me that Mary had answered a snippety "no" to something Teacher had said. Now Mrs. Thorndyke says, "*My, I'm terribly disappointed.*" There is absolute silence, and Mrs. Thorndyke says, "Matty, you're excused to go to your seat." She later told me it was because he's a general all-round talker and wouldn't quiet down. Matty goes to his seat looking very unhappy, his lips compressed. The room is silent now.
>
> Now Group 2, the poorer readers, occupy the seats deserted by Group 1. Teacher seems very tired now, and goes through the lesson mechanically. Her voice is weak and she leans against the blackboard. Time, approximately 10:50.

The interesting thing about erotization is that *it substitutes one impulse or one impulse pattern for another:* the children's excitement, whatever its affective components, is narcotized by releasing other, namely libidinal, emotional resources in the children. What is so striking in Mrs. Thorndyke is her skill in so stimulating these resources that contagion occurs: the affectivity of the teacher is spread by some children to others. Otto is a somewhat different case: he simply went into a regressive trance while enjoying the teacher's stroking.

Put in the broadest possible way, what we have seen here is Mrs. Thorndyke's effort to master, by means of narcotization, powerful *spontaneous* impulses of the children which had been placed at the service of their intellects. Thus, in the very act of releasing spontaneity, the teacher, in order not to be overwhelmed by it, narcotizes it. Obviously the effort was exhausting, for when the lesson was over, Mrs. Thorndyke was tired and listless and leaned against the blackboard for support.

While women teachers in our sample of middle-class suburban schools seem repeatedly to control the children's impulses by awakening affection and fear of loss of it, as would almost any normal middle-class mother, the question arises as to what the male teacher does in the same situation. Over the years we have been able to get good observations on only one man teacher, Mr. Jeffries, who teaches a sixth-grade class of 35 in the same school as Mrs. Thorndyke. In the classroom Mr. Jeffries takes the role of a type of contemporary middle-class American father: a Puckish imp-of-fun, buddy of the boys and sweetheart of the girls, he addresses the latter with endearments and uses nicknames and diminutives for the former as he pats them on the head or puts an arm around their shoulders. His room is a rough-and-tumble, happy-go-lucky, brink-of-chaos sort of place, much less controlled than Mrs. Thorndyke's and less overtly erotized. Mr. Jeffries calls it a "rat race" and says, "We get tired and ready to drop by the time it is over." Let us then have a look at Mr. Jeffries' room:

> 11:05. The class is having a reading lesson. Teacher says, "Galapagos means tortoise. Where are 300-pound turtles found?" A boy says, "In the zoo," and Teacher says, "Where are they native in this country?" A girl says, with a grimace of disgust, "We saw them in Marine Land in Florida. They were slaughtered and used for meat. Ugh!" John has raised his hand and Teacher calls on him. "We saw one in Wisconsin about the size of Bob's head." Teacher says, "That's plenty big." And the class laughs.
>
> Teacher asks, "What was Douglas [a boy in the story] doing on the island? Have you ever been scared, John?" "Yes," replies John. "So have I," says the teacher, and the class laughs. Teacher says, "*That's what I like about buddies.*"
>
> 11:25. Teacher says, "Let's read the story silently." He says to a girl. "Do you mind putting your beads away for the rest of the morning instead of tearing them apart?"
>
> The room is now very quiet. He walks around the aisles as the children read.

Mr. Jeffries obviously runs a "democratic" classroom, and his pupils are spontaneous and effervescent. He tells the children that he is their "buddy"; he is no aloof figure, pretending to invulnerability, but like them he is capable of fear; he is "scared" *with* them. He is right down there on the floor with the kids, so to speak: like a contemporary American *buddy-daddy*, he has leveled the distance between himself and the children. Yet by command he can suddenly get quiet when he wants it, though rarely for long. A sound curve of his class would have a relatively constant high noise plateau with occasional narrow valleys of relative quiet.

A week later we are at a grammar lesson:

> 10:15. The class is discussing types of nouns. Teacher says, "If I had lots of Ritas, she'd be a type. Maybe we're lucky we have only one." Class laughs. A girls raises her hand and Teacher says, "What is it, honey?"
>
> 10:25. The room has grown noisy during the lesson and Teacher says, "Can't

hear you, Shirley. You're not going to find out a thing by looking in that direction." His voice has risen, getting louder in order to be heard above the classroom noise.

10:40. Clatter is increasing. Eight or nine pupils are walking around the room. One boy throws a paper wad at another. Four pupils are at the pencil sharpener. Noise grows louder but *teacher ignores it.*

10:45. Teacher says, "It would seem to me that in the past five minutes you haven't accomplished a thing; you've been so busy wandering around." This creates complete silence. Then two boys stand to look at neighbor's work. Another goes to Teacher's desk to get help. Teacher and he confer. Noise is louder now.

10:55. Two boys raise hands. Two others stand next to Teacher. One girl pats his back as he bends over. She giggles.

11:00. Teacher: "O.K., put language books away, please!" He giggles as a girl asks him a question. Pupils put books in desks. Teacher: "Take a couple of minutes here. Girl with the blue hair, get up. Stretch a bit." Loud laughter from the class. Teacher: "Get up and stretch." Most of the class stands. Two boys continue writing at their desks. A boy and girl push each other. The smallest boy in the class stands alone and looks on as two girls wrestle.

At the end of the observation period on this day the Observer wrote, "I feel that the pupils are truly fond of Mr. Jeffries. They enjoy laughing together; not *at* somebody, but *with* each other." Of course, we might question the last in view of the jokes about Rita and the earlier one about the size of Bob's head. At any rate, there seems little doubt that, like Mrs. Thorndyke, Mr. Jeffries is a love object to his children. In the present observation segment, one little girl strokes his back, and he giggles with another one in a private joke during the lesson. Everybody, including the teacher, has a wonderful time. Frequently, however, the noise gets so loud that Mr. Jeffries has to shout and the students cannot hear. Suddenly at 10:45 he scolds the children for not accomplishing anything, even though he has permitted the disorder and noise to increase. At 11 o'clock the children are pushing and wrestling, but Mr. Jeffries ignores it. The following week, during a particularly hilarious and noisy arithmetic lesson, when the children can barely hear what is going on, a girl takes a boy's paper, tears it up and throws it into the wastebasket; but the teacher laughs, the class pays no attention, the paper is fished out and taped together, and the lesson continues.

About five weeks later the Observer was in this classroom when Mr. Jeffries was out sick and a substitute was on duty. The room was in its usual noisy state when the principal walked in and stood in the back of the room for a few minutes. No change took place in the class, but the principal bent over one of the little girls, embraced her, whispered something to her, then turned to the Observer, said, "Fine bunch of gals here," and left. Thus, in his behavior the principal reinforces the emphasis on impulse release at deeply gratifying levels. *Teacher, principal, children, and community are one continuous cultural system.*

As the school year entered the last month, evidence began to appear that impulse release and noise had reached a point beyond the endurance of the *children,* for the children, particularly the girls, began spontaneosly to *shush* the class:

> 10:40. The children have just finished singing. Teacher says, "Get paper, eraser, pencil." There is a loud buzz at this command, and a girl says, "What's the paper for?" Teacher says, "Now don't go wild just because you sang. Your pencils don't have to be so sharp." Observer notes that a bunch of youngsters is storming the pencil sharpener as Teacher says this. *Someone shushes the class.* Teacher says, "Fill this out the same as yesterday." He passes the sheets out very carefully, dropping the correct number on the first desk of each row. "Today's date is the eighth of May," says Teacher. "Sorry you're so noisy. Don't open your books till I tell you. Just fill out the first page. This is a reading test." The class reads in silent concentration.
>
> 11:01. The test is over. Teacher starts to issue instructions for the next activity and a girl says to the class, "*Shush!*"
>
> 11:06. A girl goes to the teacher's desk for help in spelling. He spells a word aloud as she writes, leaning on his desk for support. A girl walks by John and smacks him playfully. He gets up, walks by her, smacks her on the back soundly and sprints away. Teacher says, "I notice that most of you have finished your papers promptly. I'm very pleased. Now devote your time, the next fifteen minutes, to your spelling." A girl says, "*Shush!*" There is a loud buzz. Observer notes that this shushing has occurred several times today, *only from the pupils.*

These observations drive home the point made earlier, that responsibility for maintenance of order has shifted in such a way that the children determine when controls shall be set in motion. In the last observation, the children's efforts to hold the social structure together become overt; but throughout the term, the teacher's interest in order is so slight, he so often ignores the racket in his room that the conclusion is inescapable that the children have set their own limits because the teacher has abdicated.

INTERVIEWS WITH TEACHERS

The first section of this paper was devoted to direct observation and interpretation of teacher-pupil interaction. In the interpretation of observations, however, there is always the problem of whether the observer is "imposing his own ideas" on the data. Mindful of this difficulty, I interviewed the teachers on the subject of their ideas about classroom discipline two years after the original observations were made. The original observations of Mrs. Thorndyke were made by me; those of the other two teachers were made by my students. I give excerpts from Mrs. Olan's interview first. She says:

> In this day and age the children have more tensions and problems than when I first taught. In the one-room schoolhouse in which I first taught the children came from calm homes. There was no worry about war, and there was no TV or radio. They led a calm and serene life. They came to school with their syrup pails for lunch buckets. Children of today know more about what is going on; they are better informed. So you can't hold a strict rein on them. It is bad for

children to come in and sit down with their feet under the seat: you have to have freedom to get up and move around. When they do this they are more rested and have a greater attention span. . . .

Children need to enjoy school and like it. They also need their work to be done; it's not all play. You must get them to accept responsibility and doing work on their own.

Thus, Mrs. Olan feels that children have severe inner tensions that must not be held in close rein because it is not good for them. In answer to the question, "What would you say is your own particular way of keeping order in the classroom?" she explains simply and movingly how she manages her children:

Well, I would say I try to get that at the beginning of the year by getting this bond of affection and a relationship between the children and me. And we do that with stories; and I play games *with* them—don't just teach them how to play. It's what you get from living together comfortably. We have share times—that's the time a child can share with the teacher; and he gives whatever he wants to share: a bird's nest he has found; a tadpole that he and his dad got. Sometimes he may simply tell about something in his life—that his grandmother fell down and broke a leg and is not at home. . . . These are the things that contribute toward this discipline. Another thing in discipline: it took me a long time to learn it, too—I thought I was the boss, but I learned that even with a child, if you speak to him as you would to a neighbor or a friend you get a better response than if you say, "Johnny, do this or that." If you say, "Mary, will you please cooperate, you are disturbing us; we want to finish our reading," rather than just giving a command, they feel they are working with you and not just taking orders.

Mrs. Olan is aware of what she is doing: love is the path to discipline through permissiveness, and school is a continuation of family life in which the values of sharing and democracy lead to comfortable living and ultimately to (Mrs. Olan's own interpretation of) discipline.

With primary children the teacher is a mother during the day; they have to be able to bring their problems to you. They get love and affection at home, and I see no reason not to give it in school.

If you have the right relationship between teacher and child or between parent and child he can take harsh words and the things you say in the right spirit; and if you don't have that bond of affection, he just doesn't take it.

To Mrs. Olan, mother of a 21-year-old son, children are warm little pussycats, and you quiet them the way you do kittens. For example, in answer to the question, "Do you think children tend to be quieter if the teacher is affectionate?" she said:

If a teacher has a well-modulated voice and a pleasing disposition her children are more relaxed and quiet. Children are like kittens: if kittens have a full stomach and lie in the sun, they purr. If the atmosphere is such that the children are more comfortable, they are quiet. It is comfortable living that makes the quiet child. When you are shouting at them and they're shouting back at you, it isn't comfortable living.

Two years before this interview, observation had made clear that Mrs. Olan was no "boss," but lodged much responsibility in the children. She clarifies the matter further:

> It means a great deal to them to give them their own direction. When problems do come up in the room, we talk them over and discuss what is the right thing to do when this or that happens. Usually you get pretty good answers. They are a lot harder on themselves than I would be; so if any punishment comes along, like not going to an assembly, you have group pressure.

As I was about to go, Mrs. Olan spontaneously remarked, "My children don't rate as high [on achievement tests] as other children; I don't push, and that's because I believe in comfortable living."

Mrs. Thorndyke's response to the interview was entirely different from Mrs. Olan's. Mrs. Thorndyke has no children of her own, and we have seen how outgoing she is to her little third graders, patting and stroking them. However, when I talked to her about how she ran her class, she sounded like a strict though benign disciplinarian who hardly ever touched her pupils. The youngsters need "strong guidance," she said, and from the very first day have to be taught "who the leader is," meaning, of course, Mrs. Thorndyke. Demonstrative affection, in her opinion, is only for kindergarten and first grade; by the time the children get to her, Mrs. Thorndyke said, it should "level off." Thus, if we relied only on what she told us about herself, we would have no sound idea of what Mrs. Thorndyke was really like. If there were no direct observations of her with her children, we would think of her as a "schoolmarm" who, while laying down the law, was at the same time somewhat sensitive—rather at the mechanical "social skills" level—to children's emotional needs.

Since Mrs. Thorndyke's responses in the interview made me wonder whether her view of the teacher's role had changed or whether she was merely unaware of what she was doing, I decided to ask her permission to observe her again and she graciously consented. Her position as a teacher had changed in the intervening two years: according to new school regulations, superior students had been placed in special classes with special teachers, leaving Mrs. Thorndyke, among others, with only the slow children; and these had "a very short attention span," as she put it rather regretfully. As one watched her with these pupils, the most striking feature of her behavior was her *enormously increased mobility* in the classroom as she responded to the children's requests for help. Whereas previously, for example, as Mrs. Thorndyke walked around the room helping children in language skills, she had been able to spend more time with each child as she assisted him in his work, now she was in the midst of a constant silent clamor of hands as these children of lower IQ sought her help again and again. Whereas two years before she *sauntered* around the room, now she rushed, and though this did not prevent her from touching, tapping and stroking them in an affectionate way, her contacts were more ephemeral.

There was also a pervasive air of irritation and fatigue in her behavior. However, a striking phenomenon had entered to change the situation in an even more dramatic way: this was David, a disturbed boy with a "hopeless" mother and a "no account" father. Mrs. Thorndyke said that as long as she kept David close to her, she could help him better and keep him under control. He sat close to the front of the room near her desk, and when the other children were sitting at their places reciting, she sometimes had David right beside her at her desk. Some extracts from the record of one observation period will show what the relation was between Mrs. Thorndyke and David:

> Her hand is on David's head. He takes her hand. Now her hand is on his head again.
>
> 1:35. Now she is over near David again; he takes her hand and puts his face against it. She puts her hand on the head of Bobby. Now she touches David again; he holds her hand.
>
> 1:45. David takes her hand, really her whole arm, and holds it for about 30 seconds as he puts his face against it. She calls on him to read and he does. He has her hand again.
>
> 1:50. She is near David again and gives him her hand. He kisses it, fondles it, nuzzles it.
>
> 2:40. David is sitting close to the teacher while the rest of the children are at their seats reciting in the language skills lesson. David is a very beautiful boy. Mrs. Thorndyke puts her hand on David's arm and pats it and he places his fingers on her arm. They are like mother and child. He reads rather well. She strokes and fondles his face like that of a beloved child.

Mrs. Thorndyke says that David "needs affection" and there is no doubt that he is getting it from her. I would be inclined to say that if David could only stick with Mrs. Thorndyke long enough, it would help him. Meanwhile, one becomes aware of the fact that this restless child is held in check by his teacher's affectivity. One would be inclined to say that where affectivity is not dictated by the heart as a way of controling middle-class children, "common sense" might suggest it. Meanwhile, the problems involved in using this as an *over-all* technique have already been pointed out.

Finally, with respect to the apparent discrepancy between what Mrs. Thorndyke does and what she says she does, I would say that she is unaware of her own behavior along the dimension of "physical contact with children."

Two years after he was observed for one semester in a sixth-grade class by one of my students, Mr. Jeffries was principal of the school in which he once was teacher. His passionate involvement in teaching and in children easily won me. The following are some excerpts from a very long and thoughtful interview. He says,

> The very first day, I introduce myeslf to the children and tell them about myself. I use my family a great deal. I talk about my boy and about my daughter. I tell them about certain of my experiences, just to give them an understanding that "here is an individual."

In this way he begins to draw closer to the children. He becomes almost one with them. Speaking of himself, he says,

> They know the teacher's a friend with whom they can exchange jokes and banter. But if the teacher says, "Come on, we must get to this or that," they say to themselves, "We must do it." Maybe they say, "He's a good Joe, a good guy, so let's get the job done."

Mr. Jeffries is like Mrs. Olan in that he sees himself as working out the "criteria" for classroom management and discipline with the children in a democratic way, and he lets the children set their own punishments when they get into serious trouble, like fighting in the schoolyard. Mr. Jeffries' long explanation of how he goes about letting the children set their own rules cannot be reproduced here, but, actually, what he does is guide the children in the course of a discussion to the acceptance of his own ideas of what the "criteria" for classroom management should be.

We have seen that Mr. Jeffries' own room is a buoyant, noisy milieu. "You can't hold children in a tight rein," he says, "no more than you can hold a racehorse in a tight rein. A racehorse needs freedom and so does a child." As a matter of fact, Mr. Jeffries fears that if you hold a child in during class he will somehow break loose and "stomp" on somebody, just like a racehorse that breaks out into the fans at a steeplechase, as he put it. Children are "God-given individuals" and have a right to get up and walk around whenever they please. He says that since in this way they may find their way to an encyclopedia or a map, motility is closely related to creativity. To Mr. Jeffries, "a quiet classroom is a dead classroom" where "the children are not thinking or are afraid to think." A stranger walking into his room, he says, might think it a "riot" or that "mayhem was being committed," but he simply would not understand the basic thinking behind Mr. Jeffries' management. Furthermore, "A classroom with affection can be an awfully happy and joyous one. A quiet classroom may be an awfully fearful situation for someone."

Love, demonstrativeness, freedom, mobility, creativity, noise and thoughtfulness all go together, as Mr. Jeffries sees it. He is literally afraid of quietness and restraint.

In reviewing these findings, it is important to bear in mind that *the first section of this paper was completed before the interviewing was done, and has not been altered in any way since*. With this in mind, it can be seen that what Mrs. Olan and Mr. Jeffries *say* about what they do and why they do it confirms both observation and interpretation. In Mrs. Thorndyke, we are dealing with a person who is unaware of her affectional responses to the children.

SUMMARY AND CONCLUSIONS

Today our emphasis on creativity and spontaneity goes hand in hand with culture-weariness—a certain tiredness and disillusionment with impulse restraint, and a feeling that the Self has been sold down the river to the pirates of production, consumption and war. In these circumstances, permissiveness with children, an attitude that had been gaining strength before World War II, has invaded many phases of work with children, so that in some middle-class suburban public schools, there is a great relaxation of controls, and the teacher who is often most highly regarded is the one who lets the children be "free." These teachers are trying to be good teachers: like devoted public servants they are performing their duties as the community requires them to do. The surging impulses of the children whom they are "permitting," however, are threatening: when they are turned loose on a substitute or on one of their fellows, they can be terribly destructive. In these circumstances the teachers handle the children in accordance with their own roles in the culture of contemporary America, and in response to their own inner needs. Women teachers in these schools often manage by making themselves love objects and by making the children feel guilty. The one man in our sample played the role of one type of American *buddy-daddy,* exercising what little control there was by making himself loved the way this kind of modern American daddy is loved, and by occasionally issuing, like any suburban daddy, a peremptory command for order, the effects of which rarely lasted more than a few minutes.

Though in the very act of being released, the children's impulses are narcotized, in most cases it is not enough: the children "climb the walls" anyway. A consequence of this is impairment of the efficiency of the teachers and fatigue and obstruction of learning; for in the midst of constant turmoil, the children's capacities to hear, to concentrate and to absorb are interfered with. This explains the interesting phenomenon of the sixth graders' assuming responsibility for order in the class by *shushing* when the teacher does nothing. As a matter of fact, it would appear that under the conditions of spontaneity, as understood in this portion of Suburbia, noise and disorder destroy the very thing educators would foster.

In the broader cultural context the classroom is the children's first important experience with the administrative structure of the society. It is their first contact with what is fundamentally an impersonal mechanism for getting the culture's business done. But on the other hand, the children are prepared by the erotized atmosphere they encounter for the buddy-buddy, "false personalization" which Riesman has described for American institutions. The boys in particular will become an executive part of the impersonal structures—businesses, government bureaucracies—within which, in line with contemporary ethos, every effort is made to mix business with libido. From this point of view, life in public elementary middle-class schools of Suburbia is a preparation for work in a libidinized social structure which is at the same time basically impersonal and which pivots on "social skills."

Because of its necessary brevity, this paper is scarcely even an introduction to a single dimension of the cultural dynamics of learning. In these schools there is a great variety of ways of managing, and I have discussed but three teachers. In a limited sense, however, they present a view of one important problem: how our teachers manage under the pressure of an ideology of permissiveness and spontaneity which makes their task difficult.

In some of these rooms we get the picture of the immature yet strong egos of children manipulating a social structure which has been practically handed over to them, yet never letting it disintegrate, never actually stepping into chaos. For them this is a training in what has become known in other aspects of our culture as the art of "brinkmanship": a training in holding together in a relatively shapeless social field.

In order to round out the picture somewhat, it seems necessary to point out that the urban public elementary schoolrooms we have studied are entirely different from those discussed here. In those schools, the children are held under rigid control by the teacher, there is little talking that is not specifically permitted, the children stay in their seats, and the rooms are quiet. On the other hand, the atmosphere is also more impersonal, more attention seems to be given to rote procedures, and spontaneity is at a minimum.

In conclusion I should like to re-emphasize the fact that all of the teachers I have known in Suburbia are thoughtful, dedicated, normal human beings, trying to find within themselves the resources to deal with a dictum handed down, while at the same time they have received little instruction in how to do it. This being the case it would be wrong to make teachers the scapegoats of any adverse feeling that might be generated by the spectacle of classroom turmoil, for teachers are the instruments of their culture, as we all are.

Chapter 16

Judging Performance

16-1

BENJAMIN S. BLOOM
Quality Control in Education

16-2

EDUCATIONAL TESTING SERVICE
Multiple-Choice Questions: A Close Look

BENJAMIN S. BLOOM

Quality Control in Education

The quality of education varies greatly from school to school, and from classroom to classroom. Bloom discusses factors contributing to such differences, and outlines a program for general educational improvement. Essential in such a program, he suggests, is proper evaluation of all educational objectives. How important do you feel this is? How many kinds of objectives were measured in your own high-school learning? How many are being measured in your present college learning?

Evaluation is the systematic collection and appraisal of evidence to determine the effectiveness of some portion or the whole of an educational program. Since education is the process of changing human behavior much of the emphasis in evaluation has been on the appraisal of growth of students.

In my presentation, I will attempt to describe some of the major findings of evaluation over the past quarter of a century as well as some of the implications for education. My illustrations will range over all levels of education from the primary grades to graduate and professional education.

In recent years we have seen a frantic game of musical chairs as high school graduates seek every means at their disposal to become admitted to the college of their choice. Parents, teachers, counsellors, school administrators, and college admissions officers have been drawn into desperate efforts to get the student placed into the "right" college. Test publishers and scholarship contests have grown to proportions which many of us have difficulty in comprehending. The pressures on the secondary schools and the colleges have been so greatly increased that educators are beginning to wonder whether the major purpose of secondary education is to prepare students for the selection examinations.

Over a million students each year take one or more of the college entrance aptitude tests, and most of them take at least two of the tests. Coaching schools to prepare students for the college selection tests have begun to flourish and books on "How to Prepare" for the college selection examinations are outselling the Bible. In spite of all the increased use and emphasis on the aptitude tests, selection tests have not been appreciably improved during the past 40 years. Although we have invested millions of dollars in research on the prediction of college success, the correlation between our aptitude tests and college grades is still only +.50—the 1919 level.

About one-half of our college entrants will not complete college, with

Benjamin S. Bloom, "Quality Control in Education," *Tomorrow's Teaching,* a symposium held on January 13–14, 1961 (Oklahoma City: Frontiers of Science Foundation, 1962), pp. 54–60. Reprinted with permission.

the majority of the drop outs occurring for academic reasons in the first year or two of college. The educational waste, the sense of failure on the part of the individual, and the loss to the nation are difficult to describe in terms which will make clear what it means when annually almost one-half million individuals find their educational progress blocked.

Some recent research on this problem began with the puzzling observation that the correlation between the grades in one high school and one college (where a sizable number of students went from the particular school to this one college) was about +.65. Also the grades from another high school correlated about +.65 with the grades that the graduates of this high school received in this same college. However, when the grades from the two schools were combined, the correlations between the high school grades and the college grades went down to +.50—a figure which has been found to be true for the past half century. The research workers came to the conclusion that the basic error was the assumption that an A grade at one school was equal to the A grade of the other school, or that the grading systems of the two schools were equal. They then did studies which attempted to relate the grades of 125 high schools to each other. In these studies they found that the schools were very different in their grading standards, so different that the grade of F in one school was found to be equivalent to the grade of A in another school. They reported this research at the college level and found just as much variation in the grading standards of the colleges as they had found in the secondary schools.

After the scaling had been completed they then correlated adjusted high school grades with adjusted college grades and found the correlation to be approximately +.80. About the same relationships were obtained when they took the grades of students in *one* high school and related them to the adjusted grades these students made in the different colleges or when they took the unadjusted grades of students in *one* college and related them to the adjusted grades these students had made in the different high schools from which they had come.

There are several implications of this research. First, the counselling of students with regard to college choice can now be made with great precision in each high school. One way of putting it is that each high school can now counsel its students with respect to college choice at a level hitherto available only to a few high schools with the most capable and experienced counsellors in the country. Second, each college can now select its students in such a way as to minimize the likelihood of failure. Thus, a college which has two or more applicants for each place in its freshman class can select among these applicants so as to reduce its failure rate to one or two percent while holding to the same academic standards as it previously had. Academic failure in the future will be largely attributed to errors in selection. Third, the variations in school and college standards are such that there is literally a school and college at which almost every normal student can do acceptable academic work.

It is this third point I would like to discuss further. Why is there so much variation among schools and among colleges? The answer for the colleges is not as clear as it is for the secondary schools. Research on the variation in the achievement of high school students reveals at least three important factors. First, the educational level of the adults in the community and the cultural advantages the community possesses are highly related to the measured achievement of the secondary school students. It is reasonable to expect that the students in a community where the average adult has completed high school will be more interested in school learning than students in a community where the average adult has completed less than 10 years of school. The extent to which the home and the community stresses education and offers an environment in which music, art, and libraries are accessible to the youth will in large measure determine the academic standards of the school and the level of attainment the high school graduates will reach as measured both by achievement tests and college grades.

There is little that the school administrator can do about the number of years of school completed by the adults in the community. However, he may be able to accomplish much the same effect by helping the community become active in a great variety of adult educational activities as well as by giving leadership to raise the community's interest in cultural activities. TV, the mass media, books, art collections and music are easily within the reach of most communities in this country. The point of all this is that school standards and the educational achievements of students do reflect the cultural and educational standards of the community; a change in one is likely to be reflected in the other. We may attempt to ignore the relationship between the school and the community, but we will do so at great peril to the school.

A second factor which is highly related to the educational achievement of the high school students is the financial support for education. Although I do not believe this is as important as the educational and cultural level of the community, the research evidence is very clear in demonstrating that the amount of money spent for each student in average daily attendance is highly correlated with the achievement of the students. While I do not say that each extra dollar spent on education will affect the quality of the learning of students, there is no question about the difference between a community that annually spends 300 dollars per student and one that spends 600 dollars per student. Communities that are in the upper third in financial support for education will have better school and better learning than communities that give the average support for education and that those in the upper third in financial support will have vastly superior education for the youth than those in the lower third. The observant school administrator will recognize the many ways in which the financial support for education is related to the educational and cultural level of the community. While more research is needed on this point, it is clear that the United States is one of the few countries where the financial support for education may vary so greatly that one community may spend as much as ten times the amount that another community may spend for education. Methods of equalizing financial support for education in England and other countries result in relatively little variation in financial support for education among the different communities while still preserving a large amount of local autonomy.

A third factor accounting for the variation among the schools is the quality of the teachers. There is very clear evidence that as the quality of the teachers rises there is a corresponding rise in the educational achievement of the students. I will not go into the many indices of quality of teachers but a number of different indicators of teacher quality (salary level, professional interests and qualifications, etc.) all appear to be related to student achievement and grade standards. It should come as no surprise to educators that the quality of the output (student achievement) is highly related to the quality of the teachers. Nor should it come as any surprise to note that the quality of the output (achievement of students) is directly related to the quality and quantity of input (educational and cultural level of the community, financial support for education, quality of the teaching staff, etc.). Each conscientious school administrator spends the largest part of his working day in a constant effort to improve the quality of the input in the hopes that the output or outcomes of the educational process will be at a higher level of quality.

However, most of us eventually come to face the harsh realities that no amount of persuading, stimulating, or pushing will make a noticeable difference on the input. The community simply cannot further increase its cultural level or interest in education. The citizens refuse to increase the financial support for education. And, no matter how we try, the quality of the teaching staff cannot be raised by bringing in more and "better" teachers. At this point, the administrator must ask himself whether there are any means by which he can raise the quality of student learning without appreciably changing the input from the community, changing the teaching staff, or increasing financial expenditures. What does the educational and evaluation research of the past 25 years have to offer where input, as defined here, is constant but we wish to improve our output as measured by student achievement and learning?

So far we have been discussing output in terms of student performance on a standarized battery of achievement tests or in terms of the college achievement of our high school graduates. These are useful measures of the quality of a school but they are extremely limited. We are fond of thinking that our schools are doing more than preparing students for a widely used achievement test or for college success. But what are these other criteria for determining the quality of a school? Many of us believe that each school should have certain educational objectives in common with other schools in the nation but in addition each school is likely to have unique objectives because of the peculiar local circumstances of the teaching staff, students, and community. The criteria for determining the quality of a school and its educational functions would be the extent to which it achieves the objectives it has set for itself. Although most schools have formulated a set of educational objectives, our experiences suggest that unless the school has translated the objectives into specific and operational definitions, little is likely to be done about the objectives. They remain pious hopes and platitudes until the next step is taken which is that of determining precisely what is meant by the objectives. Schools that have succeeded in determining what evidence is appropriate in determining when an objective is achieved are most likely to demonstrate a high level of achievement of the objective. One very effective way of defining educational objectives is to determine the evaluation evidence which is appropriate and the methods of collecting the evidence—examinations, student products, observations of students, etc. Participation of the teaching staff in selecting as well as constructing evaluation instruments has resulted in improved instruments on one hand and on the other hand it has resulted in clarifying the objectives of instruction and in making them meaningful and real for the teachers.

As a result of this process over the past 25 years there is now available to education a considerable collection of evaluation instruments for every level of education. There has been a great deal of research on methods of appraisal and there are very clear formulations and operational definitions of many of the educational objectives which teachers have identified as being important desired outcomes of instruction. In retrospect one finds that the major work on objectives and evaluation has been in the area of the so-called higher mental processes including problem solving, judgment, critical thinking, and creativity. While some very good work has been done in the area of affective behavior such as interests, attitudes, and values, there is much that still needs to be done on these very difficult objectives of education.

When teachers have actively participated in defining objectives and in selecting or constructing evaluation instruments they return to the learning problems with great vigor and remarkable creativity. As they attempt to plan the learning experiences which will help students develop the types of competence, interests, and attitudes they become very resourceful in selecting materials, in planning tasks for students, and in determining the kinds of working relationships among students, between students and the teacher, and between students and the materials and problems of the subject. Perhaps my major observation on this point is that teachers who have become committed to a set of educational objectives which they thoroughly understand respond by developing a variety of learning experiences for students which are as diverse and as complex as the situation requires. The single method of instruction and the single type of learning experience quickly gives way to a variety of methods of instruction and learning experiences.

Perhaps the most severe limitations on the creativity of teachers in devising learning experiences are the fixed schedules of class meetings, the uniform size of classes, and lack of freedom in the typical school building. Some learning experiences can effectively involve a hundred or more students, while others may be effective only when the size of the group is ten or fewer students. Some learning experiences are most effective when a single student is independently pursuing a task which requires the use of the library, laboratory, or field experiences. Some learning experiences require a continuous period of several hours while others require only very brief periods of time. Some require discussions, others may be equally effective when the teacher lectures, gives a demonstration, or presents a film or recording. The point to be made is that time and facilities must be more flexible if learning experiences are to be as effective and varied as our educational objectives require.

The introduction of new learning materials in science, mathematics, English, and foreign languages which have been sponsored or developed by the National Science Foundation and other national groups will do much to help teachers provide more effective learning experiences for students. The development of TV and filmed instructional materials should prove to be valuable assets for teachers and students. The development of programmed instructional materials such as work books and teaching machines should do much to free teachers and students to devote increased effort to the more complex and, in many ways, more important objectives of education.

Most of these new materials and programs are being evaluated and evaluation is being built into the research and demonstration programs from the start. However, many of these new programs are conceived of as "crash" programs designed to bring about a rapid change in the curriculum. Without going into the merits of the particular programs, there is some question about the desirability of a quick change as contrasted with a more gradual modification in the curriculum. From the evaluation point of view, the basic problem is that of determining in what ways the new materials and ideas can be used effectively and the limits within which they are effective. If we viewed curriculum evaluation from the same point of view as the evaluation of the effectiveness of a new medical therapy, or drug, we would be as much interested in the limitations and side effects as we would be in the conditions under which it works most effectively. From this point of view, one might expect new educational procedures and materials to be tested under three conditions.

A. A laboratory investigation should be made with small groups under very carefully specified conditions. If the material or procedure proves to be effective under these conditions, then

B. It should be tried under a greater variety of conditions in the field. Under field conditions careful evaluation evidence must be gathered to determine the limits within which it works well and the conditions under which it is ineffective. One would also be interested in the side effects as well as the long term effects. Because of the great variation in communities and schools in this country, to which I have already referred, I would like to suggest that we need to create a panel of schools which can serve as experimental demonstration schools for curriculum research. A carefully selected panel of about 100 schools representing the variation in schools and communities in the country could be the ideal field tryouts for new curriculum materials and procedures. Each of these schools would need a curriculum and evaluation research person to collect the necessary evidence and to determine the conditions and limits within which the new ideas work. The teachers in these 100 schools would also need to receive appropriate training in the use of the new materials and procedures.

C. Finally, materials and procedures which are effective in the field conditions, should be reported in a type of consumer research form in such a way that the teachers in the other schools of the nation may determine ways in which they can be used effectively in their own schools. Here again, the teachers will need to collect systematic evaluation evidence to determine whether or not the new procedures continue to prove effective under the local conditions.

Perhaps the major criticism against the present emphasis on curriculum development by national agencies is that they are not integrated or related to each other in any very clear way. Each program in science, mathematics, English, etc., is developed by an independent group without careful reference to what has been done by other groups. The long term effects of such uncoordinated curriculum development is likely to be even further splitting and compartmentalization of the secondary school program at the local level.

The research and evaluation evidence on education objectives in problem solving, attitudes, and communication skills makes it very clear that significant growth is likely to take place in students only when such objectives are emphasized throughout the curriculum. Learning experiences in a single course, without corresponding emphasis and reinforcement in other courses, are unlikely to result in significant measurable growth toward such complex objectives. What is needed is curriculum planning at the local level in which school-wide educational objectives are determined by the teaching and administrative staff and then learning experiences are devised which will help students develop in the direction specified by the objectives. Such learning experiences must be evaluated to determine whether they are really effective in bringing about the changes intended. Much help can be given to the local schools by national organizations which suggest curriculum material, educational objectives, and evaluation instruments. However, until we recognize that learning takes place in a student who is interacting with teachers, material and other students, we will miss the heart of the matter. Learning does take place in the classrooms of the local schools.

We must find ways of helping local schools do a better and more complex educational task than was possible hitherto. Change in curriculum must be planned and purposive. Each new development should help the schools to move ahead systematically toward clear educational goals. Each new development must take advantage of all that we have learned in the past about learning and about students. Each new development must be supported by clear evidence of its effectiveness in helping students grow toward the major educational goals required for man's effective adaptation to a complex and rapidly changing world.

EDUCATIONAL TESTING SERVICE

Multiple-Choice Questions: A Close Look

Many believe that only essay questions can measure understanding, and that objective questions are limited to the measurement of rote, superficial factual knowledge. Nothing is further from the truth. This short extract from an ETS booklet demonstrates the intellectual penetration of good recognition items. Is there any intellectual ability that can be measured by an essay test but not by an appropriate multiple-choice test? Is it ever proper to rely solely on one type of evaluation?

[The creation of test questions is] a crucial, arduous process. It is crucial because the loftiest of objectives are meaningless if the questions in a test do not require the students taking the test to demonstrate attainment of those objectives. It is arduous because of the several important steps that must be successfully completed in the writing of the questions.

First, it is essential that the author of a test question identify and define the skill or knowledge he wishes to measure. He must satisfy himself that, among the many questions that may be asked, a particular question is worth asking. Next, he must devise a way of asking the question that will insure that the correct answer is not identified in some superficial manner. As may be apparent in the examples which follow, this consideration requires precision and artistry in the writing of test questions. A well conceived and constructed multiple-choice question should require a student to select, weigh, and apply what he knows in order to answer the question correctly.

Also, the author of the question must word the question and the answer choices so that those who indeed know what is being asked can answer correctly and those who are less knowing will, in effect, be defeated by their own ignorance. The art of writing a multiple-choice question requires, of course, a knowledge of the subject and a knowledge of how the subject is taught at the educational level for which the question is intended. Moreover, the writer of the question should be familiar not only with what students ought to have learned, but also with what they ought not to have learned. That is, he should be able to construct each question in such a way that students who have misinformation or misconceptions will be differentiated from those who are knowledgeable. Then each answer choice in a multiple-choice question will contribute to differentiating between competent and less-than-competent students. Statistical analyses of the sample questions that follow will show how this differentiating power of a question depends on the extent to which the wrong answers attract the less competent students. Questions can discriminate at different levels of ability. In effect, a question's difficulty and discriminating power depend on the sophistication required to distinguish among the answer choices.

After passing the test of expert judgment, questions must then pass a second test—the test of use. Is the question easy—perhaps too easy—or difficult—maybe too difficult? Does it differentiate between able and less able students? Is it clear and unambiguous? Even the most competent teachers and scholars may occasionally misjudge such matters. If a test is to provide reliable measurement, possible sources of error are best identified and eliminated in advance. Therefore, whenever feasible, questions are tried out experimentally before inclusion in a test. From such "pretesting" considerable information of value is derived. Each question in this booklet is followed by a statistical analysis that summarizes the kind of information obtained about the performance of those students tested with the question *before* its actual use in a test as well as after its actual use.

The difficulty of each question may be readily determined. Difficulty is represented by the percentage of students who answer a question correctly; the higher the percentage correct, the easier the question. Similarly, the attractiveness of each answer choice may be determined by the number of students who select it.

The power of a question to differentiate among students of different academic abilities is a more complex matter. To determine this, it is necessary to have for each student a measure of the ability that is being tested by the question; this measure serves as a criterion. As circular as it may at first seem, one such readily available criterion is the student's score on the total test of which the question is a part. The validity of such a technique has been confirmed by comparing the results of analysis against an internal criterion with those obtained with a less readily available independent criterion. In essence, although a committee of experts may err in the formulation of a particular question, we may assume that its judgment of what constitutes achievement in an area is generally valid. Hence the relation between students' success on a question and success on the entire test of which the question is a part is an appropriate measure of the power of the question to discriminate between more able and less able students.

But since much of the power of a multiple-choice question depends on the nature of the answer choices, obtaining measures solely of the question's over-all performance is not sufficient. If the strengths and weaknesses of a question are to be diagnosed, knowledge of the performance of each of its strategic parts must also be obtained. Therefore, for each question an analysis is made of the ability of the group of students selecting each answer choice. It seems reasonable to expect that, in general, those who are more able should select the correct response to a question and that, in general, those who are less able should more frequently find wrong answers attractive. To analyze the performance of each question, students may be divided (as illustrated in the following pages) into equal fifths based on their performance on a relevant criterion—usually total test score. When the answer choices in a question are effective, more students in the highest fifth than in the lowest fifth will select the correct response, and more in the lowest fifth than in the highest fifth will select the wrong answers. Also, the number of students selecting the correct response will generally increase in each higher fifth, while the number choosing the wrong responses will increase in each lower fifth. Information of this kind may be used by a test committee to select for its test only those questions which have proven to discriminate appropriately, or which, given the information, may be revised to make them sufficiently discriminating. The questions appearing in this booklet have all passed through such a screening.

Despite all these precautions, not every question prepared by the methods described turns out to be a good one. Even after the most careful scrutiny of an expert committee as well as a painstaking experimental screening, some do not measure adequately an important instructional goal, and some may contain errors of fact or interpretation. These, however, are the rare exceptions.

The questions which appear on the following pages have been taken from a variety of tests constructed by Educational Testing Service. Many similar questions are now in use. Those presented here are as they appeared in the original tests, with the directions, when given, as they were given to the students. Each question is followed by a statistical analysis of its performance and by a brief discussion of the thought processes involved in formulating the question and in arriving at the correct answer.

Study of this representative sample of multiple-choice questions should lead to a clearer understanding of their potentialities, and should help to dispel the myth that "objective" tests require no thought, insight, or understanding.

QUESTION 1

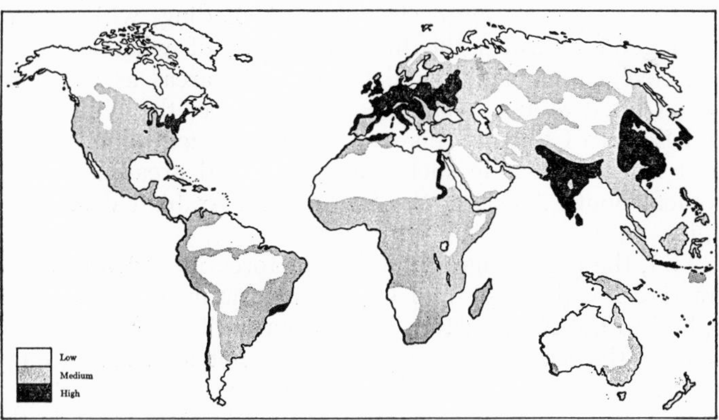

The shading on the above map is used to indicate

(A) population density
(B) percentage of total labor force in agriculture
(C) per capita income
(D) death rate per thousand of population

STATISTICAL ANALYSIS

	Students classified by total test score				
Responses	*Lowest fifth*	*Next lowest fifth*	*Middle fifth*	*Next highest fifth*	*Highest fifth*
Omit	1				
A *	45	52	53	58	58
B	6	1	2	1	1
C	6	5	1		1
D	2	2	4	1	
Total	60	60	60	60	60

* Correct answer.

Per cent of total group of 300 students answering correctly: 89%
Correlation between success on this question and total score on test: .47

In many of the multiple-choice questions included in tests in the social sciences, an attempt is made to require the student to make use of his general background of knowledge in the interpretation of materials. Thus, this question does not simply ask: What areas of the world have the highest population densities? Rather, it presents a novel situation in which the student must infer that, of the choices offered, only population density provides a plausible explanation of the shadings on the map.

This question was answered correctly by almost 90 per cent of a group of college seniors. However, although large numbers of lower ability students were successful on it, the question did differentiate between some of the very poorest students and the rest of those tested.

An examination of the map clearly shows that choice (A), population density, is the proper response. The darkest shading, which according to the map's legend indicates the highest degree of whatever the shading represents, covers such high population density areas as the northeastern part of the United States, a large part of Europe, the Nile valley, India, Japan, and Eastern China. If this were not a sufficient clue, the areas with the lightest shading include such underpopulated areas as the Arctic regions, tropical South America, the Sahara and Arabian deserts, and most of Australia.

Choice (B), the percentage of total labor force in agriculture, while possibly attractive if only India and China are examined, is clearly incorrect when applied to the Northeastern United States. This choice was taken by 10 per cent of the least able group, but was not attractive to any of the other groups.

Choice (C), per capita income, attracted moderately those in the lowest two-fifths of the group. Per capita income could be plausible only if the student's analysis of the map took in solely the dark shading in the United States and Western Europe, and even there it is not entirely correct, but the dark shading in China and India could certainly not indicate high per capita income. The reverse observation is true of choice (D), death rate per thousand of population, since the latter might be expected to be high for India and China, but low for the United States and Europe. Only nine students selected this choice.

. . .

QUESTION 2

"In a flash it came upon me that there was the reason for advancing poverty with advancing wealth. With the growth of population, land grows in value, and the men who work it must pay more for the privilege. In allowing one man to own the land on which and from which other men live, we have made them his bondsmen in a degree which increases as material progress goes on. This is the subtle alchemy that in ways they do not realize is extracting from the masses in every civilized country the fruits of their weary toil."

The person most likely to have written these words is
(A) John Jacob Astor
(B) William Jennings Bryan
(C) Thorstein Veblen
(D) Lincoln Steffens
(E) Henry George

STATISTICAL ANALYSIS

	Students classified by total test score				
Responses	*Lowest fifth*	*Next lowest fifth*	*Middle fifth*	*Next highest fifth*	*Highest fifth*
Omit	32	22	15	16	4
A	5	6	2	1	
B	15	13	22	10	9
C	7	10	13	12	16
D	8	8	9	8	4
E *	6	15	13	27	41
Total	73	74	74	74	74

* Correct answer.

Per cent of total group of 369 students answering correctly: 28%
Correlation between success on this question and total score on test: .47
(Discrepancies in total numbers in each fifth are caused by drop-out of students not completing the test.)

This question presents the student with a quotation and asks him to identify the person most likely to have made the statement. Note that the student is *not* asked to, or expected to, recognize the statement from memory. Instead, he is expected to read the excerpt carefully, to evaluate it in terms of his knowledge and understanding of American intellectual history, and then to select from the five names listed the person to whom the statement might most reasonably be attributed.

Some interesting results may be seen by examining the statistics obtained when the question was administered in a college-level American history test to a group of very able high school seniors. Because the question was a difficult one for the group, many students chose not to answer it at all rather than risk being penalized for an incorrect guess. This helped to differentiate between the able students and the less able ones. Whereas 32 of the students in the lowest fifth omitted the question, only four of the students in the top fifth did so.

Choice (A) served to attract only a few of the less able students. None of the top group thought that the statement could have been made by John Jacob Astor. An entrepreneur of the early nineteenth century who built up a vast fur trading empire in the Pacific Northwest, Astor would most likely be associated with the opening up of the Oregon country. In this huge, unsettled region where land was then readily available, he would hardly have been concerned with the particular economic problem discussed in the quotation. Moreover, anyone who recognizes the name has no reason to associate it with reform.

Choice (B) is a more sophisticated wrong answer than is (A). The students who selected William Jennings Bryan as the probable author of the passage were undoubtedly aware of Bryan's reputation as "The Great Commoner"—the self-styled defender of the people against the "dictatorship" of Wall Street, their champion in the campaign for free coinage of silver. Although the last sentence of the quotation might be slightly reminiscent of Bryan's style, the particular ideas are not those exploited by an orator who made free silver a "cause célèbre." This answer, while attractive to some of the students in the lower two-fifths, was most popular with those in the middle fifth. This may be partly explained by its greater sophistication, but the fact that most of the lower group had already chosen to omit the question probably accounts for the failure of that group to choose (B).

Choice (C), Thorstein Veblen, served to separate the better students from the very best. Few of the poorest students chose Veblen, partly because of the reasons mentioned above, and possibly also because they may not have been familiar with Veblen. The brighter students may have been more familiar with his name and ideas or at least with the fact that he was a critic of the American economic system at the turn of the century. They did not know enough, however, to realize that Veblen was not concerned with the monopoly of land as a cause of poverty.

Very few of the top group were attracted to choice (D), Lincoln Steffens. Concerned primarily with the problems of the cities, Steffens is perhaps best known for his exposure of municipal corruption.

Henry George, the correct response, was selected by over half of those in the highest fifth, but only six of the lowest group chose this correct answer. Altogether only 28 per cent of the total group could answer the question correctly, for a thoughtful understanding of the ideas of Henry George was required. The statement did not contain any of the catchwords usually superficially connected with George, such as "single tax" or "unearned increment."

QUESTION 3

In the following questions you are asked to make inferences from the data which are given you on the map of the imaginary country, Serendip. The answers in most instances must be probabilities rather than certainties. The relative size of towns and cities is not shown. To assist you in the location of the places mentioned in the questions, the map is divided into squares lettered vertically from A to E and numbered horizontally from 1 to 5.

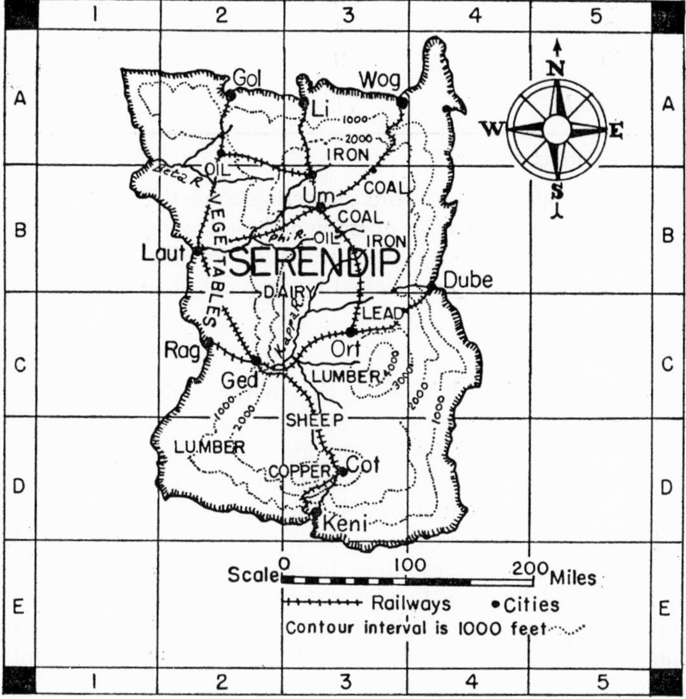

Which of the following cities would be the best location for a steel mill?

(A) Li (3A)
(B) Um (3B)
(C) Cot (3D)
(D) Dube (4B)

A map of an imaginary country, such as that shown above, offers numerous possibilities for questions which measure important understandings. One could ask several questions requiring an understanding of the symbols used on the map. To determine student comprehension of the meaning of contour lines, for example, one might ask which railroad has the steepest grades to climb. Similar questions can be developed which require knowledge of the factors influencing population distribution, economic activities, and so on.

STATISTICAL ANALYSIS

	Students classified by total test score	
Responses	*Lowest 27%*	*Highest 27%*
Omit	8	
A	10	2
B *	40	84
C	4	1
D	9	6
Total	71	93

* Correct answer.

Per cent of total group of 370 students answering correctly: 75%
Correlation between success on this question and total score on test: .43
(A somewhat different form of analysis was used for this test. Discrepancies in total numbers in each group are caused by drop-out of students not completing the test.)

The question reproduced beneath the map requires knowledge of the natural resources used in producing steel and an awareness of the importance of transportation facilities in bringing these resources together. It was part of a general achievement test given to high school seniors.

The student who knows that iron is the basic raw material of steel and that coal commonly provides the necessary source of heat would proceed to locate deposits of these resources in relation to the cities listed in the question. He would be able to eliminate Cot immediately, since there is no iron or coal in its vicinity, although Cot might be an attractive choice to students who mistakenly think that copper is a basic ingredient of steel. Both Li and Dube are located reasonably near supplies of iron, and therefore might be attractive choices. Um, however, is the more clearly "correct" response, because not only are deposits of iron and coal nearby, but they are more readily transportable by direct railroad routes.

QUESTION 4

In which of the following centuries was the piece of sculpture shown above most probably produced?

(A) The fifth century B.C.
(B) The fourteenth century A.D.
(C) The sixteenth century A.D.
(D) The eighteenth century A.D.
(E) The twentieth century A.D.

This question on art appeared in a test of general background given to college seniors and graduate students. To answer the question, the student must apply his knowledge of the characteristics of various periods in the history of sculpture in order to place the statue within its proper period.

STATISTICAL ANALYSIS

	Students classified by total test score				
Responses	*Lowest fifth*	*Next lowest fifth*	*Middle fifth*	*Next highest fifth*	*Highest fifth*
Omit	16	9	10	5	3
A	6	7	9	7	6
B	9	8	1	5	
C	8	6	5	3	
D	5	3	5	2	3
E *	27	41	44	52	62
Total	71	74	74	74	74

* Correct answer.

Per cent of total group of 370 students answering correctly: 62%
Correlation between success on this question and total score on humanities section of test: .40
(Discrepancies in total numbers in each fifth are caused by drop-out of students not completing the test.)

The statue can be identified immediately as a product of western civilization because of its subject matter and design. The sculpture most commonly associated with western art in the fifth century B.C. is that done in Greece. During that period Greek sculpture showed its characteristic idealization of the human figure. If the student contrasts a well-known statue from that period, such as Myron's "Discobolus" ("The Discus Thrower") with the statue in the picture, he can easily discover that the treatment accorded the two figures is not the same. The figure of the woman pictured is not idealized, and although the frontal pose is found in Greek sculpture, a turned head on the figure is not. Therefore, choice (A) can hardly be correct.

In some countries sculptors of the fourteenth century A.D. began to create statues for use in palaces, chapels, and tombs of private individuals, but their work retained the qualities of the representations of saints found in the Gothic cathedrals of Europe. Statues of men and women associated with Christian history were also used as architectural decorations. In the fourteenth century probably only Eve would have been carved as a nude female figure, and she would certainly have been portrayed in a more modest pose and with a fig leaf. Although, like the figure of the woman pictured, the figures of this period of Christian art are not idealized, the statue of the woman displays none of the other characteristics of medieval art, and choice (B) can be eliminated.

The fifteenth century saw the beginnings of the Italian Renaissance, and by the sixteenth century sculptors were again presenting idealizations of the human figure, most often in a Christian rather than classical context. The statue pictured above shows none of the heroic character that is found in the works of Michelangelo and none of the exaggerated stylization that appeared in the works of his followers. Thus, choice (C) can be regarded as inaccurate.

Early in the eighteenth century sculptors frequently displayed a self-conscious coy femininity in their female nudes, but by the end of that century sculptors such as Canova had adopted the classical ideals and imitated classical models. Consequently, choice (D) is not a valid one, for the statue in the photograph does not resemble an eighteenth-century interpretation of a Greek goddess or nymph. It does, however, realistically present a human figure without any attempt at idealization. The realism here is thoroughly modern. The use the sculptor makes of texture points to the modern period, for it was only late in the nineteenth century that sculpture (such as Renoir's "The Washerwoman") used nonrepresentational texture as an integral part of the design and aesthetic effect of the work of art. Minor details in the statue such as the shape of the nose, the half-closed eyes (instead of open sockets), and the line of the hair indicate that the work is not classical in origin, and at the same time they point to the twentieth century school of art. The statue is actually "Junge Frau," the work of the modern German sculptor, Georg Kolbe.

The statistics show that the question was an easy one for the particular group that took the test. The correct answer was chosen by 62 per cent of the students. However, more of the students in the highest group than in the lowest group selected the correct response, and the incorrect answers were generally more appealing to the poorer students than they were to the better students.

• • •

QUESTION 5

The sentence below has blank spaces, each blank indicating that a word has been omitted. Beneath the sentence are five lettered sets of words. You are to choose the one set of words which, when inserted in the sentence, best fits in with the meaning of the sentence as a whole.

From the first the islanders, despite an outward—,
did what they could to—the ruthless occupying power.

(A) harmony . . assist
(B) enmity . . embarrass
(C) rebellion . . foil
(D) resistance . . destroy
(E) acquiescence . . thwart

This type of question is one of several commonly used in tests in which a measure of verbal aptitude is sought. Specifically, this type is designed to measure one aspect of reading comprehension: the student's ability to recognize the consistency in logic and in style that is required of the elements in a sentence. If the student understands the implications of a sentence, he should be able to select the answer that best fulfills the meaning of the sentence. The sentences deal with a wide variety of topics that the student is likely to have encountered in general reading.

STATISTICAL ANALYSIS

	Students classified by total test score				
Responses	*Lowest fifth*	*Next lowest fifth*	*Middle fifth*	*Next highest fifth*	*Highest fifth*
Omit		2	4	1	
A				1	
B	4	1			
C	10	7	2		2
D	37	28	16	8	3
E *	9	22	38	50	55
Total	60	60	60	60	60

* Correct answer.

Per cent of total group of 300 students answering correctly: 58%
Correlation between success on this question and total score on test: .69

Examination of the question should indicate that the answer involves two words which are, in a sense, opposite in meaning, since the word "despite" carries with it the implication that the islanders acted in one fashion, while presenting a somewhat different impression to the "ruthless occupying power." With this relationship in mind, (A), (B), (C), and (D) can be eliminated since all of those answers fail to give the sense of contrast that is required. If outward harmony existed, assisting the occupying power would probably contribute to this state of harmony and strengthen it. If enmity existed, embarrassing the occupying power would be one method of expressing this feeling. Should rebellion exist, then the islanders would be doing what they could to foil the occupying power; these terms do not imply opposition. The same logic holds for "resistance . . . destroy." The correct answer, the only one implying two opposed actions, is (E).

In this analysis, 58 per cent of a group of college-bound secondary school students answered the question correctly, and it discriminated extremely well between the good students and the poor students. Performance on this question correlated .69 with performance on the test as a whole. The analysis shows that whereas nearly all of the top one-fifth answered correctly, only 15 per cent of the lowest one-fifth did so.

. . .

QUESTION 6

The question below is followed by two statements, labeled (1) and (2), in which certain data are given. In this question you do not actually have to compute an answer, but rather you have to decide whether the data given in the statements are sufficient for answering the question. Using the data given in the statements plus your knowledge of mathematics and everyday facts (such as the number of days in July), you are to select answer

(A) if statement (1) ALONE is sufficient but statement (2) alone is not sufficient to answer the question asked,
(B) if statement (2) ALONE is sufficient but statement (1) alone is not sufficient to answer the question asked,
(C) if both statements (1) and (2) TOGETHER are sufficient to answer the question asked, but NEITHER statement ALONE is sufficient,
(D) if EACH statement is sufficient by itself to answer the question asked,
(E) if statements (1) and (2) TOGETHER are NOT sufficient to answer the question asked and additional data specific to the problem are needed.

If x is a whole number, is it a two-digit number?
(1) x^2 is a three-digit number.
(2) $10x$ is a three-digit number.

STATISTICAL ANALYSIS

	Students classified by total test score				
Responses	*Lowest fifth*	*Next lowest fifth*	*Middle fifth*	*Next highest fifth*	*Highest fifth*
Omit	11	6		1	
A	9	4	7	2	1
B	4	8	9	13	14
C	2	7	3	7	1
D *	11	19	30	24	37
E	21	15	11	13	6
Total	58	59	60	60	59

* Correct answer.

Per cent of total group of 296 students answering correctly: 41%
Correlation between success on this question and total score on test: .38
(Discrepancies in total numbers in each fifth are caused by drop-out of students not completing the test.)

One of the abilities which has been receiving increasing emphasis from the elementary school through college is that of judging the relevancy of data in the solution of problems in mathematics, science, and social studies. Measurement of the extent to which a student has developed this ability near the end of the high school years is believed to be important in predicting scholastic success in college. To accomplish such measurement the type of test question presented here has been designed, validated by research, and is now in use in the College Entrance Examination Board's Scholastic Aptitude Test. This type of question is used in arithmetic, algebra, and geometry. It shifts the emphasis from rote, manipulative skills to higher level judgments and reasoning.

This question shows the very great versatility of this type, for it requires little factual knowledge and the simplest aspects of elementary algebra, but does require a considerable degree of numerical judgment.

Fact (1) alone is sufficient because the square root of any three-digit square is a two-digit number. Fact (2) alone is sufficient because, whenever a three-digit multiple of 10 is divided by 10, the result is a two-digit number. The correct answer is therefore (D).

This question and its analysis provide an interesting insight into the functioning of this type of question. When the correct answer is (D), there is a sense in which the question becomes two questions, since two separate sufficiencies must be determined. In this case, when the sufficiency of Fact 1 is considerably more difficult to determine than the sufficiency of Fact 2, a certain number of moderately able people can be expected to choose (B) as the answer. One of the reasons that may have made the sufficiency of Fact 1 difficult for them to see is that although the square root of any three-digit number is always a two-digit number, the square of a two-digit number is not necessarily a three-digit number. The latter point may have led some to conclude erroneously that Fact 1 was not sufficient. Fact 2, on the other hand, can more easily be seen as sufficient because only a two-digit number can be multiplied by 10 to produce a three-digit number. The higher ability of the 121 selecting (D) is sufficient to give the question a good index of discrimination. The 20 choosing (C) apparently failed to realize that each of the two facts is independently sufficient.

Chapter 17

Healthy Adjustment to Difficulties

17-1

FRITZ REDL
AND WILLIAM W. WATTENBERG

Diagnostic Thinking in the Classroom

17-2

W. J. MCKEACHIE, DONALD POLLIE,
AND JOSEPH SPEISMAN

Relieving Anxiety in Classroom Examinations

FRITZ REDL and WILLIAM W. WATTENBERG

Diagnostic Thinking in the Classroom

How may the teacher cope with student maladjustment? The case studies in the following article illuminate some important principles of meeting problems in the classroom. The authors do not urge a simple program of specific actions, but rather suggest diagnostic attitudes from which possible solutions may emerge. What sort of evidence do you suppose the authors have behind their recommendations?

. . . The interlocking networks of relationships which exist in a classroom may appear to be a devilish spider web designed to entangle teachers. Too many may feel baffled by the possibility that anything they may do can turn out to be a mistake.

To counteract such feelings, there is bound to be a demand that the mental hygienist give some definite, helpful answers. What can a teacher do in a classroom? How can the principles of mental hygiene be put to work?

Although no one can tell another person exactly how to handle each of the highly specific situations that could arise, it is possible to outline general approaches with which to meet the challenge of difficult situations. With practice, such ways of tackling difficult problems can become second nature. As they gradually do so, insight concerning the complex interplay of psychological forces can become a source of professional security rather than a threat to personal adequacy.

To illustrate the pattern of diagnostic thinking in the quick-as-a-wink setting of an ordinary classroom crisis, let us study a teacher in action.

A child cries without apparent cause. As the third grade was working on some arithmetic problems, Miss Queen noticed tears streaming down George's face. He was a frail boy, quiet but well liked by the others. Her first thought was that he was sick. She asked him if anything hurt him; he said "No." His voice sounded embarrassed, but he did not look sick and did not sound as though in pain. Her next guess was that maybe he had an "accident." His denial sounded convincing. During the exchange she noticed that he shot a look toward Harry, who had been watching with a glower on his face. When Miss Queen looked around the class, Harry instantly began working on his arithmetic with unaccustomed vigor. Her hunch was that there had been some set-to between the boys, but knowing

From *Mental Hygiene in Teaching* by Fritz Redl and William W. Wattenberg, copyright, 1951, by Harcourt, Brace & World, Inc., and reprinted with their permission.

the juvenile code against tattling she kept the guess to herself. However, she did want more information and pressed George to tell her what was wrong. Even as she did so it seemed as though the rest of the class was too quiet; she suspected that they knew something. George finally faltered that he had lost his lunch money. Miss Queen was sure Harry had taken it.

Her conclusions made sense to her, but the question was what should she do. Lend George the money? That would solve nothing, and she could always do that in time to see he had a good meal. Force him to tell the whole story? That would turn the class against him and give Harry social reinforcement outside school. Browbeat Harry or some other child into telling the truth? They would still blame George. She decided she had to show that George was not a tattle-tale and yet let Harry find out some social consequences of the actions she suspected him of. She had to let the class see she could protect all of them. Harry was over-age for the class, and was using his size to get power, but that problem could be tackled later. A vivid lesson now might make him more ready to accept her help later, especially if she did not attack him.

All these considerations flashed through her mind while listening to George. One possibility occurred to her, and she decided to take a chance. She told the class that George had lost his lunch money and good-naturedly admonished him to be more careful. When the arithmetic papers were collected, she said she had to go to the office and asked them to help George find his money while she was gone. To make the request more striking she dwelt a bit on how it feels to sit hungry in class all afternoon.

As she had hoped, no sooner was the door closed behind her than there was a noisy outburst. She was never sure but thought she heard voices shouting, "Give it back to him." Anyway, when she returned in five minutes the class was quiet, George had thirty cents on his desk, and Harry was drawing something on a piece of paper. All she said was, "You found his money? That's good."

There was no point in forcing anyone to think up more fibs. She remembered, of course, to work on the problem of helping Harry find ways of using his size for better purposes.

THE CONCEPT OF DIAGNOSTIC THINKING

In this simple case, Miss Queen illustrated the procedures involved in diagnostic thinking. This is the habit of mind which enables physicians, automobile repairmen, and industrial troubleshooters to work out plans of action. The essential characteristic of such thinking is that it is primarily concerned with determining the causes and finding the point of attack. Self-justification or stock remedies are kept to a minimum. With a mind open to the meaning of developments, the practitioner proceeds into action as quickly as possible.

The first hunch. As any difficulty arises, those who are in it almost immediately form a hunch as to its meaning and the appropriate remedy. Such hunches are rarely reasoned. Rather, they represent the echoes of a person's previous experiences. Beginning teachers may react in terms of how previous teachers behaved toward them and of their own feelings as students under similar conditions. The veteran has a backlog of experience in having dealt with a wide variety of conditions. Before logical thought can be brought to bear, these memories emerge and suggest a theory as to why a child or a class is behaving in a particular way and what strategy will probably work. Miss Queen, for some reason, first thought that perhaps George was sick.

Whether or not this first hunch turns out to be correct it constitutes an essential step in the process of working out a solution. By giving a focus to the collection of observations and to thought processes it prevents aimlessness. Because each child is different from all others and no two situations are ever exactly alike, the first hunch will almost always need to be modified. It is not a sacrosanct goal but a point of departure. In the illustration given, Miss Queen had to drop her first two guesses before she finally hit a promising lead.

Exercising subsurface curiosity. In testing the first hunch, the next step is to bring to bear the facts we already know and those which we can gather readily by observation. We try to determine the hidden causes of the situation. Miss Queen, for instance, gave much weight to children's aversion to tattling. This is the point at which we use our information concerning psychological dynamics. Here is where we apply facts concerning behavior at different stages of development. In the light of all our knowledge we try to check our first hunch for harmony with possible explanations. Sometimes the hunch holds up under examination. Sometimes it must be completely discarded and a new one developed. More often, the first hunch has to be amplified or altered, as Miss Queen's experience showed quite clearly.

To give another illustration: a seven-year-old boy complains to the teacher that he was hurt by a youngster who always seemed to be getting into fights. An obvious first hunch would be that here was another in a series of aggressions by a boy already unpopular for his quarreling. An investigation might reveal that the victim had been one of a group who had been taunting the "bully." Here we are dealing with a somewhat different situation than [we] at first suspected. The aggressor is being made into a scapegoat. Now, the problem is to find ways of guiding the group into a more constructive attitude toward a boy already wrestling with serious problems.

The meaning of conduct as a guide to action. Even when we may not know the cause of a bit of conduct, we may still see some meaning in it. Lest this seem like a hairsplitting distinction let us look at a simple illustration: In the course of a group discussion, a boy walks to the door with quick, tense strides, and slams the door when he leaves. Now, we cannot know on the basis of so few facts the *cause* of his action but we can see a clear *meaning*, that he was angry or disturbed. Whatever caused the boy to slam the door at this particular moment, or whatever led to door-slamming as his technique of acting out resentment, may not be known at the time. To know, however, whether his slamming the door "meant" that he was ashamed, embarrassed, fearful of further taunting by other children, angry at the teacher, jealous, or what not would be an important first clue to look for, and can often be read directly from the way the door was slammed and the circumstances which led up to the incident. Although full causation is not known, it is possible to act on the basis of our understanding of the meaning of conduct. For Miss Queen, the ways Harry and the class acted were her important clues. Our knowledge of psychological principles enables us to decide what added facts we need to know. As these are interpreted we can begin taking steps which stand a fair chance of being helpful.

Action tests the hypothesis. In any case, as soon as we feel reasonably confident of our hunches, we act upon them. Such action is regarded as a test of the accuracy of our estimates rather than as a course of behavior to which we are irrevocably committed. This is done in the same spirit in which the doctor who suspects that a patient's headaches are due to eyestrain prescribes glasses. If the headaches then vanish he feels satisfied he was right; if they persist, he looks for other causes.

Grace Arthur, in her book *Tutoring as Therapy,*[1] describes a boy, Sandy, who often played hooky. An analysis of test scores led to the hunch that his actions were a compensation for defects in reading and spelling. It was felt that, since he had normal intelligence and showed no signs of other disturbance, individual remedial tutoring would do the trick. A teacher was employed to help him. As soon as he could compete with the rest of his class, he stopped being truant. The return of George's money confirmed Miss Queen's estimate of the situation.

The initial course of action may equally well reveal that the hunches are wrong or incomplete. For instance, a girl with a very good high school record began to misbehave in the mathematics class. The teacher first suspected the difficulty was due to shame at a poor grasp of basic concepts. However, a proffer of special help was rejected with some little heat. Since this had happened only in one class the teacher decided the first guess was wrong and there must be some emotional reaction to math. A sympathetic high school counselor found that the girl was reacting against pressure from her father to become an engineer—part of the father's efforts to cover his disappointment at not having a son.

Revising estimates as events unfold. An essential characteristic of true diagnostic thinking is that it is flexible. As events unfold we change our hunches and hypotheses. Our estimates are revised not only by what happens as a result of our own treatment but also by developments in the individual or the group. Thus, in a fifth grade class we might have a boy who seemed to enjoy disrupting the flow of a lesson by getting into an argument with the teacher or a popular class member on some minor point. A friendship chart might give the information that the boy was an isolate. We

[1] New York, The Commonwealth Fund, 1946, p. 17.

might know that his father was known in the town as a truculent lone wolf. Our diagnosis, based on these facts, could be that the boy identified with his father, was also being cold-shouldered by the other children, and his argumentativeness was both cause and effect of this situation. Therefore, we would do what we could to get him accepted by the other children. Assume we were reasonably successful. Now, having won some friends, he continues to badger the teacher but not his classmates, several of whom seem to enjoy his antics. Our diagnosis would change to fit this new situation. Quite possibly he was making a better social adjustment but had taken the lead in his juvenile group's warfare against adults, as represented by the teacher.

One further word of advice on diagnostic thinking: Remember that a youngster or a group, if given a chance, will often work out problems without interference. For many individuals, trouble is a signal to bring their own resources to bear. An opportunity to think about what is happening or to talk it out in the presence of an attentive leader is all they need. The wise teacher senses those situations where the child or the group can gather added strength by being left free to work out a solution. Miss Queen, for instance, wisely realized that she could count on her class to settle the immediate problem of getting Harry to return the money.

SOME MORE ILLUSTRATIONS

All that has been said above may seem a little glib and vague. The tactics, of necessity, have been described in very general terms. They offer small satisfaction to a teacher who wants to know precisely what to do. To make the meaning somewhat more clear we will give a few more illustrations of how these tactics have been used in concrete situations.

A room becomes restless. The sophomores at Jefferson High were making a study of occupations in various local industries. Committees had gathered facts and had been presenting reports to the class. As in years past, interest had been high. Today, Betty was telling about the bus company. A bright girl, she had taken the initiative in the committee. The teacher had wondered whether Betty had not been high-handed and done all the work herself without giving the others a chance. Her report, though, was a masterpiece; she had obviously done a thorough job of getting facts from her father, who was treasurer of the company. She spoke with the smooth confidence of a self-assured executive addressing a meeting of yes-men. As she proceeded, however, the class became restive. The movable chairs creaked as students shifted their weight; an unusual undertone of whispers or mutters could be heard.

What was the cause? Did the students resent the usually popular Betty's tone of superiority? Were they bored with the contents? Were the committee members expressing their discontent with her hogging of the work? All this was possible. The teacher also recalled that the company had almost had a strike that summer, and some students came from homes of the bus company employees. Was the restlessness an echo of that conflict?

Whatever the exact reason, it looked as though the dominating flow of her report was forcing quite a few class members to bottle up observations they were itching to make. If that were the case, the cure for the restlessness was to find a way to break into her report. It might be possible to do that in such a way as to avoid throwing her on the defensive; the firm way she was talking suggested that she was afraid of that potentiality.

As she finished telling about the maintenance shops the teacher broke in with "Betty, your report is so full of facts that it might be better to take it up one section at a time. I think Joe's father has been a repairman quite a while. Maybe he can give us an idea of what training that job required."

Joe was glad to take the opportunity. A lively discussion followed. Betty was at first impatient, but was drawn in to answer some questions. No mention was made of labor troubles. Apparently, the restlessness was not due to that so much as to her monopolizing the subject. The remainder of her report was given in short snatches. Although it was not completed that hour, the feeling as the class left the room seemed good.

Children flare up at each other. There was a clatter as Tim and his chair went sprawling onto the floor. Miriam stood over him shouting, "Freshy." Miss Silver told them to stop the fighting. She picked Tim up, told him he was not hurt, and started to find out what had happened. Just then, trouble popped in another part of the room. Fred gave a cry of pain. Miss Silver turned, to find him and another boy rolling in furious combat. When she separated them their alibis were vindictively voiced: "He spit on me." "He kicked my foot."

That kind of occurrence had been happening since the beginning of the circus unit. The idea for the unit had come to Miss Silver when she noticed posters advertising a circus in the neighborhood store windows. She was sure her third graders would jump at the chance to put on a show of their own. Indeed, there had been an excited clapping of hands when she had broached the idea. She told them that they would make their own circus. Each one could be whatever he wanted. She put out a supply of construction paper and told them to go ahead and make costumes.

She had been reading some articles on the effects of too much domination of children by teachers. She wanted to do things the right way and determined not to interfere with the children's own ideas on the unit. When they came for advice she told them to do whatever they wanted. The results were bad. She had never seen so much fighting and name-calling.

Although the books all said that aggression is a product of frustration, obviously she was not forcing them to conform to her standards. Yet, something was keeping them from enjoying the experience. She could see they were not happy. Why? What was the matter? It was not the fault of the class, because up until then the group had worked well both in class and on the playground. Her first hunch grew out of a talk she had earlier when Fred asked what kind of animals they had in the circus. To her surprise she found out he had never seen a circus. She asked the whole class; three-quarters said the same thing. Her conclusion was that they were frustrated because they lacked knowledge of what to do. To counteract this condition she brought in a collection of circus books and pictures. The flare-ups subsided for a while, but soon started again.

Next she noticed that costume-making was proving too hard. George had wanted to be an elephant, but failed dismally at fashioning a trunk out of the one piece of paper which was his allotment. The wonderful ideas of the others met similar fates. In the terms of psychology texts, their level of aspiration was unrealistically high. They had set goals way beyond either their skill or the materials available. Miss Silver felt that might explain all the evidence of frustration. Accordingly, she announced that they could bring anything they wanted from home.

The day of the fights involving Tim, Miriam, and Fred was the "culminating activity," the circus itself. The children came with a choice collection of cowboy accessories, Indian suits, and the like. However, they seemed to have no idea of what to do. They switched roles constantly: Kathy, for example, was a clown one minute, a trained horse the next, and ended up by being an airplane. Once again, the group disintegrated in ill-tempered bickering.

When the principal came in to see the promised show, Miss Silver was ready to cry with vexation. In a friendly way afterwards the principal quoted to her that part of the Lippitt experiment which described the frustrating effects of laissez-faire leadership.

Miss Silver promised herself to try another unit using "democratic" techniques. Next time, she will make sure that the children have previous experience with the subject matter, that adequate supplies are available, that any construction is within the ability of the pupils, and that there is sufficient planning by the class so that they feel some security. Certainly, another debacle would not be good for the emotional health of the class, much less her own.

A child tears up his work. The new first grade teacher at the Corcoran School thought she would start off by trying to have the children enjoy being in her room. Remembering that children like big muscle activity, instead of following the local custom of introducing primers the very first day she spent the first week in games, rhythm band activity, and finger painting. Although they had seemed a very willing group of children and appeared to enjoy each activity when it was at its height, between times there was a growing undercurrent of disorder.

The new teacher's perplexity was brought to a head on the third day by something Eddie did. She had noticed him very early. Somewhat shy and anxious to please, he had come into the room carrying a shiny box full of pencils, crayons, rulers, and all the other gewgaws dear to fond parents. He was surrounded by a group of admirers, apparently friends from last year's kindergarten. At lunch the kindergarten teacher mentioned him as a dependable little leader. At the conclusion of a finger-painting session, he brought up a liberally smeared design. The new teacher had told him it was very pretty and he could take it home. The look on his face was most peculiar, as though he thought she might be joking. What he said was equally enigmatic: "Oh, pooh!"

Eddie dutifully carried the rolled paper away with him. Watching from the window the teacher was surprised to see him rip it to shreds which he flung into the gutter. Then, he gaily joined some friends in a chaotic running race. A little while later the kindergarten class emerged from the building, each child proudly holding a crude basket made of paper. Some of her first graders yelled a chant about "kindergarten babies."

The new teacher had learned enough psychology to realize that to Eddie, the work he destroyed might be a symbol of something he disliked. The attitude of her class toward the kindergarteners and the fact that those children had been taking home work suggested one possibility: Eddie had felt that he was being treated as a "baby," and his pride in first grade status was being threatened. The whole thing seemed childish and silly to the teacher.

A few thoughts later, it did not seem so silly. Maybe it was a clue to the growing disorder, the strange discontent that was troubling the class. Perhaps the activities of the first days were too much like kindergarten. Of course, it was childish, but then first graders are children. It could be that the reading and the other things that the new teacher regarded as work would be regarded at first as proud evidences of a long-awaited superiority.

When the first graders came into their room the fourth day, there was a big pile of books on the teacher's desk. She noticed they seemed fascinated. The room was quiet for once. When the books were passed out, there was an eager look on Eddie's face. The others looked equally impressed with themselves. That day the new teacher introduced the class to other "regular" subjects. She was surprised at their avid responses.

She knew that soon individual differences would take effect, and that sooner or later some would lose enthusiasm. The incident made her realize, though, that statements concerning the power of children's curiosity were true after all. She wondered a little now why she had felt otherwise. She realized that she should take into account the children's own expectations of what learning meant, in addition to her educated concept of the right technique. Anyway, teaching might turn out to be more pleasant than she expected.

"Everyone cheats on a test." It was close to the end of the third marking period, and almost all the teachers at the Buchanan High School were giving tests. That week's issue of a national picture magazine had an article showing how students at several colleges cheat on examinations. Several teachers were quite upset and bitter at the possibility that the article might put ideas into Buchanan students' heads. Jack Pugh, the assistant football coach who had been a very popular student leader seven years before and who was still regarded by the staff as an overgrown schoolboy, was frankly amused. He confided to Miss Johnson, a young science teacher, "Those old goats don't know the half of it. If every kid who cheated around here this week got caught and expelled you could count the rest on your lovely little fingers."

She was not amused. The thought that her students could be dishonest went against her grain. She had to admit to herself she was shocked. She just couldn't believe it was true. In her own classes she used an informal honor system; after giving out the papers she sat at her desk and, without looking up, corrected papers or worked on records.

To prove that Pugh was wrong she feigned her usual casualness, but watched closely. A curved mirror set up on the demonstration desk gave her a good view of part of the class without anyone suspecting they were being observed. Within ten minutes she was thoroughly disheartened. Two of the girls had open textbooks hidden beneath papers on the shelf underneath their desks. The way notes were secretly passed from one student to another, answered, returned, and read in chain letter fashion reminded her of a film in which prisoners had plotted a mass escape. Out of the corner of her eye, she saw several students look at her and when they were sure she was not watching, copy answers from the brighter members of the class. With the exception of Alice Wilkins, whom she had always disliked because of prissy mannerisms, these bright youngsters were writing in an awkward fashion that Miss Johnson realized was adopted to make such copying easier.

As her anger mounted, her first impulse was to pounce on one of the offenders and make an example of him. For a moment she debated with herself as to whom she could pick. Then she realized that would be unfair. Her next idea was to stop the examination, and denounce the whole class. That raised another question: Why penalize her students just because Pugh had tipped her off and she had been more observant?

The problem was obviously too big for her to tackle alone. This thing must be going on throughout the school. That thought settled her mind as to what to do. She would take it up with Miss Cump, the principal. There was no point in making an incident. Miss Johnson recalled having heard someone say something about how a wise teacher has to know what not to see. So she carefully refrained from any further watching that might let the students know what she had discovered.

Miss Cump was not the least bit surprised. She had suspected that the curriculum and the emphasis on grades was putting too much pressure on many students. Miss Johnson's story convinced her that the problem needed to be faced by the faculty. Within a short while committees composed of respected teachers were at work.

A teacher's pet encounters jeers. Olga was Miss Elton's favorite pupil. The girl, a fourth grader, was one of those alert, happy youngsters who work hard, learn easily, and are generally pleasant. One day, when the rest of the class had been apathetic, she came through with a very clear explanation of an arithmetic problem. Miss Elton turned to the class and said, "That is the kind of answer I like to hear. Why don't the rest of you do things the way Olga does?"

Before this speech was half finished, Miss Elton wanted to bite off her tongue. The other children seemed stonily quiet; a number glared at Olga. Miss Elton realized that she had made an error and that Olga would have rough sledding. Sure enough, on the way home, she saw a little circle jeering at Olga. The girl was angry and in tears. Miss Elton felt very bad, but did not know what to do. She drove past the group without being noticed by them.

The next day, Olga acted quite distant. She avoided Miss Elton and did not volunteer in class. However, she did work on problems at her seat. During a short quiz, Miss Elton saw her whisper an answer to Doris, who sat in front. The following day she came late, and gave a weak excuse in a belligerent voice. Miss Elton told her to stay after school, a traditional penalty at the school. Olga obeyed, but bristled defiance. Miss Elton did not know how to approach the girl. As she puzzled over the affair, the teacher reviewed what she knew of the girl. All the information agreed on one point: Olga was a stable youngster who had good sense and knew how to get along with her fellow pupils. Her actions were well calculated to overcome the reputation of being a teacher's pet. Miss Elton figured that the girl could undoubtedly work out her present problem by herself. After five minutes, Miss Elton excused her with a friendly injunction to be her usual pleasant self. She asked whether Olga's mother would be worried if she came home late. Olga replied that she usually played with some friends and was not expected home until dinnertime.

Two days later, Olga lingered for a moment after dismissal to tell Miss Elton she was sorry for having been snippy. Then she ran to join her friends. Within a week, Olga was again taking an interested part in class activities. The only noticeable differences were that she seemed to spend more time helping her friends and that she seemed to hold back giving answers to problems when several others had made errors. Miss Elton had been correct in her guess that the girl would work things out satisfactorily.

THE STRATEGY OF TIMING

The use of diagnostic thinking may be complicated by the fact that in psychological matters timing is very important. Often, the appropriate action is not a single act, but a series of acts. It is essential that we not only decide what to do but when to do it. For example, if a new boy in a class starts to clown in a way which is winning admiration of the other children our tactics have to be carefully timed. If the particular circumstances indicated that he was being successful in winning popularity, we might deliberately ignore his antics for a while. For one thing, it would be hazardous to turn the group against him. Indeed, if he became socially accepted, his reason for clowning might vanish, and we would want to let that possibility develop. Moreover, a head-on clash over clowning while it was novel and popular might make him a martyr and fix the pattern in his repertoire. Therefore we would wait. If the clowning continued, as soon as the class began to become impatient with him, as they would after a while, we could take strong measures to stop him in class, and follow those measures up with an interview in which he would be much more willing to discuss how to win the approval of his classmates. Thus, the early policy of avoiding action would be an essential feature of the long-time strategy of moving vigorously when the class feelings and his own needs had developed to the point where we could be effective.

Here is another illustration of a situation where timing can be crucial: Miss Philips had been making a special effort to win Ralph's confidence. The boy had a bad reputation in the school. He was quarrelsome and had many fights. When warned about him at the beginning of the year, she had said that with everyone against him, the boy needed a friend. She had been very pleasant to him, and lately he showed signs of gratitude. That is why her heart sank when the children came in from lunch all excited with a story that he had almost killed another boy because that boy had pushed Ralph's little sister. Soon Ralph appeared on the scene, pushed into the room by two indignant teachers. They grimly announced, "Here's your dear sweet little Ralph."

Their story was that he had beaten Jack McQuade with a stick and hurt him badly. Ralph kept shouting, "He had no right to pick on a girl." Soon an angry shouting contest was in swing. The teachers were repeating over and over again, "You almost killed him." Ralph changed his angry chant to, "Nobody can pick on my sister."

Several things were clear to Miss Philips: First, Ralph was getting in deeper water all the time. Second, he was too excited to understand anything. Third, she must satisfy the other teachers that she would take action. Fourth, Ralph and his classmates must get it clear that mayhem could not be condoned. Fifth, Ralph must continue to feel she was on his side. Obviously, the last two vital points could not be made until he was calm. Even then, she would have to do some hard thinking.

The first step, though, was to break up the angry scene then raging. She moved between Ralph and the other teachers. To them she said crisply, "I'll take care of this." She turned to Ralph and told him to take his seat. Then, she stepped out into the hall with her colleagues, closed the door, and let them tell her what they had heard and what they thought she should do until at last they were all talked out and went to their rooms.

In her own room, there was Ralph anxious to tell his side of the story. The class excitedly corroborated his claim that John McQuade had really been mean to his sister. They wanted, however, to add gory details about the stick beating. That, Miss Philips cut short, and gave the class a solemn lecture on law and order. She told them how terrible life would be if everyone took to beating or shooting anyone they thought had wronged them. Deliberately she encouraged the group to work out their excitement in fantasies of disorderly chaos. As the discussion shifted from the immediate incident, Ralph became quiet and then thoughtful. She was sure he was beginning to wonder what would be done to him. He looked at her searchingly, as if to find out what she thought of him.

The class soon had said all they had to say. She gave them some work to do, and re-established the usual routine. During the first recess period she motioned Ralph to come to her, and told him, "You and I had better find out if Jack is hurt badly." On the way to the office, he showed his worry. He stressed that he had meant only to scare Jack. In the office, Miss

Philips took the lead. The principal assured her that there had been no serious injuries. Miss Philips firmly said in Ralph's hearing that the boy was truly sorry, that this time he had learned his lesson and that she would personally guarantee his future good behavior.

After class she had a long talk with him. He told her how the other children had picked on him, and how mad it made him to see the same thing start happening to his sister. She sympathized with him, but pointedly repeated that his beating of Jack had been wrong. She dwelt a bit on possible consequences. That done, she listened as he told about how mean Jack and other children had been, and how he felt about them. He began to blubber. Just at that point the two teachers looked in the room. Seeing him in tears apparently satisfied them. Gradually, he calmed down again. She ended the interview by telling him that next time anything happened he should tell her. Not that she thought he ever would, but she wanted to be sure he knew she was his friend and she hoped that would make him think twice about starting another incident which he now could see would put her in a bad light for having come to his rescue. In this whole pattern, she was quite wise in timing her actions so that first he had time to get over his excitement, so that he felt anxious for just long enough to have an effect, and then could relax in the confidence of her backing so as to be in a proper frame of mind for the final interview.

SUMMARY

In analyzing the several incidents in this chapter it is worth while to indicate once again what they have in common. Perhaps it is easiest at first to point out some things that none of these teachers had done. None had handled the situation solely in terms of his or her own feelings. Rather, they reacted to what the children were doing. None had relied upon a single act to do everything; rather, each had made use of several measures. None had applied a stock solution; instead, they had worked out a new plan to meet a new situation. None had wandered off into an interpretation about children in general; rather, each had worked in terms of specific causes and effects operating upon the individual children as he knew them.

Through these examples we have tried to give concrete illustrations of diagnostic thinking in operation as teachers used it to cope with mental hygiene problems. The first hunches which arose as a situation developed were subjected to examination on the basis of known facts and psychological principles. Lacking complete information as to all causes operating, they relied upon the youngsters' behavior to furnish them with clues. In the light of the best estimate which could be made as to the forces at work, a program for dealing with the situation was developed. The changes in the situation after the program was applied tested the accuracy of the estimates. The analysis was flexible; it was changed as new developments threw more light on the situation.

Where did "mental hygiene" come in? In each case the children were given grounds for feeling secure in the school situation, and steps were taken to help them meet their own problems.

REFERENCES

Baruch, Dorothy W., *Parents and Children Go to School,* New York, Scott, Foresman, 1939.

Cantor, Nathaniel, *The Dynamics of Learning,* Buffalo, Foster and Stewart, 1946.

Wittenberg, Rudolph, *So You Want to Help People,* New York, Association Press, 1947.

Sheviakov, George V., and Fritz Redl, *Discipline for Today's Children and Youth,* Washington, National Education Association, 1944.

W. J. McKEACHIE, DONALD POLLIE, and JOSEPH SPEISMAN

Relieving Anxiety in Classroom Examinations

Many students worry over tests and other school matters. The authors of the article investigate one possible procedure by which a teacher may help his students to reduce tension: by encouraging students to comment upon test items. Using a method of investigation wholly different from that used in the preceding study, the authors employ a formal, subtle experiment and carefully restrict their conclusions to the quantitative evidence. Are you convinced that they have relieved anxiety?

The concept of anxiety has been one of the most widely used concepts in recent psychological theory. In this paper we will use anxiety to mean the state of an individual in a threatening situation from which he cannot immediately escape. In an earlier paper (6) the senior author suggested some of the ways in which student anxiety may be mobilized by the classroom situation and its possible effects upon his performance. This paper reports a series of investigations concerned with student performance on objective-type classroom achievement examinations. Our basic assumption in these investigations was that such a high degree of anxiety is mobilized by classroom tests that the students' performance is adversely affected.

Theory. Basically our theory was this: Most students begin a test with some anxiety as a result of their uncertainty about the outcome of the test and their high degree of motivation for achieving a "good" grade in the course. As they progress through the test they inevitably encounter some

W. J. McKeachie, Donald Pollie, and Joseph Speisman, "Relieving Anxiety in Classroom Examinations," *Journal of Abnormal and Social Psychology,* 50 (1955), 93–98. Reprinted with permission of the American Psychological Association, Inc.

questions that are too difficult or ambiguous for them to answer. Each such item adds to the student's anxiety. As he attacks the succeeding items either the anxiety, or the Zeigarnik effect aroused by the items which he has failed to pass, interferes with his performance, or in Maier's (7) terms, his behavior becomes frustration-instigated, rather than motivated problem-solving behavior.

If the effects of failing items could be diminished in some way, test performance should be improved.

EXPERIMENT I

Purpose. Our first experiment was based on the theory that if students could "blow off steam" about items that cause them difficulty, performance on succeeding items would be improved. Permitting students to write comments about difficult or ambiguous items might act to discharge feelings or to give the student more closure on the item.

Thus, our hypothesis was: Students who are encouraged to write comments about test items on their answer sheets will make higher test scores than students who have no opportunity to make comments.

TABLE 1

Effects of differing types of answer sheets upon test scores

Answer sheet	*N*	*Mean*	*SD*
Usual type	83	29.65	3.9
With space for comments	83	31.09	3.6

NOTE: Difference significant at .01 level.

Procedure. The tests upon which the experiments were performed were the regular classroom examinations in our general psychology course. They consisted of multiple-choice questions to which students responded by checking the appropriate letter on a separate answer sheet. They were given during the regular class period, and with few exceptions students completed the test in less than the class hour. Those who wished it were given additional time. In this experiment, half of the answer sheets were of the usual form, while the other half contained a blank line beside each place for responding. The instructions for the latter, or experimental group, contained these words: "Feel free to make any comments about the items in the space provided."

Results. The results of the experiment confirmed our hypothesis. Students who used the answer sheets with spaces to comment (even though many made no comments) made significantly higher scores on the test than those who used conventional answer sheets (see Table 1). Note that this experiment did not directly test our theory about discharge of anxiety, but merely indicated that an opportunity to comment was beneficial.

Discussion. The results of Experiment I were gratifying; yet in view of the many experiments in which different teaching methods failed to produce differences in objective test scores, our results seemed too good to be true. Consequently we asked ourselves a number of questions:

1. Would we get the same results if we repeated the experiment? The obvious way to find out was to repeat the experiment. We did this three times, obtaining results comparable to those of Experiment I.

2. Did the mere appearance of the answer sheet somehow influence scores on the test? To answer this question, Experiment I was repeated with the control group using answer sheets which were identical to those used by the experimental group except that instead of the instructions, "Feel free to comment . . ." their answer sheet contained the instructions, "Do not mark in this space." Again the group with instructions "Feel free . . ." made significantly higher scores.

TABLE 2

Effect of differing sets toward test

Set	*Answer sheet*	*N*	*Mean*	*SD*
Counts for grade	Space for comments	94	20.1	3.7
	Usual type	131	18.4	4.1
Just for practice	Space for comments	69	19.3	3.4
	Usual type	34	17.5	2.8

EXPERIMENT II

Purpose. If anxiety interferes with test performance, increasing student anxiety should decrease test scores. This was the hypothesis which governed Experiment II.

Procedure. The procedure used in Experiment II was the same as that in Experiment I except that some of the students were told that the test to be given would count as part of the course grade and some were told that this would be a practice test which would not count on their grades. Both groups had been warned several days in advance of the test that a test would be given, but the information that this was to be only a practice test was given to one group in the examination period. Both types of answer sheets used in Experiment I were used in both groups.

Results. While the effect of the differences between the two types of answer sheets was again significant, our hypothesis (for which we had planned to use a one-tailed test of significance) was not confirmed. The group which thought the test counted toward the course grade did not make lower scores (see Table 2).

Discussion. To attempt to explain negative results is a fascinating but dangerous pastime. One explanation was that the students' experiences with tests had generally been so anxiety ridden that our different sets were not enough to neutralize the effects of the many cues for anxiety present when the student actually took the test. Another was that the announcement that the test was "just for practice" may have so reduced motivation that performance was less. This explanation is congruent with findings that people with high need for achievement do not perform up to capacity in non-achievement situations (5).

EXPERIMENT III

Purpose. In our early experiments we had been so amazed that the experiment worked that we had not attempted further conceptualization of the way it worked. We thought that allowing students to comment reduced their anxiety, but we had never measured anxiety, and our one attempt to manipulate anxiety had failed to produce differences in behavior. Thus we were eager to learn more of the way in which permitting students to write comments about questions improved their test scores. We had four ideas:

1. When students write a comment about a test item, they must think further about that item. In thus reorganizing their thoughts about the item, they are more likely to be able to select the correct alternative.
2. In commenting about the item the student can explain the reasons for choosing the alternative, and even though this may not make the instructor mark the item right, he will see that the student has some knowledge. Thus the student does not have as great a feeling of failure and may develop a greater sense of closure about the item. This will reduce interference with later items.
3. In commenting on an item, the student can vent his emotions. Since emotions may interfere with problem solving, this release of emotional tension will permit a more rational approach to subsequent items.
4. The fact that the student is allowed to comment changes his perception of the test. He is less likely to feel that the test is intended to be punitive. He is more apt to perceive the instructor as trying to facilitate his success. Thus his anxiety about the test is reduced and whether or not he writes comments, he will be able to perform more rationally.

Our next experiment was designed to test these ideas. Specifically our hypotheses were:

1. Students' performances on a test will be improved if they are permitted to write their feelings about test items, but are not permitted to write explanations, as compared with students who have no opportunity to write comments.
2. Students' performances on a test will be improved if they are permitted to write explanations of their answers, but are not permitted to write their feelings, as compared with students who have no opportunity to write comments.
3. Giving students the opportunity to write comments affects their scores on items succeeding the item which is commented on rather than on the item upon which comments were made.

Procedures. Our procedures were much the same as in previous experiments except that we now had two experimental groups. The instructions on their answer sheets read as follows:

Group 1: "In the space provided please state your feelings, only, concerning the question. Do not explain your answer. Your comments may consist of anything whatever you feel about the question—its fairness, clarity, importance, triviality, etc. Your comments will be of aid to us in evaluating your test. Remember you may say whatever you feel."

Group 2: "In the space provided please state your explanations, only, of how you arrived at your particular answer. Do this only in those cases where a solution of the answer entails the application of a principle, fact, or method you have learned about. In other words, explain your answer wherever explanations seem necessary. These will be of aid to us in evaluating the complexity of the questions we have asked you. Use the space for explanations only."

TABLE 3

Test scores for groups given different instructions

Group	*N*	*Mean*	*SD*
Feelings	66	20.78	2.75
Explanations	75	20.86	2.25
No comments	70	20.07	2.72

To test Hypothesis 3, the obvious procedure would be to compare scores of the experimental groups with the control group on the items about which most comments were written as well as on the items immediately following. To insure that some items would attract comments and that they would not be too closely bunched together, we inserted six items which had proved very difficult to previous classes in general psychology and spaced these well apart. Unfortunately, even with these insertions no more than 20 per cent of the students wrote comments about any one item, and differences in scores on that or the succeeding item were insignificant. This led us to a different procedure for testing Hypothesis 3. If failing an item creates tension, this tension should increase throughout the test. If having an opportunity to write comments aids in reducing or releasing this tension, the improvement in performance should be more marked on the last half of the test than on the first half. Hence separate scores for each half of the test were computed.

Results. Our attempt to restrict students' comments to feelings (Hypothesis 1) or to explanations (Hypothesis 2) appeared from our results to have dissipated much of the effect of permitting comments. As indicated in Table 3, differences between the groups were not significant. However, Hypothesis 3 was verified. The groups that had been given opportunities to write comments were significantly superior to the control group on the last half of the test even though they were not superior on the first half (see Table 4).

TABLE 4

Scores on first and last halves of test for groups given different instructions

Group	*N*	*First-half mean*	*Last-half mean*	*Mean of differences*	*SD of differences*
Feelings	66	10.79	9.99	.80	1.7
Explanations	73	10.63	10.23	.40	1.8
No comments	70	10.72	9.40	1.32	1.9

NOTE: Difference of differences: Feelings vs. no comments, $p = .11$; explanations vs. no comments, $p < .01$.

In a retest of this hypothesis with other groups, comparable results were obtained with the difference in scores on the last half of the test between "feelings" and "no comments" groups having a probability of .16 and that between "explanations" and "no comments" groups having a probability of .005.

Discussion. This experiment was partly encouraging and partly discouraging. Our prediction was verified. The effects of the opportunity to comment were most pronounced on the last half of the test. Since there were no more comments on the last half of the test than on the first half, this seemed to demonstrate that comments did not affect the scores on the items about which comments were written, but rather succeeding items. This fitted in with our theory that tension is built up throughout the test and that giving opportunity to comment reduces the increasing tension. But we were surprised to find that in general neither the instructions to write explanations nor to write feelings about items seemed to have been as effective as our usual instructions to "Feel free to comment. . . ." We repeated this part of the experiment (10) with the added variation of giving one group answer sheets with the instructions: "In the space provided please state your feelings about a question *and* an explanation of how you arrived at the answer you used. Whenever you come to a question that bothers you, give any feelings you have about its clarity, fairness, triviality, etc., and also an explanation of how you arrived at the answer you used. This will help us to evaluate your test and also help in making our future tests." Surprisingly enough, none of the experimental groups was significantly superior to the group with conventional answer sheets.

The results of this follow-up were disconcerting. It now appeared that the important variable was not whether or not students released emotional feelings or gained closure by explaining their answers. Rather, it now appeared that the over-all set given by the instructions to comment was more important. Obviously, another experiment needed to be done.

EXPERIMENT IV

Purpose. Based on our previous results we now developed the hypothesis that specific instructions to comment actually increase a student's anxiety since they ask him to perform an additional task upon which he may be evaluated. Additional restraint is felt, especially when these instructions specify the kind of comment to be made. Our original instructions to "Feel free to comment" must have worked because they made the situation a permissive one. Our hypothesis for Experiment IV, then, was: Students given answer sheets with the instructions, "If you wish to make any comments about the questions on this exam, do so in the space provided," will make higher test scores than students with instructions to give their feelings and explanations of their answers on difficult items or students who are instructed not to comment.

Procedures. Our procedures were the same as in the preceeding experiments. One-third of the students were given answer sheets with the instructions, "If you wish to make any comments about the questions on this exam, do so in the space provided"; one-third of the students received answer sheets with instructions, "In the space provided, please state your feelings about a question *and* an explanation of how you arrived at the answer you used. Whenever you come to a question that bothers you, give any feelings you have about its clarity, fairness, triviality, etc., and also an explanation of how you arrived at the answer you used. This will help us to evaluate your test and also help in making out future tests"; and the remaining third of the students received answer sheets with instructions, "Do not mark in the space to the right of your answers." Except for the instructions all answer sheets were identical.

TABLE 5

Effect on performance of differing instructions

Group	*Mean*	*F*	*df*	*p*
Explanations and feelings	32.73	(1 vs. 2) 2.5	1 and 281	NS
Do not comment	33.56	(2 vs. 3) 2.4	1 and 286	NS
Free comment	34.45	(1 vs. 3) 10.5	1 and 267	<.01

NOTE: The *F* ratio when all three means were taken together was 4.89, which is just beyond the .01 level of confidence.

Results. As indicated in Table 5, our hypothesis was confirmed by our results. The students with permissive instructions made significantly higher scores than students receiving the other two types of answer sheets. Since all students in this and the other experiments finished the examination in the allotted time, the results were not due to differences in the time required to write comments

EXPERIMENT V

Purpose. The results of the four experiments conducted up to this point convinced us that test performance is influenced by the stress of the testing situation, and that this stress could be reduced by giving students the opportunity to make comments about the test. At the same time we were interested in personality variables that might make for individual differences in the amount of stress which a student feels in taking a test. To us one of the most interesting possible personality variables was the student's need for achievement. The findings of McClelland *et al.* (5) indicated that their measure of the achievement motive could differentiate students who felt motivated to excel from students who feared failure in achievement situations. We hypothesized that this latter group (low need achievement) would find the test situation more stressful, and that the opportunity to write comments would be of more aid in improving their scores than it would be for students with less anxiety about achievement.

Procedure. Students who took part in the replication of Experiment III were given the measure of achievement motivation. Students were divided at the median on this measure into two groups: (*a*) a high n Achievement group, and (*b*) a low n Achievement (fear of failure) group (5). All of these students had been given answer sheets which requested that they write comments about difficult or ambiguous items. The scores of the two groups were compared for the items on the first half of the test and for the items on the last half of the test.

TABLE 6

Errors on first and last halves of exam

Group	N	First half Mean	First half SD	Second half Mean	Second half SD
Fear-failure	12	6.5	3.6	5.6	2.8
High need achievement	12	2.8	1.9	4.6	1.8

NOTE: Difference of differences, $p = .11$.

Results. The results were not conclusive but tended to support our hypothesis. On the first half of the test, the high-achievement students scored significantly higher than the fear-of-failure group. On the last half of the examination, there was no significant difference between the scores of the two groups. The probability of the difference in gains was .11 (see Table 6). Moreover, the correlation between scores on the last half of the examination and number of comments was .73 for the fear-of-failure group and only .05 for the high-need-achievement group.

DISCUSSION AND GENERAL CONCLUSIONS

What do our experiments add up to? In the sequence of experiments our theory had been building up step by step. We now had ideas about (*a*) the sources of anxiety in the testing situation, (*b*) the effect of anxiety upon performance, and (*c*) methods of reducing the deleterious effects of anxiety upon problem solving.

Sources of anxiety. As we see it, the student's anxiety in the testing situation derives from his helplessness in relation to the instructor's power. The power of the instructor to assign a grade means that the instructor can, by assigning a low grade, bar the student from attaining some of his most important goals, such as admission to graduate professional training, the prestige of college graduation or of Phi Beta Kappa, and the material advantages of good grades in securing a job. While all student-instructor relationships possess some possible threat, the focus of the student's anxiety is course examinations, which are usually the primary basis for grade assignment. The degree of the student's anxiety will be a function of his perception of the instructor's arbitrariness and punitiveness in the use of his power. Our finding that freedom to make comments results in higher test scores could be at least partially explained, we believe, if our instructions to "Feel free to comment . . ." influenced students to perceive the instructor as being a person who was not punitive, not attempting to maintain his superior status, but one who wanted to give students every opportunity to communicate to him.

In addition, the student's anxiety is a function of uncertainty (as Sinha [9] and Cohen [1] have demonstrated). When we asked for a specific type of comment, e.g., "only feelings" or "only explanations," we did not get the improved performance which we consistently obtained when our instructions were "Feel free to comment. . . ." In retrospect, we suspect that these specific instructions were actually more ambiguous than the free-comment instructions. The student was uncertain as to how much he was expected to comment and how much his comments would influence his instructor's evaluation of him.

Finally, anxiety is a function of individual differences in motivation and security in the situation. Our results indicate that our experimental variation of instructions had little effect upon the person with high need achievement, who in need-achievement theory is presumed to be stimulated but secure in achievement testing situations. However, students fearing failure were aided by the opportunity to make comments. These results are in harmony with those of Hutt (3), who found that maladjusted children achieved higher IQ's when he followed each failed test item with an easy item. However, such a procedure did not significantly influence scores of normal children.

The effect of anxiety upon performance. While we had no direct measure of anxiety, our findings do appear to support those of Deese and Lazarus (2, 4), Sarason (8), and Maier (7), who have reported decrements in various tasks as a result of anxiety.

How can the decrement in performance due to anxiety be reduced? Obviously, reducing anxiety should reduce the detrimental effects of anxiety, and as we pointed out earlier, this is, we believe, one of the functions of giving students opportunity to comment on test questions. But the fact that scores of students who were allowed to comment improve relatively in the second half of the test suggests that commenting in itself may also be of some value in improving performance. We suspect that when a person is frustrated or anxious, the discharge of the tension through almost any available response will help decrease the effect of the anxiety on later problems. However, we cannot help speculating about the fact that each time we compared instructions to write feelings against instructions to write explanations, the explanations group made slightly, but not significantly, better scores. Can it be that merely "blowing off steam" is not effective, and that catharsis, whether of these superficial feelings or of deeply repressed emotions, should involve verbalizing cognitive as well as affective elements? Or, does the expression of negative feelings arouse fear of incurring the instructor's displeasure? Or is the important thing that the student feels that he is communicating to the person having power over him? Perhaps expression of feelings seems to communicate less than an explanation? Such speculations need to be tested by further research.

SUMMARY

The present experiments attempted to influence student scores on classroom tests by setting up conditions which would permit reduction or dissipation of anxiety.

The results showed that students who were encouraged to write comments about their questions made higher scores than students who had conventional answer sheets. Since students who could write comments did not differ significantly from the control group in their scores on the first half of the test but performed significantly better on the second half of the test, it was concluded that the effect of the comments was not to improve scores on the items about which the comments were written. When students were given specific instructions as to the type of comments to write, their test scores were lower than those of students who were told "Feel free to write comments."

On the basis of the McClelland, Atkinson, *et al.* test for achievement motivation, students who feared failure were distinguished from those with positive achievement motivation. When given opportunity to comment, students with fear of failure made lower scores on the first half of the test than students with high need achievement, but did not differ significantly on the last half of the test.

It is suggested that classroom examinations help determine the students' perception of the manner in which the instructor's power to assign grades will be used. Individual anxiety in the situation is partially a function of achievement motivation. Anxiety inhibits performance. Giving students an opportunity to write comments aids not only in reducing the threat but also in channeling the release of anxiety.

REFERENCES

1. Cohen, A. R. The effects of individual self-esteem and situational structure on threat-oriented reactions to power. Unpublished Ph.D. thesis, Univer. of Michigan, 1953.
2. Deese, J., & Lazarus, R. S. The effects of psychological stress upon perceptual-motor performance. *USAF, Hum. Resour. Res. Cent., Res. Bull.,* 1952, No. 53-19.
3. Hutt, M. L. A clinical study of "consecutive" and "adaptive" testing with the revised Stanford-Binet. *J. Consult. Psychol.,* 1947, 11, 93–103.
4. Lazarus, R. S., Deese, J., & Osler, Sonia F. The effects of psychological stress upon performance. *Psychol. Bull.,* 1952, 49, 293–317.
5. McClelland, D. C., Atkinson, J. W., Clark, R. A., & Lowell, E. L. *The achievement motive.* New York: Appleton-Century-Crofts, 1953.
6. McKeachie, W. J. Anxiety in the college classroom. *J. Educ. Res.,* 1951, 45, 153–160.
7. Maier, N. R. F. *Frustration.* New York: McGraw-Hill, 1949.
8. Sarason, S. B., & Mandler, G. Some correlates of test anxiety. *J. Abnorm. Soc. Psychol.,* 1952, 47, 810–817.
9. Sinha, A. K. P. Experimental induction of anxiety by conditions of uncertainty. Unpublished Ph.D. thesis, Univer. of Michigan, 1950.
10. Teevan, R., & McKeachie, W. Effects on performance of different instructions in multiple-choice examinations. *Mich. Acad. Sci., Arts, Letters,* 1954, 39, 467–475.

Chapter 18

Character Development

18-1

URIE BRONFENBRENNER

Soviet Methods of Character Education

18-2

RAY R. CANNING

Does an Honor System Reduce Classroom Cheating? An Experimental Answer

URIE BRONFENBRENNER

Soviet Methods of Character Education

There is great value in studying foreign systems of educational psychology. This maxim applies particularly to character education, since American educators have not given as much formal attention to shaping conforming personal behavior as, judged by this article, has the Soviet Union. Bronfenbrenner has brought a psychologist's careful eye to the analysis of Soviet theory and practice. You will be interested in analyzing the systematic use of group pressure to mold deportment. What Soviet techniques are also used in Western schooling?

Every society faces the problem of the moral training of its youth. This is no less true of Communist society than of our own. Indeed, Communist authorities view as the primary objective of education not the learning of subject matter but the development of what they call "socialist morality." It is instructive for us in the West to examine the nature of this "socialist morality" and the manner in which it is inculcated, for to do so brings to light important differences in the ends and means of character education in the two cultures. For research workers in the field of personality development, such an examination is especially valuable, since it lays bare unrecognized assumptions and variations in approach. Accordingly, it is the purpose of this paper to provide a much-condensed account of Soviet methods of character education. . . .

THE WORK AND IDEAS OF A. S. MAKARENKO

To examine Soviet methods of character training is to become acquainted with the thinking and technology developed primarily by one man—Anton Semyonovich Makarenko. Makarenko's name is virtually a household word in the Soviet Union. His popularity and influence are roughly comparable to those of Dr. Spock in the United States, but his primary concern is not with the child's physical health but with his moral upbringing. Makarenko's influence extends far beyond his own voluminous writings since there is scarcely a manual for the guidance of Communist parents, teachers, or youth workers that does not draw heavily on his methods and ideas. His works have been translated into many languages and are apparently widely read not only in the Soviet Union but throughout the Communist bloc

Urie Bronfenbrenner, "Soviet Methods of Character Education: Some Implications for Research," reprinted from the Research Supplement to the July–August, 1962, issue of *Religious Education;* copyrighted by and used by permission of the publisher, The Religious Education Association, New York City.

countries, notably East Germany and Communist China. Excellent English translations of a number of his works have been published in Moscow (1949, 1953, 1959) but they are not readily available in this country.

Makarenko developed his ideas and methods over the course of a lifetime of practical work with young people. In the early 1920's, as a young school teacher and devout Communist, Makarenko was handed the assignment of setting up a rehabilitation program for some of the hundreds of homeless children who were roaming the Soviet Union after the civil wars. The first group of such children assigned to Makarenko's school, a ramshackle building far out of town, turned out to be a group of boys about 18 years of age with extensive court records of housebreaking, armed robbery, and manslaughter. For the first few months, Makarenko's school served simply as the headquarters for the band of highwaymen who were his legal wards. But gradually, through the development of his group-orientated discipline techniques, and through what can only be called the compelling power of his own moral convictions, Makarenko was able to develop a sense of group responsibility and commitment to the work program and code of conduct that he had laid out for the collective. In the end, the Gorky Commune became known throughout the Soviet Union for its high morale, discipline, and for the productivity of its fields, farms, and shops. Indeed, Makarenko's methods proved so successful that he was selected to head a new commune set up by the Ministry of Internal Affairs (then the Cheka, later to become the GPU and NKVD). In the years which followed, Makarenko's theories and techniques became widely adopted throughout the USSR and now constitute the central core of Soviet educational practice.

To turn to the ideas themselves, we may begin with an excerpt from what is possibly the most widely read of Makarenko's works, *A Book for Parents* (1959).

> But our [Soviet] family is not an accidental combination of members of society. The family is a natural collective body and, like everything natural, healthy, and normal, it can only blossom forth in socialist society, freed of those very curses from which both mankind as a whole and the individual are freeing themselves.
>
> The family becomes the natural primary cell of society, the place where the delight of human life is realized, where the triumphant forces of man are refreshed, where children—the chief joy of life—live and grow.
>
> Our parents are not without authority either, but this authority is only the reflection of societal authority. The duty of a father in our country towards his children is a particular form of his duty towards society. It is as if our society says to parents:
>
> You have joined together in good will and love, rejoice in your children and expect to go on rejoicing in them. That is your personal affair and concerns your own personal happiness. Within the course of this happy process you have given birth to new human beings. A time will come when these beings will cease to be solely the instruments of your happiness, and will step forth as independent members of society. For society, it is by no means a matter of indifference what kind of people they will become. In delegating to you a

certain measure of societal authority the Soviet State demands from you the correct upbringing of its future citizens. Particularly it relies on you to provide certain conditions arising naturally out of your union; namely, your parental love.

If you wish to give birth to a citizen while dispensing with parental love, then be so kind as to warn society that you intend to do such a rotten thing. Human beings who are brought up without parental love are often deformed human beings (Makarenko, 1959, p. 29).

Characteristic of Makarenko's thought is the view that the parent's authority over the child is delegated to him by the state and that duty to one's children is merely a particular instance of one's broader duty towards society. A little later in his book for parents, the author makes this point even more emphatically. After telling the story of a boy who ran away from home after some differences with his mother, he concludes by affirming: "I am a great admirer of optimism and I like very much young lads who have so much faith in Soviet State that they are carried away and will not trust even their own mothers" (Makarenko, 1959, pp. 37–38). In other words, when the needs and values of the family conflict with those of society, there is no question about who gets priority. And society receives its concrete manifestation and embodiment in the *collective,* which is an organized group engaged in some socially useful enterprise.

This brings us to Makarenko's basic thesis that optimal personality development can occur only through productive activity in a social collective. The first collective is the family, but this must be supplemented early in life by other collectives specially organized in schools, neighborhoods, and other community settings. The primary function of the collective is to develop socialist morality. This aim is accomplished through an explicit regimen of activity mediated by group criticism, self-criticism, and group-oriented punishments and rewards.

Makarenko's ideas are elaborated at length in his semibiographical, semifictional accounts of life in the collective (1949, 1953). It is in these works that he describes the principles and procedures to be employed for building the collective and using it as an instrument of character education. More relevant to our purposes, however, is the manner in which these methods are applied in school settings, for it is in this form that they have become most systematized and widely used.

SOCIALIZATION IN THE SCHOOL COLLECTIVE

The account which follows is taken from a manual (Novika, 1959) for the training and guidance of "school directors, supervisors, teachers, and Young Pioneer leaders." The manual was written by staff members of the Institute on the Theory and History of Pedagogy at the Academy of Pedagogical Sciences and is typical of several others prepared under the same auspices and widely distributed throughout the USSR.

This particular volume carries the instructive title: *Socialist Competition in the Schools.* The same theme is echoed in the titles of individual chapters: "Competition in the Classroom," "Competition between Classrooms," "Competition between Schools," and so on. It is not difficult to see how Russians arrive at the notion, with which they have made us so familiar, of competition between nations and between social systems. Moreover, in the chapter titles we see already reflected the influence of dialectical materialism: Conflict at one level is resolved through synthesis at the next higher level, always in the service of the Communist collective.

Let us examine the process of collective socialization as it is initiated in the very first grade. Conveniently enough, the manual starts us off on the first day of school with the teacher standing before the newly assembled class. What should her first words be? Our text tells us:

> It is not difficult to see that a direct approach to the class with the command "All sit straight" often doesn't bring the desired effect since a demand in this form does not reach the sensibilities of the pupils and does not activate them.

How does one "reach the sensibilities of the pupils" and "activate them"? According to the manual, here is what the teacher should say: "Let's see which row can sit the straightest." This approach, we are told, has certain important psychological advantages. In response,

> The children not only try to do everything as well as possible themselves, but also take an evaluative attitude toward those who are undermining the achievement of the row. If similar measures arousing the spirit of competition in the children are systematically applied by experienced teachers in the primary classes, then gradually the children themselves begin to monitor the behavior of their comrades and remind those of them who forget about the rules set by the teacher, who forget what needs to be done and what should not be done. The teacher soon has helpers.

The manual then goes on to describe how records are kept for each row from day to day for different types of tasks so that the young children can develop a concept of group excellence over time and over a variety of activities, including personal cleanliness, condition of notebooks, conduct in passing from one room to the other, quality of recitations in each subject matter, and so on. In these activities considerable emphasis is placed on the externals of behavior in dress, manner, and speech. There must be no spots on shirt or collar, shoes must be shined, pupils must never pass by a teacher without stopping to give greeting, there must be no talking without permission, and the like. Great charts are kept in all the schools showing performance of each row unit in every type of activity together with their total overall standing. "Who is best?" the charts ask, but the entries are not individuals but social units—rows, and later the "cells" of the Communist youth organization which reaches down to the primary grades.

At first it is the teacher who sets the standards. But soon, still in the first grade, a new wrinkle is introduced: Responsible monitors are designated in each row for each activity. In the beginning their job is only to keep track of the merits and demerits assigned each row by the teacher. Different children act as monitors for different activities and, if one is to believe what the manual says, the monitors become very involved in the progress of their row. Then, too, group achievement is not without its rewards. From time to time the winning row gets to be photographed "in parade uniforms" (all Soviet children must wear uniforms in school), and this photograph is published in that pervasive Soviet institution, the wall newspaper. The significance of the achievements is still further enhanced, however, by the introduction of competition between *classes* so that the winning class and the winning row are visited by delegates from other classrooms in order to learn how to attain the same standard of excellence.

Now let us look more closely at this teacher-mediated monitoring process. In the beginning, we are told, the teacher attempts to focus the attention of children on the achievements of the group; that is, in our familiar phrase, she accentuates the positive. But gradually, "it becomes necessary to take account of negative facts which interfere with the activity of the class." As an example we are given the instance of a child who despite warnings continues to enter the classroom a few minutes after the bell has rung. The teacher decides that the time has come to evoke the group process in correcting such behavior. Accordingly, the next time that Serezha is late, the teacher stops him at the door and turns to the class with this question: "Children, is it helpful or not helpful to us to have Serezha come in late?" The answers are quick in coming. "It interferes, one shouldn't be late, he ought to come on time." "Well," says the teacher, "How can we help Serezha with this problem?" There are many suggestions: get together to buy him a watch, exile him from the classroom, send him to the director's office, or even to exile him from the school. But apparently these suggestions are either not appropriate or too extreme. The teacher, our text tells us, "helps the children find the right answer." She asks for a volunteer to stop by and pick Serezha up on the way to school. Many children offer to help in this mission.

But tragedy stalks. The next day it turns out that not only Serezha is late, but also the boy who promised to pick him up. Since they are both from the same group, their unit receives two sets of demerits and falls to lowest place. Group members are keenly disappointed. "Serezha especially suffered much and felt himself responsible, but equal blame was felt by his companion who had forgotten to stop in for him."

In this way, both through concrete action and explanation, the teacher seeks to forge a spirit of group unity and responsibility. From time to time, she explains to the children the significance of what they are doing, the fact "that they have to learn to live together as one friendly family, since they will have to be learning together for all of the next ten years, and that for this reason one must learn how to help one's companions and to treat them decently."

By the time the children are in the second grade, the responsibilities expected of them are increased in complexity. For example, instead of simply recording the evaluations made by the teacher, the monitors are taught how to make the evaluations themselves. Since this is rather difficult, especially in judging homework assignments, in the beginning two monitors are assigned to every task. In this way, our text tells us, they can help each other in doing a good job of evaluation.

Here is a third grade classroom:

Class 3-B is just an ordinary class; it's not especially well disciplined nor is it outstandingly industrious. It has its lazy members and its responsible ones, quiet ones and active ones, daring, shy, and immodest ones.

The teacher has led this class now for three years, and she has earned the affection, respect, and acceptance as an authority from her pupils. Her word is law for them.

The bell has rung, but the teacher has not yet arrived. She has delayed deliberately in order to check how the class will conduct itself.

In the class all is quiet. After the noisy class break, it isn't so easy to mobilize yourself and to quell the restlessness within you! Two monitors at the desk silently observe the class. On their faces is reflected the full importance and seriousness of the job they are performing. But there is no need for them to make any reprimands: the youngsters with pleasure and pride maintain scrupulous discipline; they are proud of the fact that their class conducts itself in a manner that merits the confidence of the teacher. And when the teacher enters and quietly says be seated, all understand that she deliberately refrains from praising them for the quiet and order, since in their class it could not be otherwise.

During the lesson, the teacher gives an exceptional amount of attention to collective competition between "links." (The links are the smallest unit of the Communist youth organization at this age level.) Throughout the entire lesson the youngsters are constantly hearing which link has best prepared its lesson, which link has done the best at numbers, which is the most disciplined, which has turned in the best work.

The best link not only gets a verbal positive evaluation but receives the right to leave the classroom first during the break and to have its notebooks checked before the others. As a result the links receive the benefit of collective education, common responsibility, and mutual aid.

"What are you fooling around for? You're holding up the whole link," whispers Kolya to his neighbor during the preparation period for the lesson. And during the break he teaches her how better to organize her books and pads in her knapsack.

"Count more carefully," says Olya to her girl friend. "See, on account of you our link got behind today. You come to me and we'll count together at home."

In the third grade still another innovation is introduced. The monitors are taught not only to evaluate but to state their criticisms publicly.

Here is a typical picture. It is the beginning of the lesson. In the first row the link leader reports basing his comments on information submitted by the sanitarian and other responsible monitors: "Today Valadya did the wrong problem. Masha didn't write neatly and forgot to underline the right words in her lesson, Alyoshi had a dirty shirt collar."

The other link leaders make similar reports (the Pioneers are sitting by rows).

The youngsters are not offended by this procedure: they understand that the link leaders are not just tattle-telling but simply fulfilling their duty. It doesn't even occur to the monitors and sanitarians to conceal the shortcomings of their comrades. They feel that they are doing their job well precisely when they notice one or another defect.

Also in the third grade, the teacher introduces still another procedure. She now proposes that the children enter into competition with the monitors, and see if they can beat the monitor at his own game by criticizing themselves. "The results were spectacular: if the monitor was able to talk only about four or five members of the row, there would be supplementary reports about their own shortcomings from as many as eight or ten pupils."

To what extent is this picture overdrawn? Although I have no direct evidence, the accounts I heard from participants in the process lend credence to the descriptions in the manual. For example, I recall a conversation with three elementary school teachers, all men, whom I had met by chance in a restaurant. They were curious about discipline techniques used in American schools. After I had given several examples, I was interrupted: "But how do you use the collective?" When I replied that we really did not use the classroom group in any systematic way, my three companions were puzzled. "But how do you keep discipline?"

Now it was my turn to ask for examples. "All right," came the answer. "Let us suppose that 10-year-old Vanya is pulling Anya's curls. If he doesn't stop the first time I speak to him, all I need do is mention it again in the group's presence; then I can be reasonably sure that before the class meets again the boy will be talked to by the officers of his Pioneer link. They will remind him that his behavior reflects on the reputation of the link."

"And what if he persists?"

"Then he may have to appear before his link—or even the entire collective—who will explain his misbehavior to him and determine his punishment."

"What punishment?"

"Various measures. He may just be censured, or if his conduct is regarded as serious, he may be expelled from membership. Very often he himself will acknowledge his faults before the group."

Nor does the process of social criticism and control stop with the school. Our manual tells us, for example, that parents submit periodic reports to the school collective on the behavior of the child at home. One may wonder how parents can be depended on to turn in truthful accounts. Part of the answer was supplied to me in a conversation with a Soviet agricultural expert. In response to my questions, he explained that, no matter what a person's job, the collective at his place of work always took an active interest in his family life. Thus a representative would come to the worker's home to observe and talk with his wife and children. And if any undesirable features were noted, these would be reported back to the collective.

I asked for an example.

"Well, suppose the representative were to notice that my wife and I quarreled in front of the children. [My companion shook his head.] That would be bad. They would speak to me about it and remind me of my responsibilities for training my children to be good citizens."

I pointed out how different the situation was in America where a man's home was considered a private sanctuary so that, for example, psychologists like myself often had a great deal of difficulty in getting into homes to talk with parents or to observe children.

"Yes," my companion responded. "That's one of the strange things about your system in the West. The family is separated from the rest of society. That's not good. It's bad for the family and bad for society." He paused for a moment, lost in thought. "I suppose," he went on, "if my wife didn't want to let the representative in, she could ask him to leave. But then at work, I should feel ashamed." (He hung his head to emphasize the point.) "Ivanov," they would say, "has an uncultured wife."

But it would be a mistake to conclude that Soviet methods of character education and social control are based primarily on negative criticism. On the contrary, in their approach there is as much of the carrot as the stick. But the carrot is given not merely as a reward for individual performance but explicitly for the child's contribution to group achievement. The great charts emblazoned "Who IS Best?" which bedeck the halls and walls of every classroom have as entries the names not of individual pupils but of rows and links. . . . It is the winning unit that gets rewarded by a pennant, a special privilege, or by having their picture taken in "parade uniforms." And when praise is given, as it frequently is, to an individual child, the group referent is always there: "Today Peter helped Kate and as a result his unit did not get behind the rest."

Helping other members of one's collective and appreciating their contributions—themes that are much stressed in Soviet character training—become matters of enlightened self-interest, since the grade that each person receives depends on the overall performance of his unit. Thus the good student finds it to his advantage to help the poor one. The same principle is carried over to the group level with champion rows and classes being made responsible for the performance of poorer ones.

Here, then, are the procedures employed in Soviet character education. As a result of Khrushchev's educational reforms, they may be expected to receive even wider application in the years to come, for, in connection with these reforms, several new types of educational institutions are to be developed on a massive scale. The most important of these is the "internat," or boarding school, in which youngsters are to be entered as early as three months of age with parents visiting only on weekends. The internat is described in the theses announcing the reforms as the kind of school which "creates the most favorable conditions for the education and communist upbringing of the rising generation" (Communist Party of Soviet Russia, 1958). The number of boarding schools in the USSR is to be increased during the current seven-year plan from a 1958 level of 180,000 to 2,500,000 in 1965 (figures cited in *Pravda,* November 18, 1958), and according to I. A. Kairov, head of the Academy of Pedagogical Sciences, "No one can doubt that, as material conditions are created, the usual general educational school will be supplanted by the boarding school" (Kairov, 1960).

If this prophecy is fulfilled, we may expect that in the years to come the great majority of Soviet children (and children in some other countries of the Communist bloc as well) will from the first year of life onward be spending their formative period in collective settings and will be exposed daily to the techniques of collective socialization we have been describing. It is therefore a matter of considerable practical and scientific interest to identify the salient features of these techniques and subject them to research study, in so far as this becomes possible within the framework of our own society.

GUIDING PRINCIPLES OF THE SOVIET APPROACH TO CHARACTER TRAINING

As a first approximation, we may list the following as distinguishing characteristics or guiding principles of communist methods of character education.

1. The peer collective (under adult leadership) rivals and early surpasses the family as the principal agent of socialization.
2. Competition between groups is utilized as the principal mechanism for motivating achievement of behavior norms.
3. The behavior of the individual is evaluated primarily in terms of its relevance to the goals and achievements of the collective.
4. Rewards and punishments are frequently given on a group basis; that is to say, the entire group benefits or suffers as a consequence of the conduct of individual members.
5. As soon as possible, the tasks of evaluating the behavior of individuals and of dispensing rewards and sanctions is delegated to the members of the collective.
6. The principal methods of social control are public recognition and public criticism, with explicit training and practice being given in these activities. Specifically, each member of the collective is encouraged to observe deviant behavior by his fellows and is given opportunity to report his observations to the group. Reporting on one's peers is esteemed and rewarded as a civic duty.
7. Group criticism becomes the vehicle for training in self-criticism in the presence of one's peers. Such public self-criticism is regarded as a powerful mechanism for maintaining and enhancing commitment to approved standards of behavior, as well as the method of choice for bringing deviants back into line.

There are of course many other important features of the Soviet approach to socialization, but the seven listed above are those which present the greatest contrast to the patterns we employ in the West. . . .

RAY R. CANNING

Does an Honor System Reduce Classroom Cheating? An Experimental Answer

Some educators believe that certain high goals of education, such as character, cannot be brought under experimental scrutiny. But when character, or the evidence of it, is defined in operational terms, it can be observed and manipulated like other behavior. Canning reports a quasi-experimental study of collegiate cheating behavior before and after some honor-system regulations were introduced. Does the author prove that the changes are the direct result of the introduction of the honor code? What other factors not controlled in this study might account for the changes?

Opportunities for experimental research in the Behavior Sciences are severely limited. However, an occasional situation arises in which human beings can be manipulated either voluntarily or without their knowledge. The classroom offers such a research environment which, in this case, was used to determine cheating practices of university students.

THE TECHNIQUE

Previous studies of honesty among students have utilized a variety of techniques,[1] some of which were used in this study to test validity and reliability. However, for the experiment reported here, one simple technique was repeated five times over a period of six years:

1. After regular examinations were collected from lower division sociology students, duplicate copies of the students' answers were carefully recorded for later comparisons.
2. These duplicate test papers were then corrected and graded, but *no* markings were made on the original examination papers.
3. At the next class session the unmarked originals were returned to their owners with the implication that the instructor had not yet had time to correct them. "Aid" from the students was solicited, and each was "permitted" to "correct" his own paper.
4. At the end of this experimental period, the papers were again collected

[1] For one example see: Harold T. Christensen, "An Experiment in Honesty," *Social Forces* (March 1948).

Ray R. Canning, "Does an Honor System Reduce Classroom Cheating? An Experimental Answer," *Journal of Experimental Education*, 24 (1956), 291–96. Reprinted with permission.

and any changes made upon the examination papers by the students were also recorded on the duplicate sheets.

5. Tabulated differences, then, became the data of this cheating experiment.

THE TIME PERIOD

In 1948, one year before an Honor System was established at the Brigham Young University, the first experiment was made upon what will be referred to as Class A. This group of students will be considered the "Before" part of the total experiment. During the years of introduction and revision of the Honor Code and System (1949–1953), three other classes (Classes B, C, and D) were studied. They constitute the "During" part of the experiment. Finally, five years after the inauguration of the System (1954), a follow-up study was made (Class E) which will be called the "Now" stage of the experiment.

THE SAMPLE

Five lower-division sociology classes were used in the experiment proper. Their 299 students were divided up as follows:

> In the "Before" group there were 48 students, 181 in the "During" group, and 70 in the "Now" group. In addition to this research sample, three classes (X, Y, and Z) containing 71, 38, [and] 96 students, respectively, were used in validity and reliability exercises. Similar experiments were made with 109 of these students but by different instructors.[2] Class Z, (96 students) was experimented with by other techniques.[3]

Although a sample of 299 students is large enough for most statistical manipulations, it is well to note that in both the "Before" and "Now" groups the number is small.

STANDARDIZATION

Attempts were made to keep tests, samples, classroom conditions, and methods of conducting the experiment comparable throughout the "Before," "During," and "Now" periods. One instructor performed all experiments; classes had considered similar subject matter; the experiment was performed at the same time in the quarter; and the approach to the class was standardized. Throughout the six year period, no information was divulged which [might] have alerted the students to the nature of the experiment.

[2] In Class X (a lower division religion class of 75 students) and Class Y (a lower division sociology class of 38 students) 45 students or 41 percent cheated in the experiment.

[3] They were made to witness cheating in the classroom in order that their reactions might be recorded. This experiment will be reported in another paper.

FINDINGS

A. CHANGES IN INCIDENCE OF CHEATING

Of all students studied during the six years of experimentation, 45 percent cheated in the controlled examinations. The total percentage is not so important, however, as the change in percentage of students cheating before, during and after the instigation of the Honor System. The "Before" period had a high 81 percent of the students who cheated. This was reduced in the "During" period to 41 percent, and finally in the "Now" period to 30 percent. See Table 1. The before-Honor System high was cut in half by the end of the first three years of the Honor System. In five years, it was reduced by nearly two-thirds (63 percent). Tests were made of these percentage reductions to determine if the differences were statistically significant.[4] There is less than one possibility in 1000 that such a difference could have resulted from chance factors. Of course, this does not prove a causal relationship between the Honor System and a reduction in cheating, but the likelihood should be noted.

B. MALE-FEMALE COMPARISONS

It may be noted also from Table 1 that in every period more female students cheated than did the males. The comparative total was 78 to 57, respectively. Of the total cheating group, 58 percent were women and 42 percent were men. This statistic by itself, however, is misleading. The proportion of cheaters of either sex must be compared to the proportion within the total sample of members of that sex. Thus the 58 percent and 42 percent above should be compared respectively to 56 percent of the total group who are females and 44 percent who are males. Table 2 shows these relationships.

TABLE 1

Number and percent of students who cheated, according to sex

	Males			*Females*			*Total*		
	No. in sample	*No. who cheated*	*% who cheated*	*No. in sample*	*No. who cheated*	*% who cheated*	*No. in sample*	*No. who cheated*	*% who cheated*
Before	18	16	89%	30	23	77%	48	39	81%
During	80	33	41%	101	42	42%	181	75	41%
Now	33	8	24%	37	13	35%	70	21	30%
Total	131	57	44%	168	68	46%	299	135	45%

Although among the students who cheated in the "Before" group, 59 percent were women, of the *total* "Before" group they comprised 62 percent. The men in this group cheated out of proportion to their number in the total group. In the "During" period the proportions by sex in both

[4] Chi square = 17.356, Df = 2. $P \leqq .001$.

the total and cheating groups were exactly the same. However, in the "Now" period of the experiment, the women cheated disproportionately, i.e., they comprised 62 percent of the cheating sample but only 53 percent of the total sample.[5] The rise and decline by sex should also be noted. The percentage among the cheaters who were male rose from 41 percent to 44 percent and then dropped to 38 percent, while among the cheaters the female percentage rose from 59 percent ("Before") to 62 percent ("Now").

TABLE 2

Percent of total group and cheating group, by sex

	Percent of total group				*Percent of cheating group*			
	MALES		FEMALES		MALES		FEMALES	
	No.	*%*	*No.*	*%*	*No.*	*%*	*No.*	*%*
Before	18	38%	30	62%	16	41%	23	59%
During	80	44%	101	56%	33	44%	42	56%
Now	33	47%	37	53%	8	38%	13	62%
Total	131	44%	168	56%	135	42%	78	58%

Similarly, there were changes in the average number of points[6] cheated. In the "Before" period, the cheating males averaged 11.6 points with a range of 4 to 24 points, while the cheating females averaged 12.9 points and a range of 4 to 30 points. By the "Now" period the males had reduced their average to 9.1 (R = 3–17) but still had a higher average than the females who had dropped to an average of 7.6 points cheated per cheating-student (R = 3–17). Again, however, standard errors of these differences indicate that they are probably products of chance.

Significance is apparent, though, when the average points cheated of the total "Before" group (12.3 points) are compared to the average of the "Now" group (8.2 points).[7] Not only are there fewer cheating, but their cheating is of lesser magnitude.

C. METHODS OF CHEATING

Four methods of cheating were discernable in the experiment: (1) wrong answers were erased or crossed through and correct answers inserted, (2) previously left blanks were filled with correct answers, (3) answers which were incorrect were not marked as such, and (4) arithmetical "mistakes" favorable to the students were made.

There were 427 individual cases of cheating divided among these four types as follows:

[5] These differences are not statistically significant. Chi-square test of the percent of women among the cheating population as compared to the percent among the total population, "Before," "During," and "Now," indicates that a greater difference could occur 40–50 times in 100 among other samples due to chance.

[6] "Points" hereafter will mean "points-per-100-possible." This designation is used in lieu of percent, inasmuch as the word "percent" is repeated so frequently in this paper.

[7] Significant beyond the .01 level of significance.

135 cases of "filled blanks" (32%)
125 cases of "changed answers" (29%)
95 cases of "'arithmetical' mistakes" (22%)
72 cases of wrong answers not checked (17%)

Although throughout the entire experiment "filling in blank answers" was the most popular form of cheating, this was not so in either the Before or During period. Before the Honor System, over half (53 percent) of the cheating cases were by "Changing-of-Correct-For-Incorrect-Answers," and during the first three years of the system, "Poor Arithmetic" was the most frequently used device (31 percent of the cases).

Sex differences are reflected in the most popular forms of cheating throughout the different periods studied. In the "Before" period "Changing Answers" was the most popular form of cheating of both sexes (M = 62 percent, F = 41 percent). In the "Now" period "Filling Blanks" (79 percent = M, 61 percent = F) was the most popular cheating technique used by students of both sexes.

The sexes "Changed Answers" and "Filled Blanks" proportionately, but the male students outdistanced the female students in "Not Checking Wrong Answers," while the women surpassed the men in "Making Favorable Arithmetic Mistakes."

D. CHEATING RELATED TO USE OF PEN OR PENCIL

Approximately 11 percent more people cheated among the students using pencils than among those using pen and ink (pens, 36 percent; pencils, 47 percent). Cheating students preferred pencils over pens by a ratio of 6 to 1; the noncheating students, 4 to 1. A three-period comparison will show a decided change in this preference: Cheaters in the "Before" period when the rate of cheating was highest had a pencil-to-pen ratio of 19 to 1, as compared to 6 to 1 in the "During" period, and 3 to 1 in the "Now" period, typified by a relatively low cheating rate.

E. CHEATING AS RELATED TO HIGH SCORES ON THE MMPI

All students in the research population who had any score on the Minnesota Multiphasic Personality Inventory of 70 or above or 60 and above on the Lie score were classified according to their cheating-non-cheating behavior in the experiment. Fifty-seven students had T scores of 70 or up on one or more of the following scales: Hypochondriasis, Depression, Hysteria, Psychopathic Deviate, Interest, Paranoia, Psychasthenia, Schizophrenia, or Hypomania. Thirty-two students had Lie scores of 60 or above. Of the 57, 28 cheated and 29 did not. Of the 32, 15 cheated and 17 did not. Thus, cheating does not seem to be differentiated in terms of high MMPI students.

F. CHEATING AND ACADEMIC PROFICIENCY

The five highest and five lowest test scores were averaged for the cheaters and non-cheaters in each of the three periods of the experiment. A marked difference was noted in each case. The mean score of these fifteen highest cheaters was 70 compared to 88 for the fifteen highest non-cheaters. The fifteen lowest scores averaged 47 for the cheaters, but 54 for the non-cheaters. Furthermore, the fifteen highest cheaters raised themselves an average of 15 points. It is clearly evident that points cheated are inversely related to test scores.

High school grade-point averages were computed for the cheaters and the non-cheaters. The cheating students averaged 1.98 grade points before coming to the University while the non-cheating students averaged 2.07 grade points.

VERBALIZATIONS VS. OVERT BEHAVIOR IN THE CHEATING EXPERIMENT

Prior to the experiment, a situational questionnaire was administered to the students in order to find the relationship between verbalizations and cheating behavior, i.e., promised and actual behavior. Among other questions posed for the students' consideration was: "You have an opportunity to change your score on an examination; (you find the instructor's roll book, or discover some other technique) WHAT WOULD YOU DO?" Twenty-six students did not answer. But of the 272 who did answer, 231 (85 percent) pledged that they would not cheat, while 41 (15 percent) said they would raise their grades. By comparison, in the experiment itself, 150 (55 percent) did not cheat and 122 (45 percent) did cheat. Thus a total of 89 people (31 men and 58 women) both cheated and lied—one-third of the total group who answered the questionnaire.

TABLE 3

Students who answered situational questionnaire "yes" or "no" according to whether or not they cheated in the experiment

	No. who answered "yes"		*No. who answered "no"*		*Total*	
Cheated:						
Males	18		31		49	
Females	15		58		73	
Both Sexes		33		89		122
Did Not Cheat:						
Males	4		60		64	
Females	4		82		86	
Both Sexes		8		142		150
Total Group		41		231		272

Table 3 will show further that 33 students (12 percent) cheated as promised but did not lie about it; 142 students (52 percent) neither cheated nor lied; and 8 students (3 percent) did not cheat in the experiment although they had previously stated they would cheat.

SUMMARY AND LIMITATIONS

After five years of testing under an Honor System at Brigham Young University, rates of cheating (of four specific types) were reduced by 63 percent in lower division sociology classes. Similarly, the average magnitude of cheating was less: Before the Honor System the average was 12.3 points per cheating student per test. After five years of the Honor System this average was reduced to 8.2 points.

Before the Honor System, male students cheated slightly out of proportion to their number in the total group, but after five years of the System, this proportion was reduced and the women students cheated disproportionately.

Although in general the favorite method of cheating was by writing in correct answers for questions which during the examination had been left blank, prior to an Honor System the favorite device was through changing answers. Male students failed to check wrong answers more frequently than did women students who, in turn, were more adept at making favorable arithmetic "errors."

Pencil-users cheated more frequently than students who used pen and ink. And the decline in cheaters' preference for pencils is directly related to the reduction in cheating itself throughout the experiment.

No differentiations were noted between cheaters and non-cheaters who scored high on any of the scales of the Minnesota Multiphasic Personality Inventory. However, in terms of high school grade-point averages, the non-cheaters surpassed the cheaters with 2.07 to 1.98 grade points. They were also differentiated by average test scores, the cheaters consistently falling below the non-cheaters. Furthermore, the number of points students raised their scores was inversely related to their correct test scores, i.e., "poorer" students "raised" themselves more points than did the "better" students.

Verbalizing about honesty was relatively easy. Of the 272 students who answered a situational questionnaire designed to test the relationship between promised behavior and actual behavior, 33 percent cheated after promising that they would not; 12 percent cheated as they promised they would; 52 percent did not lie and did not cheat, and 3 percent promised to cheat but failed to do so.

The findings of this study must be interpreted only in view of its many limitations: the small number of people involved in some classes, the lack of further controls, the "temptation" conditions for certain types of cheating, and other unknown variables. It should not be considered as representative of larger groups or other conditions than those specifically described above.

Index

Numbers in **boldface** refer to pages on which readings appear.

D E F G H I J
6 7 8 9 0 1 2 3